Lucifer

Other Books by Jeffrey Burton Russell

Dissent and Reform in the Early Middle Ages (1965)
Medieval Civilization (1968)
A History of Medieval Christianity: Prophecy and Order (1968)
Religious Dissent in the Middle Ages (1971)
Witchcraft in the Middle Ages (1972)
The Devil: Perceptions of Evil from Antiquity to Primitive Christianity
 (1977)
A History of Witchcraft: Sorcerers, Heretics, Pagans (1980)
Medieval Heresies: A Bibliography (with C. T. Berkhout) (1981)
Satan: The Early Christian Tradition (1981)

Jeffrey Burton Russell

Lucifer

The Devil in the Middle Ages

Cornell University Press

Ithaca and London

First published 1984 by Cornell University Press.
Published in the United Kingdom by Cornell University Press Ltd., London.

International Standard Book Number 0-8014-1503-9
Library of Congress Catalog Card Number 84-45153

Printed in the United States of America

*Librarians: Library of Congress cataloging information
appears on the last page of the book.*

*The paper in this book is acid-free and meets the guidelines for permanence
and durability of the Committee on Production Guidelines for Book Longevity
of the Council on Library Resources.*

For the Casebolts, Kaufmans, Ratcliffs, and Traynors, whose kindness and wisdom made my youth in Berkeley a happy one.
LAETIFICABANT IUVENTUTEM MEAM.

Contents

List of Illustrations

Preface

This third volume in the history of the concept of the Devil follows *The Devil* (1977) and *Satan* (1981). The first volume traced the concept through the period of the New Testament; the second took it to the mid-fifth century, by which time its basic lines had been drawn. The present volume describes ideas about the Devil that were prevalent in the Middle Ages. It includes Eastern Orthodox and Islamic views but emphasizes Western Christian thought, which gives the Devil most due. Because I do not know the languages requisite to a study of Islam in detail, I offer only a brief comparative description of its view of the Devil. The primary components of Christian diabology in the medieval period are patristic, scholastic, and mystical theology; art, literature, and drama; popular religion, homiletics, and saints' lives; and folklore.

Although a few medieval literary works distinguish between the persons of Satan and Lucifer, the tradition as a whole affirms their unity and uses the terms indiscriminately as names of a single personage, the Devil, the personification of evil. The name "Lucifer" was born through the association of the great prince of Isaiah 14, the morning star, Helel-ben-Shahar, who falls from the heavens through his pride, with the cherub of Ezekiel 28, who was "perfect in his ways from the day he was created until iniquity was found in him," and of both with Satan, prince of this world and obstructor of the kingdom of God. Exactly when the three concepts came together is uncertain, but Origen treated them as a unity in the third century.

Throughout these volumes I have been drawing the history of a concept. My philosophy is unabashedly idealist; it assumes that ideas are important in themselves and that the social context in which they arise is more important for understanding the ideas than the other way around. I differ from the materialism presently dominant in the historical profession and deny that modern materialism possesses any objective framework within which or by which ideas are to be judged. Rather, the first function of history is to open our minds to the infinite wealth of possible world views and to help us to understand that our own view, whatever it may be, is precarious, limited, and open to sudden and radical change.

The social context influenced diabology only in a broad sense— early medieval culture, dominated by monasticism, followed the traditional view of the Devil developed by the desert fathers; later, the rise of towns permitted the growth of universities and the scholastic approach to diabology and theology in general. But the similar development of Christian and Muslim ideas of the Devil and the closeness of seventeenth-century Protestant views to thirteenth-century scholastic ones indicate that vastly different social settings could produce nearly identical ideas.

On the whole diabology changed during this period in refined detail rather than on main points. This unusual consistency follows from the general consistency of Christian theology in the Middle Ages, which can be attributed to its relative cultural isolation and security from threatening new ideas. Only from the late seventeenth century, when Europe was awash with new ideas, did Christianity come under a broad criticism that forced it to amend its views in fundamental ways. Diabology was more consistent than other aspects of theology, probably because a useful means of dehumanizing one's opponents was to accuse them of being tools of Satan. Diabology was not subjected to serious attack until the witch craze of the sixteenth and seventeenth centuries had produced intolerable cruelties founded on and justified by belief in the Devil.

Because the sources are much more numerous for medieval than for earlier diabology, this book can offer only a rational selection. Certain themes important in themselves but tangential to the personification of evil are set aside or treated only briefly, such as hell, purgatory, death, millenarianism, minor demons, Antichrist, original sin, and all the technical details of art history and literary criticism.

I thank those who contributed to the formation of this book, especially Cameron Airhart, Joseph Amato, Milton Anastos, Theodore J. Antry, Kathleen Ashley, Hieromonk Auxentios, David Berger, Carl T. Berkhout, Alan Bernstein, Felipe Cervera, Richard Comstock, Spencer Cosmos, David Darwazeh, Hal Drake, Kathleen E. Dubs, Alberto Ferreiro, Abraham Friesen, Nancy Gallagher, Joyce Manheimer Galpern, Robert Griffin, Barbara Hambly, Wayland Hand, Kristine E. Haney, Richard Homan, Warren Hollister, John Howe, Karen Jolly, Henry Ansgar Kelly, Morton Kelsey, Moshé Lazar, Ruth Mellinkoff, Charles Musès, Raimundo Panikkar, Robert Potter, Cassandra Potts, Cheryl Riggs, Roy Riggs, Russell Riggs, Kevin Roddy, Jennifer Russell, Ellen Schiferl, Patricia Silber, Kathleen Verduin, Tim Vivian, Jack Vizzard, the late Charles Wendell, and Mark Wyndham.

In all three volumes I speak as a human being as well as a historian. It would be presumptuous and futile to deal with so fundamental a problem as evil without confronting it personally. If we take ideas seriously, we must encounter them with our whole personalities. The function of history, and of all learning, humanistic and scientific, is to look beyond our safe little studies and laboratories out into the cosmos, or into the soul, with love; but always with love, which is the burning dart that we shoot forth into the world's darkness, hoping to illuminate, if only dimly and for a moment, the green and shining landscape that stretches upward around us. Many faults must appear in these pages, as in the previous two volumes, and inconsistencies among the three. I would be a poor historian and a poorer person not to understand more at the end of the third volume than at the beginning of the first.

JEFFREY BURTON RUSSELL

Santa Barbara, California

Abbreviations

DEVIL: Jeffrey B. Russell, *The Devil: Perceptions of Evil from Antiquity to Primitive Christianity*. Ithaca, 1977.

SATAN: Jeffrey B. Russell, *Satan: The Early Christian Tradition*. Ithaca, 1981.

CCCM: Corpus Christianorum Continuatio Medievalis.

CCSG: Corpus Christianorum Series Graeca.

CCSL: Corpus Christianorum Series Latina.

CSEL: Corpus Scriptorum Ecclesiasticorum.

EETS: Early English Text Society.

Hefele-Leclercq: K. J. von Hefele and H. Leclercq, *Histoire des conciles d'après les documents originaux*, 11 vols. in 21. Hildesheim, 1973.

MPG: J. P. Migne, ed., Patrologia Graeca.

MPL: J. P. Migne, ed., Patrologia Latina.

Mansi: Johannes Mansi, ed., Sacrorum conciliorum nova et amplissima collectio.

SC: Sources chrétiennes.

All citations from medieval writers for which no specific edition is cited are to be found in MPG or MPL. Abbreviations of individual works are to be found in the footnotes with the first mention of the author or the work.

Lucifer

If intellectual activity divorces itself from life, it becomes
not only barren and alienating, but also harmful and perhaps
eventually criminal. . . . I am convinced that we live in a state
of human emergency that does not allow us to entertain ourselves
with bagatelles.

—RAIMUNDO PANIKKAR

Tot enim vulnera Satanas accipit
quot antiquarius Domini verba describit.
[The words of the Lord's historian are wounds inflicted on the Devil.]

—CASSIODORUS

1 The Life of Lucifer

Evil is real and immediate. On March 8, 1981, the *Los Angeles Times* reported the activities of the convicted murderer Steven T. Judy:

The brutal murder that made today Judy's last day to live occurred around 8 A.M. on a Saturday, April 28, 1979. Terry Lee Chasteen, 23, was taking her children—Misty Ann, 5, Steven, 4, and Mark, 2—to the baby sitter en route to her job at an Indianapolis supermarket when she was flagged to the side of the interstate highway by a man indicating there was a problem with her car. It was Judy, just five days out of jail after posting $750 bond on an armed robbery charge, playing the role of a good Samaritan. But while pretending to help, he covertly disabled her car completely and then offered the family a ride. The ride ended at White lick Creek just off a roadway where he raped the woman and then strangled her with torn bits of her clothing. When the children began to scream, Judy silenced them one by one in the river.[1]

On April 29, 1981, the *Times* reported the conviction of Lewis Norris, aged thirty-three, and his partner, Lawrence Sigmond Bittaker, aged forty:

1. W. C. Rempel, *Los Angeles Times*, March 8, 1981.

The Norris-Bittaker case included some of the most shocking testimony in American criminal court annals. From June to October, 1979, it was brought out, the two prowled the South Bay area and San Fernando Valley in a sound-proofed van they called the "Murder Mack." The five known victims ranged in age from 13 to 18. The young victims were forced to submit to repeated rapes and other sexual outrages, which in two cases lasted for two days. Some were forced to carry air mattresses and torture paraphernalia from the van to grassy knolls in the mountains above Glendora, where four of the victims were slain. The killers ripped the girls with pliers, beat them with a sledge hammer, drove icepicks into their skulls, and strangled them with wire coathangers. In the case of the first victim, Lucinda (Cindy) Schaefer, 16, who was kidnapped as she walked from church to her Torrance home, Norris and Bittaker rejected her plea to be allowed to pray before they killed her. They immediately began throttling her with a wire coathanger.[2]

Real, absolute, tangible evil demands our consideration. It threatens every one of us and all of us together. We avoid examining it at our grave peril. And on no account may we ever trivialize it. Unless the Devil is perceived as the personification of real evil, he becomes meaningless.

The heart of evil is violence. In *Violence and Responsibility*, J. Harris defines violence as that which "occurs when injury or suffering is inflicted upon a person or persons by an agent who knows (or ought reasonably to have known) that his actions would result in the harm in question."[3] Suffering is an aspect of pain, which has three distinct components. The first is the cause of pain, whether natural or deliberate violence. This action of causing harm is the active evil: it is here that Satan dwells. The second is the pain strictly defined as an acute physical response to sensory stimula. Pain in this sense is morally neutral: it can be constructive if it warns you that your foot is burning. The third is suffering, which is a response to pain that includes terror, anxiety, alarm, and fear of annihilation. Suffering is passive evil, the result of active evil.[4]

Violence can be defined as the evil infliction of suffering. Some instances of causing pain—for example, the surgeon's knife—cannot

2. R. West, *Los Angeles Times*, April 29, 1981.
3. J. Harris, *Violence and Responsibility* (London, 1980), p. 19. See also J. Ellul, *Violence* (New York, 1969); H. Arendt, *On Violence* (New York, 1969); S. Yochelson and S. Samenow, *The Criminal Personality*, 2 vols. (New York, 1977), esp. vol. 1, p. 104.
4. Drugs such as morphine do not relieve pain so much as the suffering produced by the pain. See D. Bakan, *Disease, Pain, and Sacrifice* (Chicago, 1968), p. 86. See M. Zborowski, *People in Pain* (San Francisco, 1969), for the cultural relativity of suffering.

be classified as violent because the intent is to heal, not to cause suffering. The conscious and deliberate inflicting of suffering is the heart of violence and of moral evil. "Natural evils" such as floods and muscular dystrophy are also examples of violence. They cannot be dismissed as morally neutral or as logical necessities in the cosmos. If God is responsible for the world, he is responsible for these natural evils and the suffering they entail. The doctrine of double effect cannot relieve God from responsibility. "Double effect" is the distinction between what a person strictly intends by an action and what that person foresees as its probable results; for example, if a person sees two people drowning at the same distance away, he may swim out to save one, intending what is good for him, while knowing that the other will probably drown. The limitations of "double effect" are clear from another example: a person who sets off a nuclear war with the intention of freeing the world from injustice. It seems impossible that an omniscient God does not intend what he knows absolutely will result. God knows, surely and clearly, that in creating the cosmos he creates a cosmos in which children are tortured.

Today two currents of belief run counter to one another. One of the currents is carrying us away from a sense of evil. The vague egalitarianism of our day insists that no qualitative standards exist. If no standards of value exist beyond personal preferences, then nothing is really good or really evil—including the actions of Norris and Bittaker. The other, opposite current is a renewed awareness of evil, sometimes linked with a revived interest in the Devil. One element in this current is the growth of evangelical Christianity, though this has been offset by a growing skepticism among Catholics about the existence of the Devil, in spite of the cautions of Pope Paul VI.[5] The renewed awareness of evil derives from the events of the twentieth century. Since 1914, world wars, rootlessness and crime, concentration camps, totalitarian states, the genocide of Jews and Cambodians, and widespread starvation in a world of riches have pulverized the assumptions of secular progressivism. Warplanes, missiles, and napalm are physical concretizations of the demonic in our day. The horrors of the twentieth century have provoked a reevaluation of assumptions of progress and an increased readiness to believe that evil is radically inherent in human nature and perhaps in the cosmos.[6]

5. Paul VI, Allocution of Nov. 15, 1972, *Ecclesia*, 32 (1972/II), 1605.
6. Secular progressivism suffers from a logical vacuum at its center. If no absolutes

The Devil is rooted in a perception of this radical evil. To suppose belief in the Devil outdated and superstitious is false. The question to ask about any idea is not whether it is outdated but whether it is true. The notion that new ideas are necessarily better than old is an unfounded and incoherent assumption, and no idea that fits into a coherent world view can properly be called superstitious. Those who believe in the Devil without fitting this belief into a world view may be superstitious, but those who have a coherent structure embracing the concept are not. Superstition is any belief held by any individual who has not fit that belief into a coherent world view. This definition varies from the usual dictionary definition of superstition as belief founded on ignorance. The dictionary definition does not work, because one man's ignorance is another man's wisdom. Jesuits hold beliefs that Marxists deem superstitious; Marxists hold beliefs that phenomenologists hold superstitious, and so on forever. No one has valid claim to absolute or objective knowledge.

Prior to the question of whether the Devil exists is the question of what the Devil is. The method used in this book to answer the question is the history of concepts, which is an effort to examine the bases of historical thought, to construct a coherent system of historical explanation of human concepts, and to validate that system as at least equally sure as scientific systems. In outline, the method begins, as all systems must, with epistemological skepticism, the understanding that nothing at all is known, or can be known with absolute certainty. The single exception is Nietzsche's *es denkt:* something is thinking. Absolute knowledge (knowledge$_1$) is not attainable. We can attain a lesser degree of knowledge from experience (knowledge$_2$). But knowledge$_2$ is private, not necessarily validated or socially accepted. By comparing our experiences with others' and learning from them we can eventually construct knowledge$_3$, publicly validated knowledge. If any supposed knowledge$_3$ is not validatable within a coherent system, it is not knowledge at all but superstition. All of us are superstitious some of

exist that transcend humanity, then nothing exists that could possibly be drawing humanity in any particular direction, and we are in random motion. Without a goal, motion is meaningless. If Portland is your goal you can make progress by driving a mile down the road toward Portland, but if you have no goal, then driving a mile in the direction of Portland or in any other direction is meaningless motion, not progress. That "man sets his own goals" is an evasion, because human goals shift frequently and radically. One may make progress in terms of this or that limited goal, but unless there is a general and final goal, it is not possible to speak of progress overall.

the time, and some of us are superstitious all of the time. Knowledge$_3$ can be called knowledge only when it is part of a coherent world view. Many coherent thought systems have existed and do exist; their relative value can be judged according to their degree of coherence and also according to the breadth of their ability to accommodate phenomena. Copernicus' solar system is better than Ptolemy's geocentric world, not because Ptolemy's is incoherent but because Copernicus' can embrace the phenomena more easily and simply. But no knowledge$_1$ is available by which to judge any system absolutely.[7]

Certain systems work best with certain problems. Some questions are treated best by physics, some by poetry. The best system of defining and explaining such human constructs as the Constitution or the Devil is the history of concepts. The system is best because it rests upon the fewest unproved assumptions, embraces every human concept, and does so with the greatest economy consistent with a full explanation. The definition it offers is at once the broadest and the most coherent. Other approaches to a definition of the Devil are solipsism, a priori reasoning, and ecclesiastical or other ideological authority, but each has a validation problem.[8] Why should anyone accept your view of the Devil, or your uncle's, or your pastor's, unless it fits into a coherent pattern? The historical definition, on the other hand, should be acceptable to every ideological point of view. Protestants, Catholics, atheists, Muslims, and Marxists should be able to agree as to the general lines of the development of the concept (naturally disagreement will exist on details). The Devil is what the history of his concept is. Nothing else about him can be known. The history of the concept of the Devil reveals all that can be known about the Devil, and it is the only way that the Devil can be known (in the sense of knowledge$_3$) at all. One may then decide to believe in the Devil or not, or to use the concept to illustrate some other point altogether—Marxists, for example, will be interested in it only as it illustrates social history. But everyone ought to be able to agree on the historical definition of the Devil.

7. For further discussion of the history of concepts, see DEVIL, chap. 2, and SATAN, pp. 15–29. See also S. Toulmin, *Human Understanding*, 3 vols. (Princeton, 1972–), esp. vol. 1, p. 51.

8. "Universal authority may be claimed for an abstract, timeless system of 'rational standards' only if it has first been shown on what foundation that universal and unqualified authority rests; but no formal schema can by itself prove its own applicability" (Toulmin, vol. 1, p. 63).

Christ separating the sheep from the goats. This is the earliest known portrayal of the Devil, who sits at Christ's left hand with the goats, while the good angel sits at the Lord's right hand with the sheep. The Devil is blue, the color of the lower air into which he has been thrust; the good angel is red, the color of fire and the ethereal realm in which the angels dwell. Sixth-century mosaic, San Apollinare Nuovo, Ravenna. Courtesy of Hirmer Verlag, Munich.

The history of concepts observes individual perceptions of the Devil (knowledge$_2$); it describes these perceptions constellating as they acquire social validation and become knowledge$_3$; it shows these constellations growing in time, gradually excluding the eccentric and forming the boundaries of a tradition; and it perceives the tradition as always unfinished (so long as anyone has a direct perception of evil). The concept is four-dimensional, seen throughout its entire existence in space and time up to the present.

The history of the concept of the Devil has deep implications for historical theology. In themselves God, angels, and the Devil have no history, for if they do objectively exist, historians cannot get to them in order to investigate them. Historians can only establish the human concept of the Devil. But theologians, as opposed to historians, want to ask whether the historical concept of the Devil corresponds with reality or at least is consistent with reality. Like historians and scientists, theologians are aware that they cannot obtain knowledge$_1$, that their own perceptions are private, and that whatever systems they devise or accept are, like all other systems, precarious. With these reservations in mind, the theologian begins with an assumption (all theological, historical, and scientific systems are built on assumptions) that the human mind can obtain at least some knowledge about God and the Devil that transcends merely human perceptions. The history of concepts provides the theologian with the only coherent picture of the Devil that is demonstrably consistent with historical reality. Historical theologians may personally assent to the historical tradition or reject it, but they cannot meaningfully define the Devil in terms foreign to it.

Historians draw the lines of a concept's development without making any kind of statement about its religious truth; historical theologians use these lines to distinguish legitimate from illegitimate developments, lasting ideas from those that will not fit permanently into the tradition.[9] The idea of the development of doctrine has its difficul-

9. The classical statement of the development of doctrine is of course J. H. Newman, *Essay on the Development of Christian Doctrine* (London, 1846). See Günther Biemer, *Newman on Tradition* (London, 1967); G. Ladner, *The Idea of Reform* (Cambridge, Mass., 1959); K. F. Morrison, *Tradition and Authority in the Western Church 300–1100* (Princeton, 1969); B. Tierney, *The Origin of Papal Infallibility* (Leiden, 1972); O. Chadwick, *From Bossuet to Newman* (Cambridge, 1957); J. Pelikan, *Historical Theology* (New York, 1971); the validity of the narrative historical method has been demonstrated many times, notably by A. C. Danto, *Analytical Philosophy of History* (Cambridge, 1965), and P. Munz, *The Shapes of Time* (Middletown, Conn., 1977).

ties; we no longer expect the clear answers that J. H. Newman expected. The possibility that the entire tradition is objectively false always exists; no tradition based upon false assumptions has any validity. But the only way the Devil can be defined is through his tradition, and when the tradition becomes too intricate, incoherent, or off the track, then it becomes untrue. Yet if the tradition is false, then we have no idea about the Devil at all, and any statement made about him is philosophically and literally meaningless. Wrongly used, the method might produce a tautology: we believe because we believe. But the validation of the belief is not the belief itself; it is, rather, the demonstrable tradition of what the community in space and time has believed, combined with a critical attention to eliminating distortion and unnecessary detail.

The theological alternatives to belief in tradition as a vehicle of truth, other than skepticism, solipsism, and tautology, are (1) empirical observation, which cannot be applied to beings such as the Devil that are normally unobservable by the senses; (2) democratic scholarly consensus, which is always shifting; (3) reliance upon Scripture alone, itself based upon undemonstrable assumptions that Scripture is both objectively true and the only source of revelation;[10] (4) dialectic applied to revelation—the scholastic method—which itself changes through time both as to its interpretation of Scripture and as to the function of its logic; (5) authority of ecclesiastical office through apostolic succession, again based upon undemonstrable assumptions. Only the historical approach is verifiable by and acceptable to those of any persuasion that is not doggedly irrational.

10. The effort to base theological understanding exclusively upon the Scriptures encounters numerous difficulties: (1) the Scriptures themselves depend upon tradition, the canon of the New Testament not being set before the fourth century; (2) scholars disagree as to the relative faithfulness to historical reality of the different sections of Scripture; (3) any and all readings of Scripture, emphatically including translations, are interpretations or *eisegeses;* (4) reliance upon Scripture is unacceptable to non-Christians; (5) almost all Christian doctrines, including the Trinity and Christology as well as the Devil, are only vague and inchoate in Scripture and required long discussion and debate in order to develop. The Devil's role is, of course, at least as powerful in the New Testament as in subsequent tradition. The New Testament writers "belonged to a Church which eagerly awaited the second coming of the Lord, which preferred to understand redemption not so much in the juridical categories of 'satisfaction' and 'merit' as in the more picturesque category of a victorious battle won by Christ over the Devil and evil spirits" (W. J. Dalton, *Christ's Proclamation to the Spirits* [Rome, 1925], p. 278). The oak is the acorn; but the oak is also the green and spreading tree. The truth of a concept is not to be found only in its origins, but in its entirety.

Today we have more reason than ever to be concerned with evil in that we seem to be standing at the end of time. In the nineteenth century people could assume that though things might go wrong occasionally and temporarily we had time to resolve the difficulties and eventually make things right. Marxists and other secular progressives could assume that the future would bring a better world. But now we have run out of time. J. Robert Oppenheimer and his colleagues began the end of time, and of secular progressivism. After ten billion years we, in our century, have begun the process of putting an end to evolution, to progress, to life. Only by grappling with evil now, with clear sight and with courage, can we have any chance of avoiding the ruin that looms.[11]

11. A new, excellent treatment of evil from a Jungian point of view is J. Sanford, *Evil: The Shadow Side of Reality* (New York, 1981). A new transhistorical consensus may be emerging because of the possibility of the end of time. Such is the view of R. Panikkar, "Is History the Measure of Man?" *The Teilhard Review*, 16 (1981), 39–45.

2 The Devil in Byzantium

The diabology of three civilizations—Western Latin, Eastern Orthodox, and Islamic—grew out of patristic thought. The fall of Constantinople in 1453 divides Byzantine theology from modern Orthodox theology.[1] Diabology was more extensive and precise in the

1. This volume is concerned primarily with the development of diabology in the Christian context; it treats Muslim diabology only briefly; it does not enter the complex realm of the medieval Jewish kabbalah, which drew upon Gnosticism and Christianity as well as upon rabbinic traditions. Mystical and unitive, kabbalistic thought tended to monism and on occasion could locate evil within the godhead. The book *Bahir*, the earliest kabbalistic work, dating from the late twelfth century, says that evil is a principle within God and "lies in the mouth of God." See G. Scholem, *On the Kabbalah and Its Symbolism* (New York, 1965), p. 92. Western understanding of Eastern Orthodoxy has increased in recent years. See especially E. Benz, *The Eastern Orthodox Church* (Chicago, 1963); D. J. Geanakoplos, *Interaction of the "Sibling" Byzantine and Western Cultures in the Middle Ages and Italian Renaissance (330–1600)* (New Haven, 1976); G. Maloney, *A History of Orthodox Theology since 1453* (Belmont, Mass., 1976); J. Meyendorff, *Byzantine Theology: Historical Trends and Doctrinal Themes*, 2d ed. (New York, 1979); D. M. Nicol, *Church and Society in the Last Centuries of Byzantium* (Cambridge, 1979); D. J. O'Meara, *Neoplatonism and Christian Thought* (Albany, 1982); J. Pelikan, *The Christian Tradition*, vol. 2: *The Spirit of Eastern Christendom (600–1700)* (Chicago, 1974); B. Tatakis, *La philosophie byzantine* (Paris, 1949); T. Ware, *The Orthodox Church* (Baltimore, 1963).

Latin West than in the other two civilizations, and it reflected the differences between the Western and Eastern churches. Eastern Orthodox theology, more mystical and unitive than that of the West, paid less attention to the Devil. The Byzantine church emphasized monasticism, mysticism, and an apophatic view of theology. The apophatic view is the *via negativa*, the "negative way" to God, which emphasizes his unknowableness and stresses contemplation and prayer as opposed to reason—the tendency in medieval Western thought—as the royal way to understanding.[2]

The postulates of Byzantine diabology were based on those of the fathers of the first five centuries. Byzantine heresies, sermons, and folklore, on the other hand, added details that "fleshed out" the image of the Devil. The Byzantines believed that the Devil is a creature of God rather than an independent principle; that God, not the Devil, made the material world and the human body; that the Devil and the other fallen angels were created good but fell because of pride; that the Devil and his demons tempt us, try to turn us away from God, and rejoice in our suffering and our corruption.[3]

To these fundamental assumptions Pseudo-Dionysius the Areopagite (Dionysius or Denis) brought perhaps the first thoroughgoing mystical theology in Christianity. Confused in the Middle Ages with the convert of Saint Paul and first bishop of Athens, and further confused in the West with Saint Denis the martyr of Gaul, Dionysius was in fact a Syrian monk who wrote about A.D. 500.[4] Influenced by Philo,

2. The Eastern church emphasized the beauty as well as the truth of divinity and developed icons, a religious idiom relatively unknown in the West. The early Christians were reluctant to produce any images at all, but pictures of Christ do appear in the second century, and from the fourth century the use of holy pictures became widespread. Yet no representation of the Devil is known before the sixth century. On icons, see E. Kitzinger, *The Art of Byzantium and the Medieval West* (Bloomington, 1976); E. Kitzinger, *Byzantine Art in the Making* (Cambridge, Mass., 1977); M. V. Anastos, "The Ethical Theory of Images Formulated by the Iconoclasts in 754 and 815," *Dumbarton Oaks Papers*, 8 (1954), 151–160; C. Cavarnos, *Orthodox Iconography* (Belmont, Mass., 1977); J. Lafontaine-Dosogne, "Un thème iconographique peu connu: Marina assomant Belzébuth," *Byzantion*, 32 (1962), 251–259; L. Ouspensky and V. Lossky, *The Meaning of Icons* (Boston, 1952). Personal communications from Professors L. Ayres, E. Kitzinger, and E. Schiferl confirm that no sufficient explanation for the lack of Devil pictures before the sixth century has yet been offered.

3. Pelikan, pp. 216–255.

4. For a bibliography on Dionysius see the Essay on the Sources, this volume. Works cited here are *Mystical Theology (MT); Divine Names (DN); Celestial Hierarchy (CH); Ecclesiastical Hierarchy (EH)*. The best study of the early mystical tradition is A. Louth, *The Origins of the Christian Mystical Tradition* (Oxford, 1981).

Origen, and Middle Platonism as mediated by Gregory of Nyssa and
the other Cappadocians, Dionysius distinguished between positive
and negative theology, emphasizing the apophatic, negative way and
combining the idea of the individual's kinship with God with the
understanding that God is wholly other: We know nothing about God,
who is completely beyond anything that we might understand about
him, partly because our own reason is tiny and restricted, but more
because he himself is beyond all reason. If we are to have a glimmer-
ing, we must understand him with an understanding that surpasses the
intelligence, an understanding given by God and characterized by an
irresistible desire that draws us magnetically toward that which is all
and the source of all. Yet Dionysius did not reject reason, for although
the essence of God is forever hidden, the manifestations of God—his
energeia, energies and actions—can be known: God can be seen in
things, however much they refract or distort his image. Reason tells us
that some statements about God are more untrue than others, and we
must begin by rejecting these. "We must start by applying our negations to those qualities which differ most from the ultimate goal. Surely it is truer to affirm that God is life and goodness than that He is air
or stone, and truer to deny that drunkenness or fury can be attributed
to Him than to deny that we may apply to Him the categories of
human thought."[5] Yet whatever we can say about God is only metaphorical, and Dionysius on the whole preferred distant metaphors to
close ones because the danger of confusion is less. To call God fire
misleads us less into thinking we are saying something absolute about
him than to call him eternal.

The purpose of life is to be raised up as close in unity with this
hidden God as possible. The mystic cares less about understanding
God than about union with him. This union Dionysius called *theosis*,
divinization. Now, God is what is. Everything that is comes from
him, and everything yearns to return to him. "All things are moved by
a longing for the Beautiful and the Good."[6] Things without will or

5. *MT* 3; C. E. Rolt, *Dionysius the Areopagite: The Divine Names and the Mystical
Theology* (London, 1920), pp. 198–199; V. Lossky, "La théologie négative dans la
doctrine de Denys l'Aréopagite," *Revue des sciences philosophiques et théologiques*, 28 (1939),
204–217; T. (K.) Ware, "God Hidden and Revealed: The Apophatic Way and the
Essence-Energies Distinction," *Eastern Churches Review*, 7 (1975), 125–136. Lossky, pp.
209–212, explains the difference between the "being" (οὐσία) of God and his "energy"
(δύναμις, ἄκτις). Similar ideas appear in Augustine's *Sermo de Scripturio Novi Testamenti*
52.6.16; 117.3.5.
6. *DN* 4.10; Rolt, p. 101.

intelligence seek him through natural processes; beings with will and intelligence seek him through conscious desire. The whole cosmos longs to be united with God, and God longs to gather it up to him. This is what the cosmos is about. It is very simple, but our clouded minds twist it into complexity. "Mankind at large cannot grasp the simplicity of the one Divine yearning."[7] Desire draws us to God; desire opens us up and lets him into us; the divine desire draws us to itself. In our present state, sent out from God, we are infinitely remote from him and resemble him only as a distorted image in a flawed glass. We cannot obtain unity with God through good works or study or understanding. We can only accept it as a gift. Any "knowing" of God that we may have must be acquired through "unknowing," that is, by rejecting the hope of intellectual knowledge. By passing into the cloud of unknowing we can rise to God, who surpasses all being and all understanding.[8] This is not occult cant: the cloud (*gnophos*) and the shadow (*skotos*) are part of everyone's conscious, ordinary experience, for our own minds are in a permanent state of ignorance of the true nature of God, the world, other people, and ourselves. This passage into darkness separates Dionysius from Origen and other more fully Platonist thinkers. Whereas the Platonists hoped to mount gradually through spheres of ever-increasing knowledge and light, Dionysius understood that to know is to know that we do not know.[9] If we grasp the full state of our unknowing, we will struggle against *pathē* (confused emotions and passions) and move toward *apatheia* (spiritual calm), which leads to *eirēnē* (peace) and selfless love of God. In this way our lives may become an imitation of God.[10]

God produces all the forms in the cosmos, and God draws them back to him. "The cosmos (is) a glittering sequence of hierarchies all serving to express and effect the assimilation of all things in

7. *DN* 4.12; Rolt, p. 105.
8. *DN* 7.3: ἡ θειοτάτη τοῦ θεοῦ γνῶσις ἡ δι' ἀγνωσίας γιγνωσκομένη . . . κατὰ τὴν ὑπὲρ νοῦν ἕνωσιν. *MT* 1.1; 1.3: τοῦ ὑπὲρ πᾶσαν οὐσίαν καὶ γνῶσιν . . . εἰς τὸν γνόφον τῆς ἀγνωσίας εἰσδύνει τὸν ὄντως μυστικόν.
9. God is inaccessible (ἀπρόσιτος), *DN* 7.2; invisible (ἀόρατος), *MT* 1.3; intangible (ἀναφής), *MT* 1.3; unnamable (ἀκατανόμαστος), *DN* 1.8; unobservable (ἀθέατος), *MT* 1.3. The modern philosopher Philip Wheelwright used to refer to the three radical incompletenesses of humanity: our understanding of the cosmos is never complete; our understanding of other people is never complete; our understanding of ourselves is never complete.
10. W. Völker, *Kontemplation und Extase bei Pseudo-Dionysius Areopagitica* (Wiesbaden, 1958), pp. 38–71. Compare the system of Evagrius of Pontus in SATAN, pp. 177–185.

God."[11] For if God's first creative act is an act of desire that spills the cosmos out, his second creative act is to draw back in desire what he has created in desire. Those entities closest to God are highest in the celestial hierarchy; those farthest from God are lowest in the hierarchy. The hierarchy, however, is not static but a moving scale or ladder on which the intelligences or forms may be drawn upward on their way to assimilation with God.[12] Dionysius' is the first detailed description of the celestial hierarchy, in which the angels are arranged into three hierarchies of three ranks each. The highest triad, the Seraphim, Cherubim, and Thrones, is in close contact with the *thearchia*, the divine principle that illuminates the cosmos, and receives direct illumination from it. The middle triad, the Dominations, Virtues, and Powers, receives the divine illumination as transmitted to it by the first triad, and in turn transmits the illumination to the last triad Principalities, Archangels, and Angels, which then conveys to humanity God's dispensation for the governance of the world. This hierarchical arrangement was highly influential in the East and, adapted by Gregory the Great, also spread throughout the West.[13]

Western writers, linking the idea that the Seraphim are at the pinnacle of the angelic hierarchy with the tradition that the Devil had been the greatest of angels, usually assumed that Lucifer had been a seraph. Dionysius himself could not make such an assumption, since in his system the highest orders of angels had no contact with the earth. The Devil did not play a leading role in Dionysius' thought, and he constructed no evil hierarchy to mirror the heavenly or earthly hierarchies.[14] Intensely mystical, unitive modes of religious thought tend to find little place for an active spirit of evil in a cosmos where all things proceed from God and return to him. The greater influence of mystical theology in the East than in the West is one reason why demonology did not develop as sharply or as fully there. Another reason is the influence of the "negative way" as a whole: one simply cannot say anything very secure about either God or the Devil.

Divinization—the process of return to God—embraces all forms. God knows everything that exists, of course, but not in the sense that

11. Louth, p. 178.

12. Assimilation and union: ἀφομοίωσίς τε καὶ ἕνωσις (*CH* 3.2).

13. Gregory was aware of the nine ranks though not of the three triads, and he transposed the Principalities and the Virtues.

14. The Devil and evil are discussed in *DN* 4.18–34 and appear only tangentially elsewhere in Dionysius, e.g., *EH* 3.7; *Epistolae*, 8.

In *The Temptation of Christ*, the artist revived the early medieval tradition of portraying the Devil in semihuman, rather than bestial, form. Meister of Schloss Lichtenstein, oil on canvas, fifteenth century. Courtesy of the Oesterreichische Galerie, Vienna.

they exist prior to or separate from his knowledge and then he comes to know them. Things are neither prior nor external to God. God's knowledge of things precedes them, and it is precisely what produces them. Whatever exists has existence *for the reason that* God knows it, and whatever does not exist lacks existence for the very reason that he does not know it. Things truly exist because they exist *in* God. It is less true to say that God creates the world ex nihilo than to say that God produces it out of its own being. This distancing of mysticism from ex nihilo creationism, which had been dominant since the fourth century, runs the risk of becoming pantheism. But Dionysius, though he may have been a panentheist, was far from being a pantheist. All exists *in* God and *of* God's love and knowledge. All is God in a sense, but God also surpasses all totally. God is transcendent as well as immanent.

God does not realize or actualize everything he knows. God knows contingencies that he chooses not to actualize. This does not limit God's power, knowledge, or will. Still, since the divine will, like the divine knowledge, is fixed and immutable as well as dynamic, the cosmos that is actualized and the contingencies that are realized are absolutely fixed. It is logically possible that God could have realized a different cosmos, but only logically and not really, for God's nature is eternally fixed, so that God's mind embraces the contingencies eternally and eternally chooses to realize some and not others. It is false to say that God could have created a different cosmos, because "could have" implies the impossible contradiction that the immutable will and absolute knowledge of God are mutable and limited. The cosmos is absolutely as it is, and God is absolutely responsible for it.

But now for evil. How, in a world made of God's desire, a world in which all things have their being in God, can evil exist? God is love, but God is not a custard. He is the farthest thing conceivable from being meek and mild. God is love, but God's love is like the cold winter wind that bites and penetrates and shakes and frightens and kills. God is what he is; what is, is. It is our own limitation that we wish God to conform to what we desire him to be. Dionysius' God is in part the serene God of light of the Neoplatonists, but he is also the God of Abraham, Isaac, and Jacob, whose face one cannot look upon and live.

Since God is good and all that comes from God is good, all that exists will return to him. Here Dionysius was faced with a dilemma: a thoroughgoing monist position that maintained that even evil was part of God and must, however transformed, return to God in the end would compromise the goodness of God; on the other hand a dualist position that evil is a principle independent of God would compromise God's omnipotence. Neither position fit the Christian tradition. Evil cannot come from God, since it is a contradiction of God, and it cannot be an independent principle, since all that is comes from God. Evil is therefore literally nothing in itself. It is merely a deficiency, a lack, a privation in what is. Good comes from the one universal cause; evil from many partial deficiencies. Evil is a lack of good: it has no substantial being but only a shadow of being. In one of his great showers of words, Dionysius says that evil is "a lack, a deficiency, a weakness, a disproportion, an error, purposeless, unlovely, lifeless, unwise, unreasonable, imperfect, unreal, causeless, indeterminate, sterile, inert, powerless, disordered, incongruous, indefinite, dark, unsubstantial, and never in itself possessed of any existence whatever."[15]

The cosmos is arranged in a *taxis hiera*, a holy order, God's holy dispensation, which is unchangeable and absolute. No disorderly thing (*atakton*) can exist. Harmony is the concord of all creatures with this dispensation, in which the essential unity of the cosmos rests. This union is realized as all creatures are gradually drawn up to God in the process of *theosis*, divinization. The purpose of the cosmos and the function of the hierarchies are to draw the world to God. Why does God create the diversity to begin with? Because infinite creative energy inheres in his nature. He bursts with energy, radiating out in fecund variety, power, and brilliance. It is part of the divine nature to lavish the gift of being with abandon and unlimited bounty. God builds privation into his dispensation for the cosmos, though we, with our limited understanding, do not grasp how.[16]

"How is it that the demons, if they have been brought forth from the good, are not themselves good?" Dionysius replies to his own question: the demons are not evil by nature but through their own will. The fallen angels were created good, like everything else in the cosmos, and as angels they received every good gift commensurate with their status. Evil is not inherent in matter, in the body, in animals, or in anything that exists. Evil proceeds from the evil will of

15. *DN* 4.32; Rolt, p. 127.
16. R. Roques, *L'univers Dionysien* (Paris, 1954), pp. 36–92. The idea of the plenitude of forms does not include such impossible, self-contradictory forms as a cow with wings or a duck that composes like Mozart: a duck who wrote *The Marriage of Figaro* would not be a duck.

fallen angels and fallen humans, who freely use their free will to desire that which is not good, that which is unreal. So they corrupt, weaken, and degrade themselves. This evil is not a product of nature but a distortion of nature, a subtraction from the reality that is nature. One cannot even say that the privation struggles against the good through its own power, for it is literally nonexistent. And yet this nonexistence, like a vacuum, acts to suck creatures down into the void of nonbeing.

The Devil's nature is real and good, since it was created by God. But the Devil freely turns his will toward the unreal. To the degree that he does this, he moves away from God, who is goodness, being, and reality, toward that which is privation, nonbeing, evil. Of all creatures, the Devil has moved farthest from God and closest to the void. Yet, like the low pressure in the center of a tornado, the emptiness of the Devil exerts real and terrible destruction.

Maximus Confessor (c. 580–662), an aristocrat who became a monk and an ascetic, developed and interpreted Dionysian thought and in turn influenced both the Eastern and Western churches.[17] Like Dionysius, Maximus was a mystic who emphasized the divinization of the cosmos through God's yearning. Closer to Neoplatonism than Dionysius, Maximus argued that God is a monad preceding all being and existence. The Monad, unknowable in itself, is known through its motion, its energeia. Union with God is never achievable by knowledge, but only through God's grace, which transforms our human nature into a more perfect image of God on the model of Christ. The Devil's being is good; his evil results from an ignorant misuse of his free will. His motive is envy of God and of humanity.[18] But the Devil is not only God's enemy; he is God's "servant" and "vindicator": God allows him to tempt us so as to help us distinguish between virtue and sin, to permit us to attain virtue through struggle, to teach us humility, to enable us to discern and hate evil, and to teach us our dependence upon the power of God. The Devil forces no one to sin. We sin of our own free will, but God does allow Satan to tempt us. But how, Maximus asks, can this be? How can the Devil, having been cast out of heaven, have any communication at all with the Lord God? How could Satan have stood before God's heavenly court and asked for

17. See the Essay on the Sources for a bibliography of Maximus. Works cited here are *Questions to Thalassios* (*QT*); *Chapters on Charity* (*Ch*).

18. *QT* pref.; *Ch* 4.48. Compare John Damascene, *Against the Manicheans*, 14; Procopius of Gaza, *Commentaries on Genesis*, 1.2.

permission to tempt Job? Maximus' answer is that Satan does not appear before God in heaven at all, but rather, since God is everywhere in the cosmos, Satan is in his presence wherever he appears. Though now permitted to be active in the universe for a while, Satan and his followers will after the last judgment suffer eternal separation from God, reality, and being. When the rest of the cosmos is reunited with God and divinized, those who cling to unreality and nonbeing will have forever excluded themselves from that joyous reunion.[19]

John Climacus (c. 525–600) was an anchorite who wrote a treatise on the monastic virtues entitled "The Ladder of Paradise," a description of the thirty rungs or steps leading upward toward union with God. Because the Devil and the demons retained their angelic qualities when they fell, their essence or being always remained good, but their activity in the world (*praxis*) is depraved and evil. Demons tempt us and dig three pits in the road of salvation in the hope of causing us to fall into ruin: the first pit is dug to prevent us from taking good action, the second to assure that whatever good we attempt we do not do in accordance with God's will; if the first two pits fail to trap us, the third causes us to become proud of our good lives. Only by recognizing that we can ourselves do nothing and that all goodness comes from God can we avoid this most dangerous trap.[20]

The single most influential theologian in the East was John of Damascus, or John Damascene (c. 675–c. 750).[21] Influenced by Aristotle as well as by the Dionysian tradition of Maximus Confessor and John Climacus, he digested and summarized the church fathers on all major points of doctrine, including diabology. Used extensively by subsequent Orthodox theologians, Damascene's encyclopedic work also affected the Western scholastic tradition. John's diabology is rooted in his attack upon dualism, which he found inherently illogical. If two cosmic principles existed, they would have to be in total opposition; otherwise they would share a trait or traits that preceded them which would themselves become a first principle engendering the two. If both exist, they must share at least the trait of existence, which then

19. *QT* pref., 11, 26, 31; *Ch* 2.67. Compare John Damascene, *The Orthodox Faith*," and Gregory the Great, *Moralia in Job*.

20. John Climacus, "The Ladder of Paradise" (ἡ κλίμαξ τοῦ παραδείσου), esp. chap. 26. See S. Salaville, "Saint Jean Climaque, sa vie et son oeuvre" (*Etudes orientales*, 22 [1923], 440–454).

21. See the Essay on the Sources for a bibliography of Damascene. Works cited here are *The Orthodox Faith* (*OF*); *Dialogue against the Manicheans* (*Man.*).

would be the first principle. Therefore only one principle exists, and that we call God.

But if only one God exists, whence comes evil? Either it is a part of God's creation and springs from God, or else it is a privation of God, essentially nonbeing. No other choice exists. Damascene, rooted in patristic theology, chose privation: "Evil is nothing else than a lack of the good." Both good and evil exist, but only good is real; evil's existence consists in the privation of good. Evil is only a perturbation of natural order. All that exists is good; any evil existing in creatures is a lack created by their own voluntary actions. God knows and "foresaw" that privation results from the misuse of free will, but the sole cause of privation is not God but rather the independent motion of the free will away from God. God knows that free will produces moral evil, but he also knows that a cosmos in which freedom does not exist cannot be a morally good cosmos and that the potential for good necessarily entails a potential for evil. God is responsible for creating a cosmos in which evil exists, but he neither wills nor chooses evil; in fact, he suffers and dies so that the effect of the evil can be removed.[22]

In his dialogue against the Manichees, John's Manichean opponent demands to know why God, aware that the Devil would be evil, created him. John's reply is that every creature, including the Devil, is created good. The Devil's evil consists in his free choice to abandon the good. His freedom to do evil could not be abridged without abridging his freedom to do good. His free choice of evil deprived him of his moral reality; in his fall, he lost his angelic nature and became a shadow, a hollow thing. Under the influence of John the Evangelist, Damascene emphasized the metaphor of light and darkness for good and evil. The deprivation of being and reality—evil—is analogous to the deprivation of light—shadow and darkness. The Devil fell because of his pride, and he led other angels and then people after him. In following him in evil, we turn our backs on what is real and bright and face that which is unreal and shadowy.[23] The Devil's fall removed him from his great dignity. Whatever his previous rank among the angels,

22. Words for privation frequently used by Damascene: στέρησις, ἔλλειψις, ἀπ-οβολή, ἀταξία. *OF* 2.4: οὐδὲ γὰρ ἕτερόν ἐστι τὸ κακὸν, εἰ μὴ τοῦ ἀγαθοῦ στέρησις. Cf. *Man.* 13–14, 23, 37, 47, 50, 79, and Pelikan, pp. 220–222.

23. Evil as ἀποβολή of the good that God creates: *Man.* 34–35, 68. *OF* 2.4: "in first falling away from the good, he became evil" (πρῶτος ἀποστὰς τοῦ ἀγαθοῦ ἐν τῷ κακῷ ἐγένετο).

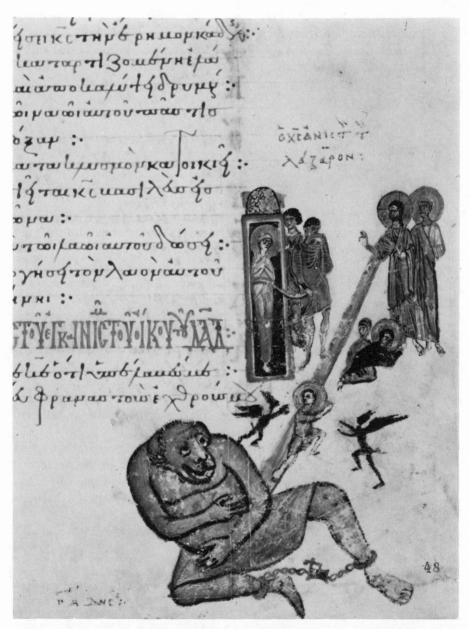

Christ raises Lazarus from the dead. The soul of Lazarus is seen rising from the clutches of a bestial Devil lying chained in hell while black imps try to impede the escape. Illumination from the Byzantine Barbarini Psalter. Courtesy Foto Biblioteca Apostolica.

he and his followers were now on the other side of the great gulf separating them from the good angels.[24]

The Devil, the cause of all the death and pain in the world, will be overcome by Christ and hurled, along with his angelic and human followers, into eternal death and fire. The Devil cannot repent, because he is a purely spiritual being, just as human souls, being spiritual, cannot repent when once removed by death from their bodies. This explanation of the Devil's inability to repent passed into Western scholastic thought, but it is a weak argument. If the angels, being purely spiritual, were able to exercise their free will in the beginning, why should their spiritual nature present them from exercising it now? Other Christian theologians have offered explanations: (1) Humans could be saved as a *genus* because Christ represented the whole genus in his sacrifice, but each angel is a genus to itself, so that no representative of all angels could exist. (This argument presumes a knowledge of, or at least a consensus about, the nature of angels, but neither exists.) (2) Humans could plead an extenuating circumstance in that they fell after being tempted by another kind of being, Satan, but the evil angels could offer no such extenuation. (No logical reason exists why lack of extenuation must mean eternal damnation.) (3) The Devil may in fact be salvaged. If God has not yet saved the Devil, it is possible that he may do so in future—or, to put it in more sophisticated terms, it is not necessary to assume that in the economy of eternity God has no room for the salvation of Satan. The means of his salvation might be quite different, and just as miraculous and bizarre, as the means of human salvation.[25]

Michael Psellos (1018–1078), an influential adviser to the imperial court and a leader of the eleventh-century revival of the university, classics, and philosophy in Constantinople, was a professor of philosophy. Unsystematic, discursive, and at times inconsistent, he discussed

24. *OF* 2.3–4, 2.30, 3.1, 4. The vast distance between the Devil and the good angels was used as a yardstick to describe the immensity of the gulf separating angels and all creation from God himself. *Man.* 46: "The Seraphim are even farther below God than the Devil is below the Seraphim" (πλέον ἀπέχει τὰ Σεραφὶμ ἀπὸ θεοῦ, ἤπερ ὁ πονηρὸς ἀπὸ τῶν Σεραφίμ). The Devil is no longer a seraph. *OF* 2.3: the good angels may or may not be equal in their essence, but they have different dignities, passing the divine light downward rank to rank, as in Dionysius. The Manicheans say that the Devil created the world, but no angel is able to create: the creative power resides in God alone.

25. *OF* 2.4, 4.4; *Man.* 45. *OF* 2.2: The Devil has no body: ἀσώματος. Cf. Dionysius, *DN* 4.1, 4.27.

diabology in a number of works, expounding his own views and exposing those of the heretics he opposed. His Neoplatonic views were influential both in Byzantium and in the Renaissance West, where Ficino used and promoted them.[26]

The Devil and demons are angels who fell, through their free will, and are unforgivable because they can offer no extenuating circumstance of temptation for their ruin. Once fallen, they form six groups, types, or orders. Here Psellos applied Neoplatonic ideas to Christianity in an original way: he offered a taxonomy of demons that bears little resemblance to the fallen angels of tradition or to the hierarchies of Dionysius. Rather, it is deeply rooted in the natural demonology of the pagan Neoplatonists, who supposed the demons to be morally ambivalent entities between gods and men rather than fallen angels. Psellos recast these natural demons as Christian fallen angels and made rather halfhearted attempts to fit them into Christian demonology. The highest demons are the *leliouria*, the shining or glowing ones, who inhabit the ether, the sphere of rarefied air beyond the moon. Then come the *aeria*, demons of the air below the moon; the *chthonia*, who inhabit the land; the *hydraia* or *enalia*, who dwell in water; the *hypochthonia*, who live beneath the earth; and, lowest, the *misophaes*, those who hate the light and dwell blind and almost senseless in the lowest depths of hell.[27]

The demons, though not matter themselves, are deeply influenced by the material nature of the regions in which they dwell.[28] The Devil

26. For a bibliography on Psellos, see the Essay on the Sources. His *On the Work of the Demons* is abbreviated here *WD*. Marsilio Ficino (1433–1499) was a Renaissance Platonist.

27. On the τάξεις, classifications, of the demons, see *WD*, 11; J. Grosdidier de Matons, "Psellos et le monde de l'irrationel," *Recherches sur le XIe siècle* (Paris, 1976), pp. 343–349; A. Ducellier, "Le diable à Byzance," in *Le diable au moyen âge* (Paris, 1979), pp. 197–212; K. Svoboda, *La démonologie de Michel Psellos* (Brno, 1927), pp. 7–12. Proclus and Olympiodorus had similar categories. Psellos' most common words for "demon" are δαίμων, δαιμόνιον, πνεῦμα, στοιχεῖον. στοιχεῖον, "element" in classical Greek, became a common late Greek word for "demon." See A. Delatte and C. Josserand, "Contribution à l'étude de la démonologie byzantine," *Mélanges J. Bidez*, vol. 2 (Brussels, 1934), pp. 207–232. Psellos' categories: λελιούρια, ἀέρια, χθόνια, ὑδραῖα, ἐνάλια, ὑποχθόνια, μισοφάες.

28. Psellos is inconsistent as to whether demons have bodies. In *WD* 10 he argues that they do, and in *WD* 7 he specifies that their bodies are real though invisible: they can take on whatever form they choose. In *WD* 8, both angels and demons have bodies, but the angels' bodies are clear and shining while the demons' are clouded and opaque. Angels' bodies are immaterial and therefore can pass through solid substances, but the

and the demons attack us and tempt us in order to frustrate God's plan for our salvation. They swarm everywhere, on land, sea, and in the air. The higher demons act directly upon human senses and indirectly upon the intellect, using their "imaginative action," *phantastikos*, to provoke images in our minds. The lower demons have minds like those of animals. These gross, grunting spirits force themselves crudely upon us, causing diseases and fatal accidents, and possessing us, which is why possessed people often exhibit animal behavior. The lower demons are entirely without intellect or free will: they act by instinct, hopping onto human beings like fleas, simply because we are warm and alive. They haunt certain places and mindlessly attack anyone entering such a place. A possessed person can be recognized by the displacement of his normal personality. Possession can be recognized in animals by alterations in their normal behavior, as when cows cease to give milk. The potential confusion of possession with disease did not escape Psellos, who argued that we ought always to seek physical causes of abnormal behavior before assuming possession. The lower demons can sometimes speak and render false oracles, but the lowest demons, the *misophaes* or "light-haters," are wholly unable to communicate, and they render persons they possess blind, mute, or deaf. The demons can be defeated by the name of Jesus, the sign of the cross, the invocation of the saints, the reading of the Gospels, holy oil or water, relics, confession, or the laying on of hands. The demons particularly feel the power of holy men and women, especially ascetics, who are able to drive them screaming with pain out of the bodies of the possessed.[29]

Psellos' bizarre schemes were inconsistent and crude. A combination of pagan philosophical ideas with popular demonological traditions, they were far too incongruent with Christian tradition to have a living or lasting effect. For one thing, such demons can only with difficulty be identified with the fallen angels, and Psellos' scheme does

---

the bodies of demons, especially those of the lower demons, are material enough to prevent such penetration. Yet in his *Life of Saint Auxentius* and elsewhere he inclines to the view that the demons are incorporeal. His argument in *Auxentius* that all the demons are equally bad and none is influenced by material surroundings is a more popular and less philosophical view. In WD 16–18 he argues that the demons are neither male nor female but are able to assume the form of either sex; they can also speak whatever language they please. When the saints strike them a blow, they feel the pain: WD 17.

29. WD 10–24. See P.-P. Joannou, *Démonologie populaire, démonologie critique au XIe siècle* (Wiesbaden, 1971), pp. 41–46; Grosdidier, pp. 343–349.

not answer whether the angelic hierarchy, after it falls, is demoted or inverted: that is, whether those angels who were highest before the fall remain the highest demons afterward, or the highest angels become the lowest demons in an inverted hierarchy. The Devil's own position is impossible to assign in the scheme. The complexity of the scheme did not respond to living perceptions of felt experience, and it serves as an example of the impracticality of taking metaphysical speculations into details that are too remote from real problems.

The dualist heresies of the East produced their own diabologies. By the eighth century the era of the great theological debates about the central teachings of Christianity was over, though Arian, Nestorian, and Monophysite heretics survived in remote areas. Medieval heresies tended to be less intellectual than the great heresies, concerned more with morality and practice than with metaphysics. On the whole, medieval heresy was less a problem in the Eastern church than in the West. The emphasis upon the apophatic, mystical approach in the East meant that it defined doctrine less precisely and left more room for variety. The ecclesiastical structure tolerated a wider diversity of opinion and practice, in contrast to the papacy of the eleventh through thirteenth centuries, which defined all teaching not in conformity with that of Rome as heretical. Yet medieval dualist heresies appeared first in the East. From the tenth century to the Turkish conquest in the fifteenth, the Byzantine church was faced with dualist views that were vocal and persistent.

The dualist heresies were rooted in Asian Gnosticism and spread through Asia Minor into Thrace and Bulgaria. The exact parentage of Byzantine dualism is disputed, and the chronology and relationship of Paulicians, Messalians (Euchites), Bulgarian Bogomils, and Byzantine Bogomils are still uncertain. The Bulgarian heresy was founded about 950 by a man named Bogomil, "Beloved of God," who took previously existing ideas from Gnosticism, Manicheism, and possibly Paulicianism and Messalianism, and wove them into a new heresy.[30] The Bogomils gained strong support in Bulgaria, possibly because of anti-Byzantine feelings among the Bulgars or anti-Bulgar feelings among their Slavic subjects, and by the eleventh century they had a strong following within the Byzantine Empire itself. In the twelfth century

30. For a bibliography on dualist heresies in the East see the Essay on the Sources. I present a composite view of Bogomilism here; in fact, considerable variations occurred in time and space.

Bogomilism began to decline in Byzantium but spread to Serbia, Russia, and western Europe. Remnants of the heresy persisted in Macedonia until the Turkish conquest of the fifteenth century. During the twelfth century Bogomilism divided into two groups, one teaching absolute dualism (the order of Drugunthia, Dragovitsa, or Dragovitch), the other preaching mitigated dualism (the order of Bulgaria). Folklore derived from Bogomil sources persisted long after the demise of the formal heresy.

Diabology was central to Bogomil thought. For the absolute dualists, the Devil was a god of darkness and evil independent of the God of goodness and light. For the mitigated dualists, the Devil was subordinate to God yet still exercised enormous and quasi-independent powers over the earth. According to one view, the true God, a God of spirit very remote from this material cosmos, has two sons, the elder being the Devil and the younger being Christ.[31] The elder son, Satanael, existed before Christ. Created good like all the other angels, he was highest in merit and sat at the right hand of the Father as the Lord's steward. But Satanael was an unjust steward (Luke 16:1–9) and grew dissatisfied with his subordinate position. In his pride he longed to set his throne as high as God's and to this purpose he rebelled. A third of the angels joined him out of respect for his high dignity and because they were used to following his command. He also promised them freedom from the tiresome liturgical duties they were obliged to perform before the throne of the Lord. As a result of their rebellion, God thrust Satanael and his followers out of heaven. Wandering in the

31. Widely different interpretations exist. H. A. Puech and A. Vaillant, *Le traité contre les Bogomiles de Cosmas le prêtre* (Paris, 1945), argued that the original Bogomils described by Cosmas thought of the Devil as God's younger son, drawing upon the parable of the prodigal in Luke 15, but M. Loos, esp. in "Satan als Erstgeborener Gottes," *Byzantinobulgarica*, 3 (1969), 23–35, denied this, claiming that the Bogomils used Luke 15 only allegorically and did not apply it to the myth of the two sons. Psellos had his own peculiar interpretation, not borne out by any other source: that the Bogomils believed that the Father, the Son, and the Devil constituted a kind of Trinity in which the Father ruled over eternal things (ὑπερκόσμια), the Devil over the things of this world (τῶν ἐγκοσμίων), and the Son over heavenly things (τὰ οὐράνια). Some heretics worshiped both Christ and the Devil, seeking reconciliation between them; some worshiped Christ only, though recognizing the power of the Devil over the earth; some, seeking the pleasures and glories of this world, worshiped the Devil only. This refinement probably existed only in Psellos' imagination. In the ninth century, Photius had already felt obliged to argue against those who believed that the Devil had a father, insisting that he had only "children," that is, sinners (Photius, *Questions to Amphilochius*, 47).

At the Last Supper, Christ points out the traitor Judas, from whose mouth the Devil issues in the form of a black imp, or *eidolon*. Illumination from the *Gospel Book of Emperor Henry III*, Germany, eleventh century. Courtesy of Dr. Ludwig Reichert Verlag.

void, the Devil determined to make a new world in which to reside. Aping God's creation, he declared that "Since God made heaven and earth, I will now make a second heaven like a second God."[32]

This "second heaven" is this cosmos. Satanael, creator of the universe in which we live, is the Creator God of the Old Testament, for any entity perverse enough to create this material world with its grossness, misery, and suffering, must be evil. The Devil, who was Moses' master, composed the Pentateuch himself, and the whole Old Testament was inspired by Satan (though some Bogomils accepted the divine inspiration of the Psalms and the prophets). Surveying his creation and finding it satisfactorily repellent, Satanael proceeded to make a sentient being, Adam, which he fashioned out of earth and water. But when he stood the thing upright, Satanael was annoyed to find it defective. Life was trickling out of Adam's right foot and forefinger in the shape of a serpent. Satanael breathed spirit into Adam, but again it trickled out, this time becoming the serpent itself. Desperate, Satanael was obliged to turn to his old enemy, the Lord, for assistance, begging him to help create humankind and promising him that if he cooperated he would be allowed to share in their governance. The Lord, wishing to fill up the ranks of the angels depleted by the ancient rebellion in heaven, agreed. A more lurid version of the story had Adam's body lying lifeless for three hundred years after Satanael had vainly tried to animate it. While Adam lay insensible, Satanael wandered the world he had created, stuffing himself with the flesh of unclean animals. Returning to Adam, he stopped up all Adam's bodily orifices with his hands and then, in order to keep him defiled and imprisoned, vomited his meal into Adam's mouth. The purpose of this unedifying scenario is to illustrate a central point of Bogomil anthropology: the human soul, a creation of the true, good God, is trapped in the human body, which is a creation of Satanael, the false god, who tricked the Lord into helping him and now holds the soul prisoner in a disgusting and defiled body.

After Adam, the Lord also helped the Devil to create Eve. Satanael, assuming the form of the serpent, had intercourse with Eve with his tail, begetting twins, Cain and his sister Calomena.[33] Later, in a natural union with Adam, Eve conceived Abel, whom Cain slew, thereby

32. Euthymius Zigabenus, *Panoply* 27.7: ποιήσω κἀγὼ δεύτερον οὐρανὸν, ὡς δεύτερος θεός. For the Devil as ape of God, see SATAN, pp. 94–95.

33. For Cain as the child of Satan and the symbol of evil, see R. Mellinkoff, *The Mark of Cain* (Berkeley, 1981).

introducing murder into the world. The Lord punished Satanael for debauching Eve by depriving him of his divine form and his power to create, so that now he became dark and ugly. Even so, the Lord left Satanael with dominion over the material universe for seven ages. Satanael gave the Law to Moses as a means of retaining his control over humanity. The Lord and the Devil are locked in a terrible struggle for the control of the cosmos, and humanity is their chief battleground. The Devil seeks to persuade us to worship and adore him rather than the Lord and assigns demons to dwell in each human soul in order to keep us bound in the shadows. Satanael's oppression of humankind was so great that we were rendered incapable of rising up out of our material integument and refilling the empty ranks of the angels, as the Lord had intended when he agreed to help Satanael create us.

But the Lord purposed to save us. After 5,500 years he produced the Son and the Holy Spirit and sent Christ, the Word of his Heart, down to earth. Christ entered the Blessed Virgin Mary through her right ear, as befitted the Word of God, and was also born through her right ear. Christ, identified with the archangel Michael, had no fleshly body (perhaps fortunately for Mary under the circumstances) but rather a wholly divine body, and therefore he did not really suffer or die on the cross. His mission was to tell humankind of their true condition, thus enabling them to unite with him and escape their imprisoning bodies. Defeated by Christ/Michael, who mounts triumphantly to heaven and takes Satanael's former place at God's right hand, Satanael is cast down out of heaven, losing the divine suffix *-el* ("Lord") and becoming merely Satan. This "second" casting down of Satan is structurally identical both with his first fall and with his final ruin at the end of the world.

In order to participate in Christ's saving act and unite ourselves with him, we must reject and despise matter, the Devil's creation and his snare. The Bogomils rejected the Christian sacraments, which used matter such as water, wine, and bread, and replaced both baptism and the Eucharist with the simple laying on of hands. They rejected the cross, which was not only material, but a lie, since Christ never really died. They despised church buildings. The demons, they said, used to live in the Temple in Jerusalem, the center of the Satanic cult promoted by Moses, but now they dwell in Hagia Sophia, the center of the Orthodox Christian imposture in Constantinople. The priesthood is worthless. Miracles, which the Catholics claim that God works in matter through the saints, are in reality tricks of demons, who love to use matter to bewilder us. Only by asceticism, spurning meat, wine, marriage, sex, and procreation, can we turn away from matter toward true spiritual reality. At the end of time, Satan will once more be loosed upon the world, but after a while Christ/Michael will return and destroy him, along with human bodies and the entire material world. The kingdom of God, justice, joy, and totally immaterial spirituality will then reign in the cosmos forever.[34]

Bogomil beliefs persisted in folklore, especially among the Slavs, long after the disappearance of the Bogomil religion. God and Satan frequently appear as comrades, brothers, or associates. God creates Satan from his own shadow. God and Satan exist together before the creation of the world. Satan and God quarrel over who should create humanity, finally agreeing that the Lord should create the soul and the Devil the body; when we die, our souls mount to heaven, but our bodies sink down into the clutches of the Devil.[35]

Why did Bogomil beliefs retain, or at least regain, their vigor after seven centuries of opposition by Christian tradition? Was it in spite of or because of their grotesqueness? Certainly the social and political

34. Psellos accused the Euchites and Bogomils of orgiastic practices, including a Satanic revel where men and women feasted and then turned the lights out and fell to promiscuous intercourse that included incest and homosexuality. Children born of these unions were brought back to the Satanic assembly eight days after birth (a parody of the usual Christian procedure in baptism), killed, offered up to Satan, and eaten. The history of such accusations is a long one. See J. B. Russell and M. W. Wyndham, "Witchcraft and the Demonization of Heresy," *Mediaevalia*, 2 (1976), 1–21. Euthymius Zigabenus also mentions Satanic practices. The idea seems to have been based upon the alleged practices of the Barbelo and Carpocratian Gnostics, especially as described in the *Panarion* of Epiphanius. Historians debate whether any truth inheres in such accusations. The main arguments against them are (1) the bias of the sources; (2) their repetition of a literary tradition going back at least as far as the reign of Antiochus IV Epiphanes in Syria; (3) the widely attested asceticism of the heretics. The main arguments in favor of them are (1) the compatibility of asceticism with libertinism whenever distinctions are made between the illumined or perfect (to whom such pleasures are denied) and the uninitiated (who are permitted everything before their perfection); (2) the natural tendency of some, realizing that the Devil is the absolute lord of this world and all its material pleasures, to decide to serve him instead of the remote, spiritual God; (3) the undisputed existence of orgiastic practices and cults in both the ancient, pagan world and in the modern world; (4) the obvious fact that someone, whether heretic or orthodox, had to think up such ideas, along with the psychological principle that whatever evil or perversion can be thought of will actually have been performed somewhere by someone. It is doubtful that the debate will ever be resolved.

35. Obolensky, pp. 277–282; Runciman, pp. 86–87. For the ancient and widespread appearance of doublets in religion (e.g., Horus/Seth) as analogous to Christ/Satan, see DEVIL, pp. 57–60, 80–84.

conditions of the eleventh century encouraged rebellion against establishment Orthodoxy, whether Catholic or Byzantine, but conditions often favor rebellions against the establishment. Why dualism in particular? First of all, Bogomil dualism, for all its lurid exaggerations, is not wholly remote from the dualism inherent in mainstream Christianity. In the spectrum stretching from absolute monism to absolute dualism, Orthodox Christianity is more to the monist side than is Bogomilism, but mainstream Christianity shares many dualistic assumptions, including a distrust of the things of this world, the encouragement of asceticism, and acknowledgment of the power of Satan, temporary and illusory though it is. Bogomil dualism is largely an exaggeration and distortion of these Orthodox views, which it cloaks in bizarre mythology. Second, the sense that we are radically alienated from a reality of beauty, truth, and light seems deeply rooted in human experience. Throughout human existence, in virtually every society and every time and place, some have felt the strong appeal of religions and philosophies that offer hope of bridging that perceived gap, of removing that sense of alienation, and of restoring us to our rightful place in reality.

Byzantine popular demonology was derived from theology and from monastic and saints' lives, as well as from pagan survivals, including magic. On balance, popular demonology was thoroughly Christian, rooted especially deeply in the literature of the desert fathers, and the pagan elements have been exaggerated by historians unfamiliar with the patristic tradition.[36] Demons could shift their shapes, taking the form of men, women, animals, or monsters. Often they were deformed in token of their privation: they might, for example, lack heads. Or they were blacks, who were popularly associated with shadow and the privation of light. In Byzantine art, demons are generally anthropomorphic, looking like angels, though often smaller, and black, occasionally having horns or a tail, but for the most part recognizably humanoid. In the fifteenth and sixteenth centuries a radical shift from the humanoid to the monstrous occurred in Greece, Rumania, and Russia, when the demons took on increasingly bestial forms. The most common animal forms in folklore are sheep, dogs, cattle, crows, and pigs. Demons demonstrate their repulsive nature by

36. On popular demonology, see especially Joannou, Ducellier; Delatte and Josserand; and M. Garidis, "L'évolution de l'iconographie du démon dans la période postbyzantine," *L'information d'histoire d'art*, 12 (1967), 143–155.

their deeds as well as by their forms: they emit terrible stenches, eat excrement, or else force those that they possess to do so. Their names betray the cultural diversity of their origins: some are barbarous gibberish; some come from ancient folk-legend, like "The Beautiful Woman of the Hills"; some indicate their activities, like "Power" or "Frenzy"; some preserve the names of ancient divinities such as Zeus or Artemis, following the patristic tradition that the old gods were really demons; and some are traditional Judeo-Christian names such as Beelzebuth or Azazel. The demons inhabit the four quarters of the earth but haunt certain localities more than others, especially pagan temples and desert places, and they are more powerful at certain hours—noon and midnight for example—than at others. They swarm in vast numbers everywhere on earth.[37]

Demons follow the Devil in their desire to hurt us, but they are also cautious and reticent, fearing defeat. Once they have possessed a person, for example, they usually want to hide in him; feeling comfortable there and fearing the pain of exorcism, they disguise or mitigate their activities unless forced by a holy man to reveal themselves. Meanwhile they cause diseases, including mental illness, and they bring about storms, shipwrecks, and other disasters. On occasion, emboldened, they take on visible shape to attack their victims with clubs, stones, or maces. A favorite mode of assault is to hurl people off precipices. Using their powers of illusion (*phasmata mēchanai*, or *mēchanēmata*), they attacked a hermit's hut with axes and torches, finally dragging it off its foundations with a rope. They emit shouts, calls for help, and other noises; they use fleas, lice, and other insects to torment us.

No physical attack is so satisfying to demons as a successful temptation, for the corruption of the soul is infinitely superior to the suffering of the body. Demons not only cause sin but are attracted by its presence, so that sinners open themselves to further temptations and even to possession. Each demon specializes in a particular vice, which he strives to promote. Sorcery, magic, and divination are favorite specialties, though Byzantine folklore, like that of the West, was ambivalent about magic. The ancient and Neoplatonic roots of magic drew from a tradition that perceived magic as a manipulation of natural, rather than supernatural, forces. Such assumptions permitted the practice of magic without sin, and many priests combined magic and prayer, invocations and supplications, for the good of their congrega-

---

37. Garidis; Delatte and Josserand, pp. 218–227; Joannou, pp. 10–26.

tions. Such magic, rather than relying upon their help, was felt to be capable of driving demons away. On the other hand, a more naturalistic view of the cosmos, derived from Aristotle, had little room for the occult, unobservable connections claimed by magic, and when combined with Christian assumptions it led to the idea that magic necessarily depends upon the agency of demons. In this view, backed as it was by the Old and New Testament injunctions against sorcery, all magic and divination were evil and the work of demons.[38]

To protect ourselves against demons we must rely upon the grace of God. We may call upon the name of Jesus, even asking specifically for the destruction of the demon, saying to him, "May Christ punish you." We may make the sign of the cross or use other holy signs. We should treat the demons with scorn, preferably refraining from doing them the courtesy of addressing them directly, but rather calling instead upon God or the saints for help. We can use magic against them (though the theologians warn against this), or, if we can get our hands on them, we can whip them, strike them, or burn them, for they fear fire intensely. The power of saints against demons is extraordinary. The presence of a saint draws the demon to reveal himself against his will and, once revealed, he can be destroyed. In dealing with any supernatural manifestation, the Christian must take care to use his power of discernment to distinguish demonic from divine apparitions. A monk who had mistaken one for the other was told that he should have demanded a proof from the spirit, such as demanding that it make the sign of the cross or sing the "Holy Holy Holy".[39]

Such beliefs indicate the pervasive sense of demonic power in Byzantine popular thought, which, like popular thought in the West, mediated the views of theologians. Pagan elements are rare, especially in diabology as opposed to minor demonology, for the Devil had no place in paganism; he thus always appears in contexts at least implicitly Christian.

These popular legends and beliefs tend on the whole to be trivial and inconsequential. Failing to confront seriously the problem of evil and suffering, they bear witness to the human tendency to lose oneself in unimportant detail and to evade issues.

38. Delatte and Josserand, pp. 227–230; Joannou, pp. 14–25.
39. Joannou, pp. 22–25; Ducellier, p. 205.

3 The Muslim Devil

Muslim tradition about the Devil is closely related to that of the other two great Western religions, Judaism and Christianity. The principles of Islam are strict monotheism and absolute submission to the will of God. For Muslims, the revelation of the Old Testament was superseded by that of the New Testament, which in turn was superseded by God's revelation of the Qur'an to Muhammad. Muhammad (c. A.D. 570–632) was born in Mecca, a cosmopolitan trading community, where as a young man he came into contact with Jewish and Christian as well as pagan Arab thought. About 610 the archangel Gabriel revealed to him the contents of a book—the Qur'an—whose prototype was in the seventh heaven. The historian identifies the intellectual components of the Qur'an, but for Muslims the holy book cannot be understood as the product of human minds or of a cultural milieu, for it is the direct word of God, written in heaven and dictated by the archangel to the prophet. In Christianity, Scripture is contingent upon the person of Jesus Christ, who himself is the Word; in Islam, Scripture has infinitely more authority than the person of Muhammad, who is the vehicle of the Word.

In the century after 622, the date when Muhammad left Mecca for Medina in the Hegira, the journey from which the Muslim calendar is dated, Islam swept the Middle East and the Mediterranean, establishing itself as one of the world's great cultural forces. During the two centuries from the foundation of the 'Abbasid caliphate in 750 to 950 the basic doctrines of Islam were set, roughly in the same way that the basic doctrines of Christianity had been set by about 450.[1]

Muslim thought was based primarily on the Qur'an and secondarily on the hadith, oral or written traditions of the practices and thoughts of Muhammad (*sunnah*). Commentaries on the Qur'an and hadith were produced, and then in a manner analogous to rabbinic and scholastic literature, commentaries on the commentaries, until a wide and detailed theology resulted. Further, a body of precedent formed around legal decisions and judicial opinions on matters of conduct. The Qur'an and hadith show close affinities with Jewish and Christian Scriptures, apocalyptic literature, and rabbinic and patristic theology. This influence is apparent not only in Muslim doctrines, but in certain ambivalences and confusions: for example, the Qur'an, like patristic writings, is unclear as to whether Satan was a being of high or of low degree before he fell.[2]

The problem of evil is inherent in and endemic to Islam, as it is to Judaism and Christianity. All three religions insist upon one, omnipotent, omniscient God. On this, Muslims are uncompromising: Allah's omnipotence is total, and nothing can happen apart from his will. But then suffering must come from God. The hadith emphasize God's omnipotence and describe a deterministic universe. God knows all suffering from all time and must have complete control over it. If one understood suffering properly, one would praise it as part of God's will. Punishment and testing are the two ways in which the Qur'an reconciles suffering with God's mercy. Suffering is a punishment for our sins. God is compassionate and merciful, but he is also just, and it is just that the sinful suffer. Even those whose lives are devoted to God endure suffering as a test. The proper response to suffering is *islam*, submission. The Qur'an has no doctrine of original sin in the Christian sense. Although the moral fall of Adam is described, his sin was not passed to his descendants. Yet it is clear that humanity is pointed in the wrong direction. "The soul of man," says the Qur'an, "is truly prone to evil."[3]

1. One of the best general surveys of Islam is M. G. S. Hodgson, *Introduction to Islamic Civilization*, 3 vols. (Chicago, 1958). A good introduction to Muslim thought is W. M. Watt, *Islamic Philosophy and Theology* (Edinburgh, 1962).

2. See W. M. Watt, *Bell's Introduction to the Qur'ān*, 2d ed. (London, 1970), and *Companion to the Qur'ān* (London, 1967). Throughout I use the sura and verse numbering of A. Y. Ali, *The Holy Qur'ān*, 3d ed. (Lahore, 1938).

3. Sura 12.53. On evil and suffering in Islam see especially J. Bowker, *Problems of Suffering in Religions of the World* (Cambridge, 1970), and J. Bowker, "The Problem of

The being and activity of the Devil is tolerated by omnipotent God for his own purposes. Islam is never dualistic, and the Devil has no independent existence of his own. God created the Devil, God permitted him to fall, and God allows him to be active in the world after his fall. All this is part of God's plan for the cosmos.[4]

The Devil has two names in the Qur'an. One is Iblis.[5] Always in the singular and always a personal name, "Iblis" occurs nine times in the Qur'an, seven in the context of his fall from grace. Some commentators argued that Iblis obtained his other name—Shaytan—as a result of his rebellion; others that the Qur'an uses the name Iblis to refer to the Devil in his relationship with God and the name Shaytan to refer to him in his relationship with humans. That Iblis and Shaytan are two names for the same evil being is clear.[6] *Shaytan* is a pagan Arabic term possibly derived from the roots "to be far from" or "to born with anger." Under Jewish and Christian influence, Muhammad defined the term in relation to its Hebrew cognate *satan*, "opponent" or "obstacle." The Qur'an also describes him as accursed, rejected, and punished by stoning. He is a rebel against God. The name Shaytan appears much more frequently in the Qur'an than does Iblis, usually in connection with the tempting and seduction of humans; the term *shayatin* in the plural also appears as the equivalent of Christian demons, evil spirits who are followers of the evil leader.[7]

The Qur'an does not make clear what kind of being the Devil is.

Suffering in the Qur'ān," *Religious Studies*, 4 (1969), 183–202. For the Christian fathers on original sin see SATAN.

4. On the Devil in Islam see B. Bamberger, *Fallen Angels* (Philadelphia, 1952), pp. 112–113; E. Beck, "Iblis und Mensch, Satan und Adam," *Le muséon*, 89 (1976), 195–244; A. J. Wensinck and L. Gardet, "Iblīs," *The Encyclopedia of Islam*, vol. 3, pp. 668–669; F. Rahman, *Islam*, 2d ed. (Chicago, 1979), pp. 31–35; H. Gätje, *The Qur'ān and Its Exegesis* (Berkeley, 1976), pp. 164–171.

5. The name *Iblis* is probably derived from the Greek *diabolos*, though alternative explanations exist, and Muhammad may have learned the term from Aramaic-speaking Christians. See W. Eickmann, *Die Angelologie und Dämonologie des Koran* (New York, 1908), p. 35; Beck, p. 217; Wensinck and Gardet. The name *Iblis* is known nowhere before the Qur'an. See A. Jeffery, *The Foreign Vocabulary of the Qur'an* (Baroda, 1938), pp. 47–48. See note 10 below for the sura references to the name.

6. See suras 4.117, 7.18–20, 19.44, 20.116–120.

7. Satan as "rejected" or "punished by stoning," suras 3.36 and 16.98; shayatin in the plural, e.g., sura 7.27–30. An evil angel 'Asra'il, or Izra'il, also appears as the angel of death who attempts to seize a person's spirit at death, but this angel is not the same as Satan. See Jeffery, pp. 187–190; L. Gardet, "Les fins dernières selon la théologie musulmane," *Revue thomiste*, 56 (1956), 427–479; 57 (1957), 246–300. The shayatin existed in pre-Islamic thought as a synonym for the evil jinn. Muhammad apparently moved the term in the direction of the Devil under Jewish and Christian influence.

Sura 18.50 states, "He was one of the jinn, and he broke the command of his Lord." Jinn are morally ambivalent spirits created by God out of fire, who may or may not have been considered a grade of angel.[8] The jinn appear to be roughly equivalent to the *daimones* or *daimonia* of Greco-Roman paganism and derived from an ancient pagan Arab distinction between gods and inferior spirits named *jinn*. The pre-Islamic Arabs associated the jinn spirits with caves, graveyards, darkness, and the underground. Pre-Muslim jinn could on occasion consort with deities, but Muslim writers downgraded them considerably. The Qur'an is unclear as to the comparative ontological ranking of angels, jinn, and humans, though angels always rank above jinn. Regardless of ontology, Allah placed humans above both angels and jinn by requiring that all spirits bow before Adam. The ontological ranking may be God, angels, jinn, humans, or God, angels, humans, jinn, or God, humans, angels, jinn. Most Muslims would say that God had placed humans above angels, but some argue that the command to the angels to bow before humans was merely a test. The Sufis even argued that Iblis failed to bow before Adam because his extreme reverence for God prohibited him from bowing before any created thing.[9]

The Qur'an teaches that the requirement to bow before Adam precipitated the fall of Iblis. Seven times the holy book repeats the story in various forms. God created Adam from clay and then called upon the angels to prostrate themselves before him. "So the angels prostrated themselves all of them together; not so Iblis: he refused to be among those who prostrated themselves."[10] Iblīs, a spirit of fire, was contemptuous of the human made of clay and outraged that God should ask him to grovel before such a lowly creature.[11] The essence of his sin was rebellion against God provoked by pride.

Was Iblis a jinni or an angel? All the passages in which the story

---

8. See Eickmann. The collective term *jinn* (sing. *jinni* masculine and *jinniya* feminine) derives from the Arabic root "to be hidden." God created the jinn: suras 51.56, 6.100. They are created from fire: suras 15.27, 55.15. Ibn 'Abbas said that the jinn were hidden from the other angels on account of their superiority, but this is out of line with tradition, which says that if the jinn are angels at all they are an inferior order. See Eickmann, p. 13. Compare the Christian ambivalence as to the rank of the Devil before his fall.

9. Beck, p. 218. The idea that Satan fell because he refused to bow to Adam derives from the first-century Jewish apocryphal "Books of Adam and Eve."

10. Sura 15.30–31. Essentially the same story appears in suras 2.34, 7.11–18, 17.61–65, 18.50, 20.116, 38.76. The story seems to be derived from the apocalyptic Christian *Life of Adam and Eve*, chaps. 12–16, where the Devil refuses to worship Adam because human nature is so inferior to angelic.

11. Iblis created from fire: sura 7.12; 38.76.

occurs put the refusal of Iblis to bow in the context of God's command to the angels. For this reason, and because of the underlying apocalyptic and Christian traditions, it seems that Iblis was an angel. Sura 26.95 refers to the "hosts of Iblis" in apparent reference to other angels who fell under his influence. And if Iblis had been only a jinni, God would not have considered it so important that he venerate Adam. In favor of Iblis' being a jinni are sura 18:50: "He was one of the jinn;" suras 7.12 and 38.76, which state that he was (like the jinn) made of fire; God's exclamation to him in sura 7.13: "Thou art the meanest of creatures;" and the traditional idea that whereas the jinn were morally ambivalent the angels were created sinless and could not have fallen. This last idea would also stand in the way of making the jinn a variety of angel.[12] The question is unresolved. In Islam as in Greco-Roman philosophy, Judaism, and Christianity, the relationships among the various genres of spirits are blurred.[13]

The Muslim account of Iblis' fall adopts the line taken by Irenaeus, who argued that the Devil had fallen out of envy for humanity, rather than the later Christian consensus that he had fallen before the creation of the material world and because of pride and envy of God. Muslims found it difficult to conceive that any creature could presume to envy the infinite Deity. The whole drama, including the fall of Iblis and the temptation of Adam, occurred in heaven. After Iblis failed to bow to Adam, God expelled him from heaven: Get out of here, you rejected and accursed being! My curse is upon you until the day of judgment. Iblis pleaded: Give me respite till the last day, when the dead will be raised. God agreed to this, and Iblis continued: Then, by your power, I will put humanity all in the wrong! Except, of course for your servants. I will surely bring Adam's descendants under my sway, all but a few. God permits Iblīs to tempt humanity and to destroy those who yield to temptation, but over those who love God the Devil has no power. God concluded the interview: I will surely fill hell with you and any who follow you. But you shall have no authority over my servants (suras 17.61–65, 38.77–85).

Though Satan was thus ordered from heaven, God did not force

12. Wensinck and Gardet. The hadith say that the angels were created from light (*nur*), while the jinn were created from fire (*nar*): the two words are linked both in sound and in etymology. The "meanest of creatures" may have been applied to Iblis only after his fall. Some commentators have argued that sura 18.50, which defines Iblis as a jinni, is a later textual addition.

13. Wensinck, p. 669: "It can in any case be said that Muslim thought remains undecided as to whether he was an angel or a djinn." See also F. Jadaane, "La place des anges dans la théologie cosmique musulmane," *Studia islamica*, 41 (1975), 23–61.

him to leave immediately, for he gave him permission to tempt Adam and Eve. Posing as a sympathetic adviser, the Devil persuaded them to eat of the fruit of the forbidden tree and "thus by deceit wrought their ruin." Now God ordered both Satan and the first humans out of Paradise (suras 2.35–36, 7.19–31, 20.117–121). Satan roams the world, and until the end of time God allows him to tempt and deceive us. He is our implacable enemy. Yet we always retain our free will. Satan himself reproaches us: "I had no authority over you except to call you, but you listened to me: then reproach not me, but reproach your own souls" (sura 14.22). No one can excuse himself by arguing that the Devil made him do it, for Satan has the power only to tempt, never to compel.[14] As in the Christian tradition, Satan tempts us to heresy, apostasy, and idolatry: he urges avarice, quarreling, drinking, gluttony, and gambling. He leads us to ignore our duty to God and to follow false prophets. He uses fear as well as blandishments, cowing us into submission when enticements fail. His treachery is limitless, and in the end he abandons even his followers to ruin, for God has ordained that all who follow Satan will suffer with him in hell. To fend Satan off we cannot rely upon the works of our own hands, but only, through prayer and the Qur'an, upon the mercy of God.[15]

This was the revelation about the Devil upon which the tradition of Islam is based.[16] But, as in Christianity, scripture left unresolved the central question of the nature of evil in a world ruled by an omnipotent and merciful God. The tendency of monotheists is always to limit God's goodness in order to preserve his omnipotence or to limit his omnipotence in order to preserve his goodness. A corollary question is whether God hates evil because it is evil or whether evil is evil because

14. Free will: suras 16.98–100; 58.10. Satan as tempter and enemy of humanity: suras 2.204–206, 3.155, 4.60, 4.116–121, 6.43, 7.175–176, 7.200, 8.11, 8.48, 12.5, 16.63, 24.21, 28.15, 29.38, 35.6, 36.60, 41.36, 43.62, 114.4–6. Satan makes promises that he does not fulfill: 4.119.

15. Heresy and apostasy: suras 2.161–165, 6.142, 59.16; idolatry: suras 4.117, 26.92, 27.24; avarice: sura 2.275; quarreling: sura 17.53; drinking, gluttony, and gambling: sura 5.93–94; forgetfulness of God: sura 6.68, 12.42, 18.63; false prophecies and revelations: suras 22.52–53, 58.10; fear: sura 3.175; abandons followers: suras 25.26–31, 59.16; God's mercy saves us: sura 4.83.

16. On further developments of the idea of evil, see W. M. Watt, *The Formative Period of Islamic Thought* (Edinburgh, 1973); W. M. Watt, *Free Will and Predestination in Early Islam* (London, 1948); G. von Grunebaum, "The Concept of Evil in Muslim Theology," *Middle East Studies Association Bulletin*, 2, no. 3 (1968), 1–3; G. von Grunebaum, "Observations on the Muslim Concept of Evil," *Studia islamica*, 31 (1970), 117–134; D. Gimaret, "Un problème de théologie musulmane: Dieu veut-il des actes mauvais?" *Studia islamica*, 40 (1974), 5–73; 41 (1975), 63–92; G. F. Hourani, "Averroes on Good and Evil," *Studia islamica*, 16 (1962), 13–40.

God hates it. In the eighth century, Hasan al-Basri preserved God's goodness by ascribing all the evil in the cosmos to the work of the Devil and his human followers. But such an interpretation, developed logically, posits a cosmic principle separate from God, an idea inadmissible in a rigorously monotheistic religion such as Islam. Al-Ashari (873–935) argued that the omnipotence of God requires us to believe that everything comes from him and that all deeds are willed by him, though some indirectly. Thus God, though not the direct cause of evil, may be its indirect cause. Al-Maturidi (d. 944) drew a distinction between God's will and God's desire. All deeds are willed by God, but some do not occur with God's good pleasure. The purpose of suffering is to test, warn, or punish humanity. The Mutazlites argued that God's power was limited by his justice, this limitation not arising from outside God's nature, which would be absurd, but rather from within his own nature. Abbad ibn-Sulayman of Basra (d. 864) contended that God had power over evil but was not the cause of it: God permits evil without willing it. But this left unanswered the question of why he permits it. The intricate difficulties in trying to square justice with mercy, goodness with omnipotence, is illustrated in a well-known story:

Let us imagine a child and a grown-up person in Heaven who both died in the True Faith. The grown-up one, however, has a higher place in Heaven than the child. The child shall ask God: "Why did you give that man a higher place?" "He has done many good works," God shall reply. Then the child shall say, "Why did you let me die so soon so that I was prevented from doing good?" God will answer, "I knew that you would grow up into a sinner; therefore, it was better that you should die a child." Thereupon a cry shall rise from those condemned to the depths of the Hell, "Why, O Lord!, did You not let us die before we became sinners?"[17]

Another aspect of the question of good and evil is human responsibility. If God is good and omnipotent, why do humans do evil? If the answer is that they have free will, then the problem is to reconcile free will with determinism. The question provokes as lively a debate among Muslims as among Christians, though in Islam the terms are different, human freedom being expressed in terms of human *qudra*, power, as against the power of God. The Qur'an and the hadith insist upon the absolute nature of divine power, and therefore divine determination has always been dominant in Islam. Yet some theologians,

17. Cited by Rahman, p. 91.

such as the Qadariyya, have argued that God delegates responsibility for actions to humans, thus allowing them to shape or at least shade their own destiny. This solution—that God's will for the cosmos involves his suspending his own omnipotence in the region of human freedom so as to produce the greater good of good freely chosen—is a logical response inevitably arising within Islam as well as Christianity. It was considered morally absurd and a severe limitation on God's justice that he should condemn and punish humans for sin if we were not to some degree responsible for it.[18] In one respect Islam differed markedly from Christianity: though the first humans ate the forbidden fruit and thus committed the first human sin, that original sin in no way passed on to their descendants. We sin, not because of inheritance or through mystical participation in Adam's disobedience, but rather from a motion of our own individual souls, provoked in large part by the conflict of bodily desires with those of the soul. The Devil exploits these perturbations of the soul, but neither he nor Adam's sin is their cause.[19]

Muslim speculation attempted to fill in the picture of the Devil presented by the Qur'an. Zamakhshari (1075–1144), for example, explained that Iblis refused to bow to Adam for the reason that he refused such honor to any but God and also because he believed that the fire of his own substance was superior to the clay of Adam's. Such interpretations of hadith sometimes became fanciful and often betrayed influences from beyond Islam. The fourteenth-century Syrian story that Iblis helped God create Adam, gathering from the earth sweet and salty matter from which Allah formed the first human, resembles the legends of Christian dualists as well as certain Shi'ite myths. The mainstream followed the Qur'anic interpretation more carefully: the Devil, motivated by pride and deceit, attempts always to

18. Rahman, pp. 100–107; Bowker, *Problems*, pp. 102, 123–126; Gimaret, p. 62; Grunebaum, "Observations," pp. 118–119; Watt, *Free Will*, pp. 238–242. The logical inevitability of some of these arguments invites critical reflection upon the sociology of knowledge. It is true that changes in social conditions may encourage shifts and developments in perceptions. But it is also true that ideas have an internal dialectic independent of social considerations. The close symmetry between Christian theology in Paris and Muslim theology in Baghdad has little to do with similar social conditions, more to do with cultural diffusion and mutual influence, and most to do with the internal dialectic of ideas. Belief in a monist God who is omnipotent, omniscient, and wholly good inevitably raises a closed set of questions, to which a closed set of answers, objections, and counterobjections inevitably respond.

19. G. Anawati, "La notion de 'Péché originel' existe-t-elle dans l'Islam?" *Studia islamica*, 31 (1970), 29–40.

thwart God's plan for the salvation of the world. But these attempts are wholly vain, for Satan exists and functions only by the permission of God, who uses him against his will for the divine purpose of testing and punishing. The Devil is clever; he can shift his shapes and make himself and his schemes seem attractive to silly humans; he exerts influence over the human body, especially the sexual organs; he hates God, humanity, and among humans Muslim believers particularly. He is immensely clever yet a total fool, since he does not understand God, or the cosmos, or his own place in it. His vision is warped and bent. His doom and ruin are sure.[20]

Theological speculation could deepen the meaning of tradition. Al-Ghazali, the practical, mystical theologian who, like the Christian nominalists and mystics, pointed out the limitations of theological assertions, followed a path similar to the via negativa of Pseudo-Dionysius. The reality of God is so much greater and broader than we can begin to understand that God is obliged to speak to us in metaphor and analogy. The Qur'an is absolutely true, but the truth that it gives us, holy as it is, can be only a pale shadow of the truth that exists in the mind of God. The Qur'an's revelation is complete so far as human understanding is able to grasp, but it is limited by the inadequacies of human speech and human concepts. God in speaking with us uses concepts such as the angel Gabriel, who draws us toward good, and the Devil, who draws us toward evil, because we are incapable of understanding reality without such concepts. Satan is a metaphor. We understand the Devil's works through psychological experience, since they manifest themselves in our own minds. The story of Satan's refusal to prostrate himself before Adam can best be understood as a metaphor for the refusal of the passions to bow to the dictates of reason. Satan is the personification of the obstacle that blocks humanity off from God, which is our own foolishness and sin.

But interpreters of al-Ghazali who did not grasp the sense of the via negativa did not understand that it transcends the metaphorical and allegorical. Al-Ghazali is not saying that Satan is only a metaphor, only an element in our psychology. He is a metaphor, but he is also not a metaphor. He is a real personality. Al-Ghazali grasps that whatever formulation we may make about reality is so precarious and so limited that we dare not ascribe it to ultimate reality. If we say, "Satan is a personality," we may have some idea of what we mean, but we have no right to assume that our idea of personality corresponds in any

20. Gätje, p. 167; G. Calasso, "Intervento d'Iblīs nella creazione dell'uomo," *Rivista degli studi orientali*, 45 (1970), 71–90, esp. 71–72, 83–88.

but the most remote way to what is in the mind of God. Thus we do not know what Satan is really, objectively, and ultimately. He is, and he is not. What we *can* know is how he (whatever he is) seems to function within our minds, so we had better dwell upon the metaphor that we can know rather than the ultimate that we cannot. We perceive, directly, evil thoughts rising in our minds. Are the evil thoughts Satan? Does Satan cause the evil thoughts? Does he exploit them? We do not know: we know only that evil thoughts arise from an evil principle and can lead to evil actions and an evil state of mind that separates us from God.[21]

The mystical tradition of the sufis, also rooted in the via negativa, emphasized that Iblis' purpose and role in the cosmos exceed our understanding. Al-Hallaj (857–922) said that when Iblis was asked to bow before Adam he refused because he knew that only Allah should be worshiped. Hallaj went so far as to declare that in all the world the only being that had as much respect for God as did Iblis, and who was as complete a monotheist, was Muhammad. For inscrutable reasons God had set Iblis an impossible task: "God cast him into the sea with his hands tied and said to him: beware lest you get wet." God strictly ordered Iblis to do what he had strictly ordered him not to do: he to whom alone the knee must bow commanded him to bend before Adam. In later mystical thought, Iblis even became the model of the perfect lover who would rather be separated from God and God's will than united with God against God's will. For some mystics he became a model of perfect loyalty and devotion.[22] The perceptions of the Qur'an and hadith and of the great Muslim theologians such as al-Ghazali, resonating as they do with the perceptions of the Christian tradition, confirm the significance of the concept of the Devil in Western monotheist religion.

21. M. Kably, "Satan dans l'‘Ithia' d'Al-Ghazālī," *Hespéris Tamuda*, 6 (1965), 5–37. The *"Devil's Delusion"* (*Talbis Iblis*) of Abu'l-Faraj Ibn al-Jawzī (1116–1200) is more an attack on al-Ghazali and the Sufis than a work on diabology. See D. S. Margoliouth, "The Devil's Delusion: *Talbīs Iblīs* of Abu'l Faraj ibn al-Jawsī," *Islamic Culture*, 19 (1945), 69–81; Margoliouth, "The *Devil's Delusion* by Ibn-al-Jauzi," *Islamic Culture*, 9 (1935), 1–21. Compare the *logismoi* of the Christian monk Evagrius of Pontus to al-Ghazali's view: see SATAN, pp. 177–183.
22. A. Schimmel, *The Mystical Dimension of Islam* (Chapel Hill, 1975), pp. 191–196; A. Schimmel, *Pain and Grace* (Leiden, 1976), p. 185. For some untraditional modern interpretations arising from Islam, see A. Schimmel, "Die Gestalt Satans in Muhammad Iqbals Werk," *Kairos*, 5 (1963), 124–137; A. Bausani, "Satan nell'opera filosofico-poetica di Muhammad Iqbal (1873–1938)," *Rivista degli studi orientali*, 30 (1955), 55–102; I. Joseph, *Devil Worship* (Boston, 1919); G. S. Gasparro, "I miti cosmologici degli Yezidi," *Numen*, 21 (1974), 197–227, and 22 (1975), 24–41.

4 Folklore

The Christian concept of the Devil was influenced by folkloric elements, some from the older, Mediterranean cultures and others from the Celtic, Teutonic, and Slavic religions of the north. Pagan ideas penetrated Christianity while Christian ideas penetrated paganism. The magical charms of Anglo-Saxon England, for example, have been shown to be largely Christian in that they were used by Christian priests for the benefit of Christian people, yet their contents are often frankly pagan.[1] As opposed to popular Christianity, folklore arises from a preconscious, unselfconscious level of storytelling or practice and leaves its traces in oral traditions that happen to have been recorded now and again in the past or set down by modern scholars. Folklore shades into popular religion, but the latter is more self-conscious, deliberate, and coherent. Popular religion consists of the beliefs and practices of people of simple or no education, and it appears most clearly in homiletic literature, the sermons, *exempla* (or formulas for sermons) of such writers as Gregory the Great, Aelfric, and Caesarius of Heisterbach.

Popular Christianity tended to present a vivid, frightening Devil.

1. Karen L. Jolly of the University of California, Santa Barbara, is preparing a doctoral dissertation on late Anglo-Saxon miracles and charms.

The domination of early medieval learning by monks meant that the colorful ideas of the desert fathers predominated, with their fierce emphasis upon the ubiquity and tangibility of demons. And the homilists dwelt upon the appalling for the explicit purpose of terrifying their auditors into good behavior. Folklore on the other hand tended to make the Devil ridiculous or impotent, probably in order to tame him and relieve the tension of fear. It is no coincidence that the period in which the Devil was most horribly immediate—during the witch craze of the fifteenth to seventeenth centuries—is the period in which he commonly appeared on stage as a buffoon. Because of the contradictory nature of these traditions, popular opinion about the Devil oscillated between seeing him as a terrible lord and seeing him as a fool.[2]

Folkloric and popular definitions are never drawn so clearly as those of theology (which are blurry enough); the folkloric Devil shades off into other concepts such as the Antichrist, giants, dragons, ghosts, monsters, weranimals, and "the little people." Over generations folklore established a number of trivial points: what clothes the Devil wears, how he dances, how cold and hairy he is, and how he may be tricked or evaded. Some of these details were long widely believed, but they do not address directly the core question of how evil is perceived.

From the fourth century through the twelfth, Christianity encountered northern pagan religions that resembled those of the Mediterranean in being polytheistic and monist, but that introduced new elements and details. From Celtic religion, for example, came the "horned god of the west," Cernunnos, lord of fertility, and hunt, and the underworld. Cernunnos, somewhat similar in traits and appearance to the Greco-Roman Pan, was assimilated to the Devil in much the same way as Pan. Yet despite the enthusiasm shown by certain modern writers for an allegedly widespread and coherent religion of a horned god or his consort the great goddess, the idea is completely rejected by all historians and anthropologists today.[3] More

2. R. Manselli, *La religion populaire au moyen âge* (Montreal, 1975), pp. 79–80.
3. The theories of Margaret Murray, *The Witch-Cult of Western Europe* (Oxford, 1921), R. Lowe Thompson, *The History of the Devil, the Horned God of the West* (New York, 1929), and Robert Graves, *The White Goddess* (New York, 1948), are only a hindrance to understanding. For a critique of the Murrayites see J. B. Russell, *A History of Witchcraft* (London, 1980), pp. 41–42. Neither does evidence exist for a widespread, coherent Druidic religion: see S. Piggott, *The Druids* (New York, 1968). On the Celts see P. F. Bober, "Cernunnos: Origin and Transformation of a Celtic

is known of Teutonic than of Celtic religions, but because the sources are virtually all foreign—Roman, for example—and late, we can have no clear idea of what these religions were like before they were influenced by Rome and by Christianity. Thus it is less proper to speak of the influence of Teutonic or Celtic concepts upon the Christian concept of the Devil than to discuss how the Christians adapted some northern motifs to their purposes. Yet the power and color of such motifs did help the Devil regain in the early Middle Ages some of the vigor he had once had in the minds of the desert fathers.[4]

The Teutonic gods, like all monist gods, are morally ambivalent. Wuotan, or Woden, ruler of gods and men, is also a god of rage (*Wut*) and destruction and a leader of the wild hunt. Thor, or Donar, is a champion of men and gods yet also appears as thunderer and hammerer, a figure of terror who, dressed in red, drives a cart pulled by two goats. Hilda, or Holda, goddess of sex, marriage, and fertility, is also a chthonic goddess of death and the underworld. Hilda can be a beautiful maiden or a terrifying hag, sharp nosed and long in the tooth, a leader of a hunt of wild women. In some accounts, the Aesir cast Hilda down into the underworld (Niflheim), where as Hel she rules the underworld and the dead. (Her name is related to the English "hell," etymologically associated with caves and holes; cf. Ger. *Hölle*, *Hohle*.) The conflict between the two classes of gods, the Aesir and the Vanir, is comparable to that found in Iranian, Hellenic, Hittite, and Hindu religions, but its origins and meaning are completely obscure. One thing is clear: it is not a struggle between "good" and "evil" gods, though the Vanir are more closely associated with the chthonic and with death.[5]

Though all Teutonic deities are ambivalent, some lean more toward evil and destruction than others. Prominent among these are the frost giants and the god Loki, all associated with the Vanir. Loki appears originally to have been an ambivalent, trickster god, analogous to the

---

Divinity," *American Journal of Archeology*, 55 (1951), 13–51; P. MacCana, *Celtic Mythology* (London, 1970); A. Ross, *Pagan Celtic Britain* (London, 1967).

4. Of course Teutonic religion varied greatly through time and place. The main sources are Old English literature (seventh to twelfth century) and Old Norse literature (ninth to thirteenth century). The power of the old gods can be felt as late as the thirteenth century but almost always with Christian coloring and interpretation.

5. H. R. E. Davidson, *Gods and Myths of Northern Europe* (Baltimore, 1964); *Scandinavian Mythology* (London, 1969), esp. pp. 94–96; G. Dumézil, *Gods of the Ancient Northmen* (Berkeley, 1973), esp. p. 4; U. Dronke, ed., *The Poetic Edda* (Oxford, 1969); Snorri Sturluson, *The Prose Edda* (New York, 1929).

Greek Hermes, but as he developed through time, particularly under Christian influence, he became more and more evil and ended as analogous to Satan. Loki's connections with evil go back at least as far as the ninth century, and by the time of Snorri Sturluson's *Prose Edda* (c. 1220), he is close to being a personification of evil. He is the father of Hel, of Night, of Fenrir the Wolf, of the World Serpent, and of Odin's steed Sleipnir. One of Loki's forms is Utgard-Loki, a frost giant of enormous cunning and power. (Often the myths distinguish sharply between Loki and Utgard-Loki, "Loki of the Outer Regions," but the name is token of their structural identity.) Loki appears at his worst in the later versions of the Baldr story. Baldr the Beautiful was a shining young god of the Aesir whom the Christian Norse identified with Christ. When Baldr was born, his mother, Frigg, summoned all of nature and caused each creature to take an oath never to hurt her beautiful son. But Frigg forgot one creature: the mistletoe. Frigg jealously guarded the secret of her son's vulnerability, but through trickery Loki discovered it. Loki made a dart out of mistletoe and, while the gods were at games, gave it to Baldr's blind brother, Hoder. The gods were amusing themselves by hurling weapons at the invincible Baldr, and Loki suggested that Hoder join in the fun. Hoder hurled the fatal weapon, and Baldr fell dead, to the consternation of the gods, who knew that his ruin presaged their own. In vengeance the Aesir pursued Loki; he escaped them momentarily by turning himself into a salmon (his ability to change his shape, like the Devil's, was a sign of his duplicity), but they captured the salmon and caused Loki to be bound in chains until the time of Ragnarok, the doom of the gods. At the end of time Loki will be loosed for a while to attack the Aesir at the head of an army of giants. For Snorri Sturluson, Loki has a beautiful exterior but a foul and corrupt spirit; he is "foe of the gods" and "forger of evil." The parallels between Loki and Satan are striking but are for the most part Christian coloring of paganism rather than the opposite.[6]

The theological distinction between the Devil as prince of evil and his followers the demons is often blurred in folklore. The use of *deofol*, "devil," as synonym for "demon" goes back in Old English at least as far as about 825 and persists to this day; French *démon*, Italian *diavolo*, and Spanish *diablo* have some of the same ambivalence, though in

6. Snorri, pp. 33–34; Davidson, pp. 176–182; G. Dumézil, *Loki* (Darmstadt, 1959); F. S. Cawley, "The Figure of Loki in Germanic Mythology," *Harvard Theological Review*, 32 (1939), 309–326.

German a distinction between *Teufel* and *Dämon* is often made. Folklore also sometimes split the Devil himself into one or more personalities. From the time of apocalyptic literature the Devil had many names, such as Satan, Belial, and Beelzebub, and the apocalyptic stories sometimes made them independent characters.[7] In medieval folklore and literature this dramatic device sometimes reappeared. In certain medieval plays, for example, Lucifer is cast as prince of hell and Satan as his messenger. But such a distinction is ignored in most of the literature and legend and is flatly rejected by theology. Such divisions were always vague and shifted in time and place, lacking consistency and coherence. Most important, the phenomenological type both in theology and in psychology is that the Devil is a single personality directing the forces of evil.

In addition to the ancient names deriving from the Judeo-Christian-Gnostic tradition such as Satan, Lucifer, Abbatōn, Asmodeus, Tryphōn, Sabbathai, and Satanael, the Devil attracts a host of popular nicknames that grow in number and variety through time. He is Old Horny, Old Hairy, Black Bogey, Lusty Dick, Dickon or Dickens, Gentleman Jack, the Good Fellow, Old Nick, and Old Scratch, with comparable sobriquets in French, German, and other languages.[8] Such names shade off into those of minor demons, themselves identified with the sprites or "little people" of paganism. Hundreds of such names exist, such as Terrytop, Charlot, Federwisch, Hinkebein, Heinekin, Rumpelstiltskin (all -lin, -kin, -lein, -le, -lot names are diminutives), Hämmerlin, Haussibut, Robin Hood, Robin Goodfellow, and Knecht Ruprecht. Such nicknames were popular not only because of their association with the "little people" but also because to give the Devil an absurd name is to offer an antidote to the fear he engendered. In the twentieth century one hears fewer diminutive names for the Devil because fewer people believe in him. Associated with such names are hundreds of usually humorous phrases or exclamations:

7. DEVIL, pp. 204–220.
8. On the Judeo-Christian-Gnostic names see C. D. G. Müller, "Geister (Dämonen): Volksglaube," *Reallexikon für Antike und Christentum*, 9 (1975), cols. 762, 791–793. See M. Rudwin, *The Devil in Legend and Literature* (Chicago, 1931), pp. 26–34, for a long alphabetical list. On the demon-scribe Tutivillus see R. Düchting, "Titivillus," *Ruperto Carola*, 58/59 (1976/1977), 69–93. On Satanael, a name originating in eighth- or ninth-century Syria and then widely adopted by the Bogomils, see M. Dando, "Satanaël," *Cahiers d'études cathares*, 30, no. 83 (1979), 3–11; 30, no. 84 (1979), 3–6; 31, no. 85 (1980), 14–32; 31, no. 86 (1980), 3–16.

what the Devil, *que diable, was in des Teufels Namen, ce n'est pas le diable* (it's not so great), *c'est un bon diable* (he's a good guy); between the Devil and the deep sea; the Devil take the hindmost; Devil-may-care (a reckless person); the Devil to pay; give the Devil his due; he's gone to the Devil; speak of the Devil; the Devil's luck, and so on. "Devil" is also a powerful negative: a "Devil-may-care" is a person who does not care at all; "Devil a one heard us" means that no one at all heard us; "to the Devil with it" signifies let us have nothing at all more to do with it.[9]

The Devil's appearance varied even more widely than his name. He was frequently identified with or associated with animals, sometimes following earlier Judeo-Christian tradition and sometimes because the animals were sacred to the pagan gods, whom the Christians identified with demons. The Devil appeared as adder, ape or monkey, asp, basilisk, bat, bear, bee or swarm of bees, boar, bull, camel, cat, centaur, chimaera (having the head of a lion, body of a goat, and tail of a serpent), crocodile, crow, deer, dog, dragon, eagle, fish, fly, fox, gnat, goat, goose, griffin, gull, hare, hawk, horse, hyena, leopard, lion, lizard, mole, ostrich, owl, phoenix, pig, raven, rooster, salamander, serpent, sheep, sparrow, spider, stag, swallow, tiger, toad, tortoise, vulture, wasp, whale, wolf, or worm. Of these the most frequent were serpent (dragon), goat, and dog.[10]

9. J. Grimm, *Teutonic Mythology*, 4 vols. (London, 1882–1888), vol. 3, pp. 984–1030; J. Orr, "Devil a Bit," *Cahiers de l'association internationale des études françaises*, 3/4/5 (1953), 107–113.

10. Some of the associations are established. The serpent and the dragon are one and the same and derive from the Genesis story; the ape is the symbol of Satan's mockery of God; the bear is associated with lust and the spotted leopard with fraud; the fox is a symbol of wiliness; the pig, of female sexuality; and the cat, of vanity. The whale is a symbol (through Jonah) of the yawning mouth of hell; it is identified with Leviathan. The horse is a symbol of male sexuality. The raven is associated both with Cain and with Odin; the cat with Freya and Hilda; the goat, with Pan and Thor. The mole is blind, dwells underground, and pulls plants (souls) down to devour them. Some animals were protected from association with Lucifer owing to their association with Christ. In 1 Peter 5:8 the Devil is described as a lion: "diabolus tamquam leo rugiens circuit, quaerens quem devoret," but the lion was seldom used because it is a symbol both of Christ (Rev. 5:5) and of Saint Mark; the Devil could never be a lamb, because Christ is the lamb of God; the Devil was never an ox and seldom (in spite of its logical appropriateness) an ass, because the ox and ass were supposed to have been in the manger and the ass also bore Jesus into Jerusalem on Palm Sunday. See B. Rowland, *Animals with Human Faces: A Guide to Animal Symbolism* (Knoxville, 1973); B. A. Woods, *The Devil in Dog Form* (Berkeley, 1959); C. G. Loomis, *White Magic* (Cambridge, Mass.,

The Devil appeared in a variety of human forms as well—as an old man or woman, an attractive youth or girl, a servant, pauper, fisherman, merchant, student, shoemaker, or peasant. He frequently made his appearance as a holy man—a priest, monk, or pilgrim. He could be a theologian, mathematician, physician, or grammarian, and in these capacities he was highly skilled in persuasion and debate. He could appear as an angel of light, as Saint Paul had warned, and occasionally he even dared masquerade as Christ or as the Blessed Mother of God. He might appear in threatening forms—as a giant, idol, or whirlwind. His proper form is invisible or amorphous, but he can shift his shape to suit his purpose.[11]

Often the Devil appears monstrous and deformed, his outward shape betraying his inner defect. He is lame because of his fall from heaven; his knees are backward; he has an extra face on belly, knees, or buttocks; he is blind; he has horns and a tail; he has no nostrils or only one; he has no eyebrows; his eyes are saucerlike and glow or shoot fire; he has cloven hooves; he emits a sulphurous odor, and when he departs he does so with stench, noise, and smoke; he is covered with coarse, black hair; he has misshapen, batlike wings. Iconographically he becomes much like Pan, horned, hooved, covered with goathair, with a large phallus and a large nose, and with Saturnine features.[12]

The Devil's color is usually black, in conformity with Christian tradition and almost worldwide symbolism. His skin is black, or he is a

1948); G. Faggin, *Diabolicità del rospo* (Venice, 1973); K. M. Briggs, *A Dictionary of British Folk-Tales in the English Language*, 2 vols. in 4 (Bloomington, Ind., 1970), vol. 2:1, pp. 45–47, 74–75, 121–122, 143; F. C. Tubach, *Index Exemplorum: A Handbook of Medieval Religious Tales* (Helsinki, 1969), items 1530–1532; H. W. Janson, *Apes and Ape Lore in the Middle Ages and the Renaissance* (London, 1952); the index of the Center for the Study of Comparative Folklore and Mythology, University of California, Los Angeles, s.v. "Devil," "Demons," etc., hereafter cited as UCLA. H. A. Kelly, "The Metamorphoses of the Eden Serpent during the Middle Ages and Renaissance," *Viator*, 2 (1971), 301–327, deals thoroughly with the transposition of serpent and dragon.

11. Loomis; Tubach, 1529, 1552–1553, 1558–1559; Briggs, vol. 2:1, 61–62; S. Thompson, *Motif-Index of Folk Literature*, 2d ed., 6 vols. (Bloomington, Ind., 1955–1958), G 303.3; M. R. James, *The Apocryphal New Testament* (Oxford, 1924), p. 149; UCLA.

12. Thompson, G 303.4, 303.4.5.6, 303.4.1.1; Briggs, vol. 2:1, pp. 47–48, 143 (Devil as three-legged hare); UCLA. For the association of Pan with the Devil see P. Merivale, *Pan the Goat-God* (Cambridge, Mass., 1969), which deals mainly with modern literature. Flaming eyes: Prudentius (348–405) has a poem *Hamartigena* which mentions them: "Liventes oculos suffundit pelle perusto / invidia impatiens justorum gaudia ferre" (Grudging the joys of the just in his envy, his burning eyes stare out from his charred pelt).

black animal, or his clothing is black. Sometimes he is a black rider on a black horse.[13] The Devil's second most common hue is red, the color of blood and fire; the Devil dresses in red or has a red or flaming beard.[14] Occasionally he is green, owing to his association with the hunt. The image of the Devil as a hunter with souls as his game was a popular metaphor of the medieval encyclopedists, and green is the traditional color of the hunter's clothing. Another connection is with the Green Man, a common Celtic and Teutonic fertility figure.[15] The Devil carries a fiery sword or an iron bar, or he wears chains and clanks them (the origin of Marley's ghost). He carries money and sometimes gives it away, but it invariably changes sooner or later into something gross.[16]

The Devil is associated with certain places and certain times of day. His direction is north, the domain of darkness and penal cold. Lapland is a favorite place of his, and there he drives reindeer. Since all churches were built facing east, north is always on one's left as one enters a

13. Loomis; Briggs, vol. 2:1, pp. 49–51, 54, 65–67; Thompson, G 303.5, 303.5.1; Tubach, 1534–1535, 1643; James, p. 345; UCLA; G. Penco, "Sopravvivenze della demonologia antica nel monachesimo medievale," *Studia monastica*, 13 (1971), pp. 34–35, on demons as Ethiopians. The Council of Toledo in 447 described the Devil as a large, black, monstrous apparition with horns on his head, cloven hooves, ass's ears, claws, fiery eyes, gnashing teeth, huge phallus, and sulphurous smell; B. Steidle, "Der 'schwarze kleine Knabe' in der alter Mönchserzählung," *Erbe und Auftrag*, 34 (1958), 329–348. Cf. Gregory the Great, *Dialogues* 2.4. In the biography of St. Afra (c. 750–850), the Devil is black, naked, and wrinkled (*Acta Sanctorum*, 5 August, 1.9). See I. Sachs, "L'image du Noir dans l'art européen," *Annales*, 24 (1969), 883–893, for the relationship of the bad image of black to black people.

14. Red was associated with evil in ancient Egypt as the color of the sterile desert and of blood. Red-haired people were commonly supposed to be evil in the Middle Ages. Thompson, G 303.4.1.3.1, 303.5.3; UCLA. See E. Kirschbaum, "L'angelo rosso e l'angelo turchino," *Rivista di archeologia cristiana* (1940), 209–248. It is possible that the common iconographic trait in medieval art of showing the Devil or demons with upswept, pointed hair is a depiction of flaming hair; another explanation is that it is in the mode of the barbarians, who greased their hair and swept it up into points in order to intimidate. See R. Mellinkoff, "Judas's Red Hair and the Jews," *Journal of Jewish Art*, 9 (1983), 31–46.

15. Thompson, G 303.5.2.2; UCLA. The Devil appears in green in Chaucer's "Friar's Tale," and green has demonic tones in *Sir Gawain and the Green Knight*. See D. W. Robertson, Jr., "Why the Devil Wears Green," *Modern Language Notes*, 69 (1954), 470–472; J. L. Baird, "The Devil in Green," *Neuphilologische Mitteilungen*, 69 (1968), 575–578. Rarely is the Devil blue, a Neoplatonic color for the demons of the lower air. See Thompson, G 303.5, and B. Brenk, *Tradition und Neuerung in der christlichen Kunst des ersten Jahrtausends* (Vienna, 1966).

16. Thompson, G 303.21; UCLA.

Cernunnos, the Celtic horned god of the wilderness, was incorporated into the iconography and folklore of the Devil. Detail from the Gundestrup cauldron, second or first century B.C., excavated in Denmark. Courtesy of the Nationalmuseet, Copenhagen.

church, and the Devil lurks on the north side of the church outside the walls, so that people prefer not to bury their dead there. Left (Lat. *sinister*) is associated with the ill-omened and dangerous in many cultures. On the medieval stage, north is the direction of hell.[17]

Anything sacred to the pagan gods may also be sacred to the Devil. Pagan temples were considered his dwelling places and were either pulled down or else sanctified as churches. Trees, springs, mountains, stiles, caves, old ruins, wells, groves, streams, and woods were also haunts of the Evil One. Sacred to the old gods because of their numinous qualities, such places were doubly feared by the Christians as both numinous and pagan. Demons can also haunt houses; an alleged "ghost" is really a demon.[18] The Devil favors noon and midnight, but he also likes dusk; he flees at dawn when the cock crows.[19] In accordance with Judeo-Christian tradition, the demons were supposed to dwell in the air or in the underworld, but they issue forth to torment people. The air is so full of demons that a needle dropped from heaven to earth must strike one; they swarm in the air like flies.[20] Lucifer is most commonly believed to dwell in the underworld. Usu-

17. It is in the north that the Lucifer of Is. 14:13 set up his throne; cf. Job 26:6–7; Jer. 1:14; Ecclus. 43:22. Bonaventure specifically placed hell in the north, heaven in the south, in his *Commentary on Ecclesiastes* 11:3. See Rudwin, *The Devil*, p. 63; UCLA; S. Shahar, "Le Catharisme et le début de la cabale," *Annales*, 29 (1974), 1185–1210, which shows that evil was associated with the north and with the left in the kabbalah. Left-handedness is widely regarded as a sign of evil, as with the Latin word *sinister*. The connections between the Devil and Santa Claus (Sinter Claes, Saint Nicholas) are pronounced. In addition to his association with the north and reindeer, the Devil can wear red fur; he is covered with soot and goes down chimneys in the guise of Black Jack or the Black Man; he carries a large sack into which he pops sins or sinners (including naughty children); he carries a stick or cane to thrash the guilty (the origin of the candy cane); he flies through the air with the help of animals; food and wine are left out for him as a bribe. The Devil's nickname (!) of Old Nick derives directly from St. Nicholas. St. Nicholas was often associated with fertility cults, hence with fruit, nuts, and fruitcake, which are characteristic of his gifts. See C. W. Jones, *Saint Nicholas of Myra, Bari, and Manhattan* (Chicago, 1978), pp. 309–323; A. D. de Groot, *Saint Nicholas: A Psychoanalytic Study of His History and Myth* (The Hague, 1965). De Groot points out that in the Netherlands, St. Nicholas is often accompanied by a little black companion, Zwarte Piet.

18. Thompson, G 303.15.3, 303.15.5; UCLA. Sometimes the demons built palaces under water: cf. Grendel's mere.

19. Briggs, vol. 2:1, pp. 56, 139–140; Thompson, G 303.6, 303.17. Müller, pp. 775–776, gives examples of Neoplatonic or Gnostic influence on the belief that there is a demon for each hour of the day and night, or each day of the week, the seven-day demons being derived from the seven planetary demons of the Neoplatonists.

20. Müller, pp. 772–773. Bonaventure: "ad modum muscorum in maximo numero" (like a great swarm of flies). Sometimes, particularly in Egypt under Neoplatonic

ally hell was placed at the center of the earth; a minor tradition set it in Iceland, whose extreme cold and groaning glaciers reminded people of a place of torment.[21]

Lucifer and his followers are active everywhere and at all times. They obsess us, attacking us physically and mentally. They cause physical and mental illnesses; they steal children, shoot arrows at people, attack them with cudgels, or even leap upon their backs. They enter the body through every orifice, especially the mouth during yawning and the nose during sneezing.[22]

The Devil is especially attracted to the vices and to sinners. He tempts people to sin and then gladly becomes the instrument of their punishment. Taking the form of a pretty girl, he enjoys tempting monks and hermits, and as a handsome youth he seduces girls, especially servants. In a typical story the handsome young Devil solicits a young girl for sexual favors; when he adds money as a further inducement, she yields; immediately he resumes his hideous form and carries her shrieking off to hell. These stories have a certain sexist bias, for the men are usually more successful in repelling temptation than

influence, "deacon demons" tried to block the soul's ascent to heaven. Calculations of the numbers of the demons were made, and though these belong more to popular religion than to folklore, they were widely accepted as testaments to the terrifying omnipresence of evil spirits. About A.D. 180 Maximus of Tyre estimated that more than 30,000 demons existed. Under the influence of Rev. 12:4 it was generally believed that one-third of all the angels fell. In the thirteenth century the abbot Richalm observed that there were as many demons as grains of sand in all the sea; the sixteenth-century scholar Johann Wier listed 1,111 legions of 6,666 demons, for a total of 7,405,926. Others, supposing 6,666 legions of angels of whom one-third, 2,222 legions, fell, calculated 133,306,668, still a low number compared with that of humans. Müller, col. 765; Rudwin, *The Devil*, pp. 17–25. A tradition existed in folklore, derived from the Gnostics and popularized by *The Voyage of Saint Brendan* and other Irish legendary literature, that in addition to good and bad angels a third group of neutral angels existed, angels who chose neither God's side nor Lucifer's. See M. Dando, "Les anges neutres," *Cahiers d'études cathares*, 27, no. 69 (1976), 3–28; Chapter 8 below, on Dante's use of the concept.

21. On hell, see DEVIL, pp. 240–241; SATAN, pp. 120–123; J. Kroll, *Gott und Hölle: Der Mythos vom Descensuskampfe* (Leipzig, 1932); K. Maurer, "Die Hölle auf Island," *Zeitschrift des Vereins für Volkskunde*, 4 (1894), 256–358; H. R. Patch, *The Other World* (Cambridge, Mass., 1950). Hell is a vast subject as well as a vast place, but as it is tangential to the subject of the Devil I leave it to the infernologists. Alan Bernstein of the University of Arizona is preparing a book on the invocation of hell in thirteenth-century France. On purgatory the master work is now Jacques LeGoff, *The Birth of Purgatory* (Chicago, 1984).

22. Whence the custom of saying "God bless you" or *Gesundheit*. Tubach, 346, 1620–1622; UCLA.

the women: when the Devil as a pretty girl tried to seduce Saint Dunstan, the monk drove her off by pinching her nose with tongs.[23] Satan enjoys playing cards, gambling, and gossiping, and at the same time he takes pleasure in punishing those mortals who follow his example. He carries off sabbath breakers, kills a clergyman who plays cards on Sunday, and punishes vain women and naughty children. He hunts the souls of sinners as well as their bodies. The didactic purpose of such stories meets the eye, but they appear in genuine folklore as well as in homiletic literature.[24]

In widely credited stories, the Devil leads the wild hunt surrounded by his demonic dogs; a similar motif is the rout of wild women, which became one of the leading elements in witch lore.[25] Like his manifestation the dragon, Satan guards underground treasures.[26] Demons hold tournaments or parliaments.[27] The Devil writes letters, some of which were allegedly preserved. The Evil One particularly loves to foment general discord in a village or town or to disrupt a congregation at prayer or divine service.[28]

He and his followers ride animals backwards.[29] The Devil loved architecture, because he took the place of the Teutonic giants, who were builders of giant artifices. Any large, mysterious object of stone was supposed to have been thrown down, built up, or dug out by the Evil One: hence there are Devil's ditches, dikes, bridges, and gorges. Meteorites are hurled down by Lucifer; he piles up sandbars in har-

23. Briggs, vol. 2:1, pp. 45, 53, 80–81, 141–143.

24. Briggs, vol. 2:1, pp. 54–56, 71–74, 79–80, 109–111, 140–141; Thompson, G 303.6.2, 303.7.1.3, 303.24; Tubach, 1202, 2452, 3503.

25. Briggs, vol. 2:1, pp. 61–62, 67–68, 74, 114, 152–153; A. Runeberg, *Witches, Demons, and Fertility Magic* (Helsinki, 1947), pp. 7, 126–132; E. H. Carnoy, "Les acousmates et les chasses fantastiques," *Revue de l'histoire des religions*, 9 (1884), pp. 370–378; J. B. Russell, *Witchcraft in the Middle Ages* (Ithaca, 1972), pp. 48–50, 79–80, 211–213. Often, motifs are mixed. For example, one version of the wild hunt has the Devil riding out with his "dandy dogs"; this was confused with the tale of the dogs of wild Parson Dando, whom the Devil carried off to hell on account of the sensuality of his life.

26. Briggs, vol. 2:1, p. 148; A. Wünsche, *Der Sangenkreis vom geprellten Teufel* (Leipzig, 1905), p. 71.

27. Tournament: Tubach, 4931; parliament: Thompson G 303.25.19.

28. Sigebert of Gembloux, *Chronica*, year 858, in MPL 160.163; Tubach, 240.

29. R. Mellinkoff, "Riding Backwards: Theme of Humiliation and Symbol of Evil," *Viator*, 4 (1973), 153–176, shows how riding backward was originally a mark of shame and then was transferred to evil. Similarly, riding, walking, or dancing widdershins, i.e., in a circle opposite to the sun's motion, is associated with evil and with the witch cult.

harbors so that ships will run aground. The custom of naming large natural features of stone—the least alive of all natural objects—after the Devil, particularly in remote or desolate areas, persisted into the twentieth century in the Devil's Kitchen, the Devil's Punchbowl, the Devil's Slide, the Devil's Tower. Of artificial constructions the Devil's favorites are bridges, though he also constructs piers, houses, roads, and even (in special circumstances) church towers. When he pipes at a wedding, the guests may turn to stone. The following story is typical: Jack and the Devil build a bridge near Kentmouth. Whatever they build up by night falls down by day. Finally Satan completes the bridge with the understanding that he will obtain the soul of the first living creature to cross the bridge, but Jack tricks him by throwing a bone across the bridge, so that the first creature to pass is a dog. The Devil also is a destroyer and pulls down by night whatever people build by day. Several parish building programs were impeded by such activity, and sometimes the location of the church had to be changed before building could be completed.[30]

As Jack showed with the dog and the bone, the Devil can be foiled and gulled by a quick wit. The function of such stories is to tame the terror. The Devil built a house for a cobbler after the cobbler promised that the Devil could have his soul when a lighted candle guttered out; but the cobbler blew out the candle before it could burn down. The candle trick was a great favorite. Lucifer wooed a servant girl and promised to marry her; a candle was lit during the service, and the girl agreed that when it burned out the Devil would have her soul; the priest saved her by swallowing the candle. A man who beat the Devil at cards claimed as wager that the Devil should plant him a fine avenue of trees. Satan agreed on the condition that when the man died he should have his soul whether he was buried in the church or outside it; the man secretly provided in his will that he be interred in the church wall. Even schoolboys outwitted the Old Boy by challenging him to cord a rope of sand or to count the letters in the church Bible. The Devil was defeated in wrestling matches, mowing or sowing contests, drinking bouts, gambling wagers, or debates (as in Stephen Vincent Benét's "The Devil and Daniel Webster"). He could even be thwarted

30. Such stories are parodies of the activities of saints as well as rooted in the folklore of giants: I have seen a staircase in New Mexico that Saint Joseph constructed in one night, and the Holy House of Loreto was moved from Palestine to Italy by the Blessed Mother of God. Thompson, G 303.9.1; Briggs, vol. 2:1, pp. 52, 60–61, 73, 85–89, 91–92, 95–96.

Si come teophiluf fait ommaige au deable.

The legend of Theophilus. In the upper panel Theophilus does homage to the Devil, placing his hands within Satan's in imitation of the feudal contract. Satan holds the contract, inscribed with the words "I am your vassal." In the lower panel Theophilus pleads with Saint Mary for forgiveness and help. Illumination from the Psalter of Queen Ingeborg, France, c. 1200. Courtesy of the Musée Condé, Chantilly, and of Photographie Giraudon.

(though this is rare in folklore) by a deathbed confession and repentance.

Sometimes Lucifer's humiliation was satisfyingly grotesque, as when he attempted to keep Saint Theobald from attending a council by removing a wheel from his cart; the saint forced him to take the wheel's place and went happily on his way with Lucifer rolling along the road beneath him. The Old One did not always stand for such treatment. A farm lad who tricked him into doing his chore of spreading muck found the muck all back in its original heaps the next morning. But on the whole the message was clear: an ordinary person, using his native wit, could make a fool of the Prince of Darkness. The ubiquity of such stories is testimony to their appeal to basic needs. Schoolboys, farmers, shoemakers, smiths, farmhands, servant girls, cobblers, and monks are common heroes of these tales; much more rarely is it a priest or a gentleman. The rich and the successful come more readily into tales in which the Devil carries off the avaricious and arrogant. Fabliaux, beast epics, and other medieval tales close to the people's hearts featured the poor making fools of the rich and the proud; and no one is more arrogant than Lucifer. The stories of the duped Devil derive from the folklore about stupid trolls and giants and are closely linked to the misadventures of the "little people." The duping of Rumpelstiltskin, a little man, a nature spirit, and/or a minor demon, is in the same genre. But the immense popularity of the tales was rooted in the resentment that the humble feel for the mighty. Such tales suggest that even the Dark Lord can be brought down by courage and common sense, and this idea agrees with the theology that the Devil, though crafty, is at bottom a fool who understands nothing.[31]

The Devil could be a silly prankster, playing marbles in church or moving the pews about. He could even genuinely help people, repaying kindnesses or finding lost objects, though the people he helps are usually socially objectionable, such as heretics or thieves.[32] The stupidity and occasional helpfulness of the Devil gave rise to such expressions as "poor Devil." Folklore was usually aimed at taming the Devil, but the opposite side of folk ambiguity sometimes expressed itself in frightening tales. "Jack of France" encountered a monk who was reciting the names of all who would die in the year to come; Jack heard him mention his name; horrified, Jack peered under the monk's

---

31. Briggs, vol. 2:1, pp. 56–59, 65–83, 92–94, 116–117, 124–128, 145–149; Wünsche, pp. 80–108; Tubach, 1567.

32. Thompson G 303.9.9, 303.22; Tubach, 953.

cowl—and saw the Devil's face. One must never call upon Satan in irritation or anger, for he may answer the call. A man irritated by his whining little daughter exclaims that he wishes the Devil would carry her off; he does. An innkeeper vowing "May the Devil take me if this be not true" wished that he had held his tongue.[33]

The Devil has aides and accomplices and even a family. His grandmother (more rarely his mother) is a persistent figure in folklore. In origin the fertility goddess Cybele, the Magna Mater, or Holda, the Devil's granddam is a terrible figure of great power, the prototype of Grendel's monstrous mother. Satan had a number of wives. His wife was sometimes a former fertility goddess. Or he could take his bride from among those women who have slept with an incubus. Still, the Devil's marriage is not always happy: he may successfully woo a woman who turns into a terrible nag and scold. The Devil's family often appeared in didactic literature. The Devil has seven daughters, representing the seven cardinal vices, or else he has two children, Death and Sin, whose incest produces the seven vices; the grandchildren delight their grandsire, who sends them out into the world to tempt humanity. The Devil has twelve disciples in mockery of Jesus. He also has sons: he impregnates a Jewish maiden of the tribe of Dan living in Babylon, thus fathering the Antichrist upon "the whore of Babylon." Or he seduces another sinful woman, begetting Merlin, Attila, Robert the Devil, Caliban, or a giant. The Devil's impregnation of a mortal woman is a mockery of the Incarnation of Christ. Since the Devil has no sex but can take on whatever form he chooses, he/she could presumably have borne a child to a man, but such an arrangement would have provided no parody of the Incarnation, and a pregnant Devil would have been grotesque and detracted too much from the dignity of the prince of hell. Beyond that is a misogynistic assumption: since the Devil, like God, is a great lord, he is assumed to be a male. It is for this reason that the Devil has no father or grandfather, though he may have a mother or grandmother. Lucifer's mother, sometimes called Lillis, or Lilith, is eager for her son the Devil to succeed. In a parody of the Blessed Mother and the angels, she joins the ranks of demons singing praises round the throne of her son. Masculine, the Devil rules the infernal roost.[34]

33. Briggs, vol. 2:1, pp. 105–106, 120–121, 132, 145–148; UCLA.

34. Briggs, vol. 2:1, pp. 153–155; Thompson, G 303.11; H. Bächtold-Stäubli, ed., *Handwörterbuch des deutschen Aberglaubens*, 10 vols. (Berlin, 1927–1942), vol. 8, col. 1844; UCLA; Tubach, 1452, 1589. The seven vices can also be represented by the seven hounds of Satan, who can also have four daughters in mockery of Peace, Mercy,

The line between the Devil and the minor demons, sometimes blurred in theology, is even more blurred in folklore. The ambivalent Greco-Roman demons were identified by Christian tradition with the fallen angels, as were the nature spirits of the Teutons, Celts, and Slavs. The most prominent fearsome spirits in the north, the giants, though they persist in medieval folklore ("Jack and the Beanstalk"), lose their prominence because the Devil seems to take over their role. The "little people" also take on more sinister characteristics: "Up the airy mountain, down the rushy glen / We daren't go a-hunting, for fear of little men." The little people—leprechauns, kobolds, trolls, dwarves, elves, goblins, *mares*, brownies—are minor nature-spirits who dwell in lakes, woods, streams, caverns, or mountains, even in the barns and cellars of civilization. They are short, dark, and often misshapen. Originally morally ambivalent and sometimes even beautiful, they were assimilated to demons by Christianity, so that their negative and destructive properties prevailed. Dwarves guarded hidden, underground treasures and killed anyone who dared violate their privacy. Trolls (who could also be ghosts of the dead) lurked under bridges in wait for unwary travelers. Elves caused disease in animals and humans by shooting them with arrows or darts—elfshot. *Mares* haunted people's sleep at night ("nightmares"). Whatever the diverse origin of these spirits, they became one in folklore with demons, like whom they frightened, harmed, and killed, but like whom too they could be tricked, cajoled, and bribed. The ancient fertility spirits of agriculture (the Green Man) and of wilderness and the hunt (the Wild Man and Woman) were powerful enough to retain much of their independence and their ambivalence, but they lent their greenness and their hairiness as well as their unbridled sexuality to the Devil and his demons.[35]

Monsters were usually distinguished from demons, though they could also blend with them. Monsters were supposed to be distorted humans, though doubts existed as to whether they had souls. They

---

Justice, and Righteousness, the four daughters of God. See H. Traver, *The Four Daughters of God* (Bryn Mawr, 1907). The daughters of the Devil can number as many as nine or ten. Medieval heretics were often represented as having twelve disciples in parody of Jesus. See G. R. Owst, *Literature and Pulpit in Medieval England* (Oxford, 1961), pp. 93–96; M. W. Bloomfield, *The Seven Deadly Sins* (East Lansing, Mich., 1952), p. 194. See also M. Rudwin, *Der Teufel in den deutschen geistlichen Spielen* (Göttingen, 1915), pp. 86–87, 141.

35. Grimm, vol. 2, p. 444, vol. 4, p. 1611; R. Bernheimer, *Wild Men in the Middle Ages* (Cambridge, Mass., 1952). The agricultural spirit lives on in fiction: Kingsley Amis, *The Green Man* (New York, 1969).

were supposed to have been created in order to show humans what physical privation is like, and what, literally but for the grace of God, we might have been. F. Gagnon has plausibly suggested that monsters fit into the ontological chain stretching away from God in the direction of less and less reality: God, angels, human rulers, human subjects, barbarians, monsters, demons, Antichrist, Lucifer. Monsters are physically deprived—they are giants or dwarves, have three eyes or none, or have faces in their bellies. This sort of physical privation is a sign of their ontological privation, which readily transposes into moral privation. Their deformity blends with that of the Devil, the most twisted and depraved of all beings.[36] Still, monsters are not properly demons but are at least one step removed from them; they were created monsters by God and thus claim some degree, however small, of goodness and beauty. A particularly persistent and sinister monster is the wer animal. Wer animals are found in most cultures (India, for example, has wer tigers, but Europe, where wolves were more prevalent, has werewolves). Vampires also are found everywhere. Wer animals are not the same as other monsters, for their monstrosity consists less in physical deformity than in their demonic ability to change shapes, and whereas monsters can be ambivalent, wer animals are essentially evil. The Devil is the chief of the shapeshifters; werewolves, vampires, and witches imitate their master in this quality in order to do his will.[37]

The most important of the Devil's many and varied accomplices is the Antichrist, whose influence permeates human affairs and who at the end of the world will come in the flesh to lead the forces of evil in a last, desperate battle against the good. Heretics, Jews, and witches are among the most prominent of Satan's human helpers. Jews and heretics may at least sometimes be unaware that they are serving the Devil, but the witches enlist knowingly in his ranks, worshiping him openly and offering him sacrifices. One can summon the Devil in many ways:

36. F. Gagnon, "Le thème médiéval de l'homme sauvage dans les premières représentations des Indiens d'Amérique," in G. Allard, ed., *Aspects de la marginalité au moyen âge* (Montreal, 1975), pp. 86–87; B. Roy, "En marge du monde connu: Les races de monstres," in Allard, pp. 74–77; J. B. Friedman, *The Monstrous Races in Medieval Art and Thought* (Cambridge, Mass., 1981); H. Schade, *Dämonen und Monstren* (Regensburg, 1962). For another identification, that of the Devil and the blacksmith, see M. Eliade, *The Forge and the Crucible* (New York, 1962), pp. 107–108.

37. D. Kraatz, "Fictus lupus: The Werewolf in Christian Thought," *Classical Folia*, 30 (1976), 57–79; M. Summers, *The Vampire* (London, 1928) and *The Werewolf* (New York, 1934) must be used with extreme caution. *Wer* is Old English for "human."

by whistling in the dark, by running widdershins around a church three times after dark, by writing him a note in Jew's blood and throwing it into the fire, by painting his picture, by looking into a mirror at night, by reciting the Lord's Prayer backward, by saying certain incantations, and so on.[38]

The most serious summoning of Satan is for the purpose of making a formal pact. The idea of formal pact goes back to a story about Saint Basil circulated by Saint Jerome in the fifth century and an even more influential story of Theophilus of Cilicia dating from the sixth.

In the Basil story as retold by Hincmar of Reims, a man who wishes to obtain the favors of a pretty girl goes to a magician for help and as payment agrees to renounce Christ in writing. The gratified magician writes a letter to the Devil in the hope that the Evil One will be pleased with his new recruit and orders the lecher to go out at night and thrust the message up into the air. This he does, calling upon the powers of evil. Dark spirits descend upon him and lead him into the very presence of Lucifer. "Do you believe in me?" asks the Dark Lord upon his throne. "Yes, I do believe." "Do you renounce Christ?" "I do renounce him." This dialogue is a blasphemous parody of baptism. Then the Devil complains, "You Christians always come to me when you need help but then try to repent later, presuming on the mercy of Christ. I want you to sign up in writing." The man agrees, and the Devil, satisfied with the bargain, causes the girl to fall in love with the lecher and ask her father for permission to marry him. The father, who wants her to become a nun, refuses. The girl struggles against the Devil's temptations but finally, unable to resist longer, yields. At last the story of the pact comes out, and with the aid of Saint Basil the boy repents and the girl is saved from a fate worse than death.[39]

The other story, the legend of Theophilus, was repeated hundreds of times in a variety of forms in virtually every European language over the span of a millennium, fathering the Faust legend and indirectly influencing the Renaissance witch craze. According to the story, an old Anatolian legend first written in Greek in the sixth century and translated into Latin in the ninth, Theophilus was a clergyman of Asia Minor who was offered the bishopric when the previous bishop died. Theophilus declined the honor, much to his later chagrin, for the new bishop proceeded to deprive him of his offices and dignities. Enraged,

---

38. Thompson, G 303.16.18.1; UCLA.

39. Hincmar interjects the tale into his *Divorce of Lothar and Teutberga*, written about 860 (MPL 125, 716–725).

Theophilus plotted to regain his influence and to seek revenge. He consulted a Jewish magician, who told him that he could help by taking him to see the Devil. Going out at night to a secluded place, they found the Devil surrounded by his worshipers bearing torches or candles. The Devil asked him what he wanted, and Theophilus replied, agreeing to become Satan's servant in return for his lost powers. He took an oath of allegiance to Lucifer, renounced his fealty to God, and promised to lead a life of lust, scorn, and pride. He signed a formal pact to this effect and handed it over to the Devil, kissing him in sign of submission. His life now increased in power and in corruption. Then the time came at last for the Devil to claim his soul in payment, and he sent out demons to torment the corrupt cleric and drag him off to hell. Terrified, Theophilus repented of his sin and threw himself upon the mercy of the Blessed Mother of God. Mary descended into hell, seized the contract from Satan, and returned it to Theophilus, who destroyed it. Mary interceded for him at the throne of God, Theophilus was pardoned, and the Devil was cheated of his due.

As the legend spread across Europe, it promoted anti-Semitism and the cult of Mary. Most significant, it initiated the idea of pact. The fathers had argued that all evildoers are limbs of Satan whether or not they are conscious of it. Thus pact was considered to include explicit homage to the Devil. Van Nuffel has shown how the idea of pact fit into both the tradition of Christian baptism and that of feudal homage. The power of the idea of pact kept growing; by the time of the witch craze it was taken as literal, historical fact and by the seventeenth century documents allegedly constituting such formal pacts were brought into evidence against accused magicians and witches in courts of law. The idea that witches were worshipers of Satan and had signed a literal, explicit pact with him was the heart of the witch craze. In modern literature, the figure of Faust sprang from that of Theophilus.[40]

40. The Theophilus story was first translated into Latin by Paul the Deacon about 840 (*Miracula Sanctae Mariae de Theophilo penitente*); the next influential version was by Hroswitha in the tenth century (*Lapsus et conversio Theophili vicedomini*); the story appeared in the writings of Marbod (11th cent.), Guibert (12th cent.), and Hartmann (12th cent.) The versions by Gautier de Coinci in the twelfth century (*Comment Théophile vint à pénitence*) and Rutebeuf in the thirteenth (*Miracle de Théophile*) were both signs and causes of its rapidly growing popularity, and many others began to appear in French, Italian, and German. See L. Radermacher, "Griechische Quellen zur Faustsage," *Sitzungsberichte der Bayerischen Akademie der Wissenschaften, philologisch-historische Klasse*, 206.4 (1930), 153–219; M. de Combarieu, "Le diable dans le *Comment Théophilus vint à pénitence* de Gautier de Coinci et dans le *Miracle de Théophile* de

Pact stories were tolerably common through the Middle Ages and Renaissance. A student at Saint Andrew's in Scotland encountered a "minister" who helped him with his assignments in return for a pact signed in blood. Sir Francis Drake defeated the Armada with the Devil's help. The favors obtained in return for the promise of one's soul are usually illusory: a scholar signs a pact in return for gold, which turns into stone; elegant feasts become offal and excrement; beautiful maidens turn into shrieking hags. In order to escape the consequences of a pact one may be obliged to journey to hell to retrieve it or else rely on the intercession of an unjudgmental saint such as the Blessed Mother. The typical pact story contains farcical elements. A knight promised to give the Devil his soul if ever he came to a town called Mouffle. The knight, confident that no such town existed, felt perfectly secure. The knight turned to the religious life, became a monk, and finally rose to the position of archbishop of Reims. Eventually he visited his home town, Ghent. There he became seriously ill and to his horror the Devil appeared at his bedside to claim him—on the ground that the real, secret name of Ghent is Mouffle.[41]

The Devil encourages Christians to make a pact with him, and thus pact became a favorite theme in sermons, poems, and theater from the thirteenth century onward, contributing to the theory of witchcraft. The popular plays *Miracles of Our Lady* by Gautier de Coinci and *Miracle of Theophilus* by Rutebeuf, Jacques de Vitry's tales for the feasts of Saint Basil and the Nativity of the Blessed Virgin, and a number of Caesarius of Heisterbach's stories all established the idea that pact with the Devil was a distinguishing mark of great sinners, especially heretics.[42] Such tales were not considered fiction. Caesarius' account

Rutebeuf," in *Le diable au moyen âge* (Paris, 1979), pp. 157–182; M. Lazar, "Theophilus: Servant of Two Masters," *Modern Language Notes*, 87, no. 6 (1972), 31–50; Tubach, 3572; H. van Nuffel, "Le pacte avec le diable dans la littérature médiévale," *Anciens pays et assemblées d'états*, 39 (1966), 27–43. On pp. 40–41, Van Nuffel offers his comparison of pact, baptism, and homage (I modify it slightly): *baptism:* introduction by godparent, question.posed by bishop, request for admission, submission, become child of God, signature, kiss of peace; *pact:* introduction by Jew, question posed by Devil, request for protection, submission, become servant of Devil, signature, kiss of peace; *feudal contract:* introduction by vassal, request for protection, submission, become vassal of lord, signature, kiss of peace. For the influence of pact on the witch craze see J. B. Russell, *A History of Witchcraft*, pp. 55–58, 76–78; Chapter 10 below.
    41. Since *mufle* is colloqual French for "slob" an element of anti-Flemish prejudice seems present here. On pact, see Briggs, vol. 2:1, pp. 111–115, 132–133, 138; Tubach 3566–3572, 4188; Thompson, F 81.2; Bächtold-Stäubli, 1842.
    42. M. Lazar, "Theophilus," *Modern Language Notes*, 87, no. 6 (1972), 31–50; G.

of the pact made by heretics at Besançon at the beginning of the thirteenth century was offered as historical fact. The heretics wandered about preaching and working wonders in order to prove the validity of their beliefs. They left no footprints after treading on floured floors; they walked on water; they ordered a hut burned down around them and emerged unhurt. The populace were so impressed that they embraced the heresy and mobbed the bishop and the priests. The bishop ordered a priest who had once himself been a magician to call up the Devil in order to find the secret of the heretics' success. The priest summoned up Satan and promised to become his man again if only he would reveal their secret. Sensing a bargain, the Devil explained that they carried their contracts with them, sewn up under the skin of their armpits. The priest reported this to the bishop, who ordered the heretics stripped, the scars in their armpits opened, and the diabolical contracts extracted. The outraged and disappointed citizens lynched their erstwhile heroes by burning them alive. The heretic (or witch) was no longer merely an unwitting tool of Satan but was considered deliberately and consciously to have made a pact with him, either an explicit pact signed and sealed, or at least an implicit one in which service was performed in return for favor.[43]

Pact became one of the keystones in the demonization of minorities, the transformation of heretics, Muslims, and Jews from ignorant souls steeped in error to conscious servants of Satan. Total misunderstanding of the religions of others (a misunderstanding no less complete today) led medieval writers to make the most improbable assumptions: the Jews, who did not believe in the Incarnation or the Eucharist, were supposed to obtain Eucharistic hosts and stab them until they bled; the rigidly monotheistic Muslims were supposed to bow down before

---

Frank, *Le miracle de Théophile*, 2d ed. (Paris, 1969). Theophilus calls the Devil "sire," line 235; the Devil tells Theophilus to place his hands in his in sign of fealty: "or joing tes mains, et si devien mes hon" (pp. 239–240); Theophilus does homage: "vez ci que je vous faz hommage" (p. 242); he makes a formal contract: "et je te refaz un couvant" (p. 245). V. F. Koenig, ed. *Les miracles de Nostre Dame par Gautier de Coinci*, 4 vols. (Geneva, 1955–1970), vol. 1, pp. 50–176: "Comment Theophilus vint à pénitance;" see M. de Combarieu, "Le diable dans le *Comment Theophilus vint à pénitence* de Gautier de Coinci et dans le *Miracle de Théophile* de Rutebeuf (I)," in *Le diable au moyen âge* (Paris, 1979), pp. 157–182; see the fifteenth-century "Chevalier qui donna sa femme au diable," in which the pact story is more developed than in Rutebeuf: T. W. Andrus, "The Devil on the Medieval Stage in France" (Ph.D. diss., Syracuse, 1979), pp. 147–150.

43. J. Strange, ed., *Caesarii Heisterbacensis monachi Ordinis Cisterciensìs Dialogus miraculorum*, 2 vols. (Cologne, 1851), bk. 5, chap. 19.

idols.[44] A typical Saracen in French epic literature is Agolaffre, whose black skin, misshapen form, long nose, huge ears, and eyes in the back of his head render him more demonic than human. One Saracen leader is called Abisme (Hell); Isembart leads an army of horned monsters bearing great hooks; another Saracen prince rips Christians apart with his great, sharp nails.[45] The German version of the *Song of Roland* by Father Konrad is even more explicit. The Muslims are pagans (*Heiden*) who worship 700 idols (*apgoten*), of which the chief were Apollo and Muhammad. All the pagans (Muslims) have put themselves under the Devil's power, and he controls them mind and body. Ganelon, the traitor to Charlemagne, is little more than a puppet manipulated by Satan, though the innocent Franks do not know that the Devil is rooted in his heart.[46]

The demonization passes the absurd. Muhammad, the human prophet of Islam, a monotheistic religion shunning all representations of the divine, becomes the chief god of the idolatrous Muslims, parallel to the Devil himself. In many plays the Devil is named Mehmet, Mahound, or another variation of the prophet's name. It followed that individual Muslims must worship the Devil and that their whole lives are in the service of the Dark Lord. Christians on crusade could be confident that they were doing God's work. The demonization of Jews is apparent in the story of Theophilus, in Chaucer's "Prioress' Tale," in the belief that the Antichrist would be a Jew of the tribe of Dan, in pictorial representations of Jews with hooked noses and bestial features, in the demonic characters of Herod and Synagoga, and above all in the sporadic pogroms and persecutions and the belief that the Jews sacrificed Christian children to the Devil or poisoned Christian wells.

The theft of children and the substitution of changelings has always been a deep terror in the human unconscious. It is a defensive explanation of one's children's disappointing behavior or the repressed fantasy

---

44. For demonization of Jews see below, Chapter 5.

45. G. Ashby, "Le diable et ses représentations dans quelques chansons de geste," in *Le diable au moyen âge* (Paris, 1979), pp. 7–21.

46. See R. A. Wisbey, *A Complete Concordance to the Rolandslied* (Leeds, 1969), s.v. *tuuele, tuvil, tuvel, tuvele, tuvil, tuvilis.* Worship of Muhammad and Apollo: "Da waren siben hundert apgot: / Machmet was der herest unter in" (3492–3493); "Uwer goete, di ir ane betet, / Appollo un Machmet, / die sint vile bose. . . . / die tuvele wonent dar inne" (805–809). Under the Devil's power: "si sich ergaben in des tuveles gewalt" (3514–3515). Ganelon manipulated by Satan: "Genelun saz mittin under in, / der tuvil gab ime den sin" (1978–1979). The Devil is rooted in Ganelon's heart: "Da wurzilt der tivel inne" (2858).

of a parent who wishes to be rid of a child; more generally it springs from terror of the transformation of the familiar into the unfamiliar, a common motif of nightmares. The happy ending of some stories of child theft or substitution reassures parents whose children's personalities have been corrupted that the earlier personality is still there and may return: thus it becomes a metaphor for spiritual growth and conversion.[47] Not only Jews stole Christian children: demons themselves did so. The following story about Saint Stephen was also told of Saint Lawrence, Saint Bartholomew, and others.

A pious Galilean woman gave birth to a son; she and her delighted husband invited their friends to a celebration. While the parents were distracted by their guests, Satan slipped into the house disguised as a human, found the infant in his cradle, and carried him off to Troy. There little Stephen was nursed by a dog, a white bitch, who spoke to Bishop Julian of Troy and told him to care for the child, for God had sent him. Julian named the boy Nathaniel and raised him carefully. One night an angel appeared to the boy, explained what the Devil had done, and told him to return to his real father. Julian sadly gave his adopted son permission to leave. After a long voyage Stephen returned, and when he got home he found a changeling in his place, a demon who had taken on the boy's form. When the changeling caught sight of the real Stephen, it shrieked in horror. Seizing the thing, Stephen demanded that it tell who it really was under penalty of being burned in the fire. The demon groaned, growled, barked, and finally fled with great commotion. The family was happily united at last.[48]

A variation of the theme is the voluntary gift of a child to the Devil by parents grateful to the Dark Lord for favors. When this occurs, the Virgin or an angel comes to the aid of the child when the Devil appears to collect him. Sometimes the Virgin appears in court as defense attorney.[49] Not only the individual soul, but the whole human race may appear in the dock; the Devil claims his rights over humankind,

47. See Maurice Sendak's children's book *Outside over There* (New York, 1981).

48. G. de Tervarent and B. de Gaiffier, "Le diable voleur d'enfants," in *Homenage a Antoni Rubió I Lluch*, vol. 3 (Barcelona, 1936), pp. 33–58; and the "Miracle de l'enfant donné au diable," discussed by Andrus, pp. 37–39, 56–57, 135–136.

49. See J.-P. Poly, "Le diable, Jacques le Coupé, et Jean les Portes, ou les avatars de Santiago," in *Le diable au moyen âge* (Paris, 1979), pp. 443–460. I am grateful to Prof. A. Bernstein for permitting me to see his unpublished paper, "Theology and Popular Belief: Confession in the Later Thirteenth Century," in which, among other things, he shows how the clergy attempted to persuade the people to go to confession by describing its efficacy in defeating the Devil.

and Christ or Mary acts as counsel for the defense. The trial of human-ity usually takes place just after the harrowing of hell. The demons hold a council in hell, and Lucifer complains that Christ has no right to take the imprisoned souls away. Sometimes the Devil claims that he has a right to the souls as a result of original sin. He names an attorney, a *procurator nequitiae infernalis*, whose name is Belial in Palladini's ver-sion of the trial of the human race. Belial goes before God the Father and demands a hearing in open court in order to put the case of hell against Christ. The court convenes in Jerusalem, and the personnel of the trial vary according to the version. When God the Father is judge, Christ is counsel for the defense, showing his wounds in argument against the Devil; when Christ is judge, the defense is undertaken by the Blessed Virgin, the *advocata humani generis*. This the Devil claims is unfair on the grounds of nepotism and because no woman can be a fit advocate in a court of law. When the judge is Solomon, the defense attorney is either the Virgin or Moses. The Devil debates his case suavely and cleverly, pulling every legal trick, quoting and glossing Scripture. He pleads that his contract with God at the time of original sin entitles him to the souls and that God himself appointed him to tempt and punish the wicked. But the judge decides in favor of hu-manity, either on the strict grounds that the Devil has broken the contract, or because humanity has been properly ransomed by Christ's death, or on the grounds that God's mercy and equity supersede strict justice. Belial appeals the verdict, and the case is settled out of court, Belial receiving assurance that the demons will be allowed to continue to keep the souls of whatever sinners they succeed in tempting, but not the souls of the just. In the end Belial returns disconsolately back into the mouth of hell.[50]

50. The idea of the trial of the human race goes back to Eznik of Armenia's fifth-century treatise "Against the Sects," in which Christ and Satan dispute in hell, Christ arguing for mercy against the Devil's claim of strict justice. Among the versions of the trial are the twelfth-century "Altercatio Diaboli contra Christum," the thirteenth-century "Pianto di Dio col nemico," and numerous sermons. It came to be a set case in legal textbooks and commentaries. The great jurist Bartolo da Sassoferrato wrote one of the most successful versions about 1359, a treatise that appeared under a number of titles, notably "Processus Satanae contra Dominam Virginem coram judice Jesu," in M. Goldast Haiminsfeld, *Processus juris joco-seriosus* (Hanau, 1611), in "Tractatus quaes-tionis ventilatae coram domino nostro Jesu Christo inter virginem Mariam advocatam humani generis ex una parte et diabolum contra genus humanum ex alia parte" in the *Opera omnia* of Bartolo (Venice, 1590), vol. 10. A fourteenth-century French version of Bartolo's treatise is the poem *L'advocacie nostre-dame*, ed. A. de Montaiglon and G.

The Devil's relationship to law in the Middle Ages appears in both theology and popular religion. If the cosmos is in fact a battleground between the forces of good and evil, the criminal must be regarded as a follower of Satan: he has lost his free will to the power of evil.[51] Certain crimes were regarded as particularly heinous and subject to diabolical inspiration: theft, sex crimes, murder, and maleficent magic. The idea of the ordeal in the early Middle Ages (it came to an end in the twelfth century) was based upon the assumption that supernatural powers were concerned in every legal case. The principle of the ordeal, and of trial by combat, is that God will intervene to distinguish the guilty from the innocent. It follows that the Devil's concern is to protect the guilty and to secure the condemnation of the innocent. Thus the ordeal is part of humanity's struggle against the Devil, and judges must be on their guard against his wiles. The assumption that God and Devil were immediately present in human affairs remained well into the Renaissance and Reformation, especially in the witch craze, when it was thought that the Devil would work every wile at his disposal in order to help his servants, the witches. Judges deemed that the punishment of the criminal was not only for the benefit of society but also for that of the criminal, for at least some legal proceedings were designed to drive the Devil out of the criminal and thus release him from the power of the Dark Lord. The degree to which exorcism may have been used in criminal trials remains a point of discussion.[52]

The Devil also wrote letters, enough in fact to constitute a whole

Raynaud (Paris, 1869—*not* 1896 as usually cited). On this see G. Gros, "Le diable et son adversaire dans *l'Advocacie nostre dame* (poème du XIVe siècle)," in *Le diable au moyen âge*, pp. 237–258. The other most influential version was by Jacobus Palladinus (Giacomo Palladini da Teramo, bishop of Spoleto), written in 1382 under the title "Consolatio peccatorum, seu Processus Belial;" it is also called the "Processus Luciferi contra Jesum coram iudice Salomone," "Compendium perbreve de redemptione generis humani," and other titles; it too is edited by Goldast Haiminsfeld. Palladini's version was widely translated and remained popular into the eighteenth century, influencing Beaumarchais and the librettist Lorenzo da Ponte. See Bloomfield, pp. 92–93; E. von Petersdorff, *Dämonologie*, 2 vols. (Munich, 1956–1957), vol. 1, pp. 290–292; D. Colombani, "La chute et la modification: Le renversement diabolique chez Gautier de Coïnci," in *Le diable au moyen âge*, pp. 133–154; P. B. Salmon, "Jacobus de Theramo and Belial," *London Mediaeval Studies*, 2 (1951), 101–115; K. Frick, *Das Reich Satans* (Graz, 1982), pp. 140–142.

51. H. von Fehr, "Gottesurteil und Folter: Eine Studie zur Dämonologie des Mittelalters und der neueren Zeit," *Festgabe für Rudolf Stammler* (Berlin and Leipzig, 1926), pp. 231–254.

52. C. DeClercq, *La législation religieuse franque de Clovis à Charlemagne* (Louvain, 1936).

satirical genre.[53] The Devil's letter, which began as a few lines quoted in twelfth-century chronicles, gained more acceptance in the thirteenth century and was widespread in the fourteenth. Its purpose was threefold: to satirize the corrupt morality of ecclesiastics, especially the Roman curia; to amuse; and finally, in its later stages, to offer instruction in the rhetorical arts. After 1350, the tenor of the letters shifted from general moral satire to an attack upon ecclesiastical governance, and they came to be closely associated first with the conciliar movement and later with Protestantism.[54] Often the form of the letter followed the form of a legal grant or charter in which the Devil bestows a reward for services rendered. He thanks the clergy for their greed, drunkenness, rapaciousness, worldly ambition, and lack of concern for their priestly duties, all of which, he says, brings many recruits down to fill hell. From the later fourteenth century, the satire took a more political turn, attacking the papacy's governance of the church. The salutation was a clever permutation of a normal legal charter: "Satan, emperor of the realms of hell, king of shadows, and duke of the deepest district, prince of pride, and eternal tormentor of all the damned, to his most faithful servant John Dominici, archbishop of Ragusa and abettor of all our works, sends good health and eternal pride."[55] The most famous letter was the "Epistola Luciferi," composed in 1351 and widely copied, translated, and adapted. After the salutation "to all the members of our kingdom, the sons of pride, particularly the princes of the modern church," it goes on to say, "we

---

53. The Devil's letter is parallel to the heavenly letters supposedly posted down from heaven by Christ. The idea of the heavenly letter goes back to the eighth century. See W. R. Jones, "The Heavenly Letter in Medieval England," *Medievalia et Humanistica*, n.s. 6 (1975), 163–178; J. B. Russell, "Saint Boniface and the Eccentrics," *Church History*, 33 (1964), 238–240.

54. On the Devil's letters in general see H. Feng's thorough work "Devil's Letters: Their History and Significance in Church and Society, 1100–1500" (Ph.D. diss., Northwestern University, 1982). I am grateful to Dr. Feng and her adviser, Professor Robert Lerner, for making her dissertation available. See also P. Lehmann, *Die Parodie im Mittelalter*, 2d ed. (Stuttgart, 1963), pp. 57–64; R. R. Raymo, "A Middle English Version of the *Epistola Luciferi ad Cleros*," in D. A. Pearsall and R. A. Waldron, eds., *Medieval Literature and Civilization* (London, 1969), pp. 233–248; W. Wattenbach, "Uber erfundene Briefe in Handschriften des Mittelalters, besonders Teufelsbriefe," *Sitzungsberichte der königlich-preussischen Akademie der Wissenschaften zu Berlin*, 1, no. 9 (Feb. 11, 1892), 91–123; G. Zippel, "La lettera del diavolo al clero, dal secolo XII alla Riforma," *Bullettino dell'Istituto storico italiano per il medio evo e Archivio Muratoriano*, 70 (1958), 125–179.

55. Lehmann, pp. 61–63.

are sending some of the eminent demons and nobles of hell to counsel and aid you; your cleverness knows very well how to acquiesce in their suggestions and add to their treacherous inventions." After a long satire on the state of the church, the letter concludes, dated "at the center of the earth in our shadowy kingdom, in the presence of hordes of demons specially summoned for this purpose to our treacherous consistory."[56] Variants of the letter of Lucifer were letters from Satan, Leviathan, and Beelzebub.

The Devil continues to prey upon our inclinations to vanity, curiosity, and the other vices, as the stories of Caesarius illustrate. In one tale, a poor Cistercian brother of decent but impoverished family had after long efforts finally learned to read. The Devil tempted him with love of books and with the hope of becoming a bishop. If only you study hard, the Devil told him, you will be bishop of Halberstadt. Deluded by vanity, the brother left the monastery, stole a horse, and rode off proudly in search of his fortune. In eighteenth-century novels such behavior was often rewarded by the temporary acquisition of a beautiful mistress and a fortune, but in the thirteenth century its end was inevitably dire: the brother was seized as a thief and hanged. The moral: do not think above your station in life.

Another story was about a knight named Henry of Falkenstein, who claimed that he did not believe in demons and in order to prove his point asked a magician named Philip to call some up for him. Philip warned him that the might of demons was dangerous and terrible, but Henry insisted, so Philip took him to a crossroads at noon and drew a magic circle round him with a sword, cautioning him not to step out of the circle and not to agree to anything the demons might suggest. Then he departed, leaving Sir Henry sitting in the circle. Soon the knight saw great floods of water sweeping toward him and heard the roaring of wind and the grunting of pigs. Then in the woods near the road he saw a hideous shadow, something like a human but taller than a tree. And this figure was moving toward him. The figure, which he realized was the Devil, approached the circle, stopped, and asked the knight what he wanted. Henry brought himself to look more closely and saw that the Devil had taken the shape of a huge man with black skin and black clothing, and of such horrible deformity that the knight

---

56. Zippel, pp. 163–166. Zippel also gives a "Sermo de quolibet statu hominum," pp. 166–175, and an "Epistola missa Clementi papae Sexto," pp. 175–179.

quickly lowered his gaze. He found the courage to speak. "You have done well to come," he addressed the dark figure, "for I have heard much about you." "Well, yes," the Devil replied, "people are always judging me and blaming me for everything. Actually I never hurt anyone. Do you suppose you could lend me your cloak?" Remembering his friend's warning, Henry refused. The Devil then asked for his belt, then a sheep from the knight's farm, and finally a rooster, but each time Henry declined, and persisted in asking his own questions. "How is it," he demanded of the Devil, "that you know so much?" The Devil replied that he knew every evil that occurs in the world and proved it by telling Sir Henry in exactly what house and at exactly what time he had lost his virginity and of other sins he had committed. The Devil resumed his own requests, but when Henry refused to accede to any of them, he reached his huge hand out toward him. Caught off guard, the knight stumbled backward and fell, calling out for his friend Philip. When Philip ran up, the Devil disappeared, and from that moment Henry never doubted the existence of demons. As a permanent mark of his experience his former healthy coloring became pale and remained so for the rest of his life.[57]

Once one has summoned the Devil, whether deliberately or inadvertently, one cannot easily escape him. Repentance and a contrite heart help, along with confession, acts of charity, recitation of the Lord's Prayer, the creed, or rosary, and sometimes one can drive him away by literally beating him. But usually one needs outside help. The pope's blessing is effective; most helpful are the saints, whom the Devil fears and shuns. Saint Gall infuriated the demons by driving them from place to place and depriving them of their rest; the Blessed Mother saves even those rash enough to sign written pacts. The signs and symbols of Christianity ward him off: the cross or the sign of the cross, holy water, the name of Jesus, the sacraments (especially the Eucharist), the words of the Bible, holy chrism, church bells. Other protections are unchristian in origin: hissing or spitting at the Devil (though the desert fathers adopted hissing), bronze, iron, fire, garlic, onions, pigs, and salt. This is largely apotropaic magic, in which things associated with the Evil One are precisely those that are most effective against him. Since he is associated with stench and smoke, he

57. Caesarius, 5.2, 5.16.

can be fumigated with incense, smoke from a yule log, or—best—
asafoetida (*Teufelsdreck:* "Devil's turd").[58]

58. Müller, 782–786; Thompson, G 303.16; 303.25.7; I. Goldziher, "Eisen als
Schutz gegen Dämonen," *Archiv für Religionswissenschaften,* 10 (1907), 41–46. Other
legends: God creates the Devil from his own shadow or his own spittle (Thompson, G
303.1.1.1 and 303.1.1.2); the Devil would do penance if assured of a return to grace
(Tubach, 1664); God creates the pleasant things of this world, but the Devil creates
such things as bats, mosquitoes, and hail (UCLA). See H. Lixfeld, *Gott und Teufel als
Weltschöpfer* (Munich, 1971); J. Bolte, "Der Teufel in der Kirche," *Zeitschrift für vergleichende Literaturgeschichte,* 11 (1897), 249–266; Thompson, A 63–64, A 2286.2.1.

5 Early Medieval Diabology

Early medieval culture in the West was isolated in and dominated by the monasteries, and its diabology thus drew deeply upon the desert fathers and incorporated admonitions as to how to deal with evil in a rough and unsettled world. Since the number of sources from the fifth through the ninth century greatly exceeds that from the first four centuries of the church, I dwell only on those whose ideas were original or widely influential: Gregory the Great in the sixth century, Isidore of Seville in the seventh, Bede and Alcuin in the eighth, and Gottschalk and Eriugena in the ninth.

Gregory the Great (pope from 590 to 604) was the most influential writer of the period and the most important transmitter of Eastern monastic ideas to the West. His letters, homilies, exegetical works, *Book of Pastoral Care*, and above all his four books of *Dialogues* and his commentary on Job, the *Moralia*, were widely used throughout the Middle Ages.[1] Gregory was the first pope to have been a monk, and the monastic point of view pervades his entire work, the *Dialogues*

---

1. For works by and about Gregory see the Essay on the Sources. The most important for diabology are the *Moralia* (*Mor.*) and the *Dialogues* (*Dial.*).

showing the influence of Cassian and the Eastern monastic tradition.[2] His *Moralia in Job*, written over a period of decades (c. 579–602) used the Book of Job as a basis for commenting upon virtually the whole human condition. He wrote the *Moralia* for the monks, who dominated theology at the time, and consequently the book is as specific and practical as it is theoretical. The *Dialogues* (c. 593–594) are even more practical. Deriving from Gregory's homilies, they were written to show God's saving activity in the world through miracles. The *Dialogues* were written for what in later times would be called an "educated audience"—not sophisticated theologians (of whom few existed at the time)—but for preachers, monks, and perhaps a few educated laymen. The first three books are narratives in a simple style, the fourth more theologically reflective.

Isidore, born in Visigothic Spain about 560, rose to be bishop of Seville about 600, and died in 636. His writings are encyclopedic and, though the underlying theological depth of his work has lately been better understood, deeply dependent upon Gregory.[3]

Bede, one of the greatest minds of the period, was born in Northumbria in the 670s, wrote numerous historical, scientific, and exegetical works, and died in 735. His diabological point of view was formed by the tradition of Augustine and Gregory, though marked by a more critical spirit than Gregory's.[4]

Alcuin, a Northumbrian born about 730, studied at York and went on to be Charlemagne's leading intellectual adviser and educational reformer before his death in 804. His numerous works were also in the tradition of Augustine, Gregory, and Bede.[5]

2. Cassian (c. 265–c. 435) brought Eastern monasticism to Marseilles about 415 after having been a monk at Bethlehem, Egypt, Constantinople, and Rome. His two great works, the *Institutions* and the *Talks* (*Collationes*), ed. E. Pichery, SC 42, 54, 64, derive from the thought of Evagrius and the other Eastern fathers. See P. Christophe, *Cassien et Césaire: Prédicateurs de la morale monastique* (Paris, 1969), pp. 67–68. See *Collationes* 7 and 8 for demonology especially. For the Devil and monasticism see SATAN, pp. 149–185.

3. For works on and by Isidore see the Essay on the Sources. The most relevant ones are the *Sentences* (*Sent.*) and the *Etymologies* (*Ety.*).

4. For works on and by Bede see the Essay on the Sources. The most useful works are the *Ecclesiastical History* (*Hist.*), the *Life of Cuthbert* (*LC*) and the *Commentary on Luke* (*CL*).

5. For Alcuin's works see the Essay on the Sources. The most helpful are the biblical commentaries, especially on Genesis (*Comm. Gen.*), Psalms (*Comm. Ps.*), John (*Comm. John*), and the Apocalypse (*Comm. Apoc.*).

The diabology of Gregory the Great was based on that of the fathers and, because of its great influence, fixed that view in medieval thought. Of all beings the Devil was the first to be created. He was a cherub, the highest of all the angels, and could have remained at the pinnacle of creation had he not chosen to sin. This view, contrary to that of Dionysius, became standard in the Middle Ages: most theologians considered the Devil the highest or one of the highest angels, whether a cherub (Ez. 28:14–19) or a seraph. Once he had sinned, he was cast as far down into the depths as he had stood high in heaven.[6] For Isidore, angels have ranks and grades reflecting both their dignity and their power. Isidore's idea of hierarchy came from Gregory and Dionysius,

6. *Mor.* 32.23: "Hunc primum condidit, quem reliquis angelis eminentiorem fecit" (He first created the angel whom he made greater than the other angels). *Mor.* 9.5: "Summus ille angelicus spiritus qui subjectus Deo in culmine stare potuisset" (That highest angel could have stood at the top if he had remained subject to God), but (*Mor.* 34.21) "tanto magis infra se cecidit, quanto magis se contra gloriam sui conditoris erexit" (The more he rebelled against the Creator's glory, the more he fell). See Chapter 2 above: Dionysius could not suppose that the Devil was the highest of the angels, but Gregory, who modified and perhaps misunderstood Dionysius, did not have this difficulty. See SATAN, p. 93, notes 38–39; pp. 129, 213. Gregory arranged the orders as follows: Seraphim, Cherubim, Thrones, Dominations, Virtues, Powers, Principalities, Angels, Archangels. This order differed from that of Dionysius in exchanging the Virtues and Principalities; Gregory's order was followed by Peter Lombard and most of the scholastics. Gregory's discussion of a tenth order of angels may have followed the tradition represented by Slavonic Enoch (2 Enoch) 29:3–4 (R. H. Charles, ed., *The Apocrypha and Pseudepigrapha of the Old Testament*, 2 vols. [Oxford, 1913] vol. 2, p. 447). Enoch declares that "incorporeal ten troops of angels" had been created, but this conflicts with Denis' nine. Gregory brought the parable of the woman with ten pieces of silver (Lk. 15:8–10) into the argument. The woman lost one of her pieces of silver; this Gregory thought analogous to the tenth group of angels, the one that fell. See Gregory, Homily 34 (on Lk. 15): 6–11, esp. 6–7: "Decem vero drachmas habuit mulier, quia novem sunt ordines angelorum. Sed ut compleretur electorum numerus, homo decimus est creatus. . . . Novem vero angelorum ordines diximus, quia videlicet esse, testante sacro eloquio, scimus angelos, archangelos, virtutes, potestates, principatus, dominationes, thronos, cherubim, atque seraphim" (A woman had ten drachmas, like the nine orders of angels, and humankind was created to fill up the number . . .). Thus Gregory posits a tenth group of angels, which can be interpreted in two ways: that group of the angels that sinned and fell; or the human saints elected to take the place of the fallen angels in heaven. Gregory is, however, clear that this tenth group does not constitute a real order, which would contradict Dionysius; rather it is a group drawn from among the angels of the other nine orders. The elect humans are taken up into heaven by entering into the various orders of angels according to their merits. The idea was discussed by Aelfric (see Chapter 6 below), Abelard (*Sic et non*, 49), Peter Lombard (*Sent.* 2.9.6 [see Chapter 7 below, n. 32]), and Aquinas and Duns Scotus in their commentaries on the *Sentences*. Langland seems to have used the idea in a peculiar way, more similar to Enoch than to Gregory (see Chapter 8 below).

but he agreed with Gregory against Dionysius that the Devil before his fall was lord of all the angels.[7] After the fall, he was prince of demons.

This view implied a firm stand against the dualism that considered the Devil independent of God. Dualist opinions deriving from Gnosticism still persisted in the sixth century. The Council of Braga in 563 took aim at the Priscillianists and other dualists. Priscillian had been bishop of Avila from 381 to 385. The leader of an ascetic, charismatic movement, he was executed for heresy at Trier in 385. Priscillian and his immediate followers were ascetics rather than dualists, but Gnostic or Manichean ideas penetrated the movement and by the sixth century may have dominated it.[8] The canons of Braga constitute one of only three major conciliar definitions on the Devil in the entire Christian record, the others being the Fourth Lateran Council of 1215 and the Council of Trent in 1546. Like the fathers of the Fourth Lateran, the Spanish bishops at Braga were concerned to deny dualism categorically, especially the following ideas: that the Devil was independent of God rather than created by God as a good angel; that the Devil is creator of this world or introduces evil things into it without God's permission; that the Devil is the creator of the human body; that the conception of a child is the work of demons in the mother's womb. The material universe, including the human body, the bishops insisted, is the work, not of the malignant angel, but of God.[9]

For Gregory, like the fathers at Braga, God is the source of all that

7. *Sent.* 1.10: "Ante omnem creationem mundi creati sunt angeli; et ante omnem creationem angelorum diabolus conditus est. . . . Primatum habuisse inter angelos diabolum" (Before the creation of the world the angels were made, and before the angels were made the Devil was made, so that the Devil held the primacy among the angels).

8. H. Chadwick, *Priscillian of Avila* (Oxford, 1976).

9. Canon 7 of Braga: "Si quis dicit diabolum non fuisse prius bonum angelum a Deo factum . . . sed dicit eum ex tenebris emersisse nec aliquem sui habere auctorem, sed ipsum esse principium atque substantiam mali, sicut Manichaeus et Priscillianus dixerunt. . . ." Canon 8: "Si quis credit, quia aliquantas in mundo creaturas diabolus fecerit et tonitrua et fulgura et tempestates et siccitates ipse diabolus sua auctoritate faciat. . . ." Canon 12: "Si quis plasmationem humani corporis diaboli dicit esse figmentum, et conceptiones in uteris matrum operibus dicit daemonum figurari. . . ." Canon 13: "Si quis dicit creationem universae carnis non opificium Dei, sed malignum esse angelorum. . . ." Mansi 9.774; Hefele-Leclercq, vol. 3, p. 177. See H. Denzinger, *Enchiridion symbolorum*, 31st ed. (Rome, 1960), nos. 237, 238, 242, 243. Fourth Lateran (1215), Denzinger, nos. 428–430. Trent (June 17, 1546), Denzinger, no. 788. A few lesser councils mention the Devil briefly, e.g., the *Statuta ecclesiae antiqua* (Gaul, c. 275); C. Munier, *Concilia Galliae A. 314–A. 506*, CCSL 148, p. 165; C. Munier, *Concilia Africae A.245–A.525*, CCSL 149, pp. 8, 62, 70–75, 264.

is, and God produces no evil. Consequently evil cannot really exist; it is only lack, privation. Those who choose evil turn away from being toward nonbeing. Satan's will to evil moves him continuously away from reality toward nothingness. The privation argument, which can seem an evasion of the issue, makes more sense when one grasps its core: God is what is, and nothing can be apart from what is. It follows that evil must not exist, or that evil is a part of God. Since Gregory and Christian tradition generally were unwilling to grasp the latter nettle, the nonbeing of evil was an inevitable doctrine. Another thorny question was natural evil, the suffering of animals and other sentient beings lacking free will. If moral evil is the result of human sin, of what is natural evil the result? Beasts, plants, and rocks cannot do evil; though they can cause suffering to a sentient being, they do not do so consciously. Still, God constructed the cosmos in such a way that this suffering is caused. God, then, must be its cause. One alternative is that the suffering is the result of original sin, humanity's own fall, which distorted the entire world. Some medieval writers suggested this option; it seems an impossible one today in light of current evolutionary views, and even in previous times it seldom achieved wide support. Another alternative is that such suffering is the result of the fall of another being, who, created at the beginning of the world, before all other creatures, upset and distorted God's plan. Thus the Devil can be blamed for all the suffering in the world.[10] Yet this ultimately is no answer, for God must then have created the cosmos knowing full well that the Devil would fill it with suffering; the responsibility cannot be thus removed from God.

The fall of the angels was not the work of God, Gregory would argue, because nothing in their nature inclined them to evil. The only precondition of their fall, the only aspect of their nature that could be blamed upon God was their mutability. But changeability, built into

---

10. *Mor.* 14.18: "a summa essentia recessit, et per hoc, cotidie excrescente defectu, quasi ad non esse tendit" (Since he fell from his high essence, and since his defect grows daily, he approaches nonbeing). Boethius (c. 480–524) had argued for privation in his "Consolation of Philosophy." Isidore, *Sent.* 1.9: "Malum a diabolo non est creatum, sed inventum; et ideo nihil est malum, quia sine Deo factum est nihil, Deus autem malum non fecit. . . . Ita et in rebus permistum est malum, ut naturae bonum ad comparationem excelleret mali. . . . Malum vero ideo natura nulla est. . . . Fecit Deus omne valde bonum; nihil ergo natura malum" (The Devil found evil rather than creating it. Evil is nothing, since God makes everything that is, and God did not make evil. Thus evil has been mixed into the cosmos so that the good would shine by comparison. Evil is by nature nothing. Since God made all things completely good, evil is nothing by nature). See G. R. Evans, *Augustine on Evil* (Cambridge, 1982), pp. 91–98.

human as well as into angelic nature, is a necessary corollary of free will. If we are free to choose good or evil, then we are free to change the good for the evil. The Devil was created able to choose between alternatives, able to change from a good life to an evil one. His choice was absolutely free and had no preconditional cause. The Devil fell because of pride; he freely chose to try to be independent of God, to be a principle in his own right. His prideful desire, the source of all sin, blotted out his proper respect and fear of God.[11] Gregory's position firmly established the view that Satan fell at the beginning of the world rather than after the creation of humanity and that his sin consisted in pride and envy of God. His envy of humanity, which led him to tempt Adam and Eve, arose later from his envy of God.[12]

Gregory used a variety of names for the Devil, all traditionally patristic, such as "the ancient enemy of the human race."[13] Before

---

11. *Mor.* 2.10, 4 preface, 4.13, 5.38, 15.4, 32.13, 34.21. See L. Kurz, *Gregors des Grossen Lehre von den Engeln* (Rome, 1938), p. 27. Isidore followed Gregory closely on this point: *Sent.* 1.10: "in superbiam eripuit"; cf. *Sent.* 2.34 and *Ety.* 7.5.

12. J. M. Evans, *Paradise Lost and the Genesis Tradition* (Oxford, 1968), p. 83.

13. J. F. O'Donnell, *The Vocabulary of the Letters of Saint Gregory the Great* (Washington, D.C., 1934), p. 142, gives a long, exhaustive list of these names. See also F. Gastaldelli, "Il meccanismo psicologico del peccato nei Moralia in Job di San Gregorio Magno," *Salesianum*, 27 (1965), 577. Gregory uses the images of Behemoth and Leviathan to fill in the picture of the Devil. Behemoth is associated with the crocodile and the serpent, hence with the Devil. The Leviathan of Job 41 is identified with that of Rev. 12 and thus associated with Behemoth, the whale, the mouth of hell, and the Devil (*Mor.* 4.9, 32.23, 34.6). Again Gregory drew on patristic tradition and made these images standard through his influence. His use of the name Lucifer was limited because he knew that it could also be a name of Christ (*Mor.* 29.32). G. J. M. Bartelink, "Les dénominations du diable chez Grégoire de Tours," *Revue des études latines*, 48 (1970), 411–432, provides an exhaustive study of the names that Gregory of Tours (538–594) gave the Devil; again they are traditional. Isidore, *Ety.* 8.11, lists a variety of names for the Devil derived from Greco-Roman or Hebrew sources, for example Phoebus, Diana, Saturn, Bel, Belphegor, Beelzebub, Belial, Behemoth, and Leviathan: these names persist right down into modern occult literature. This section of *Ety.* (compare *Sent.* 3.8) is known for its false derivations. *Daemones*, Isidore claimed, derived from δαήμονας because they know future events. *Diabolus*, he argued, derives from the Hebrew "slipping down" because he fell from heaven: "Diabolus Hebraice dicitur deorsum fluens, quia quietus in caeli culmine stare contempsit, sed superbiae pondere deorsum corruens cecidit" (*Diabolus* comes from the Hebrew for "slipping down," because he disdained to stay peaceably in the highest place in heaven, but instead, weighed down by pride, slipped and fell). This is an error based on Eucherius and Jerome, *Commentarium in Ephesios* 3.6; *Commentarium ad Titum* 2.6, in MPL 26.544. Then he proceeds to offer a more correct interpretation of the name Satan: "Satanas in latino sonat adversarius . . . transgressor . . . veritatis inimicus . . . praevaricator . . . temptator" (Satan in Latin is *adversarius*, meaning transgressor, enemy of truth, liar, tempter).

they fell, the angels had celestial bodies, but afterward they were reduced to bodies made of the lower, murky air. Though their bodies lack flesh, they can suffer the pains of corporeal fire.[14] Formed of the thick, lower air close to the earth, they are imprisoned in it, or (Gregory was as inconsistent as the earlier fathers) they wander the surface of the earth or are incarcerated underground.[15]

Gregory confronted a difficult question in the continuing power of the Devil in the world. According to the basic Christian story, Lucifer is the prince of this world, dominating humanity from the moment of original sin to the moment of salvation. Through Christ's Incarnation and Passion he broke the Devil's power and saved us from his grasp. Yet in fact when we look about, Satan seems to have lost little of his influence on humanity. How is it that after the Redemption the Devil continues to have such influence, doing his evil work among both unbelievers and the baptized? The question had puzzled Augustine and the other fathers. Augustine's tentative response was that apparently baptism erases an individual's own past sins and also the punishment due for original sin, but it does not eliminate the urge and tendency to sin inherent in every human. The question remains, next to the central question of evil itself, the most dangerous question for Christianity: why does the mission of Christ seem to have made so little practical difference in the world?[16]

Gregory posed the question squarely but answered it only allusively. He hints that the answer may lie in the power that God grants Satan over the innocent Job. Throughout the Book of Job, Satan is obliged to admit that God's is the only real authority and that he can operate only with God's permission. The Book of Job describes Satan's entering and leaving God's presence, but Gregory interprets this as follows: no matter where he is, he is in God's presence whenever he is doing God's will, but when he is doing his own will he is withdrawn from the presence of God. Wherever the demons are—in

14. *Dial. 4.30; Mor.* 29.30; Isidore, *Ety.* 8.11. That the angels became more material did not seem to have deprived them of their angelic status. Lucifer, for example, remains a seraph even after falling and becoming corporeal.

15. *Mor.* 2.20, 2.47, 26.17.

16. Gregory missed a possible explanation: God dwells outside space and time, and his every action transcends space and time. That Christ appeared on earth in Judea during the reign of Augustus does not limit the action of the Incarnation to that time and place. Thus Christ's saving mission may be said to affect all humans whatever their chronological location; human behavior then would not necessarily be better after the time of Jesus than before. For Augustine's view see Evans, pp. 130–132, 162, 170.

the air, on earth, or underground—they are in hell, separated from God and subjected to painful punishment.[17] "This is hell nor am I out of it," as Christopher Marlowe's Mephistopheles would say centuries later. God can see Satan at all times, but Satan is unable to see God or anything real, for he is like a blind man sightless in the sunlight. God sees Lucifer and knows of his sin and alienation but does not really "understand" it, for what God knows is real by virtue of his knowing it, and Satan's sin is only lack of reality, retreat from being. Satan addresses God, seeking to justify himself, accusing the elect unjustly, and asking God for permission to tempt and afflict them. God responds to the Devil in four ways: he reproaches him for his sin; he contrasts his injustice with the justice of the elect; he permits him to test their virtue, and he prohibits him from tempting them successfully (*rursumque eum a tentatione prohibet*). The contradiction in the last two points is a lame effort to cope with predestination. Gregory's idea is that God does permit the Devil to accost humanity, but in the knowledge that the elect will not yield and will only be strengthened by the assault. The core issue is the goodness and power of God. God is responsible for the cosmos that he creates; he both permits and restricts evil. He knows that the elect do not yield to temptation and so does not give the Devil real power to tempt them.

Gregory was much too practical a man to imagine that the world was actually constructed this way. No one can truthfully say that he never sins, and so everyone deserves punishment. Job led a devout life, and for the course of the action of the book he is free from sin. But being human he at one time in his life must have sinned, so his punishment was not undeserved. Often we suffer affliction unconnected with our current lives, but there is always something in our lives deserving of affliction. One is always in God's hands, because God is always in the interior heart of one's being, but when one is in a state of sin one is also in the Devil's hands, for he controls one's outward self.[18]

The Devil is the prince of this world, Alcuin later argued against the dualists, not because he is the lord of matter or of creatures, but because he is the lord of sinful human beings. The world is divided into two parts, one belonging to Christ and consisting of the just, the

17. Bede, *Hist.* 5.15; *In 2 Epistolam Sancti Petri*, 2.
18. *Mor.* 2.4–7, 2.12, 2.16, 2.20–21, 3.4–5, 3.17, 33.12; see P. Catry, "Epreuves du juste et mystère de Dieu," *Revue des études augustiniennes*, 18 (1972), 127. Isidore agreed that the Devil operates only under God's permission. The Devil never ceases tempting the elect, but God never ceases giving them the grace to resist: *Sent.* 1.10, 3.5–6.

other belonging to Lucifer and consisting of pagans, Jews, heretics, and sinful Catholics. Insofar as anyone subjects himself or herself to the Devil's will that person becomes a child of Satan.[19]

Gregory had a vivid theory of diabolical temptation, derived through Cassian out of desert monasticism.[20] He saw the world as a battleground in which we, as soldiers of Christ, stand continually in the front lines. If at any moment we withdraw our attention, the demons will swarm across the battlefield and seize us. The Devil spies on us and carefully chooses his times of attack. If he sees that we are for a moment comfortable or satisfied, or conversely that we are doubtful and unsure, or that we are at a critical juncture in our lives, then he sends his freshest troops to overwhelm us. If we open the slightest breach in our souls to sin, the demons will pour through the breach and rampage through our minds. All sins are the work of Satan. Four stages exist in the commission of every sin. First the Devil injects "suggestions" into our minds; then the suggestions provoke a response of pleasure or delight; we assent to the desire; finally, rationalizing and defending ourselves, we go ahead and commit the act. The more one tries to lead a good life, the more the Devil is eager to corrupt one, so that if ever temptations seem to slacken one may be sure that it is a devilish trick. After years of battling temptations to lust, for example, one might find oneself relatively free of that sin, but at that very moment Lucifer is preparing a new set of temptations—drunkenness or avarice for example—in order to catch one off guard. He enjoys blurring our understanding so that we do not even grasp that we are being tempted or that a moral problem exists at all, or he induces a sense of despair or helplessness in the face of temptation, so that we collapse under the crushing burden of guilt and yield to sin under the illusion that we have no chance of resisting.[21]

19. John 4:23: "Quantum vero se subjicit per liberum arbitrium diabolo, a patre diabolo est." John 6.35: Lucifer not the prince of all created things, but only of sinners. Apoc. 4.6: the division of the world into two kingdoms, Christ's and Satan's; Apoc. 4.7: Alcuin describes four evil angels who are the "body of the ancient enemy" and who rule the four great historic empires, those of the Assyrians, Persians, Macedonians, and Romans.

20. See Cassian, *Collationes* 7–9; Leo the Great, Sermons 47.9 and 89.3.

21. *Mor.* 2.8, 2.18, 2.22–23, 2.27, 4.23, 4.27, 16.18, 32.19, 32.21, 33.3; P. Boglioni, "Miracle et nature chez Grégoire le Grand," *Cahiers d'études médiévales*, 1 (1974), p. 43; Gastaldelli; *Mor.* 2.18: "Cotidie namque in acie stamus, cotidie tela tentationum eius excipimus" (Daily we stand in the battle line, taking the blows of his temptations). Isidore, *Sent.* 3.5–6, follows Gregory.

Gregory was aware that beyond human and diabolical culpability God must ultimately be responsible for the cosmos as it is. Contemplating 1 Samuel 18:10 ("an evil spirit from the Lord seized Saul") Gregory courageously admitted that this spirit really was evil and that it really did come from the Lord. But how can this be, if God is good? The spirit really is evil, he answered, because its own will and desire is to do harm. It really comes from God because God permits the evil spirit to work, not for its own evil purposes, but for the good purposes of God. The Devil would like to be able to tempt us without restraint or limitation; he would like to tear our minds, bodies, and souls to shreds. But whatever the Devil plans unjustly, God diverts to justice. Lucifer tempts us in the hope of destroying us, but God does not allow him to burden us with any trial beyond our ability to resist, and the Devil finds to his chagrin that God uses all his temptations to fortify the elect. As Thomas Merton would say a millennium and a half later, souls are like athletes: they need to struggle against competition in order to realize their potential. Satan's will is unjust, but the power God gives him is just because God uses it for justice. Those defeated by temptation are not done down by God's fault, for God has given them the strength to persevere: rather, they are brought down through their own free will. With such people the Devil enjoys apparent success in marring God's cosmos, but God turns even the consequences of sin to good, and Lucifer's knowledge that this must always be so is one of his chief torments.[22]

At the same time, the Devil really has dealt the human race a terrible blow in tempting us to original sin, which is the alienation of humanity from God. For Gregory original sin is a historical event, but it is also a metaphor for this fundamental alienation. The Devil is par excellence the alien, the other, the stranger, measurelessly removed from the reality, love, being, and glory of God.[23] His chief hope is to make us also strangers to God, and original sin is the token of his success. We are by nature balanced, centered, harmoniously in tune

22. *Mor.* 2.17–19, 3.5, 4.16, 7.16, 8.39, 32.22. *Mor.* 2.10: "Sciendum vero est quia Satanae voluntas semper iniqua est, sed numquam potestas iniusta, quia a semetipso voluntatem habet sed a Domino potestatem. Quod enim ipse facere inique appetit, hoc Deus fieri nonnisi iuste permittit" (One should realize that Satan's will is always evil, but his power is never unjust, for his will is his own but his power comes from God. Whatever he seeks to do for the sake of injustice, God seeks to do for the sake of justice alone).

23. *Mor.* 34.3–6; 12.36: "Quis vero alienus nisi apostata angelus vocatur?" See G. Ladner, "Homo Viator," *Speculum*, 42 (1967), 234–235; Boglioni, p. 46.

with God and the cosmos. Gregory calls such harmony "interiority," for the deeper we penetrate into ourselves the nearer we draw to God, who is the center of our being. But original sin distorts the harmony into hideous sound, drags us off balance, pulls us out of our true, interior selves into the state of confusion, desire, and distress that is the "exteriority" of this world. Satan rejoices in our exteriority, our distraction from reality, and God loves our "interiority," where we are true to that in ourselves which is God's image. Suffering and tribulation have the virtue that they detach us from our false and mistaken confidence in exteriority. Satan cannot penetrate our interiority, but he can use our exteriority to distract us with passions and lusts. A ruined person is one who has so lost his interiority that he cannot get back to it.[24]

Those who follow Christ constitute his mystical body; those whom Lucifer has led astray belong to the body of the Devil. "Who does not know," Gregory asked rhetorically, "that all who join themselves to Satan by evil living become members of his body? . . . The ancient enemy is one person with the whole collection of sinners." Sinners are Satan, or at least his satellites, imitators, witnesses, or offspring.[25] Isidore put it even more sharply: sinners cut themselves off from the Christian community and the body of Christ and become limbs of Satan.[26]

24. C. Dagens, *Saint Grégoire le Grand* (Paris, 1977), pp. 168–191; P. Aubin, "Intériorité et extériorité dans les Moralia in Job de Saint Grégoire le Grand," *Recherches de science religieuse*, 62 (1974), 117–166. The connection of the Eden serpent with the Devil was no longer an issue, but Alcuin's views are worth reference owing to their influence in literature: on the one hand the tempter in Eden was the Devil in serpent's form. *Comm. John* 4:22: "Diabolus . . . serpentem indutus locutus est mulieri." On the other hand, *Comm. Gen.* 60 has it that the Devil used the serpent as his mouthpiece: "Utebatur enim serpente diabolus quasi organo ad perpetrandam calliditatis suae malitiam."

25. *Mor.* 3.15–16, 4.11, 9.28–29, 12.43, 13.8, 13.34, 27.26, 28.7, 32.13, 32.16, 33.13–28, 34.4. *Mor.* 3.16: "Quis nesciat quod eiusdem satanae membra sunt omnes qui ei perverse vivendo iunguntur?" *Mor.* 4.11: "Ita antiquus hostis una persona est cum cuncta collectione reproborum." *Mor.* 13.34: "Ita quippe unum corpus sunt diabolus et omnes iniqui, ut plerumque nomine capitis censeatur corpus, et nomine corpus appelletur caput." The idea is echoed by Alcuin, who applied the term "son of the Devil" both to sinners and to the lie itself. In his *Comm. John* (4.22), referring to John 8:44, Alcuin argued that the Devil engenders the lie—the false word—just as God engenders Christ the true word: "Diabolus autem a semetipso mendax fuit, et mendacium suum ipse genuit, a nemine audivit prius mendacium. Quomodo Deus Pater genuit Filium veritatem, sic diabolus genuit quasi filium mendacium." Every person deceived by the Devil becomes a personification of the lie: "Homo vero deceptus a diabolus factus est a diabolo mendax."

26. *Sent.* 1.14–17, 1.25. *Comm. on Hebrews* 2: "Qui, dum, prave viventes, segregan-

Members of Lucifer's body could be considered Antichrists. Two different ideas of Antichrist were common. One was that all sinners—though especially heretics and Jews—were Antichrists. The figures of Satan and Antichrist often merge, and Gregory could equate the sinner as member of Antichrist's body with the sinner as member of Lucifer's. In the tenth century Adso of Monter-en-Der's treatise on the Antichrist did much to advance the alternative (and more ancient) view that Antichrist would be a single individual fostered by Lucifer at the end of the world in a last diabolical effort to block the kingdom of God. The Antichrist could be an incarnation of Satan himself, or Satan's son, or the chief of Satan's armies. The view that the Antichrist was an individual rather than a personification of continuing evils was more dramatic and more apt for eschatological speculation, and it came to dominate in theology and literature. For some writers the Antichrist was the form that Lucifer would take at the world's end when he pitches his last desperate battle against the Lord.[27]

---

tur a corpore Christi, efficiuntur membra diaboli." The heretic or sinner is separated from the church. *Sent.* 1.14: "Quia recessit a Dei populo, uterque recedentes a Christo, ad diaboli pertinet corpus." Later, Gottschalk spoke of sinners as belonging to Satan's body (*Confessio brevior*, p. 52), and Eriugena in turn called Gottschalk a heretic who was a child of Satan. For works on or by Gottschalk see the Essay on the Sources. The works cited here are his *Confessio brevior* (*CB*), *Confessio prolixior* (*CP*), the *Responsa de diversis* (*Resp.*), and the *De Praedestinatione* (*Praed.*) All citations are from C. Lambot, *Oeuvres théologiques et grammaticales de Godescalc d'Orbais* (Louvain, 1945).

27. *Mor.* 4.9, 14.21, 15.15, 15.58, 27.26, 32.15. *Mor.* 15.5: "Quis vero reproborum caput est, nisi Antichristus?" See Dagens, p. 353. Isidore, *Ety.* 8.11: "Sed et ille antichristus est qui negat esse Deum Christum." Compare Gottschalk, *Praed.* 5.31, p. 256: the civitas Dei as against the civitas Diaboli. See D. Verhelst, ed., *Adso Dervensis, De ortu et tempore Antichristi*, CCCM 45, the influential treatise by Adso. The best works on the subject are now R. K. Emmerson, *Antichrist in the Middle Ages* (Seattle, 1981); B. McGinn, "Angel Pope and Papal Antichrist," *Church History*, 47 (1978), 155–173; B. McGinn, ed., *Apocalyptic Spirituality* (New York, 1981); B. McGinn, ed., *Visions of the End* (New York, 1979); H. D. Rauh, *Das Bild des Antichrist im Mittelalter*, 2d ed. (Munich, 1979). See also K. Aichele, *Das Antichristdrama des Mittelalters, der Reformation und Gegenreformation* (The Hague, 1974). I am grateful to Professors Emmerson and McGinn for their helpful comments. Professor Emmerson would like to see more on the Antichrist in these pages, but there would be little point in reproducing his excellent work, nor is the question of the Antichrist, though the Antichrist is sometimes seen as the incarnation of the Devil, quite central to the basic question of the origin and nature of evil. The most important early texts on the Antichrist are Rev. 13:17; Hippolytus, *Treatise on Christ and the Antichrist* (c. 200); Lactantius, *Divine Institutes* (c. 300); Tyconius, *Commentary on Revelation* (c. 385). See SATAN, pp. 87–88, 158–159. For the important apocalyptic speculations of Joachim of Flora see McGinn, *Visions*, pp. 126–141, 158–167. Interest in the Antichrist rose steadily with interest in eschatology, especially during the Reformation, and reached its height in the sixteenth and seventeenth centuries. In the later Middle Ages and Reformation it was common to

Lucifer's revolt against God is defeated, and he was cast out of heaven in the morning of the world. Subsequently he successfully tempted Adam and Eve, thereby twisting and distorting human nature. The atonement—Christ's saving action in the world—is designed to save us from the effects of original sin. Before Christ, Gregory argued, the Devil possessed all humans by right; after Christ, he holds rights only over infidels and sinners. But landmines lurk in such a simple statement: Did Christ then die only for the elect? And if the Devil has lost his rights over the elect, how does he continue to tempt and torment them? The nature of the atonement and its effect are questions central to Christian theology, and it would be presumptuous to attempt a discussion of them here. Yet because they entail the question of the Devil's rights over humanity, a summary of that aspect of the problem is necessary.[28]

It was the general consensus of early medieval writers, following the fathers, that as a result of original sin humanity was in the power of the Devil. We had been, said Haymo of Auxerre, "in sorte Dei," but were after the fall "in sorte diaboli".[29] The question was whether this power of the Devil was merely a description of the state into which we had entered as a result of original sin or whether it represented a real, legal right. On this the tradition was ambivalent. On the one hand Lucifer was seen as having usurped his power over humanity by tricking Adam and Eve. On the other hand, he was perceived as having a real right (*jus*) over humanity, a right given him by God in punishment for our sins. Medieval writers sometimes found themselves arguing both positions without being quite aware of the tensions between them, or else attempting to paper over them with compromise, as Leo the Great did when he spoke of the Devil's right as a "tyrannical right," a term that later theologians and lawyers would find self-contradictory on the

---

identify Antichrist with a specific personage or institution; the Protestants liked to view the papacy as Antichrist. The triad "the world, the flesh, and the Devil" were first linked in the ninth century and became a commonplace from the eleventh: see S. Wenzel, "The Three Enemies of Man," *Medieval Studies*, 29 (1967), 47–66.

28. For a full summary see J. Rivière, *Le dogme de la rédemption au début du moyen âge* (Paris, 1934). The scenario for the temptation of Adam and Eve was set at this time: see Avitus, *De Mosaicae historiae gestis*, 2.135–143: Satan takes on the form of a serpent and approaches Eve, fearing that Adam would not listen to him. He wins Eve over by flattery, calling her "beautiful first mother"; Eve yields and then leads Adam astray.

29. Haymo, Homily 35. Rivière, *Dogme . . . moyen âge*, p. 8, summarized the common words to describe the Devil's power: "dominatus, principatus, potestas, imperium"; the words are derived from Rom. 8:38.

grounds that tyranny is by definition unjust and has no rights.[30] It was agreed that whatever rights the Devil had over us were limited by God's authority. The Devil's right is not an absolute right but one conceded to him by God. It was also agreed that whatever rights he had were justly negated by the atonement of Jesus Christ.[31]

The atonement of Christ liberated us from Satan's power. But why should God have chosen such strange means for our salvation? God could simply force Satan to loose his grip, or if the Devil had usurped his rights, God could by simple divine judgment order him to surrender them. On the other hand, if God had granted real rights under certain circumstances, he could simply revoke them under new circumstances. The painful drama of the Incarnation and crucifixion might thus have been avoided. Some of these alternatives, however, are inappropriate to God. Neither brute force nor arbitrary fiat would do. God would overcome the Devil, not by force but by just judgment.[32] If God had in fact granted the Devil some kind of right over us, then justice demanded that God pay some kind of quit-claim to the Dark Lord. If the "rights" are mere usurpation, Lucifer's power over us is a punishment that God inflicts on us, using the Devil as a kind of arm of the law. In this case the Devil's "rights" become at most a strong metaphor rather than a description of metaphysical reality, and the business of atonement is between humans and God, not between God and the Devil.

Among the early fathers two mutually incompatible views existed,

---

30. Leo I, Sermon 23: "jus tyrannicum." Compare Paschasius Radbert, *In Matthaeum*, 3; Paschasius takes a more typical position: because of our sin, the Devil has the legal right to tempt us ("diabolus nobis per legis suae jura tentandi accessum habet"). Rabanus Maurus opposed the idea of right in *De laudibus sanctae crucis*, 2.21: "Contra omne jus et omne fas servus nequissimus et fur dolossissimus sibi dominatum in alieno opere usurpaverat" (Against all right and justice the evil servant and treacherous thief seized control of another's work). Usually theologians fudged by referring to the Devil's rights in such terms as *quasi iuste* or *quaedam iustitia*.

31. Gregory, *Mor.* 17.30: "Unde accipit exterius potestatem Dominicae carnis occidendae, inde interior potestas eius qua nos tenebat occisa est. Ipse namque interius victus est, dum quasi vicit exterius" (the Devil's success is limited to the external and cannot enter into the interior soul where God's image dwells). Alcuin, *Libri carolini* 2.28: "Ratione potius quam dominatione, et iustitia potius quam potentia constrictus, praedam compulsus [diabolus] evomere" (The Devil has been forced to give up his loot by reason rather than domination and by justice rather than power). See Rivière, *Dogme . . . moyen âge*, pp. 13–14.

32. Haymo, Homily 28: "Nec potestate, sed auctoritate diabolum Dominus voluit superare."

often maintained side by side.[33] On the one hand it was argued that God chose to pay Lucifer a ransom for us. The only ransom of adequate value was Christ, but of course Christ could not really be given to the Devil. The Devil was therefore cheated of his prey, because, unaware of Christ's divinity, he eagerly seized the proffered ransom, and since it was intrinsically unjust for him to seize a sinless person, he lost by that unjust act not only Christ but all his rights over humanity as well. In the ransom theory, God hands Christ over to the Devil, but the fathers also argued the sacrifice theory, in which humanity hands Christ over to God. In the sacrifice theory the Devil has little part. Humans have alienated themselves from God, and they must offer him a sacrifice. The sacrifice must be untainted by sin; since humans are corrupted by sin, no ordinary human could be an appropriate sacrifice. Like the fathers, the early medieval writers never resolved the contradictions and evaded the issue, sometimes blithely continuing to glue the two incongruent arguments together.[34]

In the early twentieth century the question of ransom versus sacrifice still provoked partisan debate. The French anticlerical who wrote under the name of "J. Turmel" exaggerated the contradictions by arguing that the early Middle Ages were ransom-oriented and that Anselm's diabology in the twelfth century constituted a radical departure. J. Rivière, defending orthodoxy against Turmel, minimized the contradictions by downplaying the role of ransom in the earlier period. In fact a mixture of ransom and sacrifice theory existed both before and after Anselm. But sacrifice had become the more established view as early as the fifth century and remained so. Anselm's view was based upon patristic tradition; his originality lay in his use of consecutive logic to explore it.[35]

Jesus' descent to the dead after his crucifixion was another problem advanced in the early Middle Ages. The idea goes back to certain unclear notions in the Old and New Testaments. The early Christian community assumed that Jesus had been among the dead between Good Friday and Easter Sunday. Being a Palestinian Jewish commu-

---

33. See SATAN, pp. 82–86, 116–121, 138–143, 192–194, 215–218.

34. Bede, Homily 2.1: "Cum suum pro nobis corpus et sanguinem hostiam Patri obtulisset, subvertit potentiam diaboli" (When he offered his body and blood as a sacrifice to the Father for us, he undermined the power of the Devil).

35. Rivière, *Dogme . . . moyen âge;* Rivière, "Le dogme de la rédemption au XIIe siècle d'après les dernières publications," *Revue du moyen âge latin,* 2 (1946), 101–112, 219–230; J. Turmel, *Histoire du diable* (Paris, 1931).

nity, they expressed this idea in terms of a descent into the underworld rather than a Neoplatonic rising through heavenly spheres. In the underworld Jesus confronted and defeated the powers of death. Quite early this notion was used to explain a separate problem, the fate of those who had died before the Incarnation. If the Incarnation liberated humanity from the effect of original sin, what about those who lived before Christ? Christ must have led out of the kingdom of death those who had lived just lives before his birth. By the fifth century this idea was fixed by patristic commentaries, homiletic literature, and the liturgy of Holy Saturday. The fathers were unsure on one important point, however. They did not know whether all the just, or only the righteous Hebrews, were saved. One's answer conformed to one's attitudes toward pagan culture in general and Greek philosophy in particular. Was Plato saved as well as Abraham? It was agreed that only those united in faith with the Messiah could be saved. This clearly included the Hebrew patriarchs and all Hebrews loyal to the covenant. The fathers, unaware that the growth of Messianic speculation among the Hebrews had been gradual, assumed that all faithful Jews had looked for the coming of the Messiah. Some fathers extended the effects of salvation beyond the Hebrews. Origen, Cyril of Alexandria, Augustine, and Gregory Nazianzenus argued that when Christ descended among the dead he preached to the pagans and converted those who had led good lives according to conscience; Gregory the Great's twenty-second homily on the Gospels can be read as accepting this argument, which allowed Plato to be saved as well as Abraham. The doctrine of the descent among the dead, widely taught in the early church, was first formally introduced into a creed in 359 (the Creed of Sirmium). It grew in popularity in Spain in the sixth century and in Gaul in the seventh, and creeds from these areas influenced the Roman baptismal creed, which produced the "Apostles' Creed" about the eighth century. From the eighth century onward it was fixed in the liturgy.[36]

36. The biblical references are Is. 9:2, 42:6–7; Ps. 23; Hab. 3:3–13; Hos. 13:14; Mt. 27:52–53; Mk. 3:27; Acts 2:24; 1 Pet. 3:19, 4:6; Eph. 4:8–10; Rev. 20:1–2. The standard English translation is "descent into hell," but that carries much more associative freight than the original *descensus ad inferos* or *ad inferna*, where *inferna* or *inferos* can be translated simply as "the underworld" or "among the dead." Gregory the Great, Homily 22 on the Gospels: "suos in fide in actibus recognovit." On the descent see C. A. Bouman, "'Descendit ad inferos,'" *Nederlands katholieke stemmen*, 55 (1959), 44–51; J. J. Campbell, "To Hell and Back," *Viator*, 13 (1982), 107–158; M. M. Gatch, "The

A dramatic account of the descent called the *descensus ad inferos* was added to the popular apocryphal "Acts of Pilate," or "Gospel of Nicodemus," as early as the seventh century. This account, together with creeds, sermons, and liturgy, helped transpose the original idea of the descent among the dead into something more dramatic, what is called in English "the harrowing of hell," from Old English *herian*, "to make a war raid." In the harrowing, Christ sweeps down upon death, hell, and the Devil, smashes down the doors of hell, and triumphantly carries the just off to heaven. The dramatic battle between Christ and Satan at the gates of hell fits the ransom rather than the sacrifice theory and helps explain why ransom continued to be the more popular one even while the theologians gradually abandoned it.

The final episode in the "Acts of Pilate" is Satan's defeat at the end of the world. This story is badly muddled in the "Acts" and in Christian literature in general. At the time of Lucifer's initial rebellion, Christ (or Michael) casts him out into eternal darkness. He is imprisoned, yet he is also somehow free under God's permission to roam the world seeking the ruin and destruction of souls. Lucifer's second defeat is accomplished by the Incarnation of Christ; the third by Christ's resistance to the temptation in the desert; the fourth by Christ's Passion, from the agony in the garden to the crucifixion; the fifth by Christ's descent to the dead; the sixth by his resurrection; and the seventh by the second coming. The second coming will occur after a period in which the Devil will be free to attack humanity more ferociously than ever. Then, at the end, a great battle will be fought in which Christ (or Michael) will crush Satan as Christ (or Michael) did at the time of his first rebellion. Then Lucifer will forever be defeated, chained, and deprived of all liberty to move about, tempt, and afflict us. These events occupy a certain sequential order, but structurally they are all expressions of one and the same archetypal defeat. Lucifer's initial rebellion and all his subsequent strivings against the kingdom of God are inexorably doomed. Structurally the first and last

Harrowing of Hell," *Union Seminary Quarterly Review*, 36, supp. (1981), 75–88; J. N. D. Kelly, *Early Christian Creeds*, 3d ed. (London, 1972), pp. 378–383; H. C. Kim, ed., *The Gospel of Nicodemus* (Toronto, 1973). See M. R. James, *The Apocryphal New Testament* (Oxford, 1924), pp. 94–146, for a translation of the "Gospel of Nicodemus;" J. Kroll, *Gott und Hölle: Der Mythos vom Descensuskampfe* (Leipzig, 1932); C. I. Smith, "Descendit ad inferos—Again," *Journal of the History of Ideas*, 28 (1967), 87–88; R. V. Turner, "Descendit ad inferos," *Journal of the History of Ideas*, 27 (1966), 173–194. See also Chapter 6, n. 18, below. I am grateful to Dr. Kevin Roddy for allowing me to read his unpublished paper "The Descent into Hell: Medieval Literature and Medieval Myth."

The demons in hell depicted as stylized monsters. Here they are God's representatives, executing s justice. Illumination from a fifteenth-century French manuscript of Saint Augustine's *City of God*. ourtesy of the Bibliothèque Interuniversitaire Sainte-Geneviève.

defeat of the Devil is the same, which accounts for their iconographic identity in art. The difficulty arises when these structurally identical elements are taken as historically discrete events. Early medieval writers fell into this trap, and the muddle has only grown over the centuries with every well-meaning effort to sort the chronology out.[37] When the unresolvable chronological difficulties are set aside in favor of the structural solution, the substantive theological issues emerge. If Satan is eternally defeated by God, and if evil is eternally subjected to good, how is it that God permits evil at all? This question refers back almost immediately to the general problem of evil. And, if Lucifer obtains power over humankind as a result of original sin, but that power is broken by Christ, how is it that Lucifer's power now continues imperceptively diminished? These questions have never been resolved.

Early medieval writers agreed with the opponents of Origen that Satan could not be saved.[38] But they pursued the question further and offered explanations as to why he could not be. First, neither Lucifer nor his evil angels choose to be saved. Far from repenting, their initial sin sent them off into an irreversible trajectory away from reality and toward destruction. Second, the angels had been granted extraordinary powers of resistance implicit in their high nature, so their failure makes them much more guilty than humans. Third, the angels, being pure spirit, had not the excuse of being undermined by the weaknesses of the flesh. Fourth, where humanity might offer the extenuation of having been tempted by one already fallen into sin, the Devil had no such excuse: he is the originator of all sin himself. The judgment was emphatic and final: Lucifer has no hope, none at all.[39]

37. Gregory, *Mor.* 32.15, 33.20; Kurz, pp. 30–36.
38. Cassiodorus, *Expositions on the Psalms*, 9.5: the names of the fallen angels have been eternally erased from the book of life.
39. Gregory, *Mor.* 2.3, 4.2–9, 8.50, 9.50, 17.22, 34–55. *Mor.* 4.4: "apostata angelus . . . nequaquam ulterius ad lucem paenitentiae per divini respectus memoriam resurgat" (The apostate angel will never be mindful of the respect he owes God and so will never return to the light of penitence). *Mor.* 4.7: "antiquus hostis nequaquam ad meritum lucis, nequaquam ad ordinem supernorum agminum reducitur" (The ancient enemy shall never return to the light or the ranks of the heavenly powers). Isidore, *Sent.* 1.10, concurred, as did Alcuin, *Comm. Gen.* 3–4. *Comm Gen.* 3: "angelicum vulnus Deus non praedestinavit curare, hominis vero sanare praedestinavit" (God did not predestine the angelic wound to be healed, as he did the human one). *Comm. Gen.* 4: "angelus sui sceleris inventor fuit, homo vero alterius fraude seductus. Item, quanto sublimior angelus in gloria, tanto major in ruina; homo vero quanto fragilior in natura, tanto facilior ad veniam" (The angel was the author of his own crime, but man was

Gottschalk's (c. 804–c. 868/869) importance lies in the controversy he raised over predestination. Gottschalk was a monk from the archdiocese of Reims who had gone to Fulda where he encountered the great Carolingian scholar Rabanus Maurus. Rabanus took exception to his views on predestination and to the irregularity of his life—he had apparently left his monastery without permission—and sent the wandering monk back to Archbishop Hincmar of Reims with the request that Hincmar put him in confinement. Hincmar did so and in 849 called a synod at Quierzy, where Charles the Bald had founded a royal school. The synod heard Gottschalk's views and condemned him formally, imprisoning him in a monastery in the archdiocese. Confined, Gottschalk continued to write and circulate his works, the result being the most upsetting theological dispute since the Iconoclastic controversy of the eighth century. To Hincmar's consternation, the noted monastic theologian Ratramnus of Corbie took a predestinarian position not far from Gottschalk's. Hincmar called on John Scottus Eriugena, already known as the greatest mind of his day, for assistance, but Eriugena horrified him with a treatise that went to extremes on the other side. All Frankland was in an uproar. Hincmar summoned another council at Quierzy in 853 to secure support for his moderate position, but the predestinarian side called their own council at Valence, where they condemned Hincmar's views, as did the Council of Langres in 859. Hincmar now issued his own treatise on the subject, and all sides appealed to Pope Nicholas I, who died before hearing the case. Meanwhile the dust gradually settled, with Hincmar's position gradually gaining acceptance and with Gottschalk intransigent and imprisoned till his death. It was Gottschalk's stubborn virtue to refuse to accept the ambiguity about predestination and free will that was the legacy of Augustine. He faced the problem more squarely than had been done before, but the church as a whole remained unable or unwilling to resolve the question.[40]

Where Gottschalk's opponents emphasized free will, Gottschalk insisted upon the absolute need for grace. As a result of original sin we are incapable of using our free will for anything but sin: we have only a *libertas peccandi*. Only when Christ works in us through his grace do we

---

misled by another being. The angel will fall farther because his glory was greater, and since human nature is more vulnerable it may be the more readily forgiven).

40. On the controversy see M. Cappuyns, *Jean Scot Erigène* (Louvain, 1933), pp. 102–112; Hefele-Leclercq, vol. 4:1, pp. 137–235; J. Pelikan, *The Christian Tradition*, vol. 3: *The Growth of Medieval Theology* (Chicago, 1978), pp. 80–98.

have the freedom to do good and to be saved; without grace we are still free only to sin and be damned. Whoever receives grace has Christ working in him, and Christ cannot be resisted. God knows in all eternity who receives saving grace and who does not. God gives the elect the power to overcome the Devil and to avoid sin.[41] With this kind of problem Augustine had wrestled long and hard without coherent outcome. The Council of Orange (529) had argued that God predestined the elect both in the sense that he eternally knows that they are saved and in the sense that he wills their salvation; but the council also maintained that God predestined the damned only in the sense that he knows their damnation, not in the sense that he wills it. This was the line to which Hincmar tried to hew: "God has predestined what divine equity was going to render, not what human iniquity was going to commit." But Ratramnus saw the difficulty of separating divine knowledge from divine will. "God," he said, "foreknowing all things that are to follow, decreed before the ages how they are to be arranged through the ages."[42]

The degree of divine responsibility for evil therefore was a central issue. It is a delicate point, and Gottschalk moved in too boldly. On occasion he tended to the more moderate view, arguing that God had prepared and predestined hell for the Devil on the basis of the future evils that God knew he would commit.[43] But he inclined more to a severe double predestination. It was not only that God predestined the Devil to hell in the sense of predestining the punishment for sins that the Devil freely commits. God could not foreknow something without willing it, for then he would be changeable. If God in the first instance knew that the being he was creating would be damned, he need not have created that being, or at least not in that mode.[44] Among the

---

41. *Resp.*, pp. 160–161; *Praed.*, p. 185.

42. Pelikan, pp. 87–89.

43. *CB*, p. 52: "[Deus] ipsum diabolum caput omnium daemoniorum cum omnibus angelis suis apostaticis et cum ipsis quoque universis hominibus reprobis membris videlicet suis propter praescita certissime ipsorum propria futura mala merita praedestinasse pariter per iustissimum judicium suum in mortem merito sempiternam" (God has predestined the Devil, the head of all the demons, along with his apostate angels and all the wicked humans who form the members of his body, to eternal death, which they merit, for God knows in all eternity the evils that they commit and the judgment they deserve).

44. *CP*, p. 56: How could it be otherwise? "Nimirum sine causa et ipsis praedestinasses mortis perpetuae poenam nisi et ipsos praedestinasses ad eam. Non enim irent nisi essent determinati" (You would not foreordain the punishment of eternal death for them without reason and unless you had predestined them to that punishment; they would not be going to hell unless they had been predestined to do so). Otherwise God

Saint Jerome tempted to lust by a black, imp-like Devil. Illumination from the *Belles heures of Jean, Duc de Berry*, Burgundy, fifteenth century. Courtesy of the Metropolitan Museum of Art, The Cloisters Collection, Purchase 1954.

difficulties of Gottschalk's position is that it effectively eliminates real freedom of will; it entails a strong and positive, even if indirect, responsibility for evil on God's part; it implies that Christ died only for the elect and that baptism has little effect. On the whole it makes for a tightly controlled, deterministic cosmos in which there seems no point in Christ or indeed in the whole human race. That God did not die for the unbaptized or for sinners among the baptized seemed clear to Gottschalk.[45] This was at the center of the councils' condemnation of Gottschalk, for they insisted that Christ had died for all humans, not just the elect. If God truly predestines evil as well as the punishment for evil, then neither the Devil nor evil humans are fully responsible for their sins; at most they are coresponsible. And on that level of discourse it cannot be clear whether evil is really evil or simply a good that is misunderstood. In that case the Devil—the symbol of opposition to God—has no real function. The majority of Christian theologians chose not to follow double predestination.

John Scottus Eriugena, the most original theologian of the early Middle Ages, was born in Ireland in the first quarter of the ninth century. He emigrated to the kingdom of the Franks about 847, by 851 taught at Charles the Bald's royal school at Quierzy near Laon, and in the same year wrote his first work, the treatise on predestination that Hincmar commissioned. He always drew deeply upon the Latin patristic tradition, especially Augustine, but about 860 a radically new element entered his thought. The works of Pseudo-Dionysus had appeared in the West about 750, and in 860 Charles the Bald asked John to make a translation. Eriugena's attitude toward Dionysius was deeply respectful, for everyone at that time assumed that Dionysius was Paul's disciple and that his writing closely reflected the thought of the apostle. John's Greek was quite equal to the task. But his was too brilliant and original a mind to make a simple, literal translation. On the one side he modified Dionysius in the direction of Saint Augustine and according to his own originality. On the other his own ideas were transformed by those of Dionysius and other Greek mystical writers whose works he also translated, Gregory of Nyssa and Maximus Confessor. Eriugena's theology stood on its own. He "was an author who

---

would be mutable.

45. *Praed.*, p. 218: "Quod enim Deus non sit pro reprobis baptizatis passus claret illic patenter quod diabolus vincit et sibi subicit eos." Gottschalk also agreed with Augustine (against Isidore) that Lucifer did not fall at the first moment of his creation but only after a moment of reflection.

read both the Greeks and the Latins and thought for himself." His greatest work was *The Division of Nature*, composed between 862 and 867. It never had the influence it deserved, because the Neoplatonic elements brought John to the borderline of pantheism, and his ideas, viewed with suspicion from the outset, were posthumously condemned in 1050, 1059, 1210, and 1225. Now and again, in Honorius Augustinodensis, in Gilbert de la Porrée among the Cistercians, and in Nicholas of Cusa, Eriugena's thought would surface, but its use by pantheists about 1200 darkened the cloud that obscured it.[46]

Eriugena's views on evil, like the rest of his ideas, were unusual. He had less use for the concept of the Devil than his contemporaries; he assumed his existence, but the evil Lucifer did not fit his mystical cosmology.[47]

John's epistemology is basic: God is absolutely incomprehensible both to us and to himself. To know something is to define it, but God cannot be defined. Further, God is not anything at all. It is absurd to say that God is something, for that puts him into the same category as created things. Moreover, nothing can be affirmed about God, for whatever is affirmed about God denies its contrary. If we say that God is great, that denies that he is small; if we say he is light, it denies that he is darkness; and so on. But in fact God is beyond all categories, transcends all categories, and reconciles all contraries. Any affirmation about God can be only a metaphor, but a denial may be literal. For example, one may truly deny that God is limited by space or that he is light, but any statement about God that excludes any other statement about him is invalid.[48] God cannot even be said to be an essence, for

46. For works on and by Eriugena see the Essay on the Sources. The most useful are *The Division of Nature* (*Div.*), the *Commentary on John* (*Comm. John*), *Divine Predestination* (*Pred.*), and *Expositions on the Heavenly Jerusalem*" (*Ier.*). Translations are taken from I. Sheldon-Williams, ed., *Johannis Scotti Eriugenae Periphyseon*, 2 vols. (Dublin, 1968–1972) (SW). The quotation is from B. Stock, "Observations on the Use of Augustine by Johannes Scotus Eriugena," *Harvard Theological Review*, 60 (1967), 213–220.

47. In fact Eriugena used the term *lucifer* as a metaphor for the divine light of the Trinity (*Ier.* 2.3). See also *Div.* 2.20: "But the daystar of the Psalmist, while it seems to some to signify the devil, to others [seems] to signify that very bright star which is wont to precede the rising of the Sun, the star before whose appearance above the horizon tradition relates that Christ was born of a virgin" (SW, vol. 2, p. 79).

48. "Deus itaque nescit se, quid est, quia non est quid" (*Div.* 2.28; SW, vol. 2, p. 142); "Deus nec a seipso nec ab alio diffiniri potest" (Cappuyns, p. 204; compare *Div.* 2.28, SW, vol. 2, p. 138); "nulla kathegoria proprie dicitur de Deo" (Cappuyns, p. 204; cf. *Div.* 2. 28); "Non proprie de Deo predicatur quicquid habet oppositum (Cappuyns, p. 199; *Div.* 1.14, SW, vol. 1, pp. 76–77.)

The Lamb of God looks on while angels behead the Beast of the Apocalypse and cast Satan down into hell. The legend over the Devil's head is *diabolus victus*, "the Devil defeated." Illumination from the *Commentary on the Apocalypse*, by Saint Beatus, France, eleventh century. Photograph courtesy the Bibliothèque Nationale, Paris.

essence is the contrary of nothing, and God is nothing as much as he is something. It is true that one can say that God is superessential (*super-essentialis, hyperousios*), but this is really a negation, for it tells us not what God is but what he is not: he is not any essence, substance, or being. Thus God does not exist. It is absurd to maintain that God exists, as if God occupies the space-time continuum with other things that exist. A dog, a table, a star, or a woman may exist, but God does not. Yet this negative does not destroy the affirmative. Like Dionysius, John prefers negative, or apophatic, theology to positive, or cataphatic, theology, but he affirms that the truest statements are paradoxes, the coincidence of opposites. Any given statement about God resolves itself into two opposite contraries, neither of which is true and both of which are true. This is not nonsense, though it passes human reason, for God is beyond the grasp of human reason. It is true to say: God exists; God does not exist; God exists and does not exist. God neither exists nor does not exist: we cannot devise any category that can contain God.[49]

Can any sense be made out of saying that God exists and does not exist? The first distinction that Eriugena makes is between different meanings of existence or being. (1) Being may mean that which is perceivable by sense or intellect, nonbeing that which is not; (2) being may mean what is actualized, nonbeing what is only in potential; (3) being may mean that which is known to the intellect, nonbeing that which is known only to the senses. Whether God exists or not depends upon the mode that is used. God does not exist if by existence one means something that is present to the senses. If a shirt exists, then God does not. On the other hand, if one shifts the meaning of the term *existence* and says that God exists, then the shirt does not. *Being* cannot be used univocally for God and for any created thing. Whatever "being" may be for God, it is totally different from what "being" is for a shirt.

The next step is to begin the description of nature, which John does by dividing it into four stages. He makes the terms *God* and *nature* virtually equivalent, for he treats nature inclusively, as what is. Nature is more than the created cosmos. The created cosmos is God, and God is more than the created cosmos. All things are in God, and all things are God, yet God is beyond all things. "The divine nature, because it is above being, is different from what it creates within

49. *Div.* 1.14; SW, vol. 1, pp. 80–84; *Div.* 4.16.

itself."⁵⁰ What is, is; what is, is for the reason that it is God. We are not far from the modern proof that the universe exists, that being is; the difference is that Eriugena's cosmos has mind, life, and purpose. The universe is inseparable from God, it has its being, life, motion, and rest in him and of him and through him. Each creature that exists exists for the reason that God thinks it; its most basic existence is in the mind of God. In other words, if we could penetrate to the deepest level of being of a creature, we would find that that deepest level was God. How is it possible that a creature could be anything other than God? "We should not understand God and the creature as two things removed from one another, but as one and the same thing." God is above, and below, and inside, and outside, of all things, the beginning, the middle, and the end.⁵¹

Nature is God, but it is not God in the sense that it contains or limits God. Eriugena was aware that he might be seen to be a pantheist, but he briskly repudiated such a suggestion. Nature is God in that it is totally within God, but God is not limited by nature. (See figure 1.) The universe is a space-time continuum existing within God, who is beyond space and time and all other categories. A later metaphor had it that the cosmos is soaked in God like a sponge in an ocean; Eriugena would have agreed, but he would have insisted that the sponge too was the stuff of God.⁵²

It is possible, then, to divide nature, which is God, into four stages, remembering always that these are categories that our minds create and cannot be assumed to exist in God in any ultimate sense. The first division of nature is Uncreated and Creating. This is God at "the beginning." God exists in eternity, not in time, so that there is no motion, no beginning or end, in God. For us, who exist in time, the cosmos has a beginning and an end. Its beginning is this God-nature who, uncreated itself, creates. The second division is Created and Creating: this is like the Platonic world of ideas; the third is Created and Uncreating: this is the material universe; the fourth is Uncreated

50. J. J. O'Meara, *Eriugena* (Dublin, 1969), p. 51.
51. *Div.* 2.2 (SW, vol. 2, p. 12): "Num negabis, Creatorem et creaturam unum esse?" *Div.* 3.1: "Omnis universitatis principium est, et medium, et finis." *Div.* 3.17; "et fit in omnibus omnia." *Div.* 3.17: "in divina cognitione in qua omnia vere et substantialiter permanent. Est Deus supra et infra et intra et extra omnia."
52. John's position has in modern times been incorrectly described as panentheism. See figure 1.

Mainstream Christian theology

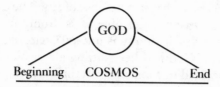

Pantheism

Eriugena (panentheism)

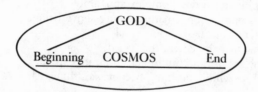

Figure 1. Three ways of conceiving of the relationship between God and the cosmos

and Uncreating: this is the God-nature when it has entered back into itself and has come to rest.[53]

God in himself is unknowable, but in what we have just called the stages of nature, God makes himself knowable. This process of the unknowable God rendering himself knowable is the process of creation. Why does God create the cosmos? Eriugena offers several answers. One is that God's nature is boundless love, that the bursting,

---

53. *Div.* 1.1: "[Natura] quae creat et non creatur . . . quae creatur et creat . . . quae creatur et non creat . . . quae nec creat nec creatur."

fecund power of that love pours itself out in an act of love. The second, rather strange one is that it is because of sin. The overarching reason is that there is no reason discernible to us: from the fact that the cosmos exists it follows that it simply is in God's nature to create it. What is, is. It is not as if God had been sitting about pondering various alternatives and decided to come up with this cosmos, or any cosmos. I AM WHO AM: God is what he is in all eternity; the cosmos is what it is; no alternative exists. For whatever reason he creates, God creates the opposites of himself and realizes himself in the coincidence of opposites.

> Every creature lives in God,
> And God is himself created in every creature
> In a way that we cannot grasp.
> Unreachable, he offers himself to us,
> Unseeable, he shows himself,
> Unthinkable, he enters our minds,
> Hidden, he uncovers himself,
> Unknown, he makes himself known,
> The unutterable Name utters the Word in which each thing is.
> Infinite and finite, complex and simple,
> He is nature above nature, being above being.
> Maker of all, he is made in all,
> Unmoving, he enters the world,
> Timeless in time, unlimited in limited space,
> And he who is no thing becomes all things.[54]

God, as Dionysius had said, is not in himself knowable, but he makes himself knowable in his manifestation, his *energeia*, and that manifestation is the cosmos.

---

54. I have taken the liberty of interpreting these passages in verse because of their lyric quality. *Div.* 3.17: "Nam et creatura in Deo est subsistens, et Deus in creatura mirabili et ineffabili modo creatur, seipsum manifestans, invisibilis visibilem se faciens, et incomprehensibilis comprehensibiliem, et occultus apertum, et incognitus cognitum . . . , et superessentialis essentialem, et supernaturalis naturalem, et simplex compositum . . . , et infinitus finitum . . . et supertemporalis temporalem, et superlocalis localem, et omnia creans in omnibus creatum, et factor omnium factus in omnibus, et aeternus coepit esse, et immobilis movetur in omnia, et fit in omnibus omnia." Div. 3.4: "Omne namque, quod intelligitur et sentitur, nihil aliud est, nisi non apparentis apparitio, occulti manifestatio, negati affirmatio, incomprehensibilis comprehensio, ineffabilis fatus, inacessibilis accessus, inintelligibilis intellectus, incorporalis corpus, superessentialis essentia, informis forma, immensurabilis mensura, innumerabilis numerus."

God creates the cosmos out of nothing. This had been Christian orthodoxy since the fourth century, but Eriugena assumed that this statement would be nonsense if taken literally rather than metaphorically. It is true that for us, nothing seems logically to precede something, but in fact we never observe something coming from nothing and in reality nothing comes from nothing. God is what is; there is no lack in God; there can be no nothing (in the sense of total lack of essence) in God. "Nothing" does not exist in God. Nor does it make any sense to suppose that God first created "nothing" and then made "something" out of it.[55] It is possible to use words differently and say that God made things out of nothing in the sense that he actualized things that were only in potential. But even this misses the mark, for two reasons. First, if things exist in potential in God's mind, they exist in the most real possible way. Second, it makes no sense (again) to imagine God waiting about for a while with things in potential before he actualizes them. God is in eternity; what he is, he is eternally; what he does, he does eternally. There was never a time when things were not. The universe is eternal as well as being created. It truly has a beginning and end for creatures who dwell within it, but it is truly eternal in the Word of God. Thus it can be said that God creates himself in his creatures.[56]

God's creating himself in his creatures is the process of the "descent of the good" (*Descensus boni*). The first stage of this descensus is the Word. Christ is the link between God and creation. In Christ the Word are all the causes, essences, ideas, exempla, wills, plans, programs, predestinations, seeds, of the whole cosmos. This is a Platonic world of ideals, but all the ideals are in Christ. When does God make this act of creation? At the beginning of time, from our point of view, and in all eternity from God's. The cosmos is a theophany, a manifestation of God.[57]

The second stage of the descensus is that which is created and does

55. That would mean that he first created nothing out of nothing in order to create something out of nothing, which is absurd. Nothing is absolutely no thing.

56. "Omnis creatura simul eterna et facta est" (Cappuyns, p. 205; *Div.* 3.16). "De universitatis eternitate in verbo Dei" (Cappuyns, p. 206, *Div.* 3.17). "De nihilo" (Cappuyns, p. 205; *Div.* 2.14). "Omnia que facta sunt in Deo, Deus sunt" (Cappuyns, p. 206; *Div.* 3.17). God creates himself in his creatures (*Div.* 1.12. SW, vol. 1, pp. 58–62). "Ac sic de nihilo facit omnia . . . de negatione omnium, quae sunt et quae non sunt, affirmationes omnium, quae sunt et quae non sunt" (*Div.* 3.20).

57. *Div.* 1.8, SW, vol. 1, p. 50. "Omnis visibilis et invisibilis creatura theophania, id est divina apparitio, potest appellari" (*Div.* 3.19).

not create: this is the material universe, the descent of the divine goodness into a world that can be grasped by both sense and intellect. Though more cloudy and shadowed and less real than the world of idea, this world too is a showing of God, proceeding (oddly) from both love and alienation, for now the question of evil emerges. Evil is privation—this Eriugena had from Augustine. Evil exists in the sense that it has effects, but in a deeper and essential sense it is nothing. Whatever is, is because God knows it. God does not know evil and thus evil is not. If God knew evil, evil would come from God, and this was not an alternative for Eriugena.[58]

Evil does not come from God. Therefore it is not natural, and neither are its effects. Evil is rather a perturbation in the natural order, a state of alienation and disharmony, and it is because of evil that God manifests himself in matter.[59] Evil *is* this state of alienation, of original sin. Original sin is not an event that happened in time. No interval elapsed between the creation and the fall of humanity. Alienation is not our natural state, because the fault is not in our intellect, our reason, or any part of our nature. But alienation is our existential state, because each of us wills to turn in upon himself or herself, seeking to cling to what we cherish in ourselves rather than reaching out to God to move and love and grow with him. God calls us to return to him, but we struggle and kick against him, digging claw and toe into what we would like to be solid rock—money, fame, pleasure—only to find it illusion. We cling to what is not rather than to what is; this alienation is more an absence of movement, a refusal to move, than anything in itself.[60]

The temptation of Adam and Eve by the Devil was a historical event occurring in time. But humanity had already fallen by then, and alienation was already at the heart of our nature. The Devil did effect this successful temptation, but his presence was supererogatory, both in Eden and in Eriugena's theology. Sin, alienation, and evil exist from the first moment of the cosmos. In the same eternal or at least coeval moment God creates us, we sin, and the consequences of our sin are set. The cosmos is the way it is. God wills to create this cosmos although (or even because?) it has in it the flaw, the privation, introduced by the sin that we all commit. Angels, like humans, are intel-

58. "Diffinitio malitiae" (Cappuyns, p. 211; *Div.* 5.26).

59. *Div.* 4.20: "in primo siquidem Adam . . . universa natura de felicitate paradisi est expulsa."

60. "De perturbato naturali ordine" (Cappuyns, p. 208; 212; *Div.* 4.11, 4.14, 5.36).

ligent creatures, so angels participate with humans at the same moment and in the same way in introducing this sin and alienation. The Devil, like humanity, fell the same moment he was created. But the whole sense of a brooding, powerful, hostile presence of the Devil that dominated so much of medieval thought is almost wholly absent in Eriugena.[61]

Eriugena viewed hell as a metaphor rather than as a locality. Hell is the permanent understanding that you have got what you want—alienation from God for your own desires—rather than what God wants, which is union with you. Your torment is your permanent realization that you have made the wrong choice. Take Christ from me, Eriugena exclaimed, and nothing good is left to me. The loss of Christ is the one and sole cause of the misery of hell.[62] Yet in the end, the evil that is in every creature will be abolished, for evil is limited. You can press away from God to the very limit of evil, but you will of necessity be drawn back toward him; even the Devil will be purged of sin, and his true, created nature will be drawn back to God. He will not cease to be, but he will cease to be the Devil.[63]

The final stage in the descent is the return of all things to God, the ascension of love back to its source. Unintellectual creatures are moved back to God naturally; intellectual creatures are moved back to God both by nature and by grace. Christ is the Word by which God brings all back to him just as he is the Word by which God sends himself out; he is the ascent as well as the descent. The Incarnation of Christ is the model of the *theosis*, the divinization, the godding of the cosmos, for as God becomes human through the Word so humanity becomes divine in the Word. When all return to God, evil and privation will be eliminated, and the ascent, the godding, will be complete. As God went out from himself in making all things, he now returns to himself, calling all things back to him, and God will be all in all, *omnia in omnibus*. The sting of evil is drawn, and the body made whole.[64]

Liturgy had broad influence in the development of the Devil, be-

61. *Div.* 4.14–15.
62. Cappuyns, p. 212; *Div.* 5.29–36.
63. *Div.* 5.26–29.
64. *Div.* 5.8; John 1.21.23: "Descendit enim verbum in hominem ut per ipsum ascenderet homo in Deum." *Div.* 3.20: "Deus fit in omnibus omnia et in se ipsum redit, revocans in se omnia, et dum in omnibus fit, super omnia esse non desinit. . . . Quando omnia revertentur in Deum, sicut aer in lucem, quando erit Deus omnia in omnibus."

cause most people encountered Christian teaching in the rites of the church more than in theology. A variety of liturgies existed in the early church, and standardization became common only from the ninth century onward. On the whole the Devil played little part in the liturgy, even, as H. A. Kelly has observed, in that of Good Friday, the one exception being the liturgy of baptism.[65]

By the third century it was common in the Western church to administer baptism at Easter. A series of scrutinies—Latin masses during which exorcisms were administered to the catechumens who were to be admitted to the church—occurred for several weeks before Easter. By the seventh century the number of scrutinies was standardized at seven.[66] Except in baptism, exorcism was never part of the liturgy, and it is unclear whether exorcism formed a part of the baptismal ceremony earlier than the third century. But at least from that time, and in the Roman Catholic church as late as 1972, exorcism was invariably part of baptism. It was assumed that the candidate remained in the power of the Prince of the Old Eon until baptism, and that to prepare the candidate for admission into the Christian community the Dark Lord had to be exorcized from his soul.

From the third century onward an order of ordained exorcists existed, but their functions were soon absorbed by the priests. In 1972 Pope Paul VI decreed the abolition of the formal order of exorcist; he provided that national episcopal councils could establish ministries with such a title but without the function. The meaning of the term *exorcism* has never been closely defined. Its origins are in Greek paganism. The word derives from the Greek *exorkizo*, "to secure by oath" or "to ask or pray deeply," from *horkos*, "oath." In its root meaning it is a solemn, intense address to someone or something and is by no means necessarily connected with demons.[67] Among the pagan Greeks and even the early Christians exorcism could be addressed to good as well as to evil powers. In the New Testament Jesus was himself "exorcized" twice, once by the high priest and once by the Gerasene demoniac.[68]

By the third century the meaning of exorcism had become more

65. For works on the Devil in the liturgy see the Essay on the Sources.
66. G. M. Lukken, *Original Sin in the Roman Liturgy* (Leiden, 1973), pp. 232–234.
67. D. M. Jones, "Exorcism before the Reformation" (master's thesis, University of Virginia, 1978), pp. 2–18; H. A. Kelly, *The Devil, Demonology, and Witchcraft*, 2d ed. (New York, 1974), p. 81.
68. The high priest: Mt. 26:63; the demoniac: Mk. 5:7.

precise: it was the ritual expulsion of harmful spirits from affected persons or objects with the help of superior spiritual powers.[69] Three kinds of exorcisms were common in early and medieval liturgies: exorcism of objects, exorcism of catechumens during the scrutinies of baptism, and exorcism of demoniacs. Originally it was assumed that the Devil or demons were not themselves exorcized, though the exorcism was indirectly addressed to them, and in the last analysis the exorcism always is an indirect prayer to Christ. Even the saints can expel demons only with the power of Christ, never with their own. For liturgical purposes holy water, incense, salt, and holy oil were exorcized directly: "I exorcize thee, creature salt . . . that this creature salt may in the name of the Trinity become an effective sacrament to put the Enemy to flight." But it gradually became more common to address the Devil or demons directly. Even in the early liturgies the two modes were combined, as in this exorcism of holy water: "I exorcize you, creature water; I exorcize you, all you hosts of the Devil."[70] Underlying exorcism is the assumption that Satan retains some power over the material world as well as over the souls of fallen humans. On this point Christian tradition was never consistent. For some, Satan's lordship over this world extends only to humans. For others, it affects the lower order of creatures as well, and among these are some who argue that this dominion is the result of original sin and others who maintain that God grants Satan the power to use material objects to tempt and test fallen humanity.[71]

The scrutinies entailed a number of confrontations with Satan, of which the exorcisms were the most dramatic. The Devil was sternly admonished to acknowledge the justice of the sentence of doom passed on him, to do homage to the Trinity, and finally to depart from the catechumen.[72] The usual formula was "Therefore, accursed Devil, depart," or something similar, but some are masterpieces of anathema, as this from the Gallican liturgy, which recapitulates the defeat of the Devil in the person of his biblical surrogates:

69. A. Angenendt, "Der Taufexorzismus und seine Kritik in der Theologie des 12. und 13. Jahrhunderts," in A. Zimmermann, ed., *Die Mächte des Guten und Bösen* (Berlin, 1977), pp. 388–409.

70. E. Bartsch, *Die Sachbeschwörungen der römischen Liturgie* (Münster, 1967), pp. 118–121; Lukken, pp. 231, 253.

71. Lukken, p. 254.

72. R. Béraudy, "Scrutinies and Exorcisms," in *Adult Baptism and the Catechumenate* (New York, 1967), pp. 57–61.

I accost you, damned and most impure spirit, cause of malice, essence of crimes, origin of sins, you who revel in deceit, sacrilege, adultery, and murder! I adjure you in Christ's name that, in whatsoever part of the body you are hiding you declare yourself, that you flee the body that you are occupying and from which we drive you with spiritual whips and invisible torments. I demand that you leave this body, which has been cleansed by the Lord. Let it be enough for you that in earlier ages you dominated almost the entire world through your action on the hearts of human beings. Now day by day your kingdom is being destroyed, your arms weakening. Your punishment has been prefigured as of old. For you were stricken down in the plagues of Egypt, drowned in Pharaoh, torn down with Jericho, laid low with the seven tribes of Canaan, subjugated with the gentiles by Samson, slain by David in Goliath, hanged by Mordecai in the person of Haman, cast down in Bel by Daniel and punished in the person of the dragon, beheaded in Holofernes by Judith, subjugated in sinners, burned in the viper, blinded in the seer, and discountenanced by Peter in Simon Magus. Through the power of all the saints you are tormented, crushed, and sent down to eternal flames and underworld shadows. . . . Depart, depart, wheresoever you lurk, and never more seek out bodies dedicated to God; let them be forbidden you for ever, in the name of the Father, the Son, and the Holy Spirit.[73]

The scrutinies also included the "exsufflation," in which the priest blew into the candidate's face. A standard part of many liturgies from the fourth century, the exsufflation showed contempt for the demons and was believed to drive them away; it was much like the desert fathers' practice of hissing or spitting at demons. The priest also touched the catechumen's ears with spittle, again to show contempt for the Devil but also because spittle has healing properties. The sign of the cross was marked on the candidate's forehead as a warning to demons against coming near. The catechumen made a formal renunciation of Satan, the "apotaxis," which usually took place during the solemnity of Easter vigil. Facing the west, the region of darkness and death, the candidate made a threefold formal statement renouncing Satan, his pomps, his works, and/or his angels, and then formally transferred allegiance to Christ while facing the east, the region of light and resurrection. The catechumen was anointed with holy oil, a seal against further assaults by the Evil One. In the actual act of baptism, the descent into the water symbolized descent into the underworld of

---

73. J. M. Neale and G. H. Forbes, *The Ancient Liturgies of the Gallican Church* (London, 1855), pp. 160–161. See Kelly, *Devil*, pp. 81–84; Lukken, pp. 232–238; Mohlberg, *Gelasianum*, pp. 44–46, 67, 249. I am grateful to Professor H. A. Kelly for his helpful comments on the Devil in the liturgy.

death, and emergence from the water symbolized rebirth and resurrection. Baptism was the culmination of the victory over Satan and was
regarded as having powers to cure illness of body and mind as well as
corruption of soul. Some early liturgies explicitly indicated that illness
was a manifestation of the Devil's oppression.[74]

In the Middle Ages the wisdom of adding these elements to baptism
was questioned, for the central function of baptism was thought to be
the initiation of the catechumen into the Christian community in the
name of the Trinity and to erase the guilt of original sin. Yet the great
canon lawyer Burchard of Worms bluntly insisted that no one was to
be baptized unless he had first been exorcized. No theologian argued
for abolishing the exorcisms during the scrutinies, though Aquinas
warned against lending them undue emphasis, and William of Auvergne tried to rationalize their incorporation by arguing that "the
exorcism does not expel the Devil, but it does signify that the Devil is
expelled by baptism itself."[75] The idea that an important function of
baptism was to expel the Devil and replace him with Christ was
integral to baptism from the earliest formal liturgies into the twentieth
century; it is therefore questionable whether a theology of baptism
that omits this element altogether can be considered continuous with
Christian practice. Yet the incoherence of modern thought is no greater than the earlier inconsistencies. If God knows the elect from all
eternity, what is the need of baptism? Why are rites needed to protect
people from the Devil when God is supposed to be protecting them
anyway? The liturgies contain prayers that God will not leave the
saints in the power of the Devil, a prayer that is by all logic super-
fluous. Such liturgies indicate that people were not at all secure as to
how much power the Devil did have, how effective Christ was in

74. Lukken, pp. 227–255. Exsufflation remained in the Catholic baptismal liturgy
into the twentieth century. A typical formula for the renunciation of Satan is Gelasianum 68: "Abrenuncias Satanae? Abrenuncio. Et omnibus operibus eius? Abrenuncio. Et omnibus pompis eius? Abrenuncio." Attached to the canons of the Frankish
council of Leptinnes in 743 is the following formula for abjuring the Devil at baptism:
"Forsachistu diobolae? Ec forsacho diabolae. End allum diobolgelde [idolatry]? End ec
forsacho allum diobolgeldae. End allum diaboles wercum? End ec forsacho allum
diaboles wercum and wordum thunaer ende woden ende saxnote ende allem them
unholdum the hira genotas sint." This renunciation, tailored for Teutonic peoples,
included a specific rejection of Thor, Wotan, and Saxnot as well as the other Teutonic
deities. Hefele-Leclercq, vol. 3:2, p. 835.

75. Burchard, *Decretum*, 4.20. William of Auvergne, *Summa aurea*, ed. P. Pigouchet
(Frankfurt am Main, 1964), p. ccliii: "Per exorcismum non expellitur diabolus, sed
significetur quod per baptismum expellitur diabolus." See Angenendt, pp. 402–408.

combatting it, who was saved by Christ, and whether he died for all or not. It was—and is—a frightening world, and apparently neither theology nor liturgy had contrived to calm the doubts of the faithful.[76]

76. The liturgies give the impression that their authors hoped that the Devil could be driven off by magniloquent insults, e.g., Gelasianum 250: "Sanguilappie, multis formis persuasor malorum, accusator veritatis, umbra vacua, inflate inanis, filius tenebrarum, angelorum iniquitas" (Bloody gobbet, many-shaped tempter to sin, adversary of truth, empty shadow, dead thing without breath, son of the shadows, iniquity of the angels). M. Férotin, *Le "Liber mozarabicus sacramentorum" et les manuscrits mozarabes* (Paris, 1912), p. 1029, gives a list of liturgical names for the Devil: *adversarius ludificus*, "mocker"; *serpens calidus* [*sic*], "clever serpent"; *veternosus pestiferus*, "ancient plaguebearer"; *apostata angelus; refuga angelus*, "emigré angel"; *deceptor*, "deceiver"; *draco*, "dragon"; *hostis antiquus*, "ancient enemy"; *hostis crudelissimus; hostis adversarius; inimicus superbus*, "proud enemy"; *inimicus bellicosus; inimicus infestans*, "ravaging enemy"; *inimicus occultus; princeps huius mundi*, "prince of this world"; *princeps superbie*, "prince of pride"; *Satan, serpens antiquus; serpens nequissimus*, "most wicked serpent"; *spiritus immundus*, "unclean spirit"; *spiritus superbus; spiritus callidus; vastator antiquus; vexator noster*, "our persecutor"; *victor antiquissimus; Zabulos* [from *Diabolos*]."

6 Lucifer in Early Medieval Art and Literature

During the period between Eriugena and Anselm, while theology was producing little new about the Devil, representational and literary art dramatized and actualized him. The history of representational art does not fit neatly into the history of concepts, because it does not always interact closely with other modes of expression. Artists often make choices for aesthetic rather than for theological or symbolic reasons; they might, for example, portray Lucifer in a certain color or attitude for reasons of composition rather than cult. No picture of the Devil survives from before the sixth century; it is not known why. The earliest representation may be a mosaic in San Apollinare Nuovo in Ravenna dating from about 520. Christ is seated in judgment; at his right hand stands a red angel below whom sheep are gathered, and on his left is a blue-violet angel standing above the goats.[1] A sixth-century

1. For the Devil in early medieval art see B. Brenk, "Teufel," *Lexikon der christlichen Ikonographie*, 4 (1972), cols. 295–300; B. Brenk, *Tradition und Neuerung in der christlichen Kunst des ersten Jahrtausends* (Vienna, 1966); O. A. Erich, *Die Darstellung des Teufels in der christlichen Kunst* (Berlin, 1931); R. Hughes, *Heaven and Hell in Western Art* (New York, 1968); A. Köppen, *Der Teufel und die Hölle in der darstellenden Kunst von den Anfängen bis zum Zeitalter Dante's und Giotto's* (Berlin, 1895); the Princeton Index of Christian Art (ICA), from which many of the examples in this chapter are taken. On San Apollinare Nuovo see particularly E. Kirschbaum, "L'angelo rosso e l'angelo turchino," *Rivista di archeologia cristiana*, 17 (1940), 209–248.

manuscript, the Rabbula Gospels, contains an illumination in which Christ expels the Devil (or demons) from the possessed.[2] Not till the ninth century did representations of the Devil become common, but from that time they increased rapidly in number and variety.[3] The reason for this rapid growth was the popularity of homilies and stories of saints' lives in which the powers of evil played conspicuous roles. Early medieval art made little distinction between the Devil and his demons, and hell was also sometimes depicted as a personage like the Devil. Death was often personified as well, but usually quite distinctly from Lucifer.

The Devil often appeared in scenes of expulsions of demons by Christ or the apostles, the fall of the angels from heaven or their expulsion by Michael, Daniel in the lion's den and his victory over Bel the dragon, the temptation of Adam and Eve, the temptation of Christ, the death of Judas, the descent into hell, and the last judgment (or particular judgment of individuals at death). Certain Old Testament figures such as Pharaoh and Goliath were symbols of Satan, and the stories of Jonah and Job offered further opportunities to portray him. His creation by God was not depicted, nor was he shown at the crucifixion he had provoked: certain moments seemed to have been too holy to blaspheme with his image.

A human or humanoid Devil appeared in the sixth century and dominated the period from the ninth through the eleventh. Another form, popular from the sixth century onward, is the tiny, misshapen being that Brenk called an *eidolon* and I shall call an imp. The animal or monstrous shape was increasingly evident beginning in the eleventh century, possibly because of the influence of monastic reform with its return to the concerns of the desert fathers. The categories are indistinctly defined, and many Devils are partly humanoid and partly bestial. The humanoid Devil could appear as an old man in a tunic, with short tail, smooth and muscular legs, and human hair and face; or as a large, naked, dark, muscular man with human hands but clawed feet and a tail; or as a giant with human features; or as a white-robed humanoid angel with feathered wings and hair to his shoulders. Rarely was the Devil female. The Devil was usually naked, though he sometimes wore a loincloth; often he was hairy. An eleventh-century manuscript shows a humanoid Devil who is close to being bestial: large and

2. SATAN, p. 102.

3. Stuttgart Psalter, in SATAN, pp. 41, 75, 86, 136, 189. Brenk, *Tradition*, 102. Brenk, *Tradition*, pp. 196–197, lists examples of the two commonest types of demons, imps and muscular humanoids, in the ninth and tenth centuries.

black, he has round, white eyes, oxlike ears, short tail, clawed feet, and short horns. The imps are tiny, naked, black, and misshapen.[4] A tenth-century manuscript at Amiens shows a tiny, naked imp with the head of an ox, long, flowing hair, bird wings, and clawed feet. In the early eleventh-century illustrations of the Old English Caedmonian poems, the angels falling from heaven into the mouth of hell become little, black, wizened imps with tiny wings and tails—except for Lucifer, who remains proudly humanoid though with flaming hair and a tail.[5]

Animal and monstrous demons tended to follow the forms suggested by Scripture, theology, and folklore, such as snakes, dragons, lions, goats, and bats. Often, however, artists seemed to select forms according to their fancy: demons with human feet and hands, wild hair, and animal faces and ears; demons with monstrous, hideous faces, or with hollow eyes and wrinkled skin; demons with human bodies, lizard skin, apelike heads, and paws. The symbolism was intended to show the Devil as deprived of beauty, harmony, reality, and structure, shifting his shapes chaotically, and as a twisted, ugly distortion of what angelic or even human nature ought to be. The didactic purpose was to frighten sinners with threats of torment and hell.[6] The fiends' animal forms denoted their demotion from angelic dignity and their animal lack of conscious purpose. Among the common bestial charactistics given them were tails, animal ears, goatees, claws, and paws (horns, not so common earlier, became standard by the eleventh century).[7]

4. Old man: ICA (Moscow, Historical Museum: Chludov Psalter, ninth century). Big and naked: Stuttgart Psalter (ninth century). Giant: ICA (Utrecht, Bibliotheek der Universiteit: ninth-century psalter). White robed: ICA (Oxford, Bodleian Library: Caedmonian poems, eleventh century). Naked demons: ICA (Paris, Bibliothèque Nationale: tenth or eleventh-century miscellany). Loincloth: ICA (Vatican City, Biblioteca Vaticana: eleventh-century psalter). Humanoid/bestial: ICA (Montecassino Monastery library: illumination of Rabanus Maurus, *De universo*, c. 1023).
5. ICA (Amiens, Bibliothèque de la Ville: Corbie psalter, probably tenth century). On the illustrations of the Caedmonian poems (Oxford: Bodleian Library Junius 11) see T. Ohlgren, "The Illustrations of the Caedmonian Genesis," *Medievalia et Humanistica*, 3 (1972), 199–212; T. Ohlgren, "Five New Drawings in the Ms. Junius 11," *Speculum*, 47 (1972), 227–233. Ohlgren is preparing an index to iconographic subjects in Anglo-Saxon illuminated manuscripts.
6. ICA (Einsiedeln, Stiftsbibliothek: illumination of Jerome, "Adversus Jovinianum," tenth century); ICA (Munich, Bayerische Staatsbibliothek: Gospel Book of Otto III, c. 1000); ICA (Hildesheim: bronze doors of the cathedral, 1008–1015).
7. Tails: ICA (London, British Library: Aelfric paraphrase, eleventh century?).

The Devil was often winged, and in the early Middle Ages his wings were often feathered like those of birds and of angels, unlike the bat wings that he wore from the twelfth century onward. Wings appear on humanoid and animal demons and were standard trappings on the imps.[8] The humanoid Devil often had sleek, dark hair, but as he became more monstrous his hair turned snakey or spikey. The reason for the upswept, spikey, or flamelike hair is unclear. It may represent the flames of hell, though flames and fire can also stand for the ethereal nature of the good angels, or it may derive from the greased, upswept hair of the barbarians who cultivated the style in order to terrify their enemies.[9] Other characteristics were glowing eyes, spewing mouths, spindly arms and legs, bloated torsos, and long, hooked noses; the last was invidiously combined with racial stereotypes to demonize Jews in later medieval art.[10] Lucifer was sometimes shown as bound in hell while his demonic servants wielded tridents or pitchforks in tormenting the damned. In earliest medieval art, as in San Apollinare Nuovo, the Devil was sometimes provided with a nimbus or halo, in this context representing power rather than holiness.[11]

The Devil was usually black, but sometimes he was blue or violet, because he was composed of the dark, thick, lower air, as opposed to the good angels, who were made of ethereal fire and were thus colored red. Sometimes he was brown, and frequently he was pale gray, the

---

Naked man with bird wings, long tail, but no horns: ICA (London, British Library: eleventh-century psalter). Horns, beard, and spiky or flaming hair: ICA (Florence, Laurenziana: eleventh-century Gospel book). See Köppen, pp. 51–55.

8. ICA (Rome, Biblioteca Casanatense: Benedictio fontis, tenth century); ICA (Vatican City, Biblioteca Vaticana: eleventh-century psalter).

9. ICA (London, British Library); ICA (Utrecht, Bibliotheek der Universiteit). A fourth-century Latin version of Athanasius' "Life of Anthony" offers a description of Satan that bolsters the interpretation that the hair represents flames: "oculi ejus ac si species Luciferi, ex ore ejus procedunt lampades incensae. Crines quoque incendiis sparguntur, et ex naribus ejus fumus egreditur, quasi fornacis aestuantis ardore carbonum. Anima ejus ut pruna, flamma vero ex ore ejus glomeratur" (*Vita Beati Antonii Abbatis*), 16.

10. Köppen, pp. 51–55. Imp with long nose, little tail, feathered wings: ICA (London, British Library, eleventh century). Brenk notes that the imp first appears in the sixth century in exorcism scenes.

11. Tridents or pitchforks: ICA (London, British Library: winged demons with instruments prodding the damned into a fiery lake, Harley 603). Bound in hell: ICA (Rome, Bib. Casanatense; Paris, Bibliothèque Nationale: Roda Bible, eleventh century); San Apollinare Nuovo, Ravenna. J. Galpern, "The Shape of Hell in Anglo-Saxon England" (Ph.D. diss., University of California, Berkeley, 1977), p. 37, argues that the gaping hell-mouth was invented in twelfth-century England.

color of illness and of death. His first clear appearance as black rather than another dark color was in the ninth-century Stuttgart Psalter. Only in later medieval art was he shown as red, the color of blood or of the flames of hell.[12]

Literature drew more specifically than representational art upon theology, popular religion, and folklore. Yet literary artists, not often being theologians, made modifications and elaborations for aesthetic or dramatic reasons. Details of the fall of the angels and of Christ's descent into hell came from the artists' efforts to get inside Lucifer's character in a way that theologians never attempted to do. Literature made the pathos and rage of Lucifer's rebellion and doom more vivid than ever before.

Such developments were more marked in vernacular literature than in Latin because it was less tied by language and scholarship to theology. Most surviving vernacular literature was written by educated authors for an audience that was often unlearned in Latin, but the power and sophistication of the vernacular was such that its appeal also reached the highly educated, and many of its ideas entered the tradition. The earliest great vernacular literature was in Old English.[13] The Old English *Genesis A*, *Genesis B*, *Christ and Satan*, and the "Harrowing

12. Black: ICA (Paris, Bibliothèque Nationale: ninth-century sacramentary of Drogo; London, British Library: Bristol Psalter, eleventh century). Blue: Kirschbaum argues that violet/blue was also the color of night and the natural color of air when sunlight is removed from it. Fulgentius of Ruspe (468–533) argued in *De Trinitate*: "corpus ergo aethereum, id est igneum, eos [angelos] dicunt habere: angelos vero malos, id est daemones, corpus aereum" (the angels have an ethereal, fiery body, while the fallen angels have an aerial body), 1. In the mosaic of Torcello (see Köppen, pp. 47–49), the Devil is blue, his hair and beard are wild and white; he holds Judas on his lap as he sits enthroned upon powerful serpents; beneath him sinners are undergoing torture; his servant demons are winged and satyr-headed. A connection between this blue Devil and the Roman river god has been suggested but not explained. Brown: Ohlgren has shown that the Junius 11 manuscript portrayed the Devil as brown except when he was disguised as a good angel, when he is red. Pale and/or gray: London, British Library; Moscow, Historical Museum; Stuttgart, Landesbibliothek. In Old English, *blac* can mean black, livid, or pale; the modern English word *livid*, like the French *livide*, is also ambiguous. See Brenk, *Tradition*, pp. 42–49.

13. The bibliography on Old English literature in general is immense. See S. Greenfield and F. Robinson, *A Bibliography of Publications on Old English Literature to the End of 1972* (Toronto, 1980); S. Greenfield, *A Critical History of Old English Literature* (New York, 1965); C. T. Berkhout brings the bibliography up-to-date regularly in the *Old English Newsletter*, *Neuphilologische Mitteilungen*, and *Anglo-Saxon England*. Old Saxon also produced an important vernacular work in this period, the *Heliand*, an anonymous ninth-century epic of Christ, where the Devil, however, plays only a minor role: M. Scott, *The Heliand* (Chapel Hill, 1966). C. Wright presented a paper, "The Fall of Lucifer in an Hiberno-Latin Genesis Commentary (MS. St. Gall 908)" at the eigh-

of Hell" present well-textured views of Lucifer, and the great epic *Beowulf* both draws upon and adds to the sense of the demonic.[14]

The psychological penetration of Old English literature, the extra richness of its new vocabulary, and its creative marriage of Teutonic and Christian ideas, continued to deepen the character of Lucifer.[15] The Teutonic hero and the Christian saint coalesced: both struggled, often alone and against overwhelming odds, against the forces of evil. Yet since the hero was often a proud man unbeholden to anyone and brought down by his pride in the end, neither Christ nor a saint quite fit the heroic pattern.[16] Ironically the most apposite traditional figure was Lucifer, the proud, the noble, standing alone in hopeless battle against an implacable foe, unyielding to the end. Teutonic heroism best explains the compelling power of the Old English Lucifer—and that of Milton. Another Teutonic concept that fit well was that of lordship—the leader surrounded by his retainers. The English term *lord* (OE, *hlaford*, "bread giver"; cf. Fr., *seigneur*, Ger., *Herr*) carries the

---

teenth annual conference on Medieval Studies, Western Michigan University, Kalamazoo, May 1983.

14. Other OE works in which the Devil or demons put in a significant appearance include: (1) Cynewulf's *Juliana*, in which Satan visits the saint in prison in order to persuade her to escape torture by renouncing God; Juliana prays to God and at his command lays hold of the Devil, whereby he confesses his sins (G. P. Krapp and E. V. K. Dobbie, eds., *The Exeter Book* [New York, 1936], pp. 113–133); (2) Cynewulf's *Elene*, where the Evil one appears to the saint when she discovers the true cross (Krapp, *The Vercelli Book* [New York, 1932], pp. 66–102); (3) the poem known as *Guthlac A*, a life of Guthlac in which the saint, like his desert forebears, is tormented by demons (Krapp and Dobbie, pp. 49–88); (4) *Guthlac B*, in which the dying saint helps restore the beauty and balance of a world distorted by sin (ibid.); (5) the prose life of Guthlac (Felix, in C. W. Jones, *Saints' Lives and Chronicles in Early England* [Ithaca, 1947]); (6) Aldhelm's Riddle no. 81, in which he identifies Lucifer the morning star with Lucifer the fallen angel: "Heu! post haec cecidi proterva mente superbus; ultio quapropter funestum perculit hostem" (R. Ehwald, ed., *Aldhelmi opera*, MGH *Auctores antiquissimi* XV [Berlin, 1919], pp. 134–135); (7) the *Christ* poems (Krapp and Dobbie, pp. 3–49), *Christ III* makes contrasts between angels and demons, bright and dull, white and black: "engla ond deofla, beorhta ond blacra . . . hwitra ond sweartra"; (8) "Judgment Day I" (Krapp and Dobbie, pp. 212–215), and "Judgment Day II" (E. V. K. Dobbie, ed., *The Anglo-Saxon Minor Poems* [New York, 1942], pp. 58–67). On *Guthlac A* see F. Lipp, "Guthlac A: An Interpretation," *Mediaeval Studies*, 33 (1971), 46–62; on *Guthlac B* see D. Calder, "Theme and Strategy in *Guthlac B*," *Papers on Language and Literature*, 8 (1972), 227–242. See A. Olsen, *Guthlac of Croyland* (Washington, D.C., 1981).

15. Some details are strictly Teutonic. R. Woolf, "The Devil in Old English Poetry," *Review of English Studies*, n.s. 4 (1953), 3, notes that the terms *feðerhama* and *haeleðhelm* found in *Genesis B*, 417 and 444, have no roots in Christian tradition.

16. Woolf, pp. 1, 11.

feudal connotations of mutual loyalty, honor, and commitment more than the Latin *dominus*, which suggests the absolute power of Roman prince. Christ is like the lord (OE, *dryhten*) of the *comitatus*, the band of Teutonic warriors that unite in loyalty around a war leader so as to obtain his protection and his bounty. Followers of Christ are his thanes (OE, *þegnas*), his military supporters. As Christ holds the lordship (OE, *dryht*) of heaven, so Lucifer holds the dryht of hell and is dryhten of darkness. The demons or fallen angels are Lucifer's thanes just as the saints are Christ's. The essence of the wrong that Lucifer and Adam committed was to violate the trust of their dryhten. This idea that sin is the disruption of the dryht blends with and colors the Christian tradition of sin as the distortion of right order.

The idea of justice that emerged in medieval thought is a similar product of the union of Teutonic and Christian ideas. *Justitia* is that state of affairs that prevails when human society is working in harmony with God's plan for the world; *injustitia* is any action, law, or rule that violates this harmony. Rebellion against one's lord is (as Dante showed by placing Judas and Brutus in the lowest level of hell) the worst violation of justice possible. The essence of Lucifer's sin for the Anglo-Saxons was the denial of his proper obedience (þegnscipe) to God. The Teutonic punishment for denial of one's lord was exile, cutting one off from the comitatus and the dryht, so that one wanders as a lordless (*hlafordleas*) outlaw without a protector. The idea fit the Christian tradition that Christ thrusts Lucifer out lordless into a lonely world.[17] Teutonic peoples could grasp the power of such a story, both in blaming Lucifer for betraying his dryhten and in sympathizing with his heroism and his inevitable doom. Satan, the shadow of God, like Grendel the *sceadngenga* (*Beowulf* 703), "the one who goes in darkness," received new psychological power in becoming the shadow of the Anglo-Saxon character. Harmony, order, and peace were the rewards of obedience to the dryhten, but the shadow always longs for resistance, disruption, and heroic pride.

"The Harrowing of Hell," a short poem in the Exeter Book, which Hulme and others called the "Old English Gospel of Nicodemus," derived from a tradition that included the "Latin Gospel of Nicodemus" and a range of texts in the liturgy of Holy Saturday, the Bible, patristic commentaries, and homiletic literature. The tradition was that between his death and resurrection Christ had descended to

17. Woolf, pp. 6–10.

the dead and freed the holy people of antiquity.¹⁸ Several other Old
English works drew upon the tradition. In one poem the Devil was
unaware of the divinity of Christ at the time of the crucifixion, and
when he tried to seize the guiltless lord he lost all his authority on earth
and freedom in hell and was clapped into eternal chains. As the demons reproached their master for his fatal error, Christ appeared,
harrowed hell, and led the dead away, exclaiming, "Lo, death, I am
your death, and hell, I am your sting."¹⁹

The account in "The Harrowing of Hell" itself was more detailed.
The Hebrew patriarchs await Christ in hell's darkness, which a light
suddenly pierces. Satan and his cruel followers are astonished and cry
out, "What is this light?" but the fathers rejoice because they know
that the Son is coming. Satan and Hell (which is personified) engage in
a desperate and acrimonious colloquy. Christ is coming, Satan warns
Hell, so stand ready to seize him. But Hell replies, Christ fears not
you nor me nor death. Nothing can withstand him, and he will bring
you eternal misery. Satan demurs. Never fear, he comforts Hell, I
have caused him to be tortured and killed already, so now I shall
capture him for you, and he will be our slave. Satan seems incoherent
on this point. Earlier he had acknowledged to Hell what he had failed
to understand at the crucifixion: that Christ is both man and God's

18. For the tradition, see SATAN, pp. 116–122, and Chapter 5, n. 36, above. The
OE prose and poetic versions of the harrowing of hell drew upon a wide tradition,
perhaps including the "Gospel of Nicodemus," which, however, may not have had any
direct influence in England until the beginning of the twelfth century. The dating of
OE materials has been thrown into doubt by recent scholarship; *Beowulf*, for example,
may date as early as the late seventh century and as late as the early eleventh; all that is
sure is that most OE literature dates from the seventh through eleventh centuries. Two
texts of the OE "Harrowing" appear in W. Hulme, ed., "The Old English Version of
the Gospel of Nicodemus," *Publications of the Modern Language Association*, 13 (1898),
457–542; S. Crawford, ed., *The Gospel of Nicodemus* (Edinburgh, 1927). Another "Descent" is published by A. Luiselli Fadda, "'Descensus Christi ad inferos,'" *Studi
medievali*, 3d ser., 13 (1972), 989–1011. See R. Trask, "The *Descent into Hell* of the
Exeter Book," *Neuphilologische Mitteilungen*, 72 (1971), 419–435, on the "Descent" edited
by Krapp and Dobbie, pp. 219–223. See also G. Crotty, "The Exeter 'Harrowing of
Hell:' A Reinterpretation," *PMLA*, 54 (1939), 349–358; P. Conner, "The Liturgy and
the Old English 'Descent into Hell,'" *Journal of English and Germanic Philology*, 79
(1980), 179–181; J. J. Campbell, "To Hell and Back: Latin Tradition and Literary Use
of the 'Descensus ad Inferos' in Old English," *Viator*, 13 (1982), 107–158; see also the
Blickling homily "Dominica pascha," in R. Morris, ed., *The Blickling Homilies of the
Tenth Century*, 2d ed. (Oxford, 1967), pp. 82–97.
19. Luiselli Fadda, citing MS Junius 121, 154r: "Eala þu deað ic beo þin deað, and
þu hell, ic beo þin bite."

An Anglo-Saxon portrayal of the magician James summoning the Devil, who rises in fierce but humanoid form from the depths of hell. Illumination from an eleventh-century manuscript. By permission of the British Library.

son; but now he suffers from the delusion that he can defeat Christ. Hell is more realistic. I could not hold Lazarus against this Christ, he complains, and now he who freed Lazarus is coming to free all the saints. The argument is interrupted by a voice like thunder: Open your gates, for the King of Glory is coming. Hell cries out to Satan in panic, Go, quickly, get to the gates, and if you have any power left, stop him from coming in! Hell excuses himself. Let the struggle be between you and him! Meanwhile the patriarchs are crying out, Let the King of Glory in! The Lord arrives; he releases the patriarchs but now seizes and binds Satan, turning him over as a prisoner to Hell. Hell reproaches Satan. Why did you cause the Savior to be killed? You knew of no guilt in him! Now all your joy has been dissolved by the Tree of the Cross.[20]

The Old English account of Genesis consists of two parts, *Genesis A* and the interpolated *Genesis B*. *Genesis A* follows the biblical account in most respects, though it is much more than a paraphrase; *Genesis B* appears to be an adaptation of an Old Saxon poem. *Genesis B* is more original and powerful than *Genesis A*. The importance of these poems for diabology is that they firmly set the rebellion and fall of the angels, which the Old Testament omits entirely, into the Genesis story.[21]

According to the Old English Genesis, God created the angels first, before making the material universe. Some of the angels rebelled out of envy and pride, following their own desires, and planned to seize a portion of God's glory. Lucifer raised a throne for himself in the north of heaven. God, angry, prepared hell for the sinful angels while at the same time confirming the loyal angels in their goodness. Further, he now proposed to fill up the ranks of fallen angels with new creatures

20. Hulme 506: "And þu nu þurh þaet treow and þurh þa rode haefst ealle þyne blysse forspylled"; Hulme 498: Satan seems to know that Christ is "godes sunu and eac man"; Hulme 500: eternal misery; Hulme 500: Satan offers Hell the hope that Christ will become their slave; Hulme 502: Hell speaks of his thanes ("ealle myne arleasan þegnas"), Hulme 506: Christ binds Satan.

21. For material on the Genesis poems, see the Essay on the Sources. One of the most interesting speculations about the poems is the possible effect that they, along with *Christ and Satan*, may have had upon Milton. Milton was a friend of the Dutch scholar Franciscus Junius, who "had the manuscripts in London before Milton went blind" (Greenfield, p. 150) and who published them at Amsterdam in 1654. The similarities in characterization, mood, and diction make it plausible that Milton had at least some acquaintance with the poems, for nowhere between the eleventh and the seventeenth centuries is the rebellious prince of hell portrayed with such strength and latent sympathy.

possessing moral freedom, so he proceeded to create the material world and, when all had been prepared, Adam and Eve.[22] At this point *Genesis B* begins. It opens in Eden in the midst of a speech by God but then retraces the fall of the angels. Lucifer had boasted that he need not serve God. He admired the beauty and brightness of his own countenance and turned his thoughts from contemplation of God to contemplation of himself. A rebellious retainer, he fondly believed that he could rely upon his own power to establish a dryht in heaven for himself. He boasted, "I can become God just like him!" He chose the northwest of heaven for his stronghold (north, land of cold and darkness, and west, land of sunset and death, are Satan's natural haunts, while God dwells in the south and east, lands of sunrise and warmth).[23] God hurled Lucifer from his high place in heaven down to the dark dales of hell; the evil lord and his angels fell for three days and nights into the pit, where they lost their angelic dignity and became demons.

Satan, the proud prince who once had been the most beautiful of the angels, now rose from his seat in hell to deliver a defiant speech to his demonic retainers. He accused the Almighty of injustice in expelling the guilty angels and reported that he had learned that God was planning to fill up their empty places in heaven with humans made of contemptible earth and soil. Oh, he exclaimed, if I could just free myself for one winter's hour, what could I do with this host of hell! But he knew that he could not escape from his divinely forged fetters.[24]

22. *Genesis A (GA)* 29: envy and pride (*aefst* and *oferhygd;* compare *GA* 22). *GA* 24: their own desires. *GA* 32: the throne in the north (in *norð*daele; compare *Genesis B* [*GB*], 275).

23. On the north in folklore and the Bible see Chapter 4 above. On the patristic origins for the site of Lucifer's throne, see P. Salmon, "The Site of Lucifer's Throne," *Anglia*, 81 (1963), 118–123; T. Hill, "Some Remarks on the Site of Lucifer's Throne," *Anglia*, 87 (1969), 303–311. *GB* 264: Lucifer boasts that he need not serve. *GB* 265–266: "cwaeð þaet his lic waere leoht and scene, hwit and hiowbeorht" (he said that his body was fair and bright, white and shining). *GB* 272–275: erect his throne in the northwest. Compare *GB* 667–668, where God has his own seat in the southeast. Lucifer's boast: "ic maeg wesan god swa he" (*GB* 283).

24. *GB* 304–305: throws him into hell, where he becomes the Devil ("hine on helle wearp, on þa deopan dala, þaer he to deofle wearð"). *GB* 307–309: fell three days and nights. *GB* 370: one winter's hour. The OE *Genesis* makes no distinction between Lucifer and Satan (see *GB* 347), unlike a few later medieval dramatic works. On the fall, see T. Hill, "The Fall of Angels and Man in the Old English Genesis B," in L.

Satan now reflected: if we have no hope of attacking God directly, we can at least pervert human beings, turn them against God, and bring them down to hell as slaves. And though Satan was bound in hell, his followers were free to roam the earth. He called upon them as a dryhten upon his thanes: If ever I bestowed treasure upon any thane while I had power in heaven, let him help me now. I shall rest more comfortably in my chains if I know that humans also have lost the kingdom of God.[25]

After a break in the manuscript, during which one of the hellish thanes apparently volunteered to be Satan's messenger to humanity, the messenger dons his Teutonic war helmet and fares upward to the Garden, in which two trees are growing, the tree of life and the tree of death.[26] Here the poem takes a liberty with the Bible, for the original story has, in addition to the tree of life, not a second, evil tree, but an ambivalent tree of knowledge of good and evil. Some modern critics have exaggerated the deviation, suggesting that the poet intended to lay all the blame on the Devil and exonerate Adam and Eve by relieving them of a choice. But the poet, though sympathetic to the plight of our first parents, in fact makes them share the guilt with Satan. As Kathleen Dubs has argued, the account is an artful interpolation illustrating the pathos of human limitations, rationalizations, and ignorance.

Satan's messenger takes the form of a serpent and approaches Adam. This is another innovation, for the biblical account has the serpent approaching Eve directly. The Anglo-Saxon audience would have been more comfortable with the idea of a great lord (good or evil) approaching Adam, the lord and master, on important business, rather than his wife. The messenger tells Adam that God wishes him to eat the fruit, but Adam, observing that this thane looks like no angel he

Nicholson and D. Frese, eds., *Anglo-Saxon Poetry* (Notre Dame, Ind., 1975), pp. 279–290. See K. Malone, "Satan's Speech: Genesis 347–440," *Emory University Quarterly*, 19 (1963), 242–246. The *craeft* (force, cunning, perverted reasoning) of the Devil is contrasted to the *handmaegen*, *handgeweorc*, or *handgescaeft*, the constructive action of God. See R. E. Finnegan, "God's *Handmaegen* versus the Devil's *craeft* in *Genesis* B," *English Studies in Canada*, 7 (1981), 1–14.

25. *GB* 406–407: pervert humans so they go to hell. *GB* 409: treasure to the thane. *GB* 414: my thanes. *GB* 434: happy if they lose the kingdom of God.

26. On the Eden passage see Hill, "Fall"; J. F. Vickrey, "The Vision of Eve in *Genesis* B," *Speculum*, 44 (1969), 86–102; R. Woolf, "The Fall of Man in *Genesis* B and the Mystère d'Adam," in S. Greenfield, ed., *Studies in Old English Literature* (Eugene, Ore., 1963), pp. 187–199; J. M. Evans, *Paradise Lost and the Genesis Tradition* (Oxford, 1968). *GB* 444: war helmet.

has ever seen, declines. The thane then approaches Eve, whose spirit he judges weaker and, complaining that Adam has misunderstood him, guilefully insists: "I am not like the Devil." He repeats his false argument to Eve and appeals to her love for Adam in order to persuade her that by eating the fruit she will be a help to her husband. Eve eats, and immediately receives what she takes to be a beautiful vision of heaven. The messenger congratulates her on her appearance, and her delusion is now so deep that she thinks both him and herself to be beautiful and shining like angels. When Eve persuades Adam to follow her, the evil thane laughs and capers, delighted that he can go back to hell with a report of his success.[27]

Adam and Eve, human, fallible, inexperienced, had believed the demonic lies, but now the deed was done, they knew that they had betrayed their lord. Why is the world so? the poet asks in anguish. "It is very strange that God would let the Lord suffer or that he would let so many people be tricked by lies parading as wisdom."[28]

The Old English poem *Christ and Satan* from the same codex as *Genesis A* and *B* is divided into three sections, "The Lament of the Fallen Angels," another "The Harrowing of Hell," and "The Temptation in the Desert." Its unity of authorship and structure has been established by recent scholarship: the unifying theme is the contrast of the humble and victorious Savior with the prideful and doomed Devil.[29] The poem begins with creation. Unlike *Genesis A*, it assumes the

27. *GB* 538–539: looks like no angel he has ever seen ("þu gelic ne bist aenegum his engla þe ic aer geseah"). *GB* 600–609: Eve's vision. Vickrey disposes of the notion that this is a real vision with the argument that the poet's audience would know immediately that no true vision could follow an act of disobedience to one's lord. Indeed the poet makes frequent clear reference to the fact that Eve throughout the passage is deluded by demonic lies (e.g., *GB* 630). *GB* 587: His bluntest lie, "I am not like the Devil" ("ne eom ic deofle gelic"). *GB* 724–725: he laughs and capers. *GB* 760–762: plans his return to Satan ("nu wille ic eft þam lige near, Satan ic þaer secan wille; he is on þaere sweartan helle haeft mid hringa gesponne"). See Evans, p. 159.

28. Þaet is micel wundor þaet hit ece god aefre wolde þeoden þolian, þaet wurde þegn swa monig forlaedd be þam lygenum þe for þam larum com" (*GB* 595–598). The poet may have had recourse to the device of the messenger demon as a means of resolving the old anomaly that Satan was bound in hell as a result of his fall yet still roamed the world: here Satan is left bound but the minor demons are allowed more freedom.

29. For editions and criticism of *Christ and Satan* (*CS*) see the Essay on the Sources. As with the other OE works, its date and origin are unknown, but C. R. Sleeth, *Studies in "Christ and Satan"* (Toronto, 1981) and R. Finnegan, ed., *Christ and Satan: A Critical Edition* (Waterloo, Ont., 1977) agree on the early ninth century. See Finnegan, *Christ and Satan*, p. 33, for the theory of the temporal progression within the poem. As with

creation of the material world at the same time as that of the angels, not afterward. It proceeds quickly to a description of the prideful angels who thought that they might themselves become lords of heaven but were cast down into hell. The collective guilt of the angels seems to equal that of their prince, who is distinguished from the others only after their ruin.[30]

Once they are established in hell, the Devil, the "old one," addresses them in stern tones.[31] We have lost our glory, he tells them, and exchanged it for the shadows of hell, bound in torment among fires that give no light. Once we sang amid the joys of heaven; now we pine in this poisonous place. The other cruel spirits blame their prince for leading them astray. You lied, they complain, in making us think that we could rebel successfully and would not have to serve the Savior.[32] You said that you yourself would be the holy God, the creator. Well, here you are, a criminal, bound tightly in the fire, and we angels must suffer it all with you.[33] Throughout their wretched colloquy Satan and his thanes rage against the reality of the cosmos as it is constructed, a perfect artistic expression of the demonic temperament and of Satan's predicament. The wretched spirits refuse to accept the world as God has constructed it, yet they can never change it. The Devil's eternal refusal to accept reality produces the eternal misery in which he dwells: he constructs his own hell.[34] The poem

---

Genesis B, the critics have exaggerated the originality and heterodoxy of the poem: no one could mistake its occasional dramatic embroideries for theological points.

30. Pride: *CS* 50, 69, 113, 196, 304, 359. Devil desires to replace Christ: *CS* 83–88, 173–174, 186–188. Hell is a horrible cavern underground: *CS* 26–31.

31. The "old one," *se alda* (*CS* 34). Other terms for the Devil in *CS*: *feonda aldor*, "prince of fiends" (76), *se werega gast*, "the wretched spirit" (125), *firna herde*," lord of sins" (159), *godes andsaca*, "God's adversary" (190, 279), *blaca feond*, "black [or pale] fiend" (195), *se awyrgda*, "the accursed one" (315), *earm aglaeca (aeglaeca, aeglece)*, "miserable wretch" (446, 578, 712), *atol aglaeca*, "cruel wretch" (160), *deofol* (636), *se balewa*, "the baleful one" (482), *se werega*, "the wretched one" (667,710), *se atola*, "the cruel one" (716), *bealowes gast*, "spirit of evil" (681), *blac bealowes gast* (718). He is named Satan. (370, 445, 691, 711), Lucifer, or *leohtberende*, "lightbearer" (366). Lines 365–374 make it clear that the poet uses Lucifer and Satan as synonymns.

32. "Þu us gelaerdaest ðurh lyge ðinne þaet we helende heran ne scealdon" (*CS* 53–55).

33. Cruel spirits: "atole gastas, swarte and synfulle" (*CS* 51–52). Thought you were "halig god, scypend seolfa" (*CS* 56–57).

34. The poet departs from the usual explanation that God prepared hell for the evil spirits and simply reports that they took up their abode there (*CS* 25).

Hell as a giant monster swallowing the damned, who are tormented by demons as Christ locks them in. Illumination from an eleventh-century English manuscript. By permission of the British Library.

achieves additional power by coloring Satan as a Teutonic hero, defeated yet proud in facing his *wyrd*, his implacable fate.[35]

Among the other lies of the Devil, the demons complain, is that his own son would become ruler of mankind. This curious passage offers poetic contrast between God the Father and his Son Christ on the one hand and the Devil with his son, the lie mentioned by the Gospel of John 8:44, on the other.[36] The poet next inserts a flashback showing how Christ had driven the demons into hell, and then returns to the dark caverns where Satan makes his reply to his thanes.[37] "Sparking" fire and poison as he speaks, Satan rehearses his reasons for rebelling.[38] I used to be a high angel in heaven, he mourns, but I plotted to overthrow the light of glory. Now I am trapped down here, full of despair, hopeless of rising again. God has thrust me down here; very well, I am God's enemy.[39] We have no place in this deep darkness where we can hide ourselves from God; though we cannot see him, he

35. Satan's followers are his *gingran*, "retainers" (*CS* 191); he is dryhten of hell as Christ is dryhten of heaven (*CS* 47, 69, 108, 163, 217); he is *aldorþaegn*, "prince," "thane-lord" (*CS* 66), but also himself a servant of hell, *handþegen helle* (*CS* 483).

36. "Segdest us to soðe þaet ðin sunu waere meotod moncynnes" (*CS* 63–64). Satan is not offering a theological argument that Christ was his subordinate, but one senses the hint of the folklore of sibling rivalry between Christ and Satan. The passage does not refer specifically to the Antichrist. Hill's suggestion ("Fall," p. 324) that "the lie" is what is intended appears to be accurate.

37. Critics have read an unnecessarily strange theology into this and subsequent passages (*CS* 81–87, 168–175, 340–347). Satan is indeed rebelling against Christ, but the poet in no way intends to distinguish a rebellion against the Father from one against the Son (*CS* 190–193, 256–258). In *CS* 83–88 and 173–174 Satan speaks of wishing to drive Christ out of heaven and put himself in his place, but what this means is that Satan envies the glory the Father gives to Christ, a traditional though not universal idea. A sophisticated view such as Eriugena's would put the rebellion at the moment after creation and thus simply make it a metaphor for the alienation that exists in the cosmos. Hill's explanation (p. 322) that the poet's emphasis upon Christ rather than the Father is natural to the dramatic unity of a poem pitting Satan against Christ seems the best explanation of any idiosyncrasy on the poet's part. That it was Christ who drove out the sinful angels is also entirely traditional: the task might be attributed to the Father, Christ, or Michael, but structurally it is all the same.

38. Sparking: "he spearcade ðonne he spreocan ongan fyre and atre" (*CS* 78; cf. "spearcum," 161). On this passage see T. D. Hill, "Satan's Fiery Speech," *Notes and Queries*, 217 (1972), 2–4; H. Keenan, "Satan Speaks in Sparks," *Notes and Queries*, 219 (1974), 283–284; R. E. Finnegan, "Three Notes on the Junius XI *Christ and Satan*," *Modern Philology*, 72 (1974/5), 175–181. These sources supply patristic precedents.

39. *CS* 96: "Ic eom fah wið god." Finnegan, *Christ and Satan*, p. 52, shows that the lament of Satan is a tradition going back to the sixth century: see Avitus of Vienne (d. c. 519), *De originali peccato*, bk. 2.

can always see us. I am imprisoned here, and though I am allowed to fly up and visit the earth I shall never again wield power there, for God has given it all over to his Son.[40] It would be better had I never known the brightness of heaven, which now is all his. At least when I visit earth I can hurt humans, but I am allowed to harm only those souls that God does not wish to keep.[41] And now Satan utters a dirge of sheer misery: "Alas, lordship's majesty, alas the protection of God's power, alas might of the Maker, alas earth, alas light of day, alas God's joy, alas angelic host, alas heaven! Alas that I am deprived of eternal joy!"[42] The passage concludes with a description of Christ resplendent in the glory that Lucifer had desired for himself.

The second portion of *Christ and Satan* deals with the harrowing of hell. The holy dead wait in hell for Christ's approach; he breaks down the doors, and a great light shines into the darkness, accompanied by angelic song as if at dawn.[43] The imagery of the harrowing, especially from line 585 onward, is structurally identical with that of the initial defeat of the angels and with that of the Last Judgment. From line 597 onward the melding of harrowing and doomsday is explicit, for the poet inserts a brief description of the last things: Christ comes in glory to divide humanity into saved and damned.

The third part of the poem treats the temptation of Christ. Satan first brings the Lord broad stones and challenges him to turn them into bread. A lacuna in the manuscript eliminates the second temptation. In the third, Satan hoists Christ mockingly onto his shoulders in order to show him the whole world. I will grant you dominion over peoples and lands, he promises: receive from me cities, broad palaces, and even the kingdom of heaven, if you are true king of angels and humans. Satan's theology is shaky, for he has no right to offer Christ dominion in heaven, yet the original biblical account is itself a bit odd in its suggestion that the Devil could credibly offer Christ the kingdom of

40. The poet clumsily glosses over the contradiction inherent in the theological tradition (109–113). Cannot see God: *CS* 100, 169.
41. "Ne ic þam sawlum ne mot aenigum sceððan butan þam anum þe he agan nyle" (*CS* 144–146). This does not refer to the harrowing of hell, but rather to the traditional view that God allows Satan to tempt sinners but only to test the elect, who are exempt from mortal sin.
42. "Eala drihtenes þrym! Eala duguða helm! Eala meotodes miht! Eala middaneard! Eala daeg leohta! Eala dream godes! Eala engla þreat! Eala upheofen! Eala ðaet ic eam ealles leas ecan dreames" (*CS* 163–167).
43. "Þa com engla sweg, dyne on daegred" (*CS* 401–402).

The harrowing of hell. Christ leads John the Baptist and the Hebrew patriarchs out of the mouth of hell. The Devil lies defeated and bound with the cross thrust like a lance into his throat. Illumination from an English manuscript, c. 1150. By permission of the British Library.

this world, which the Devil after all held only at God's pleasure.[44] Christ responds scornfully and instead sets Satan the task of returning to the darkness and measuring the length and breadth of hell with his own hands. Satan is obliged to do so and, when he has returned, reports that the grim gravehouse measures a hundred thousand miles, perhaps the largest number the poet could conceive.[45] In taking Lucifer from his proud boasts of revenge in the first part through his shocking defeat in the second to his utter humiliation in the third, the poet has depicted Christ's utter victory over the power of evil.

The greatest Old English poem, *Beowulf*, must be treated only briefly, for its influence on the tradition is unidentifiable; it refers to the Devil only by allusion, and like many masterpieces it is atypical and idiosyncratic.[46] *Beowulf* is now generally held to be a Christian poem blending Christian with pagan Teutonic motifs, Christian salvation with Teutonic heroism. *Beowulf* should be understood both as heroic struggle against monsters and as Christian combat against the forces of evil. The two interpretations are not mutually exclusive, for the poet is speaking on a number of levels at once. Beowulf faces superhuman forces both because as a hero he must confront overwhelming odds and because as a Christian hero he must face diabolical opposition to the harmony of God's cosmos.

Beowulf, a prince of the Geats in what is now Sweden, hears of the depredations of the monster Grendel at Heorot, the hall of Hrothgar, king of the Danes. He travels to Hrothgar's court and slays Grendel, but he must then do battle with Grendel's vengeful mother. The first part of the poem ends with line 2199; the second part takes place much later, after Beowulf has ruled the Geats for fifty years, and depicts his

44. Hoists him: *CS* 679–682. Compare Arnoul Gréban's *Passion*, lines 10,605–10,608 (see Chapter 9 below), where Satan asks Jesus to get up onto his shoulders so as to take him up to the pinnacle of the Temple. Offers him heaven and earth: *CS* 684–688.

45. *CS* 698–699, 705–707 (*grim graefhus*), 720–721. The measuring of hell seems to be the poet's invention.

46. The sole manuscript of *Beowulf* is British Library Cotton Vitellius A XV, dating from the late tenth or early eleventh century. The composition of the poem has been placed as early as the seventh century; the weight of opinion rests on the eighth, although recent arguments have been put forward for the eleventh. The poem used to be regarded as pagan with Christian interpolations, but in 1911–1912 Klaeber demonstrated that the Christian elements were integral, and J. R. R. Tolkien established the view that *Beowulf* is a coherent, Christian poem in his "Beowulf: The Monsters and the Critics," *Proceedings of the British Academy*, 22 (1936), 245–295. For editions and criticism see the Essay on the Sources.

struggle against the third monster, a fire-breathing dragon which he kills in single combat but which in turn wounds him mortally, and the poem ends with the death of the hero.[47]

Beowulf faces three evil monsters. Though the dragon is not so demonic as his two predecessors, there may be a hint of the unholy trinity that some Christian fathers had opposed to the divine Trinity. The situation in which Beowulf confronts the first monster, Grendel, takes place in Heorot, a dryht besieged from without and defiled from within, a hint perhaps of the Christian church or of the individual Christian soul. Heorot is threatened from without by the demonic Grendel and undermined within by stupidity and cowardice, represented by Unferth, the disaffected retainer of Hrothgar and pridefully envious of Beowulf for garnering more glory than he.[48]

Grendel can be understood on at least three levels. He is the Teutonic hero's monstrous opponent. He is also a giant (*eoten*) descendant of Cain. The poet seems to have been asserting that Grendel was human and at the same time hinting at the Christian tradition of giants that made them the demon offspring of the Watcher angels and the daughters of men.[49] Third, he is diabolical. The poet applies to Grendel terms commonly used for the Devil in Old English literature or translations of common Latin terms for the Devil.[50] More than a

47. N. Chadwick, "The Monsters in Beowulf," in P. Clemoes, ed., *The Anglo-Saxons* (London, 1959), pp. 171–203.

48. Evil trinity: SATAN, p. 116, and Chapter 4 above. Unferth: lines 499ff. C. Berkhout, "*Beowulf* 3123b: Under the Malice-roof," *Papers on Language and Literature*, 9 (1973), 428–431, defends the likeness of the *Beowulf* dragon to the dragon of Revelation 20:2: "draconem serpentem antiquum, qui est diabolus et Satanas."

49. Lines 112–113 describe the descendants of Cain as *eotenas, ylfe, orcneas*, and *gigantas*. The humanity of Grendel, line 105: *wonsaeli wer*; line 1682: *guma*. Watcher angels: DEVIL, pp. 191–197; SATAN, pp. 45–46, 64–66, and passim. On Cain and Beowulf see R. Mellinkoff, *The Mark of Cain* (Berkeley, 1981); D. Williams, *Cain and Beowulf* (Toronto, 1982).

50. See S. Wiersma, "A Linguistic Analysis of Words Referring to Monsters in *Beowulf*," (Ph.D. diss., University of Wisconsin, 1961), pp. 456–458. Among the terms are *helle haeft (captivus inferni)*, "prisoner of hell" (cf. line 788); *deað scua (mortis umbra)*, "death's shadow" (160; cf. Gregory, *Mor.* 4.5; cf. *CS* 453: *deaðes scuwan*); *werga gast*, "accursed spirit" (1747), *ellor-gaest*, "alien spirit" (1349; 1621; see above, Chapter 5, for the Devil as alien par excellence); *ealdgewinna (hostis antiquus)*, "ancient enemy"; *wiht-unhaelo*, "unholy being" (120), *gast-bona*, "soul-slayer" (177); *atol aglaeca*, "cruel fiend" (592; a common term for Satan in *CS*); *feond man-cynnes (hostis humani generis)*, "enemy of mankind" (164, 1276), *feond on helle*, "fiend in hell" (101); *helle-gast*, "hell spirit" (1274); *ellen-gaest*, "bold spirit" (86); *godes andsaca (hostis Dei)*, "God's enemy" (786, 1682); *grim-ma gaest*, "grim spirit" (102); *se aeglaeca*, "the fiend," "monster," or "demon" (159, 425,

monster, Grendel is God's adversary, the ancient enemy, the alien spirit. He dwells in the shadows; when he attempts to flee from Beowulf he seeks shelter with the demons; like Satan he is at war with God; he is received into the deadly mere as into hell; his hands are iron-clawed and bloody. Of course, he is a literary creation, the product of the author's imagination, and he cannot be equated with the Devil, yet he is clearly meant to be an aspect, a dimension, of the lord of darkness.⁵¹

Grendel's mother, like himself, is human, a female descendant of Cain.⁵² But she also is *waelgaest* (slaughtering spirit) and *geosceaftgast* (ancient or fateful spirit). The Devil is amost always seen as masculine, for the masculine reason that the ruler of hell, like the king of heaven, must be male, but he is attended and supported by female spirits, whom folklore transposes into witches. In folklore the Devil has a mother who supports him and toward whom he is always respectful, but he has no father, since a father, unlike a female ancestor, would (to the masculine mind) diminish his authority. Grendel, too, has a mother, but no one knows what evil spirit may have been his father. The hint lingers that Grendel's dam may be an analogue of Satan's mother.⁵³

The third monster, the dragon, guardian of an underground treasure trove, is basically Teutonic, yet some characteristics link him with the Devil: the obvious association with the serpent of Eden, the connection with the serpent of Revelation, and the dwelling place under the earth.⁵⁴ The poet is too great an artist to force his characters into narrow allegory. A poet, not a theologian, he can treat the monsters in modes that are theologically self-contradictory: they are creatures of Teutonic folklore; they are human descendants of Cain; and they are diabolical figures.

Occasionally something like a theological gloss enters the narrative,

---

1000; commonly used of Satan in *CS*); *feond*, "fiend" (439, 1273); *sceadu-genga*, "walker in shadows" (703); *syn-scaþa*, "wicked enemy" (707); *waelgaest*, "murderous spirit" (1331).

51. In shadows, 87; hide with demons, 755–756; at war with God, 811 (*he fag wið God;* cf. *CS* 96, *ic eom fah wið god*); pool like hell, 852; clawed and bloody, 984–990.

52. She is *ides aglaec-wif*, "terrifying woman" (1259), Cain's kin, 1261.

53. See Chapter 4 above. For the place of the witch and the hag in diabology, see Chadwick, p. 174; J. B. Russell, *Witchcraft in the Middle Ages* (Ithaca, 1972); J. B. Russell, *A History of Witchcraft* (London, 1980); Chapter 10 below. Grendel's father unknown: 1355–1357.

54. Also there is a glove made from devilcraft and dragonskins, *deofles craeftum ond dracan fellum* (2088).

The harrowing of hell. Christ lances the bestial Satan while drawing the just out of the unhappy mouth of hell. From the Miniatures of the Life of Christ, France, c. 1200. Courtesy of the Pierpont Morgan Library, New York.

as in lines 705–707, where the poet observes that people know that the wicked enemy cannot pull them down into the shadows unless God permits it. And Hrothgar's comment on the evil spirit who shoots sinful arrows under the victim's helmet into his mind is related both to the elfshot of folklore and to precedents in literature and in the writings of the desert fathers.[55]

Homilies in Old English were compiled mainly for clergy and congregations whose understanding of Latin was slight.[56] The most important Old English homilist was Aelfric (c. 955–c. 1010), abbot of Eynsham from 1005 to his death. Associated with the Benedictine reform movement, Aelfric was a colleague of another leading homilist, Wulfstan, who died in 1023 and had been bishop of London in 996 and archbishop of York in 1002. Aelfric knew no Greek but was learned in Latin and was influenced by Augustine, Gregory, and Bede. About 990 he wrote his two series of "Catholic Homilies," the first series being exegetical and the second more anecdotal along the lines of Gregory's *Dialogues*. Aelfric's forty lives of monastic saints were designed primarily for private reading and meditation.

In the beginning, Aelfric believed, God created ten hosts of angels, to whom he gave moral freedom of will. Nine of the hosts remained loyal to God, but the tenth used its freedom for the wrong purpose. From pride, disobedience, haughtiness, and envy the angels rebelled against their maker.[57] Of their own free will they followed their lead-

---

55. Lines 1745–1747. The image appears in Felix's *Life of Guthlac*, chap. 29.

56. The important collections are R. Morris, ed., *The Blickling Homilies*, 3 vols. (London, 1874–1880); M. Förster, ed., *Die Vercelli-Homilien* (Hamburg, 1932); D. Bethurum, ed., *The Homilies of Wulfstan* (Oxford, 1957); and the works of Aelfric. Aelfric's relevant works consist of three collections of homilies (HomI, HomII, HomIII), a collection of lives of saints (LS), and the Hexameron (Hex), a translation and paraphrase of the creation story of Genesis; the Hexameron appears in the "Old English Heptateuch," a paraphrase of the first seven books of the Old Testament; Aelfric was responsible for the first part of Genesis, the last part of Numbers, Joshua, and Judges. In citing the Homilies, I cite Thorpe's numbering for HomI, Godden's for HomII, and Pope's for HomIII. The Blickling Book, dating from about 975, has a Homily 9 relating to the Devil, and Homily 1 of the Vercelli Book, which dates from about 1000, is also of interest. See M. Gatch, *Preaching and Theology in Anglo-Saxon England* (Toronto, 1977). For works by and on Aelfric, see the Essay on the Sources.

57. Tradition had not set the proportion of angels that fell, but most supposed it to be about a third. Aelfric's idea of a tenth order was unusual: HomI.1: "ðaet teoðe werod abreað and awende on yfel." Compare HomI.24 and HomI.36. Aelfric drew upon Gregory the Great for this idea (see Chapter 5 above), but Aelfric was one of the few medieval writers positively to assert the existence of a tenth order. His comparison of the tenth order of angels to the tenth piece of silver lost by the woman in the parable of Lk. 10:8 states his position clearly: "To ðam teoðan werode waes mancyn gesceapen;

er, who was so beautiful and fair that he was called Lucifer, the lightbearer, but who was so puffed with pride that he set up a throne in the northern part of heaven in a vain effort to equal God. God took away his power and beauty and turned him and his followers into hideous demons and cast them all down from heaven into hell.[58] On the sixth day of creation, the same day, Aelfric believed, that Satan fell, God created Adam and the human race with the intention of using humans to fill up the ranks of the lost angels.[59] This chronology was untraditional, but it allowed Aelfric to make the dramatic point that it is our purpose to replace the angels.[60]

The Devil, angry and envious at seeing humanity ensconced happily in paradise, entered Eden in the form of a serpent. Since he has no power to compel anyone to sin, it was our own responsibility that we

---

forðan ðe þaet teoðe weorð mid modignysse forscyldigod, and hi ealle to awyrgedum deoflum wuldon awende. . . . Nu sind ða nigon heapas genemnede (here he lists the nine hosts). Þaet teoðe forwearð. Þa waes mancynn gesceapen to ge-edstaðelunge ðaes forlorenan heapas" (Mankind was created to take the place of the tenth host, for the tenth host was guilty of pride and all turned into wicked demons . . . Now the nine hosts are named. . . . The tenth perished. So mankind was created to fill the place of the lost ranks). Pride: *up-ahefednysse* (HomI.3); disobedience: *ungehyrsumnesse* (HomI.1); enmity: *wiðerweardnysse* (HomI.1).

58. Share heaven with God: HomI.1. Not God's fault: "ne naefre se yfela raed ne com of Godes geþance, ac com of þaes deofles"; Lucifer wanted to "sittan on þam norð-daele heofenan rices"; beauty of Lucifer: "ða waes þaes teoðan werodes ealdor swiðe faeger and wlitig gesceapen, swa þaet he waes gehaten Leohtberend," but he became "atelic sceocca" and his comrades "laðlicum deoflum" (HomI.1).

59. Aelfric refutes *gedwolmen* (heretics or false interpreters of Scripture), who say that Satan is responsible for the creation of certain things and God for that of others. This may be a reference to Manicheans or Priscillianists about whom Aelfric learned from Gregory.

60. HomI.1; Hex. lines 297–300; 297 is precise: Adam was created on þam ylcan daege (the very same day) as Lucifer fell. Traditional chronologies are inconsistent. *Genesis A*, for example, put the creation of the whole material world after Lucifer's fall, whereas Aelfric placed the material creation except humanity before the fall. There are various traditional scenarios: (1) God creates everything (including Adam and the angels) at once, and the fall of Lucifer and the fall of Adam are contemporary with creation; (2) God creates the angels before anything else, the angels fall at the moment of their creation, and God proceeds to create the material world; (2a), as (2), except that the angels fall a moment after creation; this moment gives scope to their free will; (3) God creates the angels and then the material world, the angels fall later, then God creates humanity; (4) the angels fall when Adam is created because of their envy of him; (5) the angels do not fall until the time of Noah (this old-fashioned view, based on the story of the Watcher angels, had by Aelfric's time ceased to find supporters). One or another version of (2), (2a), and (3) became fairly standard, for they allowed at least part of the blame for original sin to be placed upon Lucifer.

yielded to his suggestions. In falling, we joined him in his darkness and blindness; Satan stands in the light of God as a blind man stands in the light of the sun—a perfect description of the alienation of human nature from the harmony of the cosmos.[61] Satan's success in tempting us makes him lord of this sinful world, and when he shows himself he takes on terrifying forms. Aelfric describes him in the shape of a giant black man with sharp features and a full beard, his hair hanging to the ankles, his eyes shooting fiery sparks, sulphurous fires burning in his mouth, his limbs feathered, and his hands tied behind his back. In similar shapes black and terrible demons, tall as giants, with burning eyes, terrible teeth, sharp claws, and arms like logs assault the saints.[62]

Satan tried to tempt the second Adam as he had the first, and Christ in his humility allowed the temptation to occur, though of course it had no chance of success. Deceived by Christ's hunger after his fast in the desert, Satan thought that he could not be divine, and his ignorance persisted through the time of the Passion. Aelfric was still fol-

61. HomI.1. Oddly, Aelfric places Adam and Eve in the kingdom of heaven (*on heofenan rice*). He may have wished to emphasize the closeness between God and humanity, the lack of alienation before the fall; or he may simply have used the term as an equivalent of the earthly paradise. The Devil cannot compel to sin: HomI.1, 11. Blind man in sun: HomII. 30, an image Aelfric borrowed from Gregory. For names given to the Devil by Aelfric, see Nelius H. Halvorson, *Doctrinal Terms in Aelfric's Homilies* (Iowa City, 1932), p. 28. They include: *atelic sceocca*, "fearsome spirit" (HomI. 1); *atelic deofol*, "fearsome Devil" (HomI. 32); *ðaera ðeostra ealdras*, "lord of the shadows" (HomI. 4); *ealda deofol*, "old Devil" (HomI.6); *ealda sceocca*, "old Spirit" (HomII.20); *swicola feond*, "treacherous fiend" (HomI.1; HomII.19); *waelhraew deofol*, "cruel Devil" (HomI.13; HomII.23); *lyðra deoful*, "wretched Devil" (HomI.19), *reða deoful*, "cruel Devil" (HomI.17); *miccla deofol*, "mighty Devil" (HomI.14); *costnere*, "tempter" (HomI.11; HomI.24; HomII.11); *unclaena deofol*, "unclean Devil" (HomI.31); *unclaena gast*, "unclean spirit" (HomIII.4); *awyrigeda deofol*, "accursed Devil" (HomI.31; HomII.4; HomII.23; HomII.34); *awyrigeda gast*, "accursed Spirit" (HomII.11); *fleogenda sceocca*, "flying fiend" (HomII.6); *niðfulla deofol*, "base Devil" (HomII.11); *ungesewenlica deofol*, "invisible Devil" (HomII.11); *ungesewenlica feond*, "invisible fiend" (HomII.25); *ungesewenlica draca*, "invisible dragon" (HomII.11); *sweartra deofol*, "black Devil" HomIII. 27; *ðwyra deofol*, "Devil who opposes" (HomII. 12); *cwelmbaera deofol*, "tormenting Devil" (HomII.19), *ealda wregere*, "old accuser" (HomII.20); *manfulla deofol*, "dire Devil" (HomII.30); *wacola feond*, "watchful fiend" (HomII.38); *se leasa*, "the perfidious one" (HomII.34); Beelzebub, *gramlic deofol*, "cruel Devil" (HomIII.4) *hetela deofol*, "malicious Devil" (HomIII.11; HomIII.19); *syrwienda deofol*, "plotting Devil," *reða feond*, "cruel fiend" (HomIII.11.)

62. HomI.31: "he wearð ða aeteowod swylce ormaete Silhearwa, mid scearpum nebbe, mid sidum bearde. His loccas hangodon to ðam anccleowum, his eagan waeron fyrene spearcan sprengende; him stod swaeflen lig of ðam muðe, he waes egeslice gefiðerhamod, and his handa to his baece gebundene." Demons assault saints: LS, "Life of Saint Julian."

lowing the ransom theory: Satan takes Christ as the bait but swallows unawares the hook of his divinity and so forfeits his rights over his human thralls.[63] It is only at the harrowing, when Christ defeats the Devil at the gates of hell, that Satan realizes that Christ is lord and that he is doomed.

Even after Christ has fully established that the world is his, the Devil is still allowed to tempt and test until the end of time comes. But we need not fear, for God has things firmly in hand until then.[64] Then the Antichrist, man and Devil as Christ is man and God, will appear. Upon Antichrist's defeat, the world will end, and only the kingdom of God will remain.[65] Though some heretics maintain that at the end Mary and the other saints will purge Satan's evil and save him from damnation, this is a vain rationalization on the part of persistent sinners who, like the demons, have no hope of salvation.[66]

To understand early medieval diabology, one must go beyond theological speculation to the colorful stories found in homilies and saints' lives that brought home to monks and laypeople the ubiquity of the Devil and his demons. Miracle stories rooted in the old monastic tradition achieved growing popularity. Sulpicius Severus wrote that the Devil attacked Saint Martin of Tours in numerous ways, bursting into his cell roaring and brandishing a bull's horn in his bloody hand, or, in another mood, daring to put on the form of Christ, but the saint saw through the ruse and drove off the evil one, who vanished emitting a terrible stench.[67] Gregory of Tours reported that an Auvergnat

63. HomI.11; HomI.14; HomI.33; HomI.36; HomII.33.

64. Devil as lord of this world: *þises middaneardes ealdor*, "lord of this earth"; *yfel ealdor*, "evil lord" (HomIII.10). In LS, "Life of Saint Maur," God reassures the fearful saint, "*þu godes dyrling, hwi eart þu swa dreorig?*" (Thou darling of God, why are you so sad: God has all in hand).

65. HomIII.18. Wulfstan, 4, shares Aelfric's view that the Antichrist will be the Devil incarnate ("Crist is soð God and soð mann, and Antecrist bið soðlice deofol and mann" [Bethurum, p. 128]). Wulfstan is even clearer on p. 132: the very same Devil that is in hell becomes true man in the Antichrist ("se sylfa deofol þe on helle is, þaet is se þe þonne wyrð on þam earmsceapenan men Antecriste and bið soðlice aegðer ge deofol ge man"). More common explanations (see Chapter 5 above) were that all sinful beings are Antichrist, or, if Antichrist is one person, he is inspired by the Devil. The English had additional evidence that the end of the world was near in the renewed depredations of the Danes. Wulfstan, 20, saw the Danes as the hosts of Antichrist as well as retribution for the sins of the English.

66. HomII.44: those who persist in sin become like demons and dwell eternally with the Devil in the torments of hell fire.

67. Sulpicius Severus, *Vita Martini Turonensis*, ed. J. Fontaine, SC 133–135, chaps. 21–24.

bishop found his church infested by demons, the chief of whom had taken the form of a whorish woman seated on a throne. By the grace of Christ the bishop drove them out, but in revenge the demon tormented him with lustful thoughts until he fortified himself with the sign of the cross.[68]

The miracles reported by Gregory the Great in his widely known *Dialogues* often dealt with demons.[69] Some of the stories are trivial. One of the most popular described the gluttonous nun, who, while perambulating in the monastery garden, spied a luscious lettuce and, overcome by greed, seized and devoured it so hastily that she forgot to make the sign of the cross over it. Immediately the Devil laid hold of her and tormented her until at last a holy man was called in to say prayers over her. At his approach, the Devil cried out through the nun's mouth, complaining: "What did *I* do? What did *I* do? I was just sitting on the lettuce when along she came and ate me!" The saint, undeterred, forced him to depart.[70]

In another story a Jew was sleeping at night in an abandoned temple of Apollo and fearfully fortified himself with the sign of the cross (!). At midnight he awakened and saw a group of evil spirits venerating their leader. The leader quizzed each demon in turn to see what evil deeds he had done since the last meeting. One boasted that he had excited the lust of the bishop for a young nun and even caused him to give her a friendly pat on the behind. The chief was delighted with the report, for it is always better to corrupt a holy person than one whose life is already bad. The demons spotted the terrified Jew cowering in the corner, but they were unable to harm him because of the sign of the cross. Making his escape as quickly as he could, the Jew later met the bishop and decided to test the accuracy of what he had heard. He

---

68. Gregory of Tours, *Historiarum libri X*, 215. On exorcisms in hagiography see E. G. Rüsch, "Dämonenaustreibung in der Gallus-Vita und bei Blumhardt dem Alteren," *Theologische Zeitschrift*, 34 (1978), 86–94. Note that of all miracles involving demons only exorcism is rooted in the liturgy, deriving from the liturgy of baptism. On miracles see R. Swinburne, *The Concept of Miracle* (London, 1970); M. Melinsky, *Healing Miracles* (London, 1968); B. Ward, *Miracles and the Medieval Mind* (Philadelphia, 1982); B. Ward, "Miracles and History: A Reconsideration of the Miracle Stories Used by Bede," in G. Bonner, ed., *Famulus Christi* (London, 1976), pp. 70–76; N. Partner, *Serious Entertainments* (Chicago, 1977). Compare the miracle stories in Bede's *Hist.* 3.11, 4.18, 5.12 (Dryhthelm's vision of hell) and his *LC* 13, 15, 17, 41.

69. *Dial.* 1.4.7, 1.4.21, 1.10.2–5, 1.10.6–7, 1.10,9, 2.1.5, 2.8–13, 2.16.1, 2.16.2, 2.37.4, 3.6–7, 3.20–21, 3.28, 3.32, and many others.

70. *Dial.* 1.4.7.

asked the bishop whether he had been lusting for the young nun. The prelate denied it indignantly, but when reminded of the indecorous pat he broke down and confessed. Hearing how the Jew had come by the information, the bishop fell to the ground in terror, repented of his indiscretions, expelled all women from his service, and built an oratory on the site of the haunted temple. The happy ending was crowned by the conversion and baptism of the Jew.[71]

The modern mind can penetrate the grating appearance of naivete in the *Dialogues* only by recognizing that Gregory was concerned not with whether these miracles occurred scientifically or historically but rather with their internal, moral significance, their action in and upon the souls of human beings.

A third story illustrates the precision of the moral lesson Gregory wished to instill. It is a perfect moral exemplum suitable for a homily addressed to monks or clergy. One day Saint Eleutherius visited a monastery for women where a small child lived who was being tormented by an evil spirit. Eleutherius drove out the demon and then took the child home to his own monastery. But the holy man now made the mistake of boasting that the Devil, who had not scrupled to attack the child in the monastery, did not dare profane Eleutherius' own house. Immediately the Devil repossessed his victim. Through fasting and prayer the brothers saved the child again, while the saint learned his lesson about spiritual pride.[72]

Gregory intended most of the stories to be amusing enough to catch the attention of his audience, but his real purpose was serious. In the monastic tradition of Evagrius and Cassian, Gregory meant to illustrate that any sin opens a pore in the mind through which evil spirits can rush. One or another of the cardinal sins appear in at least one of Gregory's miracle stories. He made no distinction between the Devil and the demons; any one demon is a manifestation of the prince of all evil. The Devil is typically expelled by a miracle worked by Christ through the person of a holy man or woman. Indeed, the very definition of a saint was one through whom miracles were worked. Because the stories were often light, with happy endings in which the saint triumphed over his evil adversary, and because the manner of the holy

71. *Dial.* 3.7. The chief demon's examination of his followers as to their evil deeds became a standard ingredient of the witches' sabbath, as did the story in *Dial.* 3.28 ascribing to the Arian Lombards the improbable habit of ritually sacrificing a goat to the Devil after dancing round the animal and adoring it.

72. *Dial.* 3.32.

person's triumph was often humorous, these manifestations of popular religion were transposed easily into folklore. Above all they helped create the trivial and comic demon of the later Middle Ages. Yet the underlying theology is earnest. Christ works the miracles in his unceasing struggle against the powers of evil. If nature were uncorrupted by evil, miracles would have no function, but evil, distorting God's cosmos, challenges and calls forth miracles in response. Gregory intended the miracles to summon to our minds the understanding of God's eternal vigilance against the power of evil in a corrupted world.

The saints' lives of the ninth through the eleventh centuries drew deeply upon Gregory, though southern European lives may have placed more emphasis upon the Devil than the northern ones after the late eleventh century because of the influence of the monastic revival with its deliberate return to the eastern eremitical tradition.[73] On the other hand Felix's *Life of Guthlac* and the saints' lives by Aelfric indicate that there was no discontinuity in the north: the eastern tradition passed through Cassian and Gregory to the northern monastic writers as well. Satan shoots arrows of temptation against Guthlac (compare *Beowulf*, 1745–1747), and demons drive the saint to terrified despair by appearing to him with great heads, long necks, lean visages, sallow skin, unkempt beards, bristling ears, forbidding brows, savage eyes, fetid breath, equine teeth, flame-vomiting gullets, inflamed throats, wide lips, harsh voices, ashy locks, swollen cheeks, inflated chests, scabrous thighs, knock-knees, bowlegs, protuberant ankles, and splay feet. Speaking in guttural voices, they seize Guthlac, wrest him out of his cell, drag him through briars, duck him in a scummy swamp, and bear him off to the mouth of hell, where he looks down at the damned in torment. Altogether a trying day for the holy man—but one that would not have surprised the desert fathers.[74]

Aelfric retailed the story of the sorcerer Hermogenes, who had

73. This is argued by J. M. Howe, "Greek Influence on the Eleventh-Century Western Revival of Monasticism" (Ph.D. diss., University of California, Los Angeles, 1979). I am grateful to Dr. Howe for his helpful advice on this matter. Howe did a statistical study of common references to demons (not the Devil) in Greek and Latin lives of hermits between 970 and 1070 and found demons mentioned much more frequently in Italo-Greek and Italo-Latin lives than in northern ones. See also E. Rüsch, "Dämonenaustreibung in der Gallus Vita und bei Blumhardt dem Älteren," *Theologische Zeitschrift*, 34 (1978), 86–94.

74. Felix's *Life of Guthlac*, chaps. 31–32, 36, adapted from Jones, p. 139. See B. Colgrave, ed., *Felix's Life of Guthlac* (Cambridge, 1956), and T. Wolpers, *Die englischen Heiligenlegende des Mittelalters* (Tübingen, 1964).

called upon demons to assist him in combating the successful preaching of Saint James. Hermogenes sent his servant Philetus to James, but James converted him, so the furious sorcerer sent forth demons against both of them. The demons bound Philetus, but James forced them to free him, fetter Hermogenes instead, and bring the sorcerer before him. Hermogenes repented, destroyed all his magical tools, and distributed his wealth to the poor.[75] Aelfric's saints' lives are full of stories from Gregory the Great and other monastic writers recounting the assaults of demons. But Christians must despise diabolical works and temptations. When the "Devil sees that you despise him, he will grieve in his accursed mind that you are so steadfast. Angry, he will afflict you with some disease or suddenly slay some of your cattle, for he must test everyone to see whether the saints will abandon almighty God because of their trials. But you must realize that the cruel Devil cannot harm people or destroy their cattle without the Lord's permission." The choice is ours: to please Christ or to please the Devil.[76]

75. HomII.27.
76. Despise him: LS, "On Auguries." Choice: ibid. ("nu we ne magon gecwaemon criste and deofle"). Aelfric also tells the old story of Saint Basil in LS "Basilius." Other significant appearances of the Devil and demons in LS are "Eugenia," "Maur," and "The Forty Soldier Martyrs."

7 The Devil and the Scholars

The growth of literacy after 1000 led to a wide shift in cultural attitudes, including a growth of intellectual self-consciousness and critical awareness. The intellectual life of western Europe from 1050 to 1300 was dominated by scholasticism, the method taught in the cathedral schools and universities.[1] It was characterized by a strict and formal application of reason to theology, philosophy, and law. In the twelfth century scholasticism developed its own dialectical method: a question was posed, passages from Scripture and tradition were cited on both sides, and logic was summoned to resolve the question. The objections to the solution were then refuted and the next question in logical order was raised and treated. The method was refined under

1. On scholasticism in general see M. D. Chenu, *La théologie au douzième siècle* (Paris, 1957); R. Blomme, *La doctrine du péché dans les écoles théologiques de la première moitié du XIIe siècle* (Louvain, 1958); G. R. Evans, *Old Arts and New Theology: The Beginnings of Theology as an Academic Discipline* (Oxford, 1980); G. R. Evans, *Anselm and a New Generation* (Oxford, 1980); E. Gilson, *History of Christian Philosophy in the Middle Ages* (New York, 1955); D. Knowles, *The Evolution of Medieval Thought* (Baltimore, 1962); G. Leff, *Medieval Thought* (Baltimore, 1958); O. Lottin, *Psychologie et morale aux XIIe et XIIIe siècles*, 2d ed., 4 vols. (Louvain, 1957–1960; Gembloux, 1957–1959); A.-D. Sertillanges, *Le problème du mal*, 2 vols. (Paris, 1948–1951). On literacy see B. Stock, *The Impact of Literacy* (Princeton, 1983).

the influence of the writings of Plato, Aristotle, and Muslim commentators on Aristotle. In theology its tendency was radically different from that of the late twentieth century's search for common grounds and respect for diversity. Scholasticism sharpened theological points to a fine edge in order to differentiate between truth and error, orthodoxy and heresy. Though great scholastics such as Aquinas were aware of the limitations of reason and realized that any statement about God—or anything else—is precarious, the thrust of scholasticism as a whole was toward building certain knowledge into an intellectual stronghold from which truth could be defended.

Before the advent of scholasticism the twin pillars of Christian faith had been Scripture and tradition. Scholasticism added a third pillar—reason—the analytical interpretation of Scripture, tradition, and observation. A few scholastics seemed to press reason beyond the limits permitted by Scripture and tradition and found themselves censured, as Abelard (1079–1142) was by Saint Bernard (1090–1153). In the thirteenth century, theologians worried about the possible conflict between natural reason and faith, but most scholastics dutifully subordinated reason to Scripture and tradition wherever conflict seemed to arise. Saint Anselm (1033–1109) echoed Augustine's insistence that only through the illumination of the divine light within us can we understand anything.[2]

The new emphasis upon reason made advances in diabology possible by freeing theology from the servile dependence on tradition that had characterized most of the early medieval period. At the same time it created new dangers. It constructed elaborate rational superstructures upon weak epistemological bases—upon inexact observations of nature, for example. The result was a detailed, but insecure, diabology. The historian is obliged to be extremely selective in dealing with the scholastics, since the quantity of theological texts is now enormously greater than for any previous period. I therefore treat only the

2. Scholastics assumed that the Bible was literally true in the sense that the text was accurate, sound, and reported reality—but they did not assume it to mean everything in every sense, e.g., historical or scientific; that absurdity is peculiar to the nineteenth and twentieth centuries. Evans (*Anselm*, p. 69) gives an example of the application of reason to Scripture. Reading that the Devil is the ancient serpent (Rev. 12:9), the scholastics reasoned that the Devil is not really a serpent, though he may have used the serpent or taken its form. Further, the word *ancient* in this passage cannot have the same meaning as the word in the phrase "ancient of days" (Dan. 7:9) applied to God. Hence the term *ancient serpent* must be taken as a figure of speech poetically, but not physically, accurate.

most influential or most original ideas: the new theories of Anselm on the fall of the Devil and on salvation; the influential *Sentences* of Peter Lombard (c. 1100–1160); the revival of dualism by the Cathar heretics; the synthesis of Thomas Aquinas (1225–1274).[3]

Wide shifts in attitudes toward the Devil occurred during this period, sometimes in contradictory directions. The Devil became a more colorful, immediate, and present figure in art, literature, sermons, and popular consciousness. This change was the result of Cathar dualism, monastic revival of the tales of the desert fathers, and a general tendency to solidify religious figures: both Christ and the Blessed Mother became more immediate, Mary becoming Satan's most vigorous opponent. On the whole, people seemed to prefer to believe in a conscious source of evil than in blind fate or chance. Yet even while the Devil's presence grew, his importance in theology declined. Humanism, the scholastic refutation of dualism, Anselm's satisfaction theory, and Aristotelian ethics all lessened Lucifer's role in theology to the extent that he often degenerated into a caricature of rhetoric or propaganda, as when papalists referred to the antipope Clement III as "a messenger of Satan and lackey of antichrist," or as when nice debates were set: "are we to hate the Devil as much as we love Christ?"[4] The Devil also became more ridiculous and comic in sermons, art, exempla, and popular literature from the end of the thirteenth century, perhaps a logical result of reducing his theological significance while increasing the sense of his immediacy.

A step in reducing Lucifer's role was taken by Saint Anselm, monk, prior, and abbot of Bec in Normandy and then archbishop of Canterbury from 1093. The most original theologian since Eriugena, he applied to theology a careful logic derived from the liberal arts and was one of the founders of scholasticism. His *Proslogion* (1077/1078) pre-

---

3. I cannot explore such tangents as original sin, the seven cardinal sins, humanistic morality and Aristotelian ethics, hell, purgatory, or Antichrist. The most useful books on these topics are: M. Bloomfield, *The Seven Deadly Sins* (East Lansing, Mich., 1952); R. W. Southern, *Medieval Humanism* (Oxford, 1970); J. LeGoff, *The Birth of Purgatory* (Chicago, 1983); A. Bernstein, "Esoteric Theology: William of Auvergne on the Fires of Hell and Purgatory," *Speculum*, 57 (1982), 509–531; A. Bernstein, "Theology between Heresy and Folklore: William of Auvergne on Punishment after Death," *Studies in Medieval and Renaissance History*, 5 (1982), 5–44; R. Emmerson, *Antichrist in the Middle Ages* (Seattle, 1981).

4. J. Ehlers, "Gut und Böse in der hochmittelalterlichen Historiographie," in A. Zimmermann, ed. *Die Mächte des Guten und Bösen* (Berlin, 1977), p. 47; G. Evans, *Anselm*, p. 11.

sented the ontological proof for the existence of God; his *Fall of the Devil* (1085–1090) was in large part a philosophical treatise on the meaning of "nothing" as applied to evil. His later, more strictly theological works include *Why God Became Man* (1094–1098), which introduced his satisfaction theory; *The Virgin Conception* (1099–1100), written as a kind of supplement to *Why God Became Man;* and *The Congruity of Predestination and Free Will* (1107–1108).[5]

Anselm's originality has perhaps been exaggerated by some modern scholars, but he was nonetheless the first Christian theologian to confront the nature of evil and other questions with a logically systematic rational process. God gave us reason as our highest faculty, he believed, and therefore he must wish us to use it. Anselm believed that reason could act to understand reality independent of revelation— what would later be called "natural theology"—and to understand the meaning of revelation—what would later be called "revealed theology."[6]

The logically prior questions are, What is evil? and Where does it come from? Anselm addressed the questions several times but most directly in *The Fall of the Devil*. He concentrated on the fall of the Devil rather than that of Adam because of its chronological and rational priority. Adam's fall can be at least indirectly and partially explained by the temptation offered by the serpent, but in the fall of Satan no pre-existent evil blurs the question. In asking how Lucifer fell we ask how evil initially entered the cosmos, and we can confront the nature of evil abstracted from historical or mythological circumstances. *The Fall of the Devil* is essentially a philosophical treatise on the nature of evil.

Anselm's first assumption is traditional. Evil is nothing.[7] But he proceeds to analyze this concept rationally. By saying that evil is nothing, he does not mean that the word *evil* is meaningless, but rather that the concept *evil* (not good) is identical to the concept *nothing* (not anything). Such negative concepts have meaning only when referred to a good and a something, as "not John" has meaning only when it

5. For works on and by Anselm, see the Essay on the Sources. Abbreviations here: *The Fall of the Devil (Fall); Cur Deus homo (CDH [Why God Became Man]); The Virgin Conception (Virg.); The Congruity of Predestination and Free Will (Cong. [De concordia praescientiae et praedestinationis]*).

6. See M. J. Charlesworth, *Saint Anselm's "Proslogion"* (Oxford, 1965), pp. 40–43.

7. Cf. *Monologion,* 8, 19 (F. S. Schmitt, ed., *Sancti Anselmi opera omnia,* 2 vols. (Stuttgart, 1968), vol. 1 [1], pp. 22–24, 33–35).

refers to John. The word *nothing* refers only to what it negates. In the same way, the word *evil* refers only to the good that it negates. Total and complete evil is the same as total and complete nonbeing, the void. But this is incomprehensible. We are aware of evil and nonbeing only in a limited sense as they are applied to certain referents. Thus blindness is an evil: it is the negation of sight. For the sake of speech we sometimes refer to evils as existing. We say that blindness or war or cancer exist, but these are lack of sight, lack of peace, lack of health. Evil is not anything in itself, but in speech it becomes a quasi something: the word *evil* in this sense refers to certain specific lacks. Further, though nothing in itself, evil produces real results, as when a cancer kills or a thief steals. Lack of goodness produces real effects in the world.[8]

Evil is privation, lack of good. Augustine and other previous Christian writers had muddled the ontological and the moral categories of evil, and Anselm was left to struggle—not entirely successfully—with the confusion. He distinguished two kinds of privation: evil is a lack of divine perfection in created beings; it is inevitable in any created cosmos. In the other sense, it is a lack in something of a quality that it ought to possess, for example, lack of an eye in a cow. But if evil is ontological deficiency, then God has constructed a cosmos with such deficiencies and is directly responsible for evil. In the first sense, human beings are created less good than angels; in the second sense, at least some cows exist without eyes. Even if such privation is somehow necessary for the ultimate good of the cosmos, God is still directly responsible for it.

Deficiencies of the first order are easily dismissed. That horses are less intelligent, and so less "good," than humans can indeed be con-

8. *Fall*, 10–11; *Fall*, 11: "quasi-aliquid." D. P. Henry, "Saint Anselm and Nothingness," *Philosophical Quarterly*, 15 (1965), 243–246, argues that Anselm's analysis distinguishing between being *secundum formam loquendi*, according to the usage of speech, and being *secundum rem*, according to reality, is a valid one. In the former, evil can be something, or at least a quasi something; in the latter, it cannot. Aquinas followed a similar approach in *Summa theologiae* (*ST*), Ia.48.2. Real effects of evil: *Fall*, 26. S. Vanni Rovighi, "Il problema del male in Anselmo d'Aosta," *Analecta Anselmiana*, 5 (1976), 179–188, points out a central difference in the general use of the word *evil* today from that in Anselm's time. Where I, for example, began *The Devil* by arguing that evil is best understood as a condition—suffering—Anselm assumed that evil is best understood as sin—the conscious choice to do ill. Aquinas distinguished carefully between *poena* and *culpa*, roughly translatable as "suffering" and "fault." Evil can be seen as either or both, and the emphasis of our period is certainly different from that of Anselm and Aquinas.

ceived of as the necessary result of a cosmos that best expresses God's goodness by containing the maximum variety of forms. But the deficiencies of the second order present a more difficult problem: why should a cow lack eyes or a woman with cancer lack health? These are real privations occasioning suffering. Moral evil presents yet another dilemma. Moral evil can be perceived as a free-will choice or assigned an ontological cause. But if it has an ontological cause, then God is directly responsible for creating the cosmos so, and the sin is his fault, not the sinner's. Free-will choice might have originated with Adam. But it could not have, for the serpent was in Eden tempting him. Either evil was built into the cosmos and was therefore God's direct fault, or it was the result of a prior free-will choice. And here is where Christian tradition introduced the Devil as a device to explain the existence of moral evil before Adam without holding God responsible. This is why Anselm dealt with the origin of evil in a treatise on the Devil rather than in one on Adam: it enabled him to isolate the question of why and how moral evil entered the cosmos. If the first moral evil—Lucifer's sin—was caused by any pre-existing conditions, then God remains responsible for it. Augustine, with his emphasis on divine power and predestination, was never able to cut this knot.

Anselm himself went a long way round to find the answer. God, he began, did not give Lucifer the grace of perseverance in the good. But it was not God's fault that the grace was not given. If I offer you a gift, and you refuse to accept it, then I do not give it, but the fault is yours. Since Lucifer rejects the gift, God does not give it, and it is Lucifer's fault.[9] In rejecting this grace Lucifer sinned. But why did he do so? It was not that he wanted to be equal to the Creator, which he well knew was impossible, but rather that he tried to obtain happiness by his own power rather than by God's.[10] How did this happen? All creatures naturally seek God, and all intellectual creatures knowingly seek God. God had given the Devil, as he had to all creatures with self-con-

---

9. *Fall*, 2–3. It would be simpler to say that God offers the gift, Lucifer refuses it, and thus God does not give it. For God, of course, this all takes place in eternity; he is aware of Satan's refusal at the same moment as the offer.

10. *Fall*, 4: "Hoc ipso voluit esse inordinate similis Deo, quia propria voluntate, quae nulli subdita fuit, voluit aliquid" (He wanted to be like God in an inappropriate way in that he wished to obtain something through his own will, not subjecting it to God's). Albert the Great (c. 1200–1280) adopted a similar position in his *Commentary on the Sentences (Comm. Sent.)* 2.5.3; Aquinas expanded and modified the argument in *ST* Ia.63.3.

sciousness, the will to seek his own happiness (*commodum*) in the natural order. But he also gave him the choice to transcend this natural order and to seek his supernatural happiness in *justitia*, the balance and harmony that God wills for the cosmos. No one ever wills evil, for evil is nothing in itself. But we can will a lesser good in preference to a greater good. Whenever we choose a limited, selfish good over the greater good of the cosmic harmony, we sin. The Devil's sin lies in his willing the lesser good of his natural happiness over the greater good of the justice of God's cosmos.[11]

But how could the Devil will the wrong thing? Anselm investigated further. God gave Lucifer his will, so the will could not itself be evil.[12] Even the act of turning the will to evil must itself be something, or else the act of turning the will to good would also be nothing. But when Lucifer's will turned from what it should will to that which it should not, it lost its rectitude, its proper relationship to justice, and it was this injustice in which the evil consisted.[13] Still, either Lucifer's will was somehow created defective and sin derives from God, or the turning of the will to evil is an uncaused, free-will choice. The actions of the Devil's will are real and therefore part of the cosmos that God constructs, knowing its details in all eternity. It is no wonder, Anselm exclaims, that we think that God causes sins: God causes every event in the cosmos. But he does not cause the evil will that brings sins about. He wills only the good, and he merely permits the evil.[14] It might seem that God created the conditions that caused Lucifer's fall, since any conditions that exist are willed by God.

But now Anselm breaks the Augustinian mold. The conditions that

11. *Fall,* 4: "Volendo igitur aliquid quod velle tunc non debebat, deseruit iustitiam, et sic peccavit" (Wishing something that was then inappropriate to him [i.e., it was inappropriate for him to try to seize beatitude before God gave it], he deserted justice and thus sinned). The sin was that "diabolum sponte dimisisse velle quod debebat et iuste amisisse quod habebat, quia sponte et iniuste voluit quod non habebat et velle non debebat" (he freely chose not to wish what he ought and thus justly lost what he had, because he freely and unjustly chose what he did not have and ought not to wish for). See also *Fall,* 13–16.

12. *Fall,* 7.

13. *Fall,* 9: "non stetit in originali ut ita dïcam rectitudine" (he did not stay in what can be called his original rectitude).

14. *Fall,* 20: "quid mirum, si dicimus deum facere singulas actiones quae fiunt mala voluntate" (no wonder that we can say that God makes the evil actions that are done with free will); but that God permits, rather than causes evil "omnino Deum excusat et diabolum accusat" (completely exonerates God and exculpates the Devil).

surround an evil moral action are in no way its cause. At last the old knot is cut, cleanly, simply, and elegantly. No preconditions caused Lucifer's fall, none at all. Why did Lucifer sin? For no other reason than that he willed to. If a condition causing a free-will choice existed, the choice would not be entirely free. One can describe *how* Lucifer sinned in choosing *commodum* over *justitia*, but this is not a cause-and-effect relationship. "No cause preceded this act of will except that he chose to do it. 'Are you sure?' Anselm's disciple asks. 'Yes,' Anselm assures him. 'There was no reason except that he chose. This act of will has no other cause that in any way impelled or attracted it, but it is the efficient cause of itself, if I may express it so, and its own effect.'"[15] There was no cause of Lucifer's sin, none at all. This golden key unlocked a door that had been wedged shut since the days of Augustine and Pelagius. The answer inside is elegantly simple. There is no point in looking for any cause of a free-will choice. Free will is not an appearance; it is not compelled; it is not caused; it is really free. The answer is psychologically as well as theologically satisfying. We do experience the sense of real freedom of choice, and also the sense of making evil choices sometimes for their own sake. The answer is also a convincing argument that God is not the cause of moral evil.

Anselm's answer, which in retrospect seems like the invention of the wheel, was avoided by earlier theologians on account of the heavy weight of Augustine's predestinarian ideas. Anselm's answer helped resolve the predestinarian dilemma as well. Anselm argued that the terms *predestination* and *foreknowledge* are misnomers, for God is not in time looking ahead. Rather, all moments are an eternal now for God: he sees the entire cosmos from alpha to omega right now. God's own freedom is complete. This omniscient God is aware of every detail of the cosmos and is responsible for every detail. But his responsibility for some things is direct—ontological defect for example—and his responsibility for other things—sin, for example—is only indirect.[16] Since he constructs the cosmos not as a mechanical toy but as a forum for morally responsible beings, he wills that certain beings—men and angels, for example—have true freedom of will, which entails a true ability to choose evil as well as good. God destines the cosmos to be

---

15. *Fall*, 27: "Nulla causa praecessit hanc voluntatem nisi quia velle potuit. . . . non nisi quia voluit. Nam haec voluntas nullam aliam causam qua impelleretur aliquatenus aut attraheretur, sed ipsa sibi efficiens causa fuit—si dici potest—et effectum."

16. *CDH* 2.17: "voluntatem vero eius nulla praecessit necessitas."

what it is. But he wills some things for themselves, and other things— moral evils—he wills only indirectly in the sense of creating a cosmos in which they inhere. He tolerates them for the greater good of creation, but he does not will them. In other words, God builds real, true freedom into his cosmos. Humans and angels are really responsible, conscious creatures with freedom and dignity. "Although God destines these things (caused by free-will action), he does not cause them by compelling the will, nor by restraining it, but by leaving it to its own power. . . . Some things are predestined to occur through free choice."[17] This answer achieves a viable resolution of the ancient contradiction between predestination and free will, but it does not resolve the problem of evil. Though it relieves God of responsibility for sin, it leaves him with direct responsibility for the blind cow. Further, it does not explain why, if moral evil must exist, it should cause so much suffering.

The free-will sin of Lucifer introduced moral evil into the world. Desiring to spread that evil, he tempted Adam and Eve. Since Adam and Eve are fully responsible for their own free choice, logic does not require any diabolical temptation. Original sin could have occurred without it. Anselm, respecting tradition, never thought of removing the Devil from the scene, but elsewhere he was able to describe original sin and its effects without substantial reference to the Devil. God creates human nature to dwell in harmony with the cosmos and with him. Harmony entails the obedience of humans to God's plan. Animals and plants exist in the cosmos naturally and unselfconsciously, and they have no freedom to accept or reject it. But humans have the free choice to live in harmony with the cosmos or to reject it. Sin is the conscious, voluntary desertion of God's pattern in the cosmos. Original sin is the choice of the human race in Adam not to render God his just due.[18] Original sin introduced disruption, disharmony, disorder, injustice, dissonance, and imbalance into the cosmos and alienated the human race from God.[19] We do not have the power to take from God

17. *Cong.* 2.3; *Cong.* 3.14: In good events he wills both the event and the good; in evil events he wills the event but not the evil.

18. *Virg.* 1–4, 9–10, 26–27. *CDH* 1.11: "Non est itaque aliud peccare quam non reddere Deo debitum" (Sin is nothing other than failing to render God his just due). *CDH* 1:15: "Dei honori nequit aliquid, quantum ad illum pertinet, addi vel minui. Idem namque ipse sibi est honor incorruptibilis et nullo modo mutabilis" (One cannot take from or add to God anything that is proper to him, for his honor is incorruptible and immutable).

19. *CDH* 1.15: "Quae cum vult quod debet, Deum honorat; non quia illi aliquid

anything that pertains to his divine essence, but we can take from him the harmonious existence that he wills for us.[20]

Original sin is so called, Anselm continues, because it exists at the origin of each person, as soon as he or she acquires a rational soul. It cannot have existed at the origin of the race, for we were created in sinless harmony with God; instead it was introduced by Adam and Eve, in whom all humans sinned.[21] As a result of original sin, God granted the Devil limited powers to tempt and punish humanity, but Lucifer holds these powers at God's command and has no right (*jus*) over us at all. Whatever we owe as a result of our sin we owe to God and not to the Devil.[22]

The theory that the Devil has no rights accompanies an important shift in salvation theory from ransom toward sacrifice. By the fifth century, sacrifice theory generally prevailed, but ransom had never been eliminated and enjoyed a certain revival in the early Middle Ages. The scholastics renewed the debate.[23] The most important contribution to this soteriological debate was Saint Anselm's treatise *Cur*

---

confert, sed quia sponte se eius voluntati et dispositioni subdit, et in rerum universitate ordinem suum et eiusdem universitatis pulchritudinem, quantum in ipsa est, servat. Cum vero non vult quod debet, Deum, quantum ad illam pertinet, inhonorat" (When one wills what one should, one honors God, not by giving him anything, but by freely submitting to his will and plan and preserving his order and the beauty of the universe insofar as one is able. But he who does not will what he ought dishonors God to the extent he is able).

20. *CDH* 1.23: "Nonne abstulit Deo, quidquid de humana natura facere proposuerat? Non potest negari" (Does not [the sinner] take away from God what he had proposed for human nature? It cannot be denied).

21. See Anselm, *Virg.*, passim, for theories of transmission of original sin, which is irrelevant to this book.

22. *CDH* 1.7, 2.19: "Siquidem diabolo nec Deus aliquid debebat nisi poenam, nec homo nisi vicem, ut ab illo victus illum revinceret; sed quidquid ab illo exigatur, hoc Deo debebat non diabolo" (God owes the Devil nothing except punishment, and humanity owes the Devil nothing except a representative who will defeat him and regain what he has taken, and whatever God demands of that representative is owed to God not to the Devil).

23. On soteriology (salvation theory) in this period, see especially J. Rivière, *Le dogme de la rédemption au début du moyen âge* (Paris, 1934); J. P. Burns, "The Concept of Satisfaction in Medieval Redemption Theory," *Theological Studies*, 36 (1975), 285–304; D. E. De Clerck, "Questions de sotériologie médiévale," *Recherches de théologie ancienne et médiévale*, 13 (1946), 150–184; J. Pelikan, *The Christian Tradition*, vol. 3: *The Growth of Medieval Theology* (Chicago, 1978), pp. 129–138. On Anselm's theory in particular see A. Atkins, "Caprice: The Myth of the Fall in Anselm and Dostoevsky," *Journal of Religion*, 47 (1967), 295–312; J. Hopkins, *A Companion to the Study of St. Anselm* (Minneapolis, 1972), pp. 122–212; B. P. McGuire, "God, Man and the Devil in Medieval Theology and Culture," Université de Copenhague: Institut du moyen âge grec et latin: *Cahiers*, 18 (1976), 18–79; J. McIntyre, *St. Anselm and His Critics: A Re-interpretation of*

Deus homo (*Why God Became Man*). Anselm's originality in this question has been exaggerated by some modern writers. Sacrifice theory was already a well-established option, and ransom had already been widely rejected.[24] Yet Anselm did move the discussion onto a new plane of sophistication. He was the first to face the incoherencies openly and to try to resolve them through logic. Writing for a general intelligent audience as well as for theologians, he drew upon common sense and experience as well as logic, thinking of his argument less as a categorical logical proof than as a rationally coherent explanation. Rejecting the ransom theory completely, he formulated an original variant of sacrifice theory known as satisfaction theory.[25]

---

the *Cur Deus Homo* (Edinburgh, 1954); R. W. Southern, *Saint Anselm and His Biographer* (Cambridge, 1963), pp. 77–121, esp. the excellent summary on pp. 92–93.

24. For the importance of sacrifice theory earlier see SATAN, pp. 82–86, 116–121, 138–143, 192–194, 215–218; F. M. Young, "Insight or Incoherence," *Journal of Ecclesiastical History*, 24 (1973), 113–126.

25. *CDH* 1.7. Anselm was not the first to use the term *satisfaction* in soteriology, but he was the first to work it into a coherent theory. See Rivière, p. 161. G. R. Evans, "The *Cur Deus Homo*," *Studia theologica*, 31 (1977), 33–50, offers a good description of Anselm's mode of reasoning. The famous ontological argument for the existence of God in Anselm's Proslogion has engendered debate among contemporary scholars as to whether the argument proves or disproves the existence of the Devil, the greater interest in such arguments being in testing the validity of the argument for God. See P. E. Devine, "The Perfect Island, the Devil, and Existent Unicorns," *American Philosophical Quarterly*, 12 (1975), 255–260; W. L. F. Gombocz, "St. Anselm's Disproof of the Devil's Existence in the *Proslogion*: A Counter Argument against Haight and Richman," *Ratio*, 15 (1973), 334–337; W. L. F. Gombocz, "St. Anselm's Two Devils but One God," *Ratio*, 20 (1978), 142–146; W. L. F. Gombocz, "Zur Zwei-Argument-Hypothese bezüglich Anselms Proslogion," *Quarante-septième bulletin de l'Académie St. Anselme*, 75 (1974), 95–98; C. K. Grant, "The Ontological Disproof of the Devil," *Analysis*, 17 (1957), 71–72; D. and M. Haight, "An Ontological Argument for the Devil," *The Monist*, 54 (1970), 218–220; R. J. Richman, "The Ontological Proof of the Devil," *Philosophical Studies*, 9 (1958), 63–64; R. J. Richman, "The Devil and Dr. Waldman," *Philosophical Studies*, 11 (1960), 78–80; R. J. Richman, "A Serious Look at the Ontological Argument," *Ratio*, 18 (1976), 85–89; J. B. Stearns, "Anselm and the Two-Argument Hypothesis," *The Monist*, 54 (1970), 221–233; T. Waldman, "A Comment upon the Ontological Proof of the Devil," *Philosophical Studies*, 10 (1959), 49–50. The argument for the proof of the Devil follows that for the proof of God: the most evil of all possible beings must exist, because an evil that exists only in your mind is less evil than one that exists in reality; since you can conceive of the most evil of all possible beings, it exists in your mind, and because it is most evil, must exist in outside reality as well. The argument for the disproof of the Devil: if evil is nonbeing, then the most evil of all possible beings is completely not-being and cannot exist at all. As Gombocz observed, either argument can work, depending on the assumptions. If evil is nonbeing, then the argument does disprove the existence of *id quod nihil minus cogitari potest*. If evil has being, then the argument proves the existence of *id quod nihil peius cogitari potest*. Neither argument affects Anselm's Devil, who was not the least possible being, because he was

In this new theory Anselm used some terms that today may seem offensive or silly, such as his legal metaphors and his concept of God's honor. But R. W. Southern and other critics have shown that these metaphors are irrelevant to the logic of the argument, which proceeds perfectly without them.[26]

The essence of the argument is that God's fairness and rectitude restore to harmony a human nature that we had distorted by original sin. The theory brings humanity concretely into the picture. Salvation is no longer an abstract cosmic transaction between God and the Devil, but a free act involving real human beings.

In the scenario of satisfaction theory Lucifer has little role. God created humanity in a state of harmony and justice; we shattered the harmony; God could leave us alienated from him, for in strict justice he is under no obligation to save us. But his mercy and love make it inherent, fitting, and proper in him to do so.[27] God therefore chooses to save us. But he cannot restore alienated humanity by simple force or fiat without violating justice. We humans had unbalanced the scales of justice, and we now had to restore the balance by offering restitution. Yet if we simply restored the scales to where they had been before our sin, we would be offering no compensation for the act that unbalanced them. In compensation we need to offer God something that we do not already owe him. But we owe God everything already, including love and repentance. We have nothing extra, nothing of our own, to offer him. Further, the satisfaction must be proportionate to the scale of the sin, but even the smallest sin against God is greater than the whole

---

created with real existence, and who may or may not be the worst possible being. Further, the worst possible being need not exist. As Anselm pointed out, the ontological argument works only for God, who is the only being who can be said to exist absolutely. The perfection of other things is subject to limitation. The most perfect island is subject to erosion, the most perfect unicorn to its imaginary status, and the most perfect evil to its contingency upon good, but the most important being as being cannot be contingent. The argument continues, but its subtler distinctions are not relevant to this book.

26. It is also necessary to grasp what Anselm understood by God's honor. It was no divine arrogance but rather that divine attribute that holds the cosmos in perfect harmony, or the obedience that we owe to God, or the integrity of God's plan for the cosmos. It was certainly colored, however, by contemporary feudal concepts, especially that of the *servitium debitum* that the vassal owes the lord. See Southern, *Saint Anselm*, pp. 107–114; J. F. Niermeyer, *Mediae Latinitatis lexicon minus* (Leiden, 1976), s.v. *honor*, esp. meanings 1 and 2.

27. *CDH* 1.7, 1.9, 1.12, 1.19, 1.24, 2.8–9. In a sense God cannot do what is not fitting and proper to him, for that would be a contradiction of his nature. *CDH* 1.19: "quia non convenit, facere non potest."

world; the price paid, therefore, must be greater than the whole world, yet the only thing worth more than the cosmos is God, and this humanity clearly does not possess. Most of all, we must offer what we offer freely and willingly, but because we are ruined and bound by sin we are unable to make a free offering to God.[28]

Humanity thus owes God a huge debt, but a debt it is incapable by itself of paying; God is capable of paying it, but he owes no debt. If any other being (an extraterrestrial?) saved us, we would become that being's servant (here Anselm makes a commonly held feudal assumption). So the being who saves us must be God. But if God merely paid the price to himself, justice would not be restored, for, again, it is humanity that is in debt: we are the ones who must pay. It follows that the only being who can pay the price is a God/man.[29] Christ's Passion is a sacrifice offered to God by the God/Man. Christ freely willed the sacrifice. God permits this free-will choice of sacrifice on Christ's part and indeed constructs the cosmos with the knowledge that it occurs. But God neither forces nor commands it; the theory removes from God the cruel charge of ordering or willing the death of his Son.[30]

As for the Devil, he is not saved by Christ's Passion; neither can any satisfaction be made for his sin. As it required one of the same species to save humanity, it would require one of the same species to redeem Lucifer, and this is impossible, since each angel constitutes its own species. Also, since the Devil fell untempted, he would have to return to grace unaided, which is impossible. Such traditional arguments lack the logic and elegance of Anselm's other theories.[31]

Satisfaction was an elegant improvement on previous soteriology, but many of Anselm's successor scholastics ignored it and continued to produce the ancient muddle of ransom and sacrifice. But although ransom theory has never disappeared entirely, satisfaction theory has

28. *CDH* 1.15: "necesse est ut omne peccatum satisfactio aut poena sequatur" (it is necessary that satisfaction or punishment follow every sin); *CDH* 1.11–14; *CDH* 1.19: "nam Deus nulli quicquam debet, sed omnis creatura illi debet" (for God owes no one anything; rather, every creature owes him); *CDH* 1.20–21, 2.6; *CDH* 1.22: "ex vulnere primi peccati concipitur et nascitur in peccato" (because of the wound inflicted by original sin we are conceived and born in sin).

29. *CDH* 2.6: "necesse est ut eam [satisfactionem] faciat deus-homo" (it is necessary that the satisfaction be made by a God/Man).

30. *CDH* 1.8: "non enim eum invitum ad mortem ille coegit aut occidi permisit, sed idem ipse sponte sua mortem sustinuit" (God did not force him unwilling to death, but rather he suffered death of his own free will); see *CDH* 1.19, 2.11, and C. Armstrong, "St. Anselm and His Critics," *Downside Review*, 86 (1968), 354–376, on why death was fitting.

31. *CDH* 2.21.

generally prevailed since the thirteenth century. Its effect was to rele-
gate the Devil to an unnecessary and subsidiary role in the central
doctrine of Christianity. For Anselm, the Devil was not a necessary
hypothesis in explaining either the fall of humanity or our redemption.

Peter Lombard (c. 1100–1160) taught at the cathedral school at Paris
from 1140 to 1159 and wrote the *Four Books of Sentences [Opinions]* about
1155 to 1158. Relying upon the fathers, especially Augustine, Peter
introduced no novel ideas but arranged theological questions in logical
order and investigated each dialectically, stating the views and au-
thorities on both sides and concluding with an opinion or *sententia*.
The *Sentences* became the standard theology textbook of the later
twelfth and thirteenth centuries and formed the basis of commentaries
and explications by later scholastics such as Albert the Great and
Aquinas. The following summary of scholastic diabology draws upon
Peter and other standard writers of the period. For the most part these
opinions merely restate earlier views and can be passed over quickly;
new ideas, such as Abelard's salvation theory, deserve fuller attention.[32]

The standard view that evil was privation, lacking any ontological
reality in itself, was argued all the more vehemently in this period
owing to the need to combat the dualist heresies that began to appear
in Latin Europe in the 1140s. Yet it was also agreed that although evil
is nothing in itself, its operation produces real effects, as (we would say
today) a vacuum can disrupt and destroy.[33] Abelard was condemned
at Sens in 1140 for allegedly arguing that God neither could nor should
prevent evil actions, but he really had said only that God *ought* not to
do so because that would interfere with the operation of free will.[34]

The traditional view that angels and demons have bodies of ethereal

32. Peter Lombard, *Sentences (Sent.)*, *Libri IV Sententiarum studio·et cura patrum collegii Sancti Bonaventurae in lucem editi*, 3d ed., 2 vols. (Grottaferrata, 1971–1981). See D. Van den Eynde, "Essai chronologique sur l'oeuvre de Pierre Lombard," in *Miscellanea Lombardiana* (Novara, 1957), 45–63; P. Delhaye, *Pierre Lombard* (Paris, 1961).

33. Abelard, *Sic et non*, 143; B. Boyer and R. McKeon, eds., *Peter Abailard Sic et non* (Chicago, 1977); cf. also *Sic et non* 29–31, 37, 46–47, 54, 77, 143. See also Alan of Lille (d. 1203), *Contra haereticos libri quattuor*, 1.4.

34. Sens, canon 17: "quod Deus nec debeat nec possit mala impedire." H. Denzinger and K. Rahner, *Enchiridion symbolorum*, 31st ed. (Rome, 1960), no. 375. See also J. Rivière, "Les 'capitula' d'Abélard condamnés au concile de Sens," *Recherches de théologie ancienne et médiévale*, 5 (1933), 5–22, at p. 16; G. Delagneau, "Le Concile de Sens de 1140: Abélard et Saint Bernard," *Bulletin de la Société archéologique de Sens*, 37 (1933), 80–116; E. Buytaert, ed., *Abailardi opera theologica*, 2 vols., CCCM 11–12, pp. 455–480. On Abelard see L. Grane, *Peter Abelard: Philosophy and Christianity in the Middle Ages* (New York, 1970).

or aerial matter persisted among some scholastics, Bonaventure, for example, but was rejected by Albert the Great and Aquinas, who argued that they were purely spiritual substances on the grounds that spiritual but contingent creatures were needed to fill what the scholastics perceived as a gap between God (pure spirit and uncontingent) and humans (spirit/matter and contingent).[35] Most scholastics held Satan to be the highest of all the angels, but the question proved bothersome. If angels have ranks, then Lucifer might have had his equals. If he were a seraph, it was difficult to explain how he could have been driven out of heaven by Michael, a mere archangel. In exploring such concerns the scholastics seem to have pressed reason beyond reasonable bounds.[36]

35. Yvo of Chartres (c. 1040–1116) held the traditional view in his *Panormia*, 8.68. An unusual view was held by Witelo (Vitellio), a Polish scholar at Paris in the thirteenth century. Drawing upon the ancient Platonic doctrine that demons were beings intermediate between humanity and the gods, Witelo treated them as natural beings superior to humans and inferior to angels, *mediae potestates*. They were composed of body and soul and were mortal. According to the natural perfection of their nature, they were unable to sin; faith teaches that they did, so their sin must be supernatural. See A. Birkenmajer, *Etudes d'histoire des sciences en Pologne* (Warsaw, 1972), pp. 122–136; E. Paschetto, "Il 'De natura daemonum' di Witelo," *Atti dell'Academia delle Scienze di Torino: Filosofia e storia della filosofia*, 109 (1975), 231–271.

36. Satan as the highest angel: Peter Lombard, *Sent.* 2.6.1; Hugh of Saint Victor, *Summa sententiarum*, 2.4; Albert the Great, *Commentary on the Sentences*, 2.6.1. On Albert see B. Geyer, ed., *Opera omnia Alberti Magni*, 8 vols. to date (Munster, 1951–); A. Borgnet, ed., *Opera omnia*, 38 vols. (Paris, 1890–1899); T. F. O'Meara, "Albert the Great: A Bibliographical Guide," *The Thomist*, 44 (1980), 597–598; J. Auer, "Albertus Magnus als Philosoph und Theologe," *Beiträge zur Geschichte des Bistums Regensburg*, 14 (1980), 41–62. Robert Pullen argued that Lucifer was either a cherub or a seraph: *Liber sententiarum*, 6.45–48. In *ST* Ia.63.7, Aquinas presents a logical argument for Lucifer's being the highest of the angels. The highest angel is the most likely to fall because his high status makes him most susceptible to the sin of pride. Duns Scotus (1266–1308) argued that the angels within a given order were not equal: *Commentary on the Sentences*, 2.9. Duns' works are edited by L. Wadding, *Opera omnia*, 12 vols. (Lyon, 1639); see esp. vol. 6:1–2, *Commentary on the Sentences*, and vol. 11:1, *Reportata Parisiensia*; see E. Gilson, *Jean Duns Scot: Introduction à ses positions fondamentales* (Paris, 1952). Satan would have liked to have worn a handsome and appealing shape when he appeared to Adam and Eve, but God would not let him, lest the temptation he offered be irresistible; neither did God allow him to take his own grotesque shape, which would have been too repellent. He was therefore obliged to speak through the serpent. See Peter Lombard, *Sent.* 2.21.2: "Sed quia illi per violentiam nocere non poterat, ad fraudem se convertit, ut dolo hominem supplantaret, quem virtute superare nequiret. Ne autem fraus illiciter manifestaretur, in sua specie non venit, ne aperte cognosceretur et ita repelleretur. Iterum, ne nimis occulta foret fraus eius, quae caveri non posset, et homo simul videretur iniuriam pati, si taliter circumvenire permitteret eum Deus, ut praecavere non posset, in aliena quidem forma venire permissus est diabolus, sed in tali, in qua eius malitia facile posset deprehendi. . . . Venit igitur ad hominem in serpente, qui

All agreed that Lucifer's sin was pride, but no agreement was reached as to what this meant. Albert followed Anselm, but Hugh of Saint Victor (c. 1096–1141), Honorius Augustodunensis (early twelfth century), and Peter Lombard indicated vaguely that Satan somehow wanted to be God's equal.[37] Peter the Eater emphasized Lucifer's envy of humanity, whom God had chosen to fill the place of the fallen angels in heaven. Peter Lombard noted that Lucifer and the other angels were created with natural goodness (*boni*); they were neither naturally evil (*mali*) nor damned (*miseri*). Yet since they were also not confirmed in goodness (*beati*), they were prone to sin.[38]

Abelard's subjectivist view enabled him to look at the problem from a different angle. For Abelard, the essence of sin is the intention to do wrong, the deliberate movement of the will toward violating divine justice, regardless of the action that results. Thus it was unimportant what the Devil *did*: what was important was the motion of his will toward evil.[39] The other angels followed Lucifer simultaneously, also through pride. Though Lucifer offered them persuasion, he was not the cause of their sin, which was their own free will as individual

---

forte si permitteretur, in columbae specie venire maluisset. . . . Diabolus enim per serpentem tentabat, in quo loquebatur" (But because he couldn't harm him through violence, he turned to fraud, so that he might undermine man instead of conquering him by force. In order to hide himself, he did not come in his own shape, lest he be recognized and repulsed. But it was not fitting that his fraud be so completely subtle that man would suffer injury by having no way of being alerted, and therefore the Devil was allowed to take only a form in which his malice could easily be discovered. He therefore came to man in the form of a serpent, for only this was permitted him, although he would have preferred to appear as a dove. The Devil tempted man through the serpent, through whom he spoke).

37. Albert, *Comm. Sent.* 2.5.3; Albert, *ST* 5.21.1; Honorius, *Elucidarium*, 1.7–8; Hugh, *Summa sententiarum*, 2.4; Peter Lombard, *Sent.* 2.6.1: "similis quidem esse Deo voluit non per imitationem, sed per aequalitatem potentiae" (he did not want to imitate God but rather to possess equal power). Rupert of Deutz (c. 1070–1129), *De victoria verbi Dei*, ed. Rhaban Haack (Weimar, 1970), 1.6–27; Alexander of Hales (c. 1186–1245), *Comm. Sent.* 2.6.2. See I. Herscher, "A Bibliography of Alexander of Hales," *Franciscan Studies*, 26 (1945), 435–454. Bonaventure (1217–1274), *Comm. Sent.* 2.5.1.2. Bonaventure's works are edited by the Franciscans of Quaracchi, *Sancti Bonaventurae Opera omnia*, 11 vols. (Quaracchi, 1882–1902); see E. Gilson, *La philosophie de Saint Bonaventure*, 2d ed. (Paris, 1943).

38. Petrus Comestor (d. 1178), *Historia scholastica Liber Genesis*, 21; Peter Lombard, *Sent.* 2.3.6; Duns Scotus, *Reportata*, 2.4.

39. Abelard, *Ethica*, ed. D. E. Luscombe, *Peter Abelard's Ethics* (Oxford, 1971), trans. J. R. McCallum, *Abailard's Ethics* (Oxford, 1935). See J. G. Sikes, *Peter Abailard* (Cambridge, 1932), pp. 179–189.

angels.[40] The number of fallen angels is indeterminate but great, and some of each rank fell, retaining their relative status after their ruin.[41] Abelard's conceptualist position in the controversy between nominalists and realists had deep implications for the study of the Devil that were not understood until recently: the Devil is not merely a word, as the nominalists had it, nor necessarily an objectively existing entity, as the realists had it, but rather a real concept that the word *Devil* points to without defining.

The scholastics resolved the question of when the Devil fell. Although traditionally Lucifer was generally supposed to have been corrupt from the beginning, Peter Lombard and others observed that if he had really been evil from the moment of his creation, that would mean that God had denied him free will and created him evil. On the other hand, he could not have delayed long in making his choice, because angelic intelligences grasp the nature of the cosmos immediately and intuitively. Angels do not learn through sensory observation or reason, so no new information could ever have entered his mind to change it. Therefore at least a small delay—*moracula*—must have intervened between his creation and his fall, during which he must have recognized his own limited nature as opposed to God's and freely chosen to disobey his master.[42] The fallen angels had been created naturally

40. Rupert, *De victoria*, 1.6–27; Alexander of Hales, *Summa theologia*, 2a2ae.3.2; Albert, *ST* 5.20.2.

41. Hildebert of Le Mans (1056–1133), Sermon 49; *Tractatus theologicus*, 19–21; William of Auvergne (c. 1180–1249), *De universo*, 2.2.6–13, 2.3.8, in *Guilelmi Alverni . . . opera omnia*, 2 vols. (Paris, 1674). See William's *De bono et malo*, ed. J. R. O'Donnell, *Mediaeval Studies*, 8 (1946), 245–299, and 16 (1954), 219–271; Albert, *ST* 10.42.1–5, which disagrees with the idea of the infernal hierarchy and argues that the demons fell before the celestial hierarchy was established and therefore lack ranks.

42. Abelard, *Sic et non*, 46–47; Peter Lombard, *Sent.* 2.3.4; William of Auvergne, *De universo*, 2.2.48, 23.1–26: book 3 deals exclusively with demons; Albert, *Summa de creaturis*, 4.62–69; Aquinas, *ST* Ia.63.5. The University of Paris resolved the question in 1241 and again in 1244 by affirming the delay as necessary to preserve the goodness of God. Bonaventure held that the angels were created on the first day along with the Empyrean, matter, and time: Gilson, *Saint Bonaventure*, p. 196. Compare Duns Scotus, *Reportata*, 2.4. The question of the introduction of the moral anomaly of sin into the cosmos has curious analogies to modern cosmological problems. Physics tends to assume that the initial state of the cosmos in the first moment was perfectly symmetrical. Asymmetry or distortion may have been introduced (it is not known how) as a discontinuity a tiny fraction of a second (*moracula*) after the first moment. If it were not for this first, minuscule asymmetry at the beginning of the cosmos, the cosmos would have developed with perfect symmetry, like a perfect, frozen crystal, without diversity, life,

good with natural grace, but they had not been confirmed in supernatural grace. At the moment of their fall, the loyal angels were confirmed in supernatural grace and were now *beati* as well as *boni*, but the evil angels were confirmed in their evil.[43] The evil angels are fixed in their own choice and cannot be saved. First, unlike Adam and Eve, they cannot plead the extenuation of an external tempter who was a superior being. Second, their natural intellect being so much greater than that of humans, their fault was correspondingly greater. Third, they are purely spiritual beings and do not possess the mobility of nature proper to humans. A spiritual creature is completely bonded to its choice: this is why human souls after death are also unable to repent. Fourth, after their fall, their angelic qualities are diminished. They retain much of their sharp intellect, but in an impaired form, and though they do not lose their free will, they lose the power actually to choose between good and evil.[44]

The scholastics disagreed as to the relationship of the creation of humanity to the fall of the angels, most arguing that God created humanity for the purpose of filling up the ranks that the evil angels had depleted with the souls of the elect (a source of the modern pietism that good people "become angels" when they die). This view provided an added poignancy to Satan's assault upon Adam: to his desire to block God's plan for the cosmos he added a burning envy for the beings created to take his place in heaven.[45] All these arguments were de-

---

intelligence, or freedom. The asymmetry created a kind of turbulence in the cosmos that, once begun, naturally expanded, increased, and multiplied, producing the apparent randomness and divergency that are necessary to the development of life and intelligence. I am grateful to Dr. Charles Musès, Professor Robert Schrieffer, and other natural scientists kind enough to discuss these issues with me; they are not responsible for any scientific inaccuracies. This modern physical problem is analogous to the medieval ethical one: once sin is introduced to disrupt the perfection of the cosmos, it spreads in ever-widening circles—Lucifer corrupts the other angels and then humanity—but the existence of that evil was necessary for the diversification of the cosmos and for freedom to exist. The scholastics saw no contradiction between creation in a single instant and creation in seven days, however interpreted. Creation was a single, initial moment followed by whatever time was necessary to complete the process.

43. Bonaventure, *Comm. Sent.* 2.4.12, agreed. Compare Aquinas, *Commentary on the Sentences (CS)*, 2.4.1.3; Aquinas, *ST* Ia.62.3; Duns, *Comm. Sent.* 2.4–6; Duns, *Reportata*, 2.4.

44. Albert, *ST* 2.7.1–5; Peter Lombard, *Sent.* 2.7.5. The scholastics believed that one could have free will yet not be able to choose between good and evil. God, for example, has free will but cannot choose evil; the damned have free will but cannot choose good.

45. Hildebert, Sermon 49; Peter Lombard, *Sent.* 2.21 and *Commentarium in*

signed to explain how the idiot, grinning menace of evil had intruded into a cosmos designed to be harmonious. The next set of questions dealt with the Lord's restoration of his shattered cosmos.

Anselm's satisfaction theory made some headway in the twelfth century, but considerable incoherence in soteriology persisted, with Honorius, Rupert, the Victorines and others continuing to believe in both ransom and sacrifice without regard for their incompatibility. Some theologians took overtly conservative positions, especially William of Champeaux (1068–1122), Anselm of Laon (d. 1117), and Anselm's brother Ralph. Though the Devil may have no rights vis-à-vis God, the school of Laon argued, he does have rights over humanity, and God respects those rights. God's providence provides for the Devil's committing a crime of such magnitude as to cancel them—his effort to seize the sinless God/Man Jesus Christ.[46] This is pure ransom theory, and it was still in use at the time of Innocent III complete with the metaphor of bait and hook. In keeping with crusading mentality the metaphor sometimes changed from angling to warfare: Christ, like a wise warrior lurking in caves and rocks to surprise his enemy, hid in the womb of the Blessed Mother, thus disguising his divine nature under the appearance of humanity. Behind the striking inelegance of such metaphors lies a reasonable proposition. If we knew God and his laws directly and absolutely we would be overwhelmed and would have no choice but to obey; God hides his divinity so that we may have untrammeled use of our free will.[47]

Other scholastics were moderately conservative. Peter Lombard, Rupert, and Bernard of Clairvaux (1090–1153) limited the Devil's rights yet granted him wide powers.[48] Still others, such as William of

---

Psalmum 118. Alan of Lille (*Contra haereticos* 1.14) argued that humanity would have been created anyway in order to ornament the heavenly Jerusalem: "non propter supplendam ruinam tantum, sed potius ad coelestem Hierusalem exornandum."

46. Ralph, *Sententias excerptas*, 31, ed. G. Lefevre, *Anselmi Laudensis et Radulfi fratris eius sententias excerptas* (Evreux, 1895): "Diabolus dicitur juste possidere hominem, quia Deus juste hoc permittebat et homo juste patiebatur quod promeruerat" (The Devil is said to possess humanity justly because God justly permitted it and humanity justly suffered what it deserved). Anselm, *Sent.* 9: God became human so that the Devil might lose his power over humanity ("per hoc suam potestatem amitteret"). See also *Sent.* 8. A recent challenge to the idea that a school of Laon existed is V. Flint, "The 'School of Laon,'" *Recherches de théologie ancienne et médiévale*, 43 (1976), 89–110.

47. Innocent III, Sermon 29: "virgam et lineam, hamum et escam" (hook, line, and sinker, *lit.*, pole, line, hook, and bait). See also Rivière, *Le dogme*, pp. 224–225, citing a sermon in Paris Bibliothèque Nationale Lat. 14958 fol. 115r-v.

48. Bernard was inclined to the view that humanity suffers justly, God permits the

Auvergne, Honorius, Robert Pullen, Alexander of Hales, and Albert the Great, supported the Anselmian position by denying all rights to the Devil and eschewing ransom theory completely.[49]

Abelard agreed with Anselm that the Devil had no rights and that ransom theory would not hold up, but he exceeded Anselm in daring. Christ saved only the elect, who had never been in Satan's power, so that Christ really delivered no one from Satan's dominion. The Devil has power only over the unjust, and that only because God uses him as a jailer. Abelard was condemned at the Council of Sens in 1140 for going this far, and he recanted. No one was yet ready to resolve the underlying question of predestination and free will. If God determines who is saved from all eternity, what effective power could the Devil have over the elect? How can he be said to tempt those who are destined not to yield? Aquinas would answer that the Devil really tempts the elect, and the elect really have freedom to choose, yet God knows in eternity that they choose to resist and they resist successfully. Abelard's theory avoided both ransom and sacrifice and, in accordance with his subjective theory of morality, emphasized the subjective action of God in the Passion. The effects that may have proceeded from God's action on the cross were not to Abelard the essential point, but rather God's intention. By becoming human, God ennobled humanity; by suffering on the cross he shared our human suffering and dismissed the reproach that he who constructed a universe full of pain avoids that pain himself. All this God did in humility and for love of his creatures. The free, generous, unmerited outpouring of God's love for humanity engenders love in return, and in this way the alienation

---

suffering justly, and the Devil himself has no just rights. But Bernard sometimes leaned in the other direction, not so much in opposition to Anselm as in reaction against Abelard. Peter, *Sent.* 3.19–20; Bernard, *Tractatus de erroribus Petri Abelardi* 5.14: "hoc ergo diaboli quoddam in hominem jus, etsi non jure acquisitum, sed nequiter usurpatum; juste tamen permissum. Sic itaque homo juste captivus tenebatur, ut tamen nec in homine, nec in diabolo illa esset justitia, sed in Deo" (Thus the Devil holds a certain right over humankind; though it was not acquired by right and unjustly usurped, nonetheless it is justly permitted. Thus humankind is justly held captive, but the justice lies neither in the human nor in the Devil, but only in God). See Rivière, *Le dogme*, pp. 206–221.

49. Robert, *Sententiae* 4.13–14: "quippe diabolus in homine, quem malo dolo deceperat, nihil iuris habebat [4.13]" (surely the Devil has no right over mankind, which he deceived with an evil trick). See Rivière, *Le dogme*, pp. 164, 416; Burns, pp. 293–295.

Saint Michael disputes the fate of a soul with a demon. At left, a demon tries as usual to tip the balance in the favor of hell; at right, an angel offers the redeemed soul to heaven. Catalan painting, altar frontispiece of the church of Soriguerola (Gerone), thirteenth century. Courtesy of the Museu d'Art de Catalunya.

between humans and God is bridged. This attractive view was too far beyond the limits of tradition to prevail.[50]

The scholastics floundered with the question of where the fallen angels dwell. It had always been unclear whether they had been cast down into the air or under the earth. If in the air, how could they now be tormented by fire or do their job of torturing the souls of the damned? But if underground, how can they wander the world seeking the ruin and destruction of souls? Some argued that they roamed the air until the last judgment, after which they would be thrust into hell, but that did not resolve the difficulty; neither did the idea that the Devil himself was bound in hell while the subsidiary demons roamed loose. Most strained of all was the theory that the demons spent some of their time in the air, tempting, and other times in hell, ascending and descending as their duties required. The best resolution of the tangle would be to take hell as a state of deprivation of God's presence rather than as a place: "This is hell, nor am I out of it." Unfortunately such a solution, though respected by Aquinas, was not widely held, for it went against the scholastic desire to pin down details.[51]

Some things the Devil does may appear to be good, but in fact his every move is aimed at the destruction of God's harmonious cosmos. God permits him to tempt and afflict us in order to test our souls and give wide range to our free-will choice between good and evil. The Devil cannot gain direct access to a person's soul, but God permits him under certain circumstances to manipulate natural phenomena against us.[52] He may create illusions in our minds, giving impressions of

50. Abelard, *Commentaria in epistolam Pauli ad Romanos*, 2; *Theologia Christiana*, 4, ed. E. Buytaert, *Petri Abelardi opera theologica* (Turnhout, 1969), vol. 2. The proposition condemned at Sens, no. 4 (Denzinger no. 371): "quod Christus non assumpsit carnem ut nos a jugo diaboli liberaret" (that Christ did not take on flesh to free us from the Devil's yoke).

51. Hildebert, *Tractatus theologicus*, 19–20; William of Auvergne, *De universo*, 2.3.11; Peter Lombard, *Sent.* 2.6.2–3; Aquinas, *CS* 2.6.1.3, and *ST* Ia.64.4; Bonaventure was convinced that the demons live in the air, not the underground, though some of them descend to torment the damned from time to time: "locus, ante diem judicii, non est infernus subterraneus, sed aer caliginosus, licet probabile sit nonnullos eorum ad torquendas animas eo descendere" (*Comm. Sent.* 2.6.2).

52. Peter Lombard, *Sent.* 2.7: God permits demons to perform magic to warn or test the faithful or to deceive the fraudulent; Abelard, *Ethics* 4; William of Auvergne, *De universo*, 2.3.6–7; Peter Lombard, *Sent.* 2.8.4: "Daemones non substantialiter intrent corda hominum, sed propter malitiae suae effectum; de quibus pelli dicuntur cum nocere non sinuntur" (Demons enter human hearts, not substantially, but by the effect of their evil will, hence they are said not to be able to harm our bodies). Peter Lombard, *Commentarium in Psalmum 77*: God permits demons to punish as well as tempt.

wondrous things as a stage magician does, but these are only marvels (*mira*), not real miracles (*miracula*). The Devil can take any shape he likes or manipulate nature, though only within natural laws. When his deeds appear to contravene nature, it is either an illusion or else a natural event beyond our ability to understand. For example, that angels and demons can transport people or things through the air is in accord with nature, just as people or animals can transport things on the ground. The Devil manipulates nature not only to tempt but also to afflict us physically with disease or possession.[53]

Such speculations have journeyed on tortuous logical roads a long way from serious attention to the problem of evil. Yet such intellectual abstractions, popularized in sermons, were accepted both by the educated and by the unlettered, in whose minds the abstractions took on immediacy and power. The degree to which they were taken seriously in the eleventh century by an intelligent, learned person who was not a theologian appears in the autobiography of Guibert of Nogent.[54] Guibert's accounts of twenty-two cases of demonic activity include not only abstractions and clichés but also three incidents that he alleges actually happened to him or others he knew personally. When Guibert reports that he experienced a terrifying noise unaccompanied by words or visual manifestations, we need not be skeptical: such an experience may well have proceeded (with or without demonic influence) from his unconscious. His description of the Devil's suggestion to a monk that it is sweeter to lie in bed in the morning than to rise for prime is scarcely unbelievable, and his report of his mother's harrassment by an incubus while his father was away at war is less likely an invention of Guibert's than an actual subjective event in the life of his mother. Guibert's stock description of a demon that haunted him conventionally—skinny neck, emaciated face, black eyes, furrowed brow, puffed up mouth, thick lips, spiky hair—does not invalidate the

---

53. Albert, *Comm. Sent.* 2.43.3: "potest diabolus multis modis formare formas et illas offerre oculis sive sensui; sensus autem objectas volens nolens apprehendit" (the Devil can produce many kinds of forms and set them before the eyes or other senses, and the senses are forced to observe such things). William of Auvergne, *De universo*, 2.3.12–13; Honorius, *Liber quaestionum*, 11; Walter Map, *De nugis curialium*, 5.6; Abelard, Council of Sens, no. 16 (Denzinger no. 383).

54. Guibert, *De vita sua*, ed. and trans. J. Benton, *Self and Society in Medieval France: The Memoirs of Abbot Guibert de Nogent* (New York, 1970); J. Paul, "Le démoniaque et l'imaginaire dans le 'De vita sua' de Guibert de Nogent," in *Le diable au moyen âge* (Paris, 1979), pp. 373–379. R. Colliot, "Rencontres du moine Raoul Glaber avec le diable d'après ses histoires," in *Le diable au moyen âge*, pp. 119–132.

erunt eq; adiuisione omni carni. Post ad
uentu aute dni et bestie damnatione.
quis occidetur gladio amanifestis auib;
comedendus, cu corpora tunc resur
gant. ut homines integri iudicentur.
EXPLICIT.

INCIPIT DE ALIO ANGELO ET CLA
VE ABISSI

Et uidi alium angelum descenden
tem de celo habentem claue abissi.
et catenam magnam inmanu sua.
et tenuit draconem angue anticu
qui est diabolus et satanas. Lib.
gauit eu annis mille. et misit eum
inabyssum. et clausit et signauit
sup eu ne seducat amplius gentes usq;
dum finiantur mille anni. Post hec
oportet eu solui modico tepore. Exelu.

INCIPIT EXPLANATIO SVPRASCRIPT
STORIAE. RECAPITVLATA PASSIONE.

Et uidi aliu angelum descendente de
celo. dnm ihm xpm dicit primo ad
uentu. Habentem claue abissi. et catena
magnam inmanu sua. et tenuit dracone
anguem anticu qui est diabolus et sa
tanas. et ligauit eu annis mille. et misit
eum inabyssum. et clausit et signauit
sup eu ne seducat amplius gentes usq;
dum finiantur mille anni. Inteuas
hic nobis inuocandus est dns. ne in mille
annoru numeru. multoru sim consen
tientes erroribus. neq; p excessu ppum
ipsi nuquam ur erore. sed custodiet
fide nram. ipse qui fidelis uocat et ueiax.
Ipse dns dicit in principio libri huius qua
ego sum primus et nouissimus. uuus. et fui

UBI ANGLS LIGA
UIT DRACONEM
ID EST DIABOLU
IN ABISSUM

The archangel "binds the dragon, that is, the Devil, in the abyss." Illumination from the *Commentary on the Apocalypse*, by Saint Beatus, France, eleventh century. Photograph courtesy of the Bibliothèque Nationale, Paris.

experience, for we naturally supply the details of every experience from our own hoard of assumptions.

One can approach such tales psychoanalytically, as John Benton did, or phenomenologically, as Jacques Paul did. Every individual interprets subjective events in accord with the mental universe that he has constructed for himself; our personal mental universes are likely to reflect the general assumptions of our times. An event occurring to a person whose mental universe has room for the Devil is likely to interpret such an event quite differently from a person with a differing mental universe. In a society in which demonic activity is assumed to be natural, certain subjective events are likely to be interpreted as the work of demons, and then such experiences of demons become part of the evidence for demonic activity. One need not accept the objectivity of the conclusion to observe that this is a respectable mental process. Some modern writers persist in being astonished that intelligent people could believe in such things. This is to ignore the coherent (if not necessarily objective) world that Guibert and his contemporaries had constructed for themselves and also to forget that one's own world view is equally a construction resting upon unproved epistemological assumptions.[55]

The theory of incubi, one of which so troubled Guibert's mother, was one of the roots of belief in witchcraft: the witches were supposed to invite such intercourse. The idea of incubi does not seem to derive from folk belief, and though the desert fathers told tales of demons taking on the forms of attractive young men or women, incubi do not become significant in European thought before the twelfth century. The concept seems to arise from scholastic theory. Demons, who have no proper form or sex of their own, can take any shape they please. As incubi they take on the shape of men to seduce sleeping women; as succubi they assume the shape of women to seduce men. This they do, not for lust, which they are incapable of feeling, since they have no real bodies, but only to humiliate and corrupt their victims.[56]

The scholastics' tendency to point up every theological detail was sharpened by their sense of the need to defend orthodox teaching against a variety of opponents. As Christian society increased its commercial and cultural contacts with other societies, orthodox Christians

55. Personal construct psychologists understand this; see for example D. Rowe, *The Construction of Life and Death* (New York, 1982).

56. William of Auvergne, *De universo*, 2.3.2; Albert, *Comm. Sent.*, 2.7.5. See J. Russell, *Witchcraft in the Middle Ages* (Ithaca, 1972), pp. 115–119.

became more aware of the challenge posed by Jews, Muslims, and heretics, though their actual understanding of other religions was minimal.[57] Heretics, who seemed to challenge Christianity from within, accepting some doctrines but veering off in strange directions, seemed the most dangerous of all. Heresy is a Christian theological view opposed to the teaching of the Christian community as a whole. By definition, those ideas receiving general assent or official approval were considered orthodox, and those rejected heretical. The heresies of the early church (before the eighth century) were generally intellectual in nature—relating, for example, to the definition of the Trinity—but medieval heresies were usually ethical in nature, dealing, for example, with whether laymen ought to preach or the degree to which the bishop must be obeyed.[58]

Medieval heresy grew rapidly from the middle of the eleventh century, owing in part to growing political stability, widening literacy, the growth of centers of learning in the cities, and the exchange of ideas through commercial intercourse. Popular heretical movements were numerous, but intellectual dissent had at least as great an effect on theology. Theologians modified and sharpened doctrine through dialogue with the intellectual heretics, and their usual response to social heresy was to translate it into intellectual terms for the purpose of refuting it.[59] Heresy focused the attention of theology on certain areas that might otherwise have been neglected, and heretical ideas often crept into art and literature even when rejected by theologians. The heretics did not consider themselves heretical but believed that they were following true apostolic tradition. The only workable definition of heresy in the Latin Middle Ages is an artificial one: a doctrine unacceptable to the papacy at a given time. Modern historical thought treats heretical and orthodox thought as arising from the same cultural

57. See R. W. Southern, *Western Views of Islam in the Middle Ages* (Cambridge, Mass., 1962).

58. On heresies in general see C. T. Berkhout and J. B. Russell, *Medieval Heresies: A Bibliography* (Toronto, 1981). The best general work is M. D. Lambert, *Medieval Heresy* (London, 1977). Note that the sect of the "Luciferans," once supposed to have existed in the fourteenth century, is a fiction. Orthodox writers of the period took Augustine's account of fourth-century Luciferans, followers of Bishop Lucifer of Cagliari (who had nothing to do with the Devil) and applied it to certain Waldensian groups in their own time, on the basis that any heretics were followers of the Devil and might properly be termed Luciferans. See R. Lerner, *The Heresy of the Free Spirit in the Later Middle Ages* (Berkeley, 1972).

59. G. R. Evans, *Anselm and a New Generation* (Oxford, 1980), p. 146.

and social environment rather than drawing categorical distinctions between them.

The revival of dualism by the Cathar heretics from the 1140s onward influenced diabology deeply.[60] The Cathars, whose roots were in Gnosticism, derived directly from two sources: earlier Reformist heresy, which sometimes led to extreme asceticism and rejection of the world, and Bogomilism, imported into Italy by Bulgarian missionaries beginning in the 1140s. Spreading from northern Italy into southern France, Aragon, the Rhineland, and the Low Countries, Cathar dualism posed the greatest heretical challenge to the medieval church, and it was finally exterminated only by crusade and inquisition. The dualist doctrines of the Cathars varied from group to group, the largest general difference being that between the "absolute dualists," who maintained that the Devil was a principle completely independent of God, and the "mitigated dualists," who held that he was a creature who had usurped God's powers.[61]

The Cathars' principal theological concern was with the problem of evil, and they took the figure of the Devil in deadly earnest. Their emphasis upon Lucifer worked on the one hand to make him more real to the popular consciousness and on the other to provoke an orthodox reaction against belief in his importance. But the difference between Catholics and Cathars on the question of dualism has been oversimplified. The debate was not between two extremes but rather where on the spectrum between dualism and monism the truth lay. Orthodox Christianity is itself a quasi-dualist religion—in the place it has traditionally given the Devil, in its tendencies to reject the world, and in its efforts to relieve God of the responsibility of evil. On the other side, even absolute Catharism was ambivalent in assuming an ultimate triumph of the good principle, and mitigated Catharism, with its idea that Satan is God's subordinate, was close to the middle of the spectrum and to orthodox Christianity.

Essentially the Cathar view of the Devil was intended to save the goodness of God by limiting his power, to account for the conflict between good and evil that we observe in life, and to respond to the

---

60. See Chapter 3 above for the Bogomil antecedents to Catharism. The best book on Catharism is A. Borst, *Die Katharer* (Stuttgart, 1953); see also Berkhout and Russell, nos. 290–709.

61. On Cathar doctrines see especially Borst; M. Loos, *Dualist Heresy in the Middle Ages* (Prague, 1974); G. Schmitz-Valckenberg, *Grundlehren katharischer Sekten des 13. Jahrhunderts* (Munich, 1971).

Judas receiving his payment for betraying Christ. The Devil, black and bestial, hovers behind him in encouragement. Giotto (1276–1337), oil on canvas, in the Arena chapel, Padua, 1306. Courtesy of Archivi Alinari.

conflict between the two that we perceive within ourselves. The Ca- ·
thar religion expresses a poignant yearning to transcend this hopelessly
corrupt and ruined world to a beautiful and perfect world beyond.
Mitigated dualism did not advance the discussion, for like Catholicism
it envisioned the Devil as God's creature; only absolute dualism offered a real alternative to Christianity.

The absolute dualists argued that evil came from an evil principle, a
being wholly independent of the good God. This must be, they argued, because if only one principle exists, it must be either good or
evil, since one principle cannot embrace opposites. If the one principle
is good, where does evil come from? But if it is evil, where does good
come from? The dilemma cannot be resolved, they maintained, unless
two principles are assumed. They rejected the mitigated position on
the ground that if the Devil were a creature of the good God he would
be unable to do anything against God's will, and God would still be
responsible for evil. How could an all-good and all-powerful God
construct a cosmos such that he would regret what occurs in it? Only
four solutions exist: one is atheism; the second is absolute dualism; the
third is the coincidence of opposites, which asserts that one principle
can in fact contain opposites—the position of the mystics; the fourth is
that evil has no being—the position taken by the scholastics.[62]

The line between absolute and mitigated Cathar doctrines was not
always clear. It is best therefore to treat all Cathar views on the Devil
in topical order. Three basic points of view on the nature of the Devil
existed, the first being that he was absolutely independent of God.
This view made him so abstract that it was frequently modified or
replaced by one of the other two views. The second was that Lucifer
was a son of God, the brother of Christ. To defend this position the
Cathars sometimes used the parable of the prodigal son, with Christ as
the loyal son and Satan the one who wandered in sin; or the parable of
the vintner who has two sons, of whom one helps him in the vineyard
and the other does not.[63] The third view was that Lucifer was the son,

62. The fullest known absolute Cathar exposition is the *Liber de duobus principiis*, a
thirteenth-century Lombard treatise, ed. C. Thouzellier, *Le livre des deux principes*
(Paris, 1973). "The Secret Supper," Bogomil in origin but extant in many versions, is
another. E. Bozóky, ed., *Le livre secret des cathares* (Paris, 1980); R. Reitzenstein, ed., *Die
Vorgeschichte der christlichen Taufe* (Leipzig, 1929), pp. 297–311; W. Wakefield and A.
Evans, *Heresies of the High Middle Ages* (New York, 1969), pp. 458–465.

63. See the *Manifestatio heresis*, ed. A. Dondaine, "Durand de Huesca et la polémique anti-cathare," *Archivum fratrum praedicatorum*, 29 (1959), 228–276; Loos, pp. 34–
35; see also F. Talmage, "An Hebrew Polemical Treatise, Anti-Cathar and Anti-
Orthodox," *Harvard Theological Review*, 60 (1967), 323–348. Texts used by the Cathars

not of the good God, but rather of the evil principle. Here the evil principle becomes as remote and hidden as the hidden good Lord, while Satan/Lucifer is real and concrete. Lucifer somehow made his way into heaven and wormed his way into God's confidence, obtaining the post of his steward (here the Cathars used the parable of the unjust steward). He seduced the angels (or, in another version, created them). But this whole construction, making Lucifer the son of the evil principle instead of the evil principle itself, is meaningless, for in that case Lucifer/Satan is not the "true" Devil at all and his activities in no way explain the origin of evil.

Whatever the Devil's origin, all Cathar groups believed that he is prince of this material world, its maker and its ruler. All agreed that the true God created only spirit. The absolutists said that the Devil created the material world at the same time as God created the spiritual world or earlier; the mitigated dualists said that God created the spiritual cosmos first and then the Devil imitated it crudely by making formless matter and molding it into creatures; he could give these unfortunate things no life, so he went to heaven to seduce the angels so as to stuff them into inanimate matter and procure a captive population for this earth.

Human bodies are a particularly repulsive manifestation of matter, for the Devil creates them for the purpose of incarcerating captured spirits inside them—the fallen angels or (in some versions) the souls descended from the fallen angels. Sex is a diabolical invention to engender new bodies to serve as more prisons for souls. The human body is a gross indignity foisted upon us by Satan.

The God described in the Old Testament is not the true, good God at all, but the Devil himself. Anything attributed in the Pentateuch to God really refers to the Devil. This the Cathars deduced from the following contrasts: the New Testament God of love is a contradiction of the vindictive Old Testament God; the Old Testament God is changeable; the Old Testament God is cruel; the Old Testament God set up a tree of temptation for Adam and Eve; the Old Testament God regretted having created humanity. Most of all, the Old Testament

---

to establish the divine origin of Lucifer: Ez. 35.3; Ps. 46.10, 80.9–10, 81.1, 95.5; Mal. 2.11; Mt. 2, 21.28; Jn. 8.44, 14.30; 2 Cor. 4.3–4; Eph. 2.3, and others. "Lucifer" is the name that the Cathars preferred for the Devil, for it hints at his divine origin. It may be that this Cathar preference influenced the French and German dramas in which Lucifer appeared as king of hell and Satan as his servant (see Chapter 8 below).

God is called the creator of the material world, which is known to be wholly evil.[64]

Since bodies are evil, Christ could not have had a material body, nor could he have died on the cross for us. Rather, his saving act consisted in bringing us the news that we are in fact imprisoned in the flesh and that if we accept his illuminating knowledge we will be able when we die to escape the body and mount up into the true, spiritual world of God. Souls who do not accept this illumination are doomed to be reincarnated again and again until they do.

The Catholic response to dualism was summed up in the Fourth Lateran Council of 1215, the most influential ecumenical council of the Middle Ages, which treated the Cathar threat seriously enough to address it in its very first canon. The assembled fathers affirmed that the true, good God created all things from nothing. The Devil and the other demons were created good in their nature, but they made themselves evil by their own free will. The human race sinned in yielding to the Devil's temptation. At the resurrection at the end of the world all persons shall receive their just deserts, the evil suffering perpetual torment with the Devil, the good enjoying eternity with Christ.[65] The

---

64. Cathar opinions varied as to how much of the Old Testament was evil. It was agreed that the Pentateuch was evil, that Moses and the patriarchs were demons or demoniacally inspired, and that the Mosaic law was an imposture of the Devil. To get around the fact that Christ quoted Moses, some resorted to the device of two different Moses. Such beliefs may have encouraged the anti-Judaism that had been growing since the late eleventh century. Cathar skepticism extended to small portions of the New Testament as well—John the Baptist was sometimes regarded as another demonic figure.

65. Canon 1 of Fourth Lateran, Denzinger nos. 428–430: "Diabolus enim et alii daemones a Deo quidem natura creati sunt boni, sed ipsi per se facti sunt mali. Homo vero diaboli suggestione peccavit. . . . Recipiant secundum opera sua, sive bona fuerint sive mala, illi cum diabolo poenam perpetuale, et isti cum Christo gloriam sempiternam." Some tendentious recent writers argue that the council did not really intend to affirm the existence of the Devil but only that God was the sole creator. The singularity of the divine principle was certainly the main point, but Ozaeta has shown that Innocent III frequently referred to the Devil in his writings without the slightest doubt as to his existence—hardly surprising, since no theologian up to that time had ever expressed a doubt about it—and thus the doctrine was clearly intended to be implicit in the conciliar canon (J. M. Ozaeta, "La doctrina de Innocencio III sobre el demonio," *Ciudad de Dios*, 192 (1979), 319–336). Quay argues persuasively that the pope and council did indeed intend to define the existence of the Devil, the point being that the source of evil must be located outside both God and humanity (P. Quay, "Angels and Demons: The Teaching of IV Lateran," *Theological Studies*, 42 (1981), 20–45).

scholastics argued against the dualists that evil is nonbeing and that two opposed eternal principles are logically impossible. (1) Since evil has no essence it cannot be the source of anything. (2) Evil may diminish good but cannot consume it; otherwise nothing would be left in which evil could reside, and it would destroy itself. (3) Since evil has no being, it cannot cause anything except *per accidens* in that it resides in a good that causes something. (4) A principle of incoherence and disorder cannot exist, since these are mere negations of coherence and order. (5) If two eternal principles were absolutely balanced, the cosmos would be in stasis between them, but if they were *not* absolutely balanced, one would eternally exclude the other. (6) An absolutely evil being cannot exist, because absolute evil is absolute nothing; further, such a being is self-contradictory, because it would hate and cancel its own essence: were there anything in itself that it loved and cherished at all, it would not be entirely evil.[66] In fact an odd convergence of Catholic and Cathar views lies beneath the surface. If evil does exist absolutely, then it has its own kind of existence totally different from that of good. Thus, rather as antimatter is to matter, evil can be being in the Devil's sense but nonbeing in God's sense. Both sides were really affirming, in different terms, the utterly alien, non-Godness of evil, but rational discussion degenerated into angry conflict. The real action of evil, however defined, was demonstrated in the ruthless extirpation of the Cathar religion by crusade and inquisition.

Other heresies contributed little to the concept of evil, though many of the accusations that became standard during the witch craze were lodged originally against heretics. The most common of such accusations were sexual orgy, sacrifice to the Devil, infanticide, and cannibalism. Though heretics may have occasionally committed some of these crimes, historians agree that organized, widespread Satanism did not exist. The belief in such things seems to be the result of a combination of antiheretical propaganda with negative psychological projection. The ancient tradition that heretics were at least unwitting servants of the Devil and part of his mystical body encouraged such illusions. The elements of demonization of heretics had long existed in the theory that those opposed to the church were followers of Satan,

---

Quay's article also presents an excellent summary of modern views. On the councils see J. Alberigo, J. Dossetti, P. Joannou, et al., *Conciliorum oecumenicorum decreta*, 3d ed. (Bologna, 1973).

66. Anselm, *Monologion*, 4; Aquinas, *ST* Ia.2.3, 5.3, 48.3, 49.3, 65.1; Aquinas, *Summa contra gentiles (SCG)*, 3.7, 3.15.

Satan, king of hell, tortures the damned while he is bound to a fiery grill, as in the *Vision of Tundale*. ...mination from the *Très riches heures du Duc de Berry*, Burgundy, fifteenth century. Courtesy of the ...sée Condé, Chantilly, and Photographie Giraudon.

and in an era when the diabolical presence was felt to be particularly immediate, demonization became intense.

Jews and Muslims were also demonized, Jews more often because of their more immediate presence in the cities of western Europe. Jews were accused of kidnapping and sacrificing Christian children, desecrating the Eucharist or holy images, and poisoning wells. The blame for the crucifixion of Christ was laid upon them (rather than upon all humanity), and their persistence in refusing to accept Jesus as the Messiah was held to be a sign that Satan dwelt among them, hardening their hearts.[67]

One of the questions that must be asked is what effects belief in the Devil has. To what extent was Christian diabology responsible for the vicious anti-Semitism of the late Middle Ages, Renaissance, and Reformation? It seems to have borne bitter fruit. Yet if no idea of the Devil had existed, the course of anti-Semitism would probably have been little different. First of all, it had as many social as religious causes. Second, the religious causes consisted of ancient barriers between Jews and Christians, each group excluding the other from its community. Without a Devil, Christians would still have excluded

67. On the Devil and the Jews see M. Barber, "Lepers, Jews, and Muslims: The Plot to Overthrow Christendom in 1321," *History*, 66 (1981), 1–17; B. Blumenkranz, "La polémique antijuive dans l'art chrétien du moyen âge," *Bolletino dell'Istituto Storico Italiano per il medio evo e archivio Muratoriano*, 77 (1965), 21–43; N. Cohn, *Europe's Inner Demons* (London, 1975); G. Langmuir, "From Ambrose of Milan to Emicho of Leiningen: The Transformation of Hostility Against Jews in Northern Christendom," in *Gli Ebrei nell'Alto Medioevo* (Spoleto, 1978), pp. 313–373; G. Langmuir, "Medieval Anti-Semitism," in H. Friedlander, ed., *The Holocaust: Ideology, Bureaucracy, and Genocide* (Millwood, N.Y., 1980), pp. 27–36; R. Mellinkoff, "Cain and the Jews," *Journal of Jewish Art*, 6 (1979), 16–38; R. Mellinkoff, *The Horned Moses in Medieval Art and Thought* (Berkeley, 1970); R. Mellinkoff, *The Mark of Cain* (Berkeley, 1981); R. Mellinkoff, "The Round-Topped Tablets of the Law: Sacred Symbol and Emblem of Evil," *Journal of Jewish Art*, 1 (1974), 28–43; L. Poliakov, *The History of Anti-Semitism*, vol. 1 (New York, 1974), esp. pp. 124–169; F. Raphael, "Le juif et le diable dans la civilisation de l'Occident," *Social Compass*, 19 (1972), 549–566; "La représentation des juifs dans l'art médiéval en Alsace," *Revue des sciences sociales de la France de l'Est*, 1 (1972), 26–42; J. Trachtenberg, *The Devil and the Jews* (New Haven, 1943). See Chapter 10 below for demonization during the witch craze. See also B. Blumenkranz, *Juifs et Chrétiens dans le monde occidental 430–1096* (Paris, 1960); B. Blumenkranz, *Le juif médiéval au miroir de l'art chrétien* (Paris, 1966); I. Schachar, *The Judensau* (London, 1974); D. Iancu-Agou, "Le diable et le juif," in *Le diable au moyen âge* (Paris, 1979), pp. 261–276. On the demonization of Muslims, see H. Backes, "Teufel, Götter, und Heiden in geistlicher Ritterdichtung," in A. Zimmermann, ed., *Die Mächte des Guten und Bösen* (Berlin, 1977), pp. 417–441. Muslims were identified as pagans and therefore absurdly accused of idolatry. Eulogius of Córdoba called Mohammed an *angelum Satanae et praevium Antichristi*, "angel of Satan and precursor of the Antichrist" (Backes, p. 426).

Jews, blamed them for the crucifixion, and regarded them as sinners cut off from the mystical body of Christ, the corporation of the saved. Diabology was a handy weapon, but it was just that: a weapon, not the cause, of anti-Semitism, which has recently flourished independently of Christian diabology. Christianity's theological tradition bears much responsibility for anti-Semitism, but diabology is not the chief culprit. In fact, as the Devil has faded in recent centuries, the projection of evil upon others has increased. If we have no Lucifer on which to project our shadow, we choose Jews, capitalists, Catholics, communists, Russians, Arabs, blacks—the list is long, though Jews have always been unfortunate enough to be at the top of it. The concept of the Devil is an effect, not a cause. Both the image of the Devil and the demonization of minorities seem to draw upon a sink of idiotic cruelty within ourselves.

In the mid-thirteenth century, when these turmoils were in temporary abeyance, the most influential of the scholastics appeared, Thomas Aquinas (1225–1274), one of the most coherent, precise, and inclusive philosophers of all time. Thomas' *Commentary on the Sentences* dates from the 1250s; his greatest works were produced in the period after 1259: the *Summa contra gentiles*, the *Summa theologiae* and his treatise *De malo* (*On Evil*). His prodigious intellectual activity was abruptly terminated on December 6, 1273, when he had a mystical experience that led him to view all that he had written as straw by comparison. He ceased writing and died on March 7, 1274, on a journey to the Ecumenical Council in Lyon.[68]

Aquinas' view of the Devil is entailed in his search for understanding of evil. He beings with Neoplatonic assumptions long built into Christianity. God is pure actuality, wholly realized, perfect good, perfect being. Things exist insofar as they participate in the being of God. Therefore all that exists is good; goodness and being are essentially the same thing.[69] Nothing can properly be called evil in itself but

68. The bibliography on Aquinas, like that on Augustine and Luther, is enormous. For editions of the most relevant works and some modern works on his treatment of the Devil and evil, see the Essay on the Sources. The *Summa theologiae* dates from 1266–1273. The *Summa contra gentiles* has been dated variously: it may have been begun as early as 1259 or as late as 1270. See T. Murphy, "The Date and Purpose of the Contra Gentiles," *Heythrop Journal*, 10 (1969), 405–415. The *De malo* (*DM*) has been dated as early as 1259–1268 and as late as 1269–1272; see O. Lottin, "La date de la question disputée 'De malo' de saint Thomas d'Aquin," *Revue d'histoire ecclésiastique*, 24 (1928), 373–388.
69. *SCG* 4.39; 4.95; *ST* Ia.5.1: "bonum et ens sunt idem secundum rem" (the words "good" and "being" signify the same thing).

only insofar as it lacks being and goodness. Evil has no essence itself and can exist only in something good, as blindness can exist only in the eye.[70] Every natural thing moves naturally toward realizing itself fully by moving toward God, in which everything has its being. Evil is a pulling away from that natural movement, a turning away from the direction of reality toward the direction of nothingness. Every evil therefore proceeds from desire for a good, as when a father's wish for the security of his family causes him to embezzle money from his firm.[71]

Thomas distinguished among four evils. He dismisses (1) absolute evil (*malum simpliciter*) as an abstraction having no referent in reality, since absolute evil is absolutely nothing. (2) He also dismisses "metaphysical evil," the fact that created beings are necessarily less perfect than God, because such a situation is a logical necessity. He considers seriously (3) the evil of privation, a lack in a creature of what it ought by nature to have, such as sight in a woman, and (4) the evil of sin, a lack of moral good.

Plotinus and Augustine had argued that metaphysical evil was inherent in any cosmos. Because God's energy pours itself out into the cosmos to the fullest extent, it fills the cosmos with a plenitude of forms, the greatest possible diversity of creatures. This means that some creatures are closer to God/reality/goodness than others. To the degree that things are farther from God they are less real, less good, and therefore more "evil." Aquinas rejected this analysis decisively. "Something is called evil," he said, "only owing to the fact that it causes injury." It is not evil that some things are necessarily farther from God than others, not evil that a stone is not a fish or a cow is not a woman. Only when a creature is deprived of something properly belonging to it can we speak of an evil. "Evil is a given subject's failure to reach its full actuality." Each creature is naturally drawn to realize itself fully in God/being/good, and evil is the measure of the extent that it is blocked from this realization. A deaf woman is not a fully

70. *SCG* 3.11: "every evil is in a good thing"; *SCG* 3.7: "evil has no essence." *SCG* 1.71: "cognoscuntur mala per bona" (evils are known only through the good they inhabit); *ST* Ia.5.1–3, Ia.47–49, IaIIae.19, Ia.2.3; *ST* Ia.5.3.2: "nullum ens dicitur malum inquantum est ens sed inquantum caret quoddam esse, sicut homo dicitur malus inquantum caret esse virtutis, et oculus dicitur malus inquantum caret actione visus" (nothing is called evil insofar as it is a thing, but insofar as it lacks something, as a man is called evil when he lacks virtue or an eye bad when it lacks sight).

71. Everything has being in God: *ST* Ia.48.1. Evil proceeds from desire for good: *SCG* 2.162, 3.10, 3.13–14; *ST* Ia.49.2, IaIIae.19.

realized woman, so deafness is an evil in a woman. A woman lacking hearing lacks something proper in a woman and so suffers a privation, but the fact that she does not possess angelic nature is a mere negation, not a privation. Of the two, Aquinas considers only privation evil.[72] Yet Thomas bowed to the older position in arguing that the diversity of the cosmos also entails degrees of corruptibility. In this sense a kind of metaphysical evil does come into play: everything is created good, but from some things the goodness departs more than from others.[73]

The center of Aquinas' teaching on evil is privation. Blindness is an evil, but it is lack of sight, not anything in itself. Only the lack of a good which a creature ought naturally to have is an evil.[74] Blindness in a jockey is an evil, but not lack of wings (however desirable these might be), because sight is natural to a jockey and wings are not. The problem with this notion of evil as privation is that it depends upon artificial Platonic categories that cannot be defined meaningfully. What is the normal state of water, liquid, solid, or gas? Is ice water deprived of liquidity, or is the water in my swimming pool ice deprived of its solidity? And where are the boundaries? It is not normal for a child to be blind, but it is normal for a blind child to lack sight. The difficulties in the Platonic, "realist" philosophy held by many of the scholastics have led in recent centuries to the demise of most such assumptions. Some modern writers have suggested defining natural evil out of existence by reserving the term *evil* to moral fault. But

---

72. *SCG* 3.11; 4.7; *ST* Ia.48.2: evil is not "sicut pura negatio sed sicut privatio" (not like pure negation but like privation). *ST* Ia.48.5: "Malum . . . est privatio boni" (Evil is privation of good). *ST* Ia. 48.3: "Non autem quaelibet remotio boni malum dicitur. Potest enim accipi remotio boni privative et negative. Remotio igitur boni negative accepta mali remotionem non habet, alioquin sequeretur quod ea quae nullo modo sunt mala essent; et iterum quod quaelibet res esset mala ex hoc quod non habet bonum alterius rei. Sed remotio boni privative accepta malum dicitur, sicut privatio visus caecitas dicitur" (Not every absence of good is an evil, for absence of good can be understood both as privation and as negation. Absence of good in the sense of negation is not evil, for otherwise things that simply did not exist would be evil, and other things would be evil just because they lacked the quality appropriate to something else. But the absence of good in the sense of privation is an evil, as blindness can be seen as a privation of light).

73. *SCG* 3.71; *ST* Ia.48.2.

74. *ST* Ia.48.3: "subjectum mali sit bonum"; *SCG* 3.3–15; *SCG* 1.71: "malum non dicit esse nisi inquantum est privatio boni" (one does not call something evil except insofar as it is the privation of good); *DM* 1.1: "malum . . . non est aliquid, sed est ipsa privatio alicuius boni" (evil is nothing in itself; it is the privation of a certain good); *ST* Ia.49.1: "malum enim est defectus boni quod natum est et debet haberi" (evil is the lack of a good that the creature ought to have according to its nature).

Thomas had the courage to recognize natural evils as real. Cancer is an evil because it causes suffering; to define *evil* in such a way that cancer is not "evil" does not alleviate the problem of evil, since it leaves us with the cancer and the suffering it causes. If Thomas had, for example, defined blindness as a simple negation of sight in a *blind person* rather than as privation of sight in a *person* he might have avoided a Platonist pitfall, but he would have evaded the problem of evil in an unworthy, and meaningless, manner.

But how then reconcile the existence of cancer with that of a good God? At the very beginning of the *Summa theologiae* Thomas admits that the existence of evil in the cosmos is the best argument against the existence of God.[75] To this he opposed the five rational proofs for the existence of God and then turned back to the problem of reconciling the existence of God with that of evil.

God is responsible for the entire cosmos. No other principle can exist, no independent cause of evil or *summum malum*. Total evil is total nonbeing; it is nothing. Evil is ultimately dependent upon good. Every evil has to be based on some good, and that element of good renders it not entirely evil. Anything that exists is good at least to the extent that it exists. Evil, being nothing, can cause nothing, so every evil is caused by a good. The most evil possible being would seek its own utter destruction and so perish. God, who is infinite, annihilates his opposite—totally, so that it never exists at all. The Devil therefore cannot be an entity independent of God. He must be a being whose being comes from God and is basically good no matter how perverted.[76] Everything that exists or occurs in the cosmos is the direct result of God's will, except only the moral acts of free-will creatures. No blind fate exists, no chance, no random events.[77] To what extent is God

75. *ST* Ia.2.3: "videtur quod Deus non sit. Quia si unum contrarium fuerit infinitum totaliter destruetur aliquid. Sed hoc intelligitur in hoc nomine Deus quod sit quoddam bonum infinitum. Si ergo Deus esset, nullum malum inveniretur. Invenitur autem malum in mundo. Ergo Deus non est" (it seems that God does not exist, for if any contrary is infinite, it destroys its contrary. But God is defined as infinite good. Thus if God existed, evil would not. But evil does exist. Therefore God does not).

76. *SCG* 3.15; *ST* Ia.49.2–3.

77. *ST* Ia.22.2. Thomas would interpret modern theories of random motion as Einstein did: that some principle of causation must be operating in or through what appears to be random. This is not an assumption of quantum theory, but nothing in quantum theory suggests that randomness may not be compatible with order. The idea of randomness is, like all other ideas, a product of the human mind and simply describes a situation in which the observer presently does not (and possibly can never)

responsible for each category of evil? Since "metaphysical" evil is not really evil, the question is the extent to which God is responsible for *natural* evil and for *moral* evil.

Every evil has a cause.[78] Using Aristotelian terms, Thomas argues that evil lacks a formal or final cause, being nothing in itself, but it does have a material cause—the good in which it resides—and an efficient cause—the agent that brings out the defect. Natural evil always has a natural cause. Any defect in nature is caused by some other preceding defect in nature. It seems that God is ultimately the cause of such defects. But these defects are only accidental by-products of a good. Bacteria cause suffering in others only *per accidens:* they are good in themselves. A boulder, good in itself, causes pain *per accidens* by rolling onto a passing car. God never wills the defect, the evil, but only the good in which it resides. God can be said to be the cause of natural evil only *per accidens.* Having no defect in himself, God cannot be the direct cause of any. He wills no evil; yet he also does not will evils to disappear. What he does, then, is permit evils to occur for a greater good; his providence extracts good from every evil.[79] The perishability and corruptibility of creatures are necessary in a cosmos diverse enough to express and reflect its divine creator fully. A cosmos in which nothing were perishable would be static and monolithic. The spider could not live without eating the fly; the weasel would perish unless it devoured the mouse. "Tell that to the mouse" is not an

---

scientifically observe causation for certain events (for example, the emission of alpha particles from an atomic nucleus) and therefore describes them as random and deals with them only statistically. Randomness is a statement about the limitation of the observer's powers rather than a statement about the nature of the cosmos. Both the statement that the universe is ordered and purposeful (a cosmos) and that it is not (in that case it is a chaos) are compatible with randomness. Further, seemingly random events produce a resonance, so that randomness on a microlevel seems always to produce order at a higher level, as anyone using chi-square operations knows. Science may or may not ever discover a principle operating behind apparent randomness. In any event, theology has no problem with randomness, for it does not and cannot contradict the idea of a governing principle. My thanks to Charles Musès and David Darwazeh for discussing this problem with me.

78. *ST* Ia.49.1: "omne malum aliqualiter causam habeat."

79. *ST* Ia.49.1.3: "unde numquam sequitur malum in effectu, nisi praeexistat aliquod aliud malum in agente vel materia" (no evil is ever effected unless some other evil existed in the agent and/or the material). *CS* 2.46; *ST* Ia.19.9: "Deus igitur neque vult mala fieri, neque vult mala non fieri, sed vult permittere mala fieri. Et hoc est bonum" (God neither wills evils to be done or not to be done, but he permits them to be done for the greater good). Cf. *ST* Ia.2.3.

adequate retort, because the theory takes the mouse's suffering fully into account. It is simply not possible to build a cosmos bursting with life and vigor without corruptibility and perishability and the suffering they entail.[80]

Thomas' God, then, does not will natural evil, but he accepts it as the necessary price for the existence of the cosmos. Is that existence worth so much suffering, or is so much suffering compatible with the idea of a good God? Thomas assumed so. Not everyone would agree. But removing God from the equation does not avoid the problem of evil. The argument against the existence of God strikes not only at God but at all ideas of a cosmos, a universe that is in any way rational, orderly, or purposive. No orderly cosmic principle could produce such a flawed universe. The argument from evil, if it is valid, destroys the notion of all cosmic principles, not just the one we call God.[81] By destroying all order and principle it renders all judgments of value completely subjective. It leaves us with no reason whatever to condemn an extermination camp or a black-baiting sheriff. And then a curious thing happens: the original argument is destroyed by a paradox. If no order or purpose exist, all human values and aspirations are absurd, and good and evil exist only as subjective constructs of human minds. Since evil, then, does not exist objectively, it cannot be adduced against the existence of God. The argument from evil is circular and invalid. One may still deny any order in the cosmos and thus the existence of God, but one may not logically use the argument from evil against the existence of God. On the other hand, one maintaining the existence of God must offer an explanation for the existence of natural evil, and this Thomas' privation answer fails to do, for it is possible to conceive of a diverse cosmos that contains and limits suffering to a much greater extent than does this cosmos. The mouse, for example, might not have to suffer fear or pain but instead find happiness in offering itself up to the weasel.

Moral evil (*culpa*) raised other incongruities.[82] On the one hand

---

80. *ST* Ia.46.1.3, Ia.47.1, Ia.65.21; *CS* 1.39.2; 1.46.1.3.

81. E. Harris, *The Problem of Evil* (Milwaukee, 1977), pp. 4–5: "A world that engenders human beings who seek fulfillment in valued ends, yet implacably frustrates their desires [is irrational]. Either human aspirations must be absurd and unnatural . . . or . . . it must be a perverse world."

82. Thomas distinguished between *poena*, a privation in a morally free creature not proceeding from choice, e.g., lack of analytical ability, and *culpa*, a fault involving free choice of the will. *ST* Ia.48.5: "culpa habet plus de ratione mali quam poena" (culpa is more properly evil than poena). Aquinas' poena, by the way, applies only to defects in rational creatures, not in lower creatures.

Thomas wanted to assert that everything in an ordered universe has a cause, but on the other he wanted to affirm free will and to absolve God of responsibility for sins. The first tendency led him to assert that moral evil was a form of privation and that some defect in the will and/or intellect must be the cause of sin. (This led him to mix, as Augustine had done, ontology and morality.) Virtue draws us toward reality, actualization, and happiness; sin pulls us toward the void. But if a defect in will or intellect causes the sin, what is the cause of the defect? The answer has to be either some other defect or God.[83] The second tendency led in the other direction: God cannot in any sense be the cause of sin. Sin is not caused by God or by any precondition, but by a free act of the will. Now, will (*voluntas*) is drawn naturally toward God, but in intellectual and rational creatures voluntas has an attachment, free will (*liberum arbitrium*), which can affirm, suspend, or ignore the natural movement of voluntas. Moral evil, sin, is the knowing, free choice of evil.[84]

Aquinas sought to reconcile these two tendencies. To solve the problem he needed to isolate a defect that was voluntary (otherwise it would have a cause in nature) but not evil in itself (for then it would itself be the sin and require a cause). Without these qualifications, an infinite recession of causes would result and offer no solution. He found what he wanted in the deliberate refusal of a free creature to consider the rule, measure, and harmony of God's cosmos. This refusal is wholly free, but it is not a sin, for only an act can be a sin. It is a simple negation, not a privation; it is free, not rooted in nature. This uncaused defect may then cause the sin, which is an evil action that the will takes while it is refusing to consider the rule. The solution is brilliant, but in perspective it works less well than Anselm's simple insistence that no cause of sin exists. The voluntary decision to set the rule aside could itself be seen as evil (though not as complete an evil as the act that follows); not only reason, but Jesus' condemnation of sins "in the heart" would support such a view. In Aquinas' solution God is not responsible for moral evil, because moral evil is the free and direct choice of the agent. God's predestination and providence govern the entire cosmos, but his providential plan embraces free will and its consequences.[85]

83. *DM* 1.3–4, 16.2; *SCG* 3.4, 3.16.2; *ST* IaIIae.1–5, IaIIae.75–80.
84. *ST* IaIIae.6–17 (esp. 13.6), IaIIae.78.1, IaIIae.79.1.2; *SCG* 3.10.
85. *DM* 1.3, 16.2.4–7; *SCG* 3.71–73, 159, 163; *ST* Ia.22–23. Aquinas here opposed Abelard's subjectivist view and insisted that sin involved action and a thing evil in itself rather than motive only (*ST* IaIIae.19–20). See J. F. Dedek, "Intrinsically Evil Acts:

Aquinas was inconsistent on the question of whether angels could sin naturally. God cannot sin by definition; creatures without intellect or reason cannot sin, because they lack free will; but humans (free, rational creatures) and angels (free, intellectual creatures) are able to sin.[86] Had God confirmed all angels and humans in grace so that sin could not exist, freedom would have been a sham, and unless there is free choice to do good, moral good is a sham.[87] Angels therefore are capable of sinning naturally. Yet angels cannot sin, because they are pure spirit and so cannot suffer any defect of intellect. Unlike humans, rational creatures who need to think things out, purely intellectual creatures know things surely by immediate intuition. Angels therefore cannot sin naturally.[88] Thomas could have resolved the dilemma by applying to angels the free-will explanation of sin he evolved for humans. The Devil could have known that it was appropriate to follow God's will yet chosen to set it aside anyway, for no reason other than malice. Instead, Thomas took another, unnecessarily complex, approach. The Devil could not sin naturally, but he was able to sin supernaturally.[89] God presented Lucifer with a gift of supernatural

---

An Historical Study of the Mind of St. Thomas," *The Thomist*, 43 (1979), 385–413.

86. Lacking bodies, however, angels are not tempted by bodily passions. *ST* Ia.59.4, 63.1; *CS* 2.5.1.1, 2.3.1.1–2, 2.8, 4.44.3; *SCG* 4.90.

87. Demons (fallen angels) can sin: *SCG* 3.108–110. A ministorm blew up among Thomists in the 1950s over the issue of the peccability of the angels, some steadfastly trying to find an underlying consistency. But Thomas was arguing two opposing lines of thought. See, for example, C. Courtès, "La peccabilité de l'ange chez Saint Thomas," *Revue thomiste*, 53 (1953), 133–163; A. Hayen, "Le péché de l'ange selon Saint Thomas d'Aquin," *Teoresi*, 9 (1954), 83–176; Philippe de la Trinité, "Du péché de Satan et de la destinée de l'esprit," in Bruno de Jésus-Marie, ed., *Satan* (Paris, 1948), pp. 44–97; Philippe de la Trinité, "Réflexions sur le péché de l'ange," *Ephemerides carmeliticae*, 8 (1957), 44–92; J. de Blic, "Saint Thomas et l'intellectualisme moral à propos de la peccabilité de l'ange," *Mélanges de science religieuse*, 1 (1944), 241–280; J. de Blic, "Peccabilité de l'esprit et surnaturel," ibid., 3 (1946), 163. The Devil was an angel, perhaps the highest: *DM* 16.3–4; *CS* 2.3–11; *ST* Ia.63.7. A purely intellectual substance, he was created good in his nature and with free will.

88. *SCG* 3.108–110.

89. *ST* Ia.58.5: "et in his quae naturaliter ad rem pertinent, non decipiuntur; sed decipi possunt quantum ad ea quae supernaturalia sunt" (the angels cannot sin naturally, but they can sin in regard to supernatural things). *DM* 16.3: "peccatum diaboli non fuerit in aliquo quod pertinet ad ordinem naturale, sed secundum aliquid supernaturale" (the Devil's sin did not relate to the natural order, but to the supernatural order). Aquinas defined the supernatural sharply (unlike today's blurry usage): it is anything that goes beyond what is proper to a creature's nature. Angels and demons are not supernatural but a part of nature. Still, God may give them supernatural grace, i.e., grace transcending their natural powers.

grace that would have conferred beatitude upon him. Having perfect intellect, Lucifer well knew that this was better than any natural happiness, but he chose to set aside consideration of the highest good and to act in the absence of that consideration. This was his sin.[90]

The Devil's sin has both content and quality. The content is his choice to reject God's free gift of supernatural grace in order to pursue natural happiness. It was impossible that the Devil, one of the highest angels, should have believed that he could actually equal God. He wanted to be like God, not in the sense of being equal to his Maker, but in the sense of being free to command his own salvation, to obtain his own beatitude by his own powers, and immediately, at the moment he wanted it. In this way he wished to be independent of God. Duns Scotus disagreed, arguing that the Devil could have wished to be equal to God even though he knew that he could not be. If I will to rob a bank but refrain only because I judge that I cannot succeed, this conditional act of will on my part is fully sinful. The Devil's will to equal God, restrained only by his knowledge that he could not succeed, was fully sinful.

The quality of the Devil's sin is pride, which lay in his wish to seize happiness through his own resources, to be like God in being master of his own fate, and to owe no debt of gratitude to the Lord. Again Duns demurred, arguing that although the Devil's sin involved pride, it also involved the other sins, chiefly lust, for Lucifer loved himself beyond all order and reason.[91]

Lucifer's sin did not take place at the moment of creation, for that would allow his free will no scope, and God would be responsible for creating him sinful. It must therefore have occurred after a moment's delay, a moment when the angel realized that he was not God, that his

90. *ST* Ia.63.1.4: "non cum ordine debitae mensurae" (not within the order of due measure).

91. Pride brought envy of God and humanity. *ST* Ia.63.2: "nisi per hoc quod in tali affectu superioris regula non servatur; et hoc est peccatum superbiae"; *ST* Ia.63.3: "voluit hoc habere per virtutem suae naturae, non ex divino auxilio secundum Dei dispositionem" (he wanted to obtain his happiness through the powers of his own nature, without divine help, as God wished it). *ST* Ia.13: the only two sins of which angels are capable by nature are pride and envy. *CS* 2.5.1, 2.21.1: pride and envy. Duns' discussion of Satan's wish to be God's equal is in *Reportata Parisiensia*, 2.6.1 and in his *Commentary on the Sentences*, 2.4–7. Duns divides acts of will into two kinds: (1) *simplex*, in which one wills a deed one believes one can accomplish; this is an efficacious act; (2) *cum conditione*, in which one wills a deed one cannot or thinks one cannot accomplish. In *Reportata*, 2.6.2, Duns argues that the chief element in Lucifer's sin was lust, in that he loved himself inordinately.

being depended upon God, and that he had the choice of accepting this state of dependence or not.[92] This is an astute extrapolation from human experience. The rage that occurs when we first discover that we are not God—that our will need not be done, that we will be disliked and ignored, that we will die—is the primal rebellion. Alone among the creatures of this planet we humans are aware that we are not one with the cosmos, and in that awareness lies our alienation.

Aquinas, along with Cassian, Gregory the Great, Rupert of Deutz, and most other medieval writers, interpreted chapter 12 of the Book of Revelation to mean that after Satan's sin a war broke out in heaven, with the just angels under the leadership of Michael the Archangel driving the Devil and the other apostate angels out. This dominant theological opinion, however, was not reflected in the mystery plays, which portrayed the expulsion of the demons as being effected by the simple fiat of the divinity. An alternate view was that the war referred to in Revelation applies to the struggle of the church against worldly tyrants. But the war in heaven became the standard view for both later theology and later literature, notably for Milton's *Paradise Lost*.[93]

Thomas' rather abstract Devil is responsible for other evils in the cosmos only in an indirect way. The Devil's action upon us is only external. He can persuade and tempt us, but he can never infringe upon our freedom by causing us to sin. He can compel your body by external force, but he can never cause you to assent to evil. Since the Devil does persuade other creatures to sin, he may be called an indirect cause of sin, but this is only a manner of speaking, for the sinner himself or herself is always the direct uncaused cause of sin. The Devil therefore is not necessary to explain the act of sin. Moreover, he is not even necessary to explain temptation. If the Devil did not exist, humanity would still be subject to temptations to sin owing to the passions of the body.[94] Having already shown that an evil principle independent of God cannot exist, Thomas' logic leads him to a point where an evil being dependent upon God is also unnecessary to explain evil.

92. *ST* Ia.56.3; *ST* Ia.63.5–6: "in primo instanti omnes fuerunt boni, sed et in secundo fuerunt boni a malis distincti" (in the first moment all the angels were good, but in the next moment the good and evil angels were separated from one another).

93. *ST* Ia.63–68. See S. P. Revard, *The War in Heaven*. (Ithaca, 1980).

94. *ST* Ia.114.3; *ST* IaIIae.80: "manifestum est quod diabolus nullo modo potest necessitatem inducere homini ad peccandum" (it is clear that the Devil can in no way cause a human being to sin).

Christian Scripture and tradition require belief in the Devil, but natural reason and logic do not.

Being a Christian, Thomas could not doubt the existence of a being fully affirmed by Christian tradition. But if he is not the cause of sin, what is the Devil's function? Thomas' answer is that he is the head (*caput*) of all evil creatures, their chief, prince, ruler, and lord.[95] Not only is he their leader, but he incorporates them into one being with him. As the faithful are members of Christ's mystical body, united with him in grace, so sinners are members of Satan's mystical body, united with him in alienation. Not the principle or the cause of evil, Satan is the focal point and unifying force of all evil.[96]

The Devil and the other fallen angels were punished as soon as they sinned. They were cast out of heaven into the lower air and under the earth. The heart of their punishment is their awareness that they are deprived of their natural union with God.[97]

Once the angels' choice is made they cannot reverse it. The angels that chose to accept God's free gift of grace are confirmed forever in beatitude and are incapable of sin. Lucifer and his followers are forever damned and can never be saved.[98] Thomas passed over the older arguments for this position quickly so as to reach his own argument: that unlike humans, who are rational creatures relying on sense and reason, angels are purely intellectual beings who grasp the truth intuitively and immediately without the need for either sense or reason.

95. *ST* IIIa.8.7: "omnium malorum caput est diabolus, inquantum illum imitantur" (the Devil is the head of all evildoers insofar as they follow him). *ST* IIIa.8.8: this applies also to Antichrist, who is a manifestation of the Devil; the two are really one head of evil: "antichristus est membrum diaboli, et tamen ipse est caput malorum. Diabolus et antichristvs non sunt duo capita sed unum."

96. *ST* Ia.63.8; Lucifer does not cause the other angels to sin; he induces them to, but their choice is their own ("non quidem cogens, sed quadam quasi exhortatione inducens"). Fallen angels as demons: *CS* 2.6.1, 2.8.1. They form an infernal hierarchy: *ST* Ia.109; *CS* 2.6; 2.9. Lucifer induced, but did not cause original sin among humans: *ST* IaIIae.81–85, IIaIIae.163.1. See J. B. Kors, *La justice primitive et le péché originel d'après S. Thomas* (Paris, 1930); O. Magrath, "St. Thomas' Theory of Original Sin," *The Thomist*, 16 (1953), 161–189.

97. *ST* Ia.64.3–4. Some are now in hell to torment the damned; some are in the air to tempt humanity; at the end of the world after judgment they will all be confined to hell. *SCG* 4.90; *CS* 2.8, 4.43: though incorporeal, demons can suffer from fire, because God puts them under its power. On all these points Thomas mercifully seems to have taken little interest, and his arguments are perfunctory.

98. *ST* Ia.62.8; *ST* Ia.64.2: "mali vero peccantes sunt in peccato obstinati" (the evil angels who sinned are fixed in their sin).

Hence their understanding of the situation was absolutely complete at the first moment. No new information can ever reach them through sense, reason, or any other faculty. Because they know all that they can ever know, and because they made their choice in the full light of that knowledge, literally nothing can occur that could change their minds.[99] It is here that the argument for the supernatural rather than natural choice of the angels fits. For one objection is that if pure spirits are unable to change, they would have been unable to change and choose evil in the first place. In that event, of course, the angels would not have had free will. But Thomas' supernatural argument carries him further. It is true that angels were naturally unable to sin initially, since their intellect grasped the situation and their *voluntas* pointed toward God. But God offered them a choice beyond nature that allowed their *liberum arbitrium* to come into play. The simpler solution—that the angels' *liberum arbitrium* is always really free and could change at any time—would have violated the ancient tradition that Satan cannot be saved. Once set in sin, evil angels and damned humans live in total contempt for justice and joy and in burning hatred of the happiness of those who hope for glory. They loathe everything good or real and try to pull it down into the void.[100]

Thomas' salvation theory was based on Anselm's. Salvation involved satisfaction offered to God and restoration of humanity to communion with God. Christ's Passion freed us from the power that God permitted Satan to wield as a result of original sin, but the Devil never had any rights over us. The terms *ransom* and *redemption* may be used, Thomas said, so long as we understand that it is to God that Christ pays our debt and not to the Devil.[101] This argument was an effective

99. *ST* Ia.64.2. In this they are like the souls of humans after death, which are likewise immutable in choice because no new sensory or rational information can enter their minds, which are now pure spirit (*SCG* 4.93–95). For the older arguments, see *ST* IaIIae.80.4: "peccatum diaboli fuit irremediabile, quia nec aliquo suggerente peccavit, nec habuit aliquam pronitatem ad peccandum ex praecedenti suggestione causam" (no one tempted the Devil, and there was no preceding cause; the demons also cannot be saved by Christ, since his merits apply only to his own species, humanity).
100. *CS* 4.50.2.1: "in damnatis erit perfectissimum odium. . . . Mali de omnibus bonis dolebunt; unde et felicitas sanctorum considerata eos maxime affligit" (In the damned exists a perfect hatred. The evil resent every good thing, and the happiness of the saints particularly offends them).
101. *ST* IIIa.49.2; *CS* 3.19.1; *SCG* 4.39–42; *ST* IIIa.48.4: "et ideo per respectum ad Deum justitia exigebat quod homo redimeretur, non autem per respectum ad diabolum. . . . Non erat pretium solvendum diabolo, sed Deo. Et ideo Christus sanguinem suum, qui est pretium nostrae redemptionis, non dicitur obtulisse diabolo, sed Deo"

reconciliation of sacrifice and ransom theory, and, once again, the Devil was not an integral part of the solution.

The eclipse of the old ransom theory undermined the dramatic idea of the harrowing of hell, where Christ smashes the gates to free the souls of the dead. If Satan had no rights over the dead, then God had no need to combat him at the mouth of hell. Nonetheless, the image of the harrowing was so powerfully fixed in the imagination of the age that it persisted until relatively modern times, reinforced by the also popular image of Christ as victorious military/feudal commander: *Christus victor*.[102] Some earlier writers had argued the liberal position that Christ preached to the deceased pagans in hell and thus freed all the good souls who had lived and died before his advent. Abelard took the even more liberal view that the just pagans had all been illuminated and saved by the Word during their lives.[103] The majority of the scholastics, however, including Peter Lombard and Saint Bernard, took a narrower view, and so did Aquinas. Only those who believed in the Messiah could be saved, and that meant only the ancient Hebrews who had been faithful to the covenant. The good pagans, even the philosophers, are therefore not among the saved, though they were provided under the doctrine of limbo with a quiet and dignified after-life, deprived of beatitude yet free from care. Thus Vergil, who guided Dante through hell and purgatory, could not mount with him to heaven.[104]

Thomas could not resolve the ancient inconsistency in Christian thought between the idea that the Passion of Christ broke Satan's power and the observation that sin and evil continue. The Devil is allowed to tempt and punish us as before. Yet Christ's Passion protects all who have faith in him, so the Devil's efforts to tempt the faithful are vain.[105] A solution might have been found in an extrapolation from Abelard's position. That God was incarnate in one particular place and time is unimportant. Christ died for all human beings wherever they are in space or time. His sacrifice was built into the plan of salvation

---

(man had to be redeemed with respect to God's justice not with respect to the Devil. The price had to be paid to God, not the Devil. Therefore Christ offered up his blood, the price of our redemption, to God, not to the Devil).

102. G. Aulén, *Christus victor* (Paris, 1949).

103. *Sic et non* 84. See R. V. Turner, "Descendit ad Inferos: Medieval Views on Christ's Descent into Hell and the Salvation of the Ancient Just," *Journal of the History of Ideas*, 27 (1966), 173–194.

104. *ST* IIIa.52. Limbo is the highest circle of hell.

105. *ST* IIIa.49; *CS* 3:19.1.

for all eternity, and it affects those who came after the incarnation no more than those who came before. Thus no reason exists to expect an improvement in human behavior after the Incarnation, which affects all time and space.

Demons attack humans in order to impede the kingdom of God. Though they may actually on occasion do a small good in order to achieve a greater evil, they always intend the evil. God justly allows them to tempt and punish us, and though the Devil cannot cause sin he everywhere encourages it. Every sinner aids the Devil in his warfare against God and humanity, and every sinner, whether or not he knows it, is a servant of Satan.[106] All actions of the Devil are subject to the permission of God and the limitation of natural laws. The Devil can do nothing that violates natural process: he cannot change a prince into a frog. But he can work through nature, deluding the mind by suggesting illusions internally or by forming external illusions observable to the senses. To tempt us he may use external material objects such as gold or real estate, or he may act through internal ones such as bodily members and fluids. Though having no body himself, the Devil may assume a body in which he can (for example) have sexual intercourse, though neither as incubus nor as succubus can he engender offspring. He may also possess the body of a victim for a period of time, though he may never impair the free will or conscience of the possessed. Even the greatest philosophers may be led by the assumptions of their time to transgress the boundaries of good judgment.[107]

The ingenious solutions of the scholastics to the ancient questions of diabology were far too ingenious. They take us into a realm that paradoxically combines abstraction with gross detail. It goes far beyond the human experiences that provoked the idea of the Devil to begin with. Our experience is of the presence of something dark, cruel, idiotic, and destructive in the pits of our minds and the secret

---

106. *ST* Ia.114, IaIIae.80.2–3; *ST* Ia.65.1: the Devil is lord of this world, not in the sense of the universe but in the sense that those who lead a worldly life serve him ("non creatione, sed quia saeculariter viventes ei serviunt").

107. *CS* 2.8.1 on incubi and succubi; *SCG* 2.154; *ST* Ia.57, Ia.110–114, IIIa.43.2; *DM* 16.9. Earlier in the twentieth century, when Thomism was the semiofficial philosophy of the Catholic church, a debate raged between Thomists and anti-Catholics on the question of Thomas' responsibility for the witch craze. Now that the smoke has cleared it is evident that the debate was foolish from the start. Thomas clearly went to absurd lengths in describing the work of demons, but he did no more than follow a long tradition going back to the early fathers. The Christian theology that underpinned witch beliefs was not the invention of Aquinas.

places of the stars, raging for ruin. The scholastics present us with a pure intellect, setting aside the rule of order for a fatal moment. Can this explain the child molester who, I hear on the radio as I write this paragraph, raped a four-year-old child and slashed his throat? They also present us with snickering demons who humiliate sleeping persons as incubi and succubi. Can this explain the magnitude of a power that may well destroy the earth with atomic weapons? For a concept to continue to live it must respond to human perceptions; here it nearly ceases to do so. Artists and mystics were able to grasp the diabolical reality more intensely and convincingly.

8 Lucifer in High Medieval Art and Literature

Art and literature followed, rather than led, the theology of the Devil, yet they dramatically enlarged and fixed certain points in the tradition. The effort to create artistic unity, to make the story a good one and the development of the plot convincing, led to a scenario in some ways more coherent than that of theologians. The Devil went through several movements of decline and revival in the central and late Middle Ages. The fading of Lucifer in the theology of the twelfth and thirteenth centuries was matched by the growth of a literature based on secular concerns such as feudalism and courtly love, and later by the growth of humanism, which attributed evil to human motivations more than to the machinations of demons. Thus many of the greatest writers and works—Chrétien de Troyes, Wolfram von Eschenbach, Hartmann von Aue, and Chaucer; the *Chanson de Roland*, the *Nibelungenlied*, and *El Cid*—usually treated the Devil in a perfunctory manner or as a metaphor for the vices or evil in general. On the other hand the colorful and concrete Devil of the desert fathers, Gregory, and Aelfric remained alive in homiletic literature and in the poetry and drama that drew upon homiletics, liturgy, and theology. The triumph of free-will nominalism in the fourteenth and fifteenth centuries and the terrifying famines and plagues of the same period made the Devil an intensely threatening figure in much of later medieval art and literature.[1]

The pictorial arts followed theology less closely than did literature. Pictorial artists tend to think less in conceptual terms than poets or philosophers, and the Devil's shape depends in part upon the materials used: in sculpture, a human or quasi-human form is easier to portray than a little, black imp; in the cramped confines of an illuminated manuscript the imp is easier; no ivory shows a black devil. Theology and literature permit a careful distinction to be made between the Devil and demons; in art, where precise theological distinctions are difficult to make, the amalgamation of the two is common.[2]

Efforts to trace the development of artistic representations of the Devil yield no clear results. Trends are mostly local in time and place and often reverse themselves. Until the eleventh century the Devil was generally portrayed either as a human or as an imp, and this tendency persisted in Byzantine art. In the West, beginning in England about 1000 and spreading to Germany about 1020 and then beyond, the Devil tends to be a monstrous composite of human and animal. The grotesque was brought to artistic heights in the fifteenth and sixteenth centuries by Derek Bouts, the Van Eycks, Hans Memling, Hiero-

---

1. Far too much material exists to allow more than a survey of the Devil in the art and literature of the period 1100–1500. One can only take representative samples and keep in mind that this is a history of the personification of evil, not a study of art, poetry, and theater in themselves. There is no room for excursions into the jungles of related topics such as the art of Bosch, the development of hell, limbo, or purgatory, the Antichrist, or the tradition of vision literature. On the Antichrist, see R. Emmerson, *The Antichrist in the Middle Ages* (Seattle, 1981), chap. 4, "Antichrist in Medieval Art," and chap. 5, "Antichrist in Medieval Literature." On the vision literature see D. D. R. Owen, *The Vision of Hell* (Edinburgh, 1970); on purgatory see J. LeGoff, *The Birth of Purgatory* (Chicago, 1982).

2. I follow writers better trained in art history than I, with special thanks to Joyce Galpern, Kris Haney, Ellen Schiferl, and others. See B. Brenk, *Tradition und Neuerung in der christlichen Kunst des ersten Jahrtausends* (Vienna, 1966); B. Brenk, "Teufel," *Lexikon der christlichen Ikonographie*, 4 (1972), 295–300; F. Klingender, *Animals in Art and Thought to the End of the Middle Ages* (Cambridge, Mass., 1971); J. M. Galpern, "The Shape of Hell in Anglo-Saxon England" (Ph.D. diss., University of California, Berkeley, 1977); G. Schiller, *Iconography of Christian Art*, 2 vols. (Greenwich, Conn., 1971–1972); H. Seidlmayr, "Art du démoniaque et démonie de l'art," in E. Castelli, *Filosofia dell'arte* (Rome, 1953), pp. 99–114; A. Wienand, "Heils-Symbole und Dämonen-Symbole im Leben der Cistercienser-Mönche," in A. Schneider, ed., *Die Cistercienser* (Cologne, 1974), pp. 509–554. I have also surveyed more than 450 representations of the Devil in Christian art from 1050 to 1500 in the Princeton Index of Christian Art, including illuminated manuscripts, paintings, frescoes, murals, ivories, glass, and sculpture.

nymous Bosch, Pieter Brueghel, Jan Mandyn, and Peter Huys. As has long been understood, the grotesque work of Bosch and others is no perversity but an exploration of the psychology of the unconscious in more or less traditional religious terms, set forth in terms of monsters and demons. It is also a moral statement of the problem of evil: Bosch portrays this world as a mirror of hell, in which sin, stupidity, and futility rule.[3] Bosch remained in the medieval didactic tradition of art. And this raises the question of the demonic in art. "Demonic" art can have two meanings: the portrayal of the demonic by artists such as Bosch, concerned to set a moral example to their viewers;[4] and art in which the artists themselves are consciously or unconsciously serving the demonic. In the latter, disharmony, meaninglessness, and distortion mirror the evil that obstructs God's plan for the cosmos, and the art is used not to satirize or repel but to allure and entrap.[5] The purpose of this chapter is to indicate the iconographic tendencies of the former.

Lucifer is sometimes closely associated with other threatening figures such as Hell or Death (after the eleventh century Death and the Devil are usually portrayed separately, though on occasion they still accompany one another, or the Devil's head is shown as a skull to suggest the association). Into the eleventh century Satan is usually human or humanoid; from the eleventh century onward he is more likely to be animal or a human/animal monster; from the fourteenth century becomes increasingly grotesque. The monstrous Devil, with horns on knees, calves, or ankles and with faces on chest, belly, or buttocks reflects Lucifer's inner moral monstrosity. The small, black imp common in the earlier Middle Ages persists but gradually yields to the grotesque.[6]

The Devil is usually black or dark, but the opposite is also common:

3. See M. Lazar, "Caro, mundus, et demonia dans les premières oeuvres de Bosch," *Studies in Art*, 24 (1972), 106–137.

4. See Galpern, pp. 29–31. Medieval artists, like monastic and mendicant homilists, often used scenes of horror to frighten viewers into leading a good life; Augustine had early recommended dwelling on scenes of hell in order to instruct the rustics.

5. See R. Hammerstein, *Diabolus in musica* (Bern and Munich, 1974), pp. 16–19; Seidlmayr, pp. 105–113.

6. The monstrous does not always indicate the demonic. The monstrous Devil blurs into the "monstrous races" of humanity (see above, Chapter 4), gargoyles, and simply comic grotesques. When the Devil has seven heads, crowned or uncrowned, or ten horns, the representation draws directly upon Rev. 12.3. Occasionally he will have three heads or faces, like Hekate (see DEVIL, p. 130) and in mockery of the Holy Trinity.

he is livid or pallid, a hue associated with death, heretics, schismatics, and magicians.[7] He is usually naked or wears only a loincloth, the nakedness symbolizing sexuality, wildness, and animality. His body is often muscular, often, too, very thin, but seldom fat; before the twelfth century he is occasionally handsome or pleasant looking. He is very seldom female, but he can disguise himself in any form he pleases.[8] As an animal, he is most frequently an ape, dragon, or serpent. The serpent with a human face appears in the art of many cultures; such representation seems to have become common in Christian art in the thirteenth century. The serpent's human head related it to Adam and Eve more convincingly; the artistic tradition may have drawn upon the theater, where the serpent had to be able to talk. It also symbolized the complicity in sin between human and Devil. In addition, misogynistic tradition emphasized Eve's guilt more than her husband's, so the serpent more often looked like Eve than like Adam.[9] His most common animal characteristic after the eleventh century was horns, which also still carried the ancient connotation of power.[10] The second commonest animal characteristic was a tail; the third was wings, divided about equally between the feathery wings appropriate to an angel and the sinister bat wings more fitting to the caverns of hell. The Devil's hair is often swept upward into spikey points, whether to represent the flames of hell or to refer to the practice of the barbarians, who swept their hair up into greased points in order to intimidate their enemies.[11] Demons have long, hooked noses, a charac-

7. See above, Chapters 4 and 6. For literary analogies, see Caesarius of Heisterbach, *Dialogus miraculorum*, ed. J. Strange (Cologne, 1851), 5.2 (pallor), and 5.5, 5.8 (shadowy).

8. Brenk, *Tradition*, pp. 178–179.

9. J. K. Bonnell, "The Serpent with a Human Head in Art and in Mystery Play," *American Journal of Archeology*, 21 (1917), 255–291. See Bonnell and J. M. Evans, *Paradise Lost and the Genesis Tradition* (Oxford, 1968), p. 170, for Peter Comestor's statement that the Devil chose the shape of a serpent with a maiden's face ("elegit etiam quoddam genus serpentis virgineum vultum habens"). Peter seems to have been the first to use this idea in his *Historica scholastica: Liber Genesis*, 21. See Chapter 9 below for the serpent on the stage.

10. See R. Mellinkoff, *The Horned Moses in Medieval Art and Thought* (Berkeley, 1970), for the continuation of the iconography of the horns of power into the Middle Ages; unfortunately the symbol was widely misunderstood, for the horns of Moses were thought to represent the evil of the Jews, and the Jews themselves then came to be depicted as horned.

11. The possessed in early Christian art sometimes are shown with hair sticking up into points. See Brenk, *Tradition*, pp. 132, 176. The motif goes beyond Europe: Japanese demons have similar upswept hair. See DEVIL, p. 100.

teristic transferred to Jews in the process of demonization. Other characteristics are hooves or paws, claws, hairiness, and goat legs (though demons' skin can also be leathery). The Devil rarely has an aura or halo (originally a mark of power, not necessarily of holiness). He can breathe fire and shoot arrows (like Death or elves) to kill the soul. Demons carry tridents, pitchforks, hooks, and other instruments of torture; their fearsome employment in hell as executioners of the damned was one of the commonest scenes in which they appear. Other frequent scenes were the exorcism of the possessed (though this became less common in the later Middle Ages, as interest shifted from biblical scenes to the immediate, current presence of the Devil in everyday life); the fall of the angels into hell, where they were transformed into twisted and scorched demons as they pelted down; Christ or Saint Michael spearing or trampling the Devil; the contest at the scales of justice between a demon and an angel over the soul of a dying person (an ancient motif in Egypt, where Anubis weighed the soul in the scale against justice [*ma'at*]). The most dramatic scene was the harrowing of hell, where Christ casts down the gates of hell; this scene transposed readily into that of the Last Judgment, where Lucifer is finally defeated and the souls of the blessed are led to heaven.[12]

From the eleventh century, medieval literature became increasingly diverse and sophisticated. Lyric, romance, epic, history, beast fables, and other genres now complemented, and to an extent supplanted, sermons and saints' lives. The variety is reflected in *The Canterbury Tales*, where Chaucer displayed a virtuoso control of numerous styles, genres, and levels of sophistication. In the eleventh century, Old English had been the only Western European language other than Latin with a substantial amount of serious literature, but by the next century French, Provençal, German, Italian, Spanish, and other vernacular literatures were emerging. This shift, celebrated in Dante's "De vulgari eloquentia," meant that writers such as Chaucer, Langland, Wolfram, and Chrétien composed in languages more natural to them than Latin and more readily available to a wide audience. Much was still being written in Latin—theology, history, philosophy, lyric poetry, hymns, liturgical drama, and homiletic literature (sermons and exempla)—but Latin was understood only by the clergy and a few other educated individuals. Therefore vernacular versions of saints' lives began to appear in the eleventh century, vernacular sermons were

12. Brenk, *Tradition*, p. 177.

composed, and liturgical plays were performed in the vernacular as well as Latin.

Homiletic, liturgical, and hagiographic literature was the hinge between traditional Latin genres and the new vernacular and between the theology of the elite and the beliefs of the uneducated public. Homiletic literature was popular, not in the sense that it derived from the uneducated, but in the sense that it was written to be understood by the people and took their experience into account. Theological ideas were blended with legendary materials and dramatic stories in order to make an impression upon the audience. Homiletic literature thus drew deeply from hagiography (saints' lives), which affected the idea of the Devil, for saints' lives were still much what they had been in the days of the desert fathers, when Satan was at large in the world and snuffling at every door. Ancient and medieval world views tended to perceive things as static rather than developing through time. All times were one in the mind of God, and all things and individuals on earth manifestations of his eternal ideas. A saint is a saint is a saint, just as a king is a king is a king. A king of one country in one period is just like a king of another country in another period, because essentially a king *really* is a representation of God's eternal idea of king. What saints did, therefore, remained the same through the centuries. The form of the saint's life had been set first by lives of the desert fathers such as Athanasius' *Life of Anthony* and then by medieval lives imitating them, such as Gregory the Great's *Life of Benedict*. Consequently the Devil played a lively role in medieval hagiography as the challenger and opponent of the saints and the chief of all evil forces, the power behind all sins, vices, and worldly concerns. While the Devil was paling among the theologians, he remained vivid in the saints' lives, and though he was always defeated, he retained his ability to terrify. Saints' lives, always popular, had long been a part of the liturgy on appropriate feast days. Preachers found in these colorful and dramatic stories an infinite number of moral exempla, and they realized that ghastly stories of hellfire were effective deterrents to sin. Far from playing down Lucifer's role as the theologians were doing, homilists played it up for dramatic and didactic purposes. But any notion that they were exploiting the idea to "control the poor" misses the point that the clergy were at least as terrified of the Devil as their flocks were. The influence of saints' lives on sermons and liturgy and upon the numerous genres, such as theater, that sprang from them, was one of the chief reasons for the Devil's continued grip on the mind of the later Middle Ages and Renaissance.

The literature includes exempla, sermons, and spiritual anecdotes for the instruction of novices. Alan Bernstein cautions that we must distinguish manuals of preaching and exempla from sermons actually given, for few sermons survive as actually presented. These genres included a wide range of topics. Caesarius of Heisterbach, for example, recounted stories dealing with the origins of the evil angels, their free will, their fall, their knowledge and powers, their temptations and corruption of souls, possession, means of protection against demons, the battle between demon and angel for custody of the soul of a deceased person, and punishment by demons of sinners in hell.[13]

The literature of visions of the other world, which goes back at least to the third century, produced in the eleventh a masterpiece, *The Vision of Tundale*, which influenced Dante and subsequent artistic and literary portraits of Lucifer. *Tundale* gives a thorough description of the torments of the damned in the fiery, sulphurous pit of hell, and offers

13. I am grateful to Professor A. Bernstein for letting me read his unpublished paper "Theology and Popular Belief: Confession in the Later Thirteenth Century" and for numerous suggestions and ideas, which form the basis of this paragraph. See also G. R. Owst, *Literature and Pulpit in Medieval England* (Oxford, 1961); J.-P. Perrot, "Le diable dans les légendiers français du XIIIe siècle," in *Le diable au moyen âge* (Paris, 1979), pp. 429–442; J. Poly, "Le diable, Jacques le Coupe, et Jean des Portes, ou les avatars de Santiago," in *Le diable au moyen âge*, pp. 443–460; J. Schneyer, *Repertorium der lateinischen Sermones des Mittelalters für die Zeit von 1150–1350, Beiträge zur Geschichte der Philosophie und Theologie des Mittelalters*, 8 vols. (Münster, 1969–1978); G. de Tervarent and B. de Gaiffier, "Le diable voleur d'enfants," in *Homenage a Antoni Rubio I Lluch*, vol. 2 (Barcelona, 1936), pp. 35–38; T. Wolpers, *Die englische Heiligenlegende des Mittelalters* (Tübingen, 1964); J.-T. Welter, *L'exemplum dans la littérature religieuse et didactique du moyen âge* (Paris, 1927); J.-T. Welter, *La tabula exemplorum secundum ordinem alphabeti* (Paris, 1926). Exempla are brief statements of themes that can be incorporated into sermons. See also A. V. Murray, "Religion among the Poor in Thirteenth-Century France," *Traditio*, 30 (1974), 285–324. The most important of these didactic works were the Dominican Stephen of Bourbon's *De diversis materiis praedicabilibus*, partially edited by Lecoy de la Marche, *Anecdotes historiques* (Paris, 1877); J.-C. Schmitt is editing the version in Paris, Bibliothèque Nationale, Lat. 15970. The Cistercian Caesarius of Heisterbach's *Dialogus miraculorum* was edited by J. Strange in 2 volumes (Cologne, 1851). Richalm of Schöntal, another Cistercian, was edited by B. Pez in his *Thesaurus anecdotorum novissimus*, 6 vols. (Augsburg, 1721–1729), vol. 1:2, col. 324ff. The "Legends of the Saints" of Jacques de Vitry became so popular all over Europe that they gained the name of "The Golden Legend." The edition is by T. Graesse, *Jacobi a Voragine Legenda aurea*, 2d ed. (Leipzig, 1850); see J. Greven, *Die Exempla aus den sermonen feriales et communes des Jakob von Vitry* (Heidelberg, 1914); G. Franklin, ed., *Die Exempla des Jacob von Vitry* (Munich, 1914).

two striking pictures of demons and one of Lucifer himself. Tundale saw "a beast of unbelievable size and inexpressible horror. This beast exceeded in size every mountain that he had ever seen. His eyes were shining like burning coals, his mouth yawned wide, and an unquenchable flame beamed from his face." He saw another demon having two feet and two wings, with a long neck, an iron beak, and iron talons. This beast sat atop a pool of frozen ice, devouring as many souls as he could seize. These souls, as soon as they were reduced to nothing in his belly, were excreted onto the frozen ice, where they were revived to face new torments. And at last Tundale saw

the prince of darkness, the enemy of the human race, who was bigger even than any of the beasts he had seen in hell before. . . . For this beast was black as a crow, having the shape of a human body from head to toe except that it had a tail and many hands. Indeed, the horrible monster had thousands of hands, each one of which was a hundred cubits long and ten cubits thick. Each hand had twenty fingers, which were each a hundred palms long and ten palms wide, with fingernails longer than knights' lances, and toenails much the same. The beast also had a long, thick beak, and a long, sharp tail fitted with spikes to hurt the damned souls. This horrible being lay prone on an iron grate over burning coals fanned by a great throng of demons. . . . This enemy of the human race was bound in all his members and joints with iron and bronze chains burning and thick. . . . Whenever he breathed, he blew out and scattered the souls of the damned throughout all the regions of hell. . . . And when he breathed back in, he sucked all the souls back and, when they had fallen into the sulphurous smoke of his maw, he chewed them up. . . . This beast is called Lucifer and is the first creature that God made.[14]

The most important development of the Devil in literary art oc-

14. On the vision literature, see M. Dods, *Forerunners of Dante* (Edinburgh, 1903); H. R. Patch, *The Other World* (Cambridge, Mass., 1950), esp. pp. 89–120. The most influential of these visions were *The Vision of Saint Paul*, originally third-century Greek and translated into Latin in the sixth century; the Irish version of Adamnán, ninth to eleventh century; the *Vision of Tundale* (Tnugdal), written in Germany by an Irishman in the twelfth century, and the *Purgatory of Saint Patrick*, twelfth century. The Latin and German versions of the *Vision of Tundale* are edited by A. Wagner, *Visio Tgndali: Lateinisch und Altdeutsch* (Erlangen, 1882). See also V. H. Friedel and K. Meyer, eds., *La vision de Tondale: français, anglo-normand, et irlandais* (Paris, 1907); E. Gardiner, "The Vision of Tundale: A Critical Edition of the Middle English Text" (Ph.D. diss., Fordham University, 1980); P. Dinzelbacher, *Vision und Visionsliteratur* (Stuttgart, 1981); D. D. R. Owen, *The Vision of Hell* (Edinburgh, 1970); H. Spilling, *Die Visio Tngdali* (Munich, 1975); J. C. D. Marshall, "Three Problems in the Vision of Tundal," *Medium Aevum*, 44 (1975), 14–22. For quotations, see Wagner, pp. 16, 27, 35. Compare A. di Paolo Healey, ed., *The Old English Vision of St. Paul* (Cambridge, Mass., 1978).

curred in the vernacular poetry of the later Middle Ages. The outpouring of such poetry was so vast that only a few of the most influential writers can be treated. Many of the great writers of epic and romance, such as Chrétien de Troyes, Wolfram von Eschenbach, and Hartmann von Aue treated the Devil only tangentially or metaphorically. But he was a negative center in the work of both Dante Alighieri and William Langland.[15]

Dante (1265–1321) is by common consent the greatest medieval poet and lay theologian. His *Comedy*, written in the last fifteen years of his life and called by later admirers the *Divine Comedy*, is a complex mystical poem in which the Devil, though seldom "on stage," is a powerful force operating throughout both hell and earth. Dante's diabology drew upon Christian tradition, scholasticism, vision literature, and Greco-Roman and Muslim thought.

The inner meaning of the *Divine Comedy* appears in its most striking feature: the structure of its cosmos. Dante's arrangement drew upon Aristotelian, Ptolemaic, and Neoplatonic philosophy and science, but the poet did not intend to write an astronomical, a geographical, or in any modern sense a physical or scientific treatise on the universe. Rather he wished to portray the cosmos according to its moral design. For Dante and his contemporaries the ultimate meaning of the cosmos is ethical, not physical, although as a careful artist he wished his ethical world to be as closely analogous to the physical universe as possible. In the *Comedy*, the physical cosmos is a metaphor of the real, ethical cosmos, rather than the other way round. Dante would not have been surprised or troubled to learn that no mountain of purgatory existed on the face of the physical globe, no cavernous hell in its depths. His intention was to describe the inner moral reality of the cosmos, not its external manifestations.

Dante's cosmos, like Ptolemy's, was arranged in a series of concentric spheres, the earth being the sphere at the center of the universe. Above the earth was the sphere of the moon and then in order those of Mercury, Venus, the sun, Mars, Jupiter, Saturn, the fixed stars, and the *primum mobile*, the sphere that moves the whole universe.

15. On medieval literature in general and on Dante and Langland in particular see the Essay on the Sources. On the influence of courtly love and lyric on Dante see T. Bergin, *Dante* (New York, 1965); on that of the scholastics see E. Gilson, *Dante et la philosophie* (Paris, 1939); on Muslim influence see M. Asín Palacios, *Islam and the "Divine Comedy"* (New York, 1926). On possible Indian influence see A. de Gubernaitis, "Le type indien du Lucifer chez le Dante," *Giornale Dantesco*, 3 (1895), 49–58.

Beyond that was heaven, the dwelling place of God, the angels, and the blessed. In the center of the earth is hell, and at the very center of hell, imprisoned in the darkness and the ice, is Lucifer.

With this cosmos Dante worked out a mystical vision not unlike that of Dionysius. Every being in the cosmos moves either toward God or toward the Devil. God is ultimately far up and out; the Devil is ultimately far down and in. When we are filled with our true human nature, which is made in the image of God and buoyed by the action of the Holy Spirit within us, we rise naturally up toward God, we spread out, widen our vision, open ourselves to light, truth, and love, with wide vistas in fresh air, clean, beautiful, and true (Paradise 1.135–138). The mystic rose at the threshold of heaven opens out infinitely and eternally. But when we are diverted by illusion and false pleasure, we are weighed down by sin and stupidity, and we sink downward and inward away from God, ever more narrowly confined and stuffy, our eyes gummed shut and our vision turned within ourselves, drawn down, heavy, closed off from reality, bound by ourselves to ourselves, shut in and shut off, shrouded in darkness and sightlessness, angry, hating, and isolated (Parad. 1.134). Each circle of hell as we descend is narrower and darker. There is nothing in that direction, literally nothing: silence, lack, privation, emptiness. God is expansion, being, light; Satan, drawn in upon himself, is nothingness, hatred, darkness, and despair. His isolation stands in utter contrast with the community of love in which God joins our minds with the first star (Parad. 2.29–30).

Dante's journey from the dark forest on the surface of the earth into the center of hell is a moral journey downward, in which he sees represented all the sins that draw the world, each individual, and Dante himself, downward toward ruin. Theologically one cannot go to hell and return, but one can understand and experience hell by grasping the nature of sin and its consequences. Understanding, one can change and transform one's life. When Dante at last reaches the horrible center, he turns. The poet vividly describes that painful turning on the grotesque flanks of Satan, a turning that heads him upward out of hell and toward the light, where at last he sees the stars again (Inferno 34.139: "uscimmo a riveder le stelle"). Dante's descent into hell is the story of everyman, drawn down by sin and then offered the chance of a metanoia, a conversion, a turning back to the light; it is also an allegory of Christ's descent into hell and his resurrection. Dante's central insight was that the cosmos is a moral as well as a physical entity, that it is in a state of tension between good and evil, as opposed to the modern, strangely anthropomorphic view that it is neutral and that evil is entirely limited to the individual human consciousness. For Dante, ethics rules the sciences as the primum mobile rules the heavens, and all knowledge is morally relevant (*Convivio* 3.15: "la moralitade è bellezza de la filosofia").

This cosmology, morally powerful as it is, nonetheless suffers from difficulties. The Neoplatonic scheme from which Christian cosmology largely derived was in origin a vertical, linear one with the One at the top, emanating the cosmos down rank by rank; at the bottom was *hyle*, pure matter, farthest away from the One and least real. (See figure 2.) By bending (as it were) this cosmos downward at the ends and making a circle or sphere out of it, this conception could be wedded to Ptolemy's cosmology. Here the earth was at the center, with the planetary spheres in orbit around it, then the sphere of the fixed stars, also in orbit, and outmost the primum mobile, the slowly moving sphere within which the whole cosmos turns. This scheme was adopted by most early Christian writers, who placed God out beyond the primum mobile, the earth at the center, and, usually, hell under the surface of the earth. It was logical (and original) of Dante to complete the vision by putting hell at the very center of the earth and Satan at the very center of hell. (See figures 3 and 4.)

The difficulty posed by this system is that it seems to place the Devil rather than God at the center of the cosmos. Dante addressed the difficulty in two ways. First and most important, he meant God to be placed at the real, moral center of the cosmos, but he could not represent this spatially and indeed went to pains to deny that the moral center can be located in space or time. It is not in space and has no pole (Parad. 22.67); heaven has no other "where" than in the mind of God (Parad. 27.106–110); it is the point at which all times are present (Parad. 17.17–18: "il punto a cui tutti li tempi son presenti"); the point

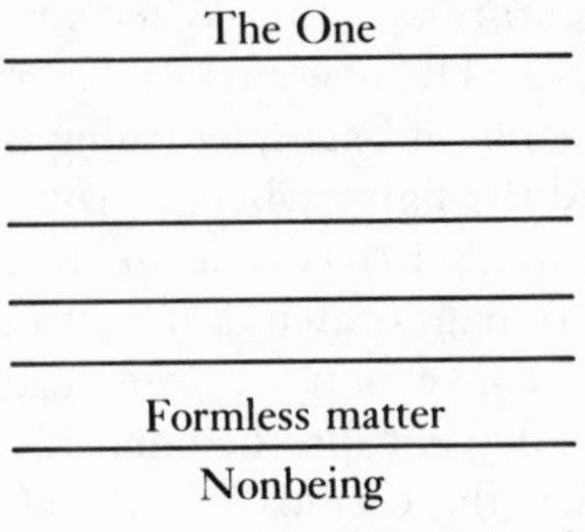

The One

Formless matter

Nonbeing

Figure 2. The Neoplatonic chain of being

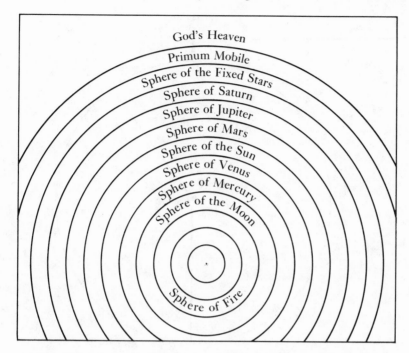

Figure 3. The heavenly spheres (adapted from William Anderson, *Dante the Maker*, London, 1980, p. 265)

at which every "where" and every "when" converge (Parad. 29.11–12: "là 've s'appunta ogne *ubi* e ogne *quando*"). As Freccero put it, Satan is the "center of the physical world and beyond the outermost circumference of the spiritual world," but God is "at the center of the spiritual world and is the circumference of the physical."[16] And of course Dante accepted the idea of Gregory the Great that God was deep inside every individual soul as well.

Each individual has the choice of opening himself or herself to the light or of closing himself off from it. Those who open themselves to the light have all their pretenses and defenses melted away like snow under sun, and then God fills them with such living light as seems to dance when you behold it (Parad. 2.109–111: "voglio informar di luce sì vivace, che ti tremolerà nel suo aspetto"). People also have the choice of aligning themselves along straight lines that look right up to God or

16. J. Freccero, "Satan's Fall and the *Quaestio de aqua et terra*," *Italica*, 38 (1961), 112–113.

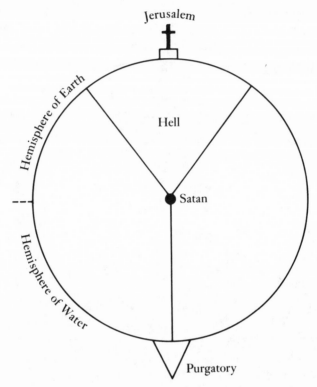

Figure 4. Earth in the *Comedy* (adapted from William Anderson, *Dante the Maker*, p. 254)

of twisting across the lines. It is as if the cosmos that God extends from himself is a sphere with radii running straight and true out from the divine center to the surface. God draws everyone and everything toward him, and everything when seen and used rightly bears toward him (Parad. 28.19: "tutti tirati sono e tutti tirano"; cf. Parad. 5.5–6). But individuals sometimes fail to see the point or recognize the goal. Then, following a false path, they swerve from the course in some other direction. The impulse that God implants in every one of us to seek him is thus diverted and misses its goal (Parad. 1.129–135). Whenever we are in the cosmos we can look straight along the radii toward the truth at its center; whenever we see straight, we see God. When we cut across the lines and force the pattern, our lives become more difficult, since we are going against the grain and trying to wrench the cosmos around to fit our own view of what it ought to be.

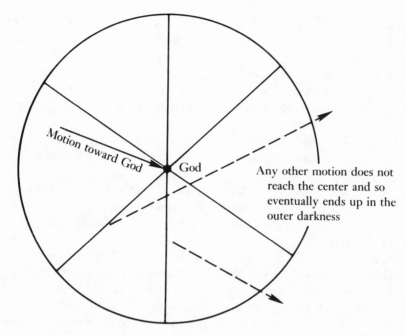

Figure 5. God as the focus of life

Within the figure:

Motion toward God

God

Any other motion does not reach the center and so eventually ends up in the outer darkness

The direction of such motion leads us inevitably away from God, for only motion toward the center can reach him; the trajectory of any other movement takes us sooner or later right out of the cosmos, out of community, love, and light, to the outer darkness from which no reentry is possible. For the light at the center is the only light; it is the light with which all other lights shine. "I believe, from the keenness that I felt from the living light, that I would have been ruined had I turned my eyes away from it" (Parad. 33.76–78). One whose eyes are open to that light could never consent to leave it for anything else, for it is the very life and wholeness of every thing (Parad. 33.100–105); it is the love that moves the sun and other stars (Parad. 33.145: "l'amore che move il sole e l'altre stelle"). The pathos and horror of Satan is that he is isolated forever from that love. (See figure 5.)

The second and more concrete resolution to the problem was to use Aristotelian physics, in which everything seeks its natural place in the universe, a view that Saint Augustine had approved.[17] From the

17. Augustine, *Confessions*, 13.9.

sphere of the moon upward, natural movement is curvilinear, orbital; below the moon, and on and inside the earth, movement is rectilinear. Fire moves naturally upward, water naturally downward. When this view of physical locomotion is translated into ethical terms, virtue is seen as rising naturally upward, sin as sinking naturally downward. The love that rules the cosmos raises us with its light (Parad. 1.74–75: "amor che'l ciel governi . . . che col tuo lume mi levasti"). The center of the cosmos is the point toward which all heavy, sinful things sink; it is the point farthest away from God (Inf. 14.118: "là dove più non si dismonta"; Inf. 34.110–111: "'l punto al qual si traggon d'ogne parte i pesi"; cf. Inf. 34.93). It is the logical place for the Devil to dwell.

Another difficulty is that this system not only places the Devil at the center of the world but can be misunderstood to thrust God out beyond the boundaries of the cosmos and make him remote—exactly the contrary of what Dante wished to convey. Another system was theoretically possible. If the original Neoplatonic scheme is turned *upward* at the edges, forming a circle, then it is God who stands at the center of the cosmos. Such a scheme would in many ways have fit Christian tradition better. Augustine and Gregory frequently spoke of interiority, the need to seek God within, the reality of the interior man as opposed to the exterior man. The Neoplatonist conception may be expressed by a series of spheres emanating outward from the One, and such a modification underlay the thought of Dionysius and Eriugena. The overall ethical conception that God is at the center of all things, drawing them toward him, is more congenial to a mystical—or indeed any Christian—conception, and it was fundamental to Dante's thought. But this scheme was virtually impossible to represent in art or in literary description. Moreover it could not be expressed in scientific analogy, for it contradicted Aristotelian physics and Ptolemaic cosmology. If God is at the center, radiating the cosmos out from him, then the material earth must be out beyond all the spheres of fixed stars and planets. It must be represented as an entity of indeterminate shape and locality, or as a globe in an orbit impossible to reconcile astronomically with the other heavenly orbits. These problems made it too difficult for Dante to describe the physical universe theocentrically. The view that came to be called Copernican, with the sun and light at the center, would have made a better metaphor for Dante's system, but it was a view favored by few medieval cosmologists. (See figure 6.)

God had created the cosmos good, but Lucifer spoiled its perfection by introducing sin. His pride caused him to try to attain beatitude

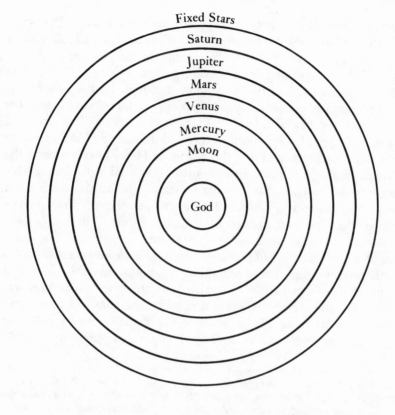

Figure 6. A theocentric physical universe (after Simon Marmion, c. 1460).

immediately and by his own efforts rather than waiting for God (Parad. 19.48: "per "principio del cader fu il maledetto superbir di colui che tu vedasti"; cf. Parad. 27.26–27.) The angels underwent a supernatural test soon after their creation, a test that lasted only a moment (Parad. 29.49–51). Some of the angels chose to remain loyal; others chose sin; still others refused to choose at all.[18] The angels that fell are intelligences exiled from their true native land above; they rained down from heaven, a despised crew driven down from bliss. One tenth of the angels joined in their ruin, a number that God makes up

18. On the neutral or trimmer angels, "quel cattivo coro de li angeli che non furon ribelli nè furon fedeli a Dio" (that wicked choir of angels who were neither rebels nor faithful to God, Inf. 3.37–39), see M. Dando, "Les anges neutres," *Cahiers d'études cathares*, 27, no. 69 (1976), 3–28; J. Freccero, "Dante and the Neutral Angels," *Romanic Review*, 51 (1960), 3–14; M. Rossi, "Sur un passage de la *Chanson d'Esclarmonde* (vs.

by the creation of humanity and the salvation of the saints.[19] Lucifer
had been the highest of the angels (Parad. 19.47: "che fu la somma
d'ogne creatura"; Inf. 34.46: his six wings identify him as a seraph).
But he fell like lightning from heaven, plunging through the spheres
and hurtling toward earth. The point at which he fell was in the
southern hemisphere at the polar opposite of Jerusalem, where the
earth would be healed by the Passion of the Savior. The dry land
shrank back from his approach in fear and disgust, pulled away from
the impact, and retreated into the Northern Hemisphere, leaving the
southern half of the globe almost entirely covered with water. "Almost," because when Satan actually struck the earth, the impact
opened a huge crevasse into which he hurtled all the way to the center
of the globe. The land, created by God and governed by God's love,
retreats from God's antithesis as if by inverse magnetism. The heav-
iness of Satan's sin was so ponderous that he sank into creation like a
plumb into pudding. A cave or "tomb" was hollowed out by his fall, a
"tomb" that became hell.[20] The earth from this giant excavation was
thrust up to the surface, where it formed the mountain of purgatory.

 After one has (like Dante) sunk to the very depths of hell, one
"turns" at that center and ascends up the mount of purgatory to heav-

---

2648–2826)," *Le diable au moyen âge* (Paris, 1979), p. 465. Rossi shows that the idea had
precedents in Christian literature and cites the *Chanson d'Esclarmonde* as an example.
This third group of angels must wander the world (*Esclarmonde*) or else dwell in the
circle of trimmers (Dante). Possibly the idea drew strength from the growing belief in
purgatory; the third state of the angels could be seen as paralleling the third state of
human souls after death.

 19. *Conv.* 3.13: "intelligenze che sono in esilio de la superna patria" (intelligences
exiled from their heavenly home); *Conv.* 2.5: "di tutti questi ordini si perderono ali-
quanti tosto che furono creati, forse in numero de la decima parte; a la quale restaurare
fu l'umana natura poi creata" (Some from each of these orders fell almost as soon as they
were created—about a tenth of them—and human nature was then created to make up
the lost number). Dante does not speak of a tenth order of angels, but rather of one
tenth of angels of all ranks. Inf. 7.11–12: Michael throws them out; Inf. 8.83: "da ciel
piovuti" (rained down out of heaven); Inf. 9.91: "cacciati del ciel, gente dispetta" (a
despised race driven out of heaven). Cf. Parad. 29.50–54. The fallen angels become the
demons guarding the battlements of the infernal city of Dis (Inf. 9.91–97).

 20. Inf. 34.122–126: "e la terra, che pria di qua si sporse, per paura di lui fé del mar
velo, e venne all emisperio nostro; e forse per fuggir lui lasciò qui il loco vòto quella
ch'appar di qua, e sù ricorse" (and the land that was here made a veil of itself for fear of
Satan and withdrew to the northern hemisphere; and to flee him, the land that was in
the midst of the earth left a hollow space for hell and moved up onto the surface). Cf.
Purgatory 12.25–27; Parad. 29.55–57. See Freccero, "Satan's Fall." Dante implies that
God created the whole cosmos before the fall of Satan; if Satan had fallen earlier, the
earth would not have been there to receive him.

en. In physical reality one descending from the surface of the earth at Jerusalem would not turn in order to ascend to the opposite point on the globe but rather would keep going straight ahead. Apparently Dante imagined Vergil (with Dante on his back) descending feet first as one would a ladder and then when he reached the center of gravity turning around to climb up the ladder.[21] Since Dante's journey is a descent toward evil, which now must be reversed into an ascent toward good, the reversal is dramatically symbolized in a turning unforgettable in its grotesque drama. Satan is at the very center of the cosmos, his head sticking up toward Jerusalem and the north, his buttocks frozen in the ice, his huge, hairy legs rearing up toward purgatory and the south. Vergil is obliged to turn himself laboriously with Dante on his back while clinging to the Devil's furry hide, so that they may direct their journey upward toward purgatory and the clear stars above.

When the Devil makes his rare appearances onstage, notably in the last canto of Inferno, he is more pathetic and repulsive than terrifying. Some critics have suggested that Dante simply failed to produce as impressive a Devil as Milton later did, but this explanation misses his point.[22] Dante specifically intended Lucifer to be empty, foolish, and contemptible, a futile contrast to God's energy. Dante viewed evil as negation and would have thought Milton's Devil much too active and effective. Lucifer's formal absence from wide tracts of the *Comedy* and from the Inferno itself indicates Dante's agreement with scholastic theology in limiting the Devil's role. One of Lucifer's most dramatic parts in medieval literature is at the harrowing of hell, but Dante's reference to the harrowing (Inf. 4.52–63) mentions him not at all. Neither does the poet's discussion of soteriology in canto 7 of Paradise refer to the Dark Lord. Dante distanced himself from ransom theory, and rejection of ransom meant relegating the Devil to a peripheral role in the economy of salvation. The lack of dramatic action on the part of Dante's Lucifer is a deliberate statement about his essential lack of being.

Satan's true being is his lack of being, his futility and nothingness. There he is in the dark at the very dead center of the earth, where sins have sunk to their proper place. As one descends into hell, each circle is filled with graver, heavier sins, until in the lowest circle, the circle of treason, Satan is at the dead center with his buttocks stuck in the ice at

21. Singleton's edition (See the Essay on the Sources) vol. 1:2, p. 634.
22. For the relationship between Dante and Milton, see I. Samuel, *Dante and Milton* (Ithaca, n.d.).

the dead point of the turning world, where all the heaviest weights converge. At that point there can be no motion more; the heaviest weights have found their true place and press together in an eternally immobile mass, where Satan is compressed by all the weight of the world (Parad. 29.57: "da tutti i pesi del mundo costretto"). This stalemate is the sign of the futility, meaninglessness, darkness, and nonbeing of this lifeless point.[23] If all things are drawn to God, what can be drawn to Lucifer? Only the nothingness and meaninglessness of sin. As we close upon ourselves when we turn away from God toward unreality, so the center of hell is a dark mass turned infinitely in upon itself, cut completely and forever off from reality. Satan, the symbol of this nothingness, can have no real character except negation, and so his futile immobility is precisely what Dante wished to portray.

Satan's nothingness permeates everywhere, a cold counterpart to the warm presence of the Dove. Cold and dark, it emanates up from the dead center, seeping up through all the cracks of hell onto the sinful earth. Satan's force acts like gravity throughout the earth, pulling men and women down toward its glamour and weighting them down toward hell. This gravity is the exact opposite of the force exerted by God, who draws things toward him to the extent that they are light, spirit, and good. Lucifer's blind, empty idiocy, like a vacuum, sucks and drains the life and color from the earth. While still wandering in the dark wood before his first descent into the underworld, Dante encountered three beasts—the *lonza* (leopardess), *leone* (lion), and *lupa* (she wolf)—a triune symbol of sin, ferocity, and Lucifer (like him, their names begin with "l"), whose triune face they prefigure. In every circle of hell the influence of his idiocy is felt, even in the circle of the good pagans, who would not be in limbo if it were not for the fall of Adam and Eve, which Lucifer engineered. Throughout the circles of hell, other sinister demons are his avatars: Charon (Inf. 3), Minos (5), Cerberus (6), Pluto (7), Phlegyas (8), the Furies and Medusa (9), the Minotaur and Centaurs (12), Geryon (17), the giants (31), and others.[24] The assimilation of these figures to the Devil is clearest in the figure of Pluto, in Inferno 7.1. Over the gate of hell leading to Pluto's realm is the phrase "pape Satàn, pape

23. F. Fergusson, *Dante* (New York, 1966), p. 119: "stalemate."

24. Since the time of the early fathers it had been conventional to portray the pagan gods as demons, but Dante's love of classical civilization made him replace the gods with mythological figures that had been sinister to the classical mind itself. Other medieval writers did the same. Arnoul Gréban's Passion play has a demon named Cerberus, for example, and *Eneas*, a French adaptation of the *Aeneid*, assimilated a number of classical mythological figures such as Charon and Cerberus to demons. See Owen, pp. 142–143.

Satàn, aleppe," words of uncertain meaning that nevertheless make the association of Pluto and Satan explicit. It is an unusual feature of Dante's hell that more traditional Christian demons, like Satan himself, seldom appear on stage. Where medieval art and drama loved to portray demons tormenting the damned with cruel tools, Dante's condemned suffer well-defined torture appropriate to their sins, torture usually inflicted without the visible presence of demons. In this Dante held closer to theological than to artistic and literary trends.[25]

The figure of Lucifer down at the motionless center of hell is a contrast with that of God in every way. The lowest three circles of hell, Cocytus, or the City of Dis, are ruled by Lucifer directly rather than through his surrogates. Here dwell the violent, fraudulent, and malicious. The ninth and lowest circle, Giudecca, the place of Judas, is occupied by traitors to kindred, country, and guests. Lowest of all are traitors to benefactors. Treason is in the lowest pit of hell because of all sins it most twists the just order of the cosmos. Treason against God is the ultimate sin and absurdity: betraying for one's own dark and limited ends the principle of light and justice upon which the whole cosmos, and therefore one's self, depends. As Judas betrayed God the Son, so at the beginning of time Lucifer betrayed God the Father. And such treason is futile. God's light and God's justice still and always inform the cosmos, but Satan and Judas will never see them: they are wrapped up in their own dark terror and pain forever. Traitors and all sinners deceive and betray themselves with their own blind idiocy. Deception and self-deception, blocking out God's light, are the key to all sin.

The nothingness of the Devil is underscored by his absurdity. He is imprisoned and entombed in the lightless cavern of Giudecca with his legs protruding into the air.[26] The narrowness and darkness of this prison, contrasted with the infinite light and space of God's world,

25. Demons do appear in the fifth of the evil ditches (*malebolge*) of the eighth circle of hell, where the fraudulent are imprisoned. Here they have some elements of the comic stage demons. Though the idiocy of the Devil is so cold as to freeze any sense of laughter, the stupidity of minor demons can have elements of humor. Dante used the term *demonio* for "demon" most frequently, but *diavolo* is an occasional equivalent, as in Inf. 28.37. Dante's usual name for the Devil is Lucifer, e.g., Inf. 31.143, 34.89, but he also calls him Satan (Inf. 7.1) and Beelzebub (Belzebù; Inf. 24.127). When Vergil, who was naturally unaware of the Judeo-Christian tradition, speaks, he uses the classical name Dis (Dite) for the lord of the underworld (Inf. 11.65, 12.39, 34.20).

26. Lucifer's tomb is a parody of Holy Sepulchre, the tomb of Christ. See A. Cassell, "The Tomb, the Tower, and the Pit: Dante's Satan," *Italica*, 56 (1979), 331–351.

Saint Wolfgang and the Devil shows a strongly stylized Devil with all the standard iconog
characteristics: horns, tusks, hooves, wings, tail, lolling tongue, face on buttocks. He has no
over the saint, who can repulse him with the sign of the cross. Michael Pacher (active 1467–14
on canvas. Courtesy of the Bayerischen Staatsgemäldesammlungen.

Dante with hell at his right, purgatory behind him, the heavenly spheres above him, and heaven, the City of God, at his left. Tempera on wood, Italian, fourteenth century. Courtesy of Archivi Alinari.

symbolize his deliberate blindness and self-imposed ignorance. The darkness of Lucifer contrasts with the light that floods heaven (Parad. 1.79–81; 2.109–111; 5.118: "lume che per tutto il ciel si spazia"; 29.136–138: "la prima luce, che tutta la raia, per tanti modi in essa si recepe, quanti son li splendori a chi s'appaia"). The icy lake that holds him immobile is frozen too hard to creak, a sign of death and absolute cold, a symbol of the spirit closed off from God and an allegorical antinomy of the life-giving waters of baptism.[27] The immobility of Satan is the opposite of the mobility of the angels and the blessed spirits, his frozen hatred the opposite of God's love, which moves the world (Parad. 1.1–3; 14.23–24; 21.80–81; 23.103; 24.16–17; 24.130–133: "io credo in uno Dio solo ed etterno, che tutto 'l ciel move, non moto, con amore e con disio"). Satan's forced motionlessness is also contrasted to God's voluntary serenity, which moves without moving (Parad. 19.64–65: "dal sereno che non si turba mai"). As Jesus was immersed up to his waist in the life-giving Jordan, so Satan is stuck up to his waist in the mortal ice, water that is dead and buried, unlike the warm and living waters of God's love (Parad 33.10–12: "meridiana face di caritate, e . . . fontana vivace").

Below each of his three faces Lucifer has a pair of huge wings, six in all, like the six wings of the Seraphim (Parad. 9.78). But these are not the feathery wings of angels, burning with living gold (Parad. 30.13–15) but leathery bat wings, a symbol of his darkness and blindness.[28] The heavy wings beat the frozen air vainly, unable to take off, stirring up winds that freeze the streams of hell as they sink into Cocytus and, seeping up through the earth, stir mortal minds to sin, just as God's light shines out to touch all earthly hearts.[29] The frozen wind of Satan is in direct contrast to the fire of love that blows in the breath of the Holy Spirit (Parad. 22.32: "la carità che tra noi orde") and to the kindling of joy (Parad. 21.88: "l'allegrezza ond'io fiammeggio").

The nonbeing of Satan is further manifest in his giant size: he is a towering mass of moribund matter. Theology held that angels remained angels after their fall, though some said that the fallen angels

27. Also the lake, *lago* (Inf. 32.23) harks back to the Latin *lacus*, which means "pit" as well as "lake," and was used as such by Jerome in the Vulgate (Is. 14.15) to designate the place to which Satan fell.

28. Inf. 34.46: "sotto ciascuna uscivan due grand'ali"; Inf. 34.49–50: "non avean penne, ma di vispistrello era lor modo."

29. He can even (Inf. 33.139–148) animate the bodies of the dead. Dante had believed that Branca Doria and Michel Zanche were alive on earth, but he hears that they are actually dead and are being used like puppets by Satan.

took on the heavy, lower air, as opposed to the good angels, who were made of the rarer ether. But Dante extrapolated a shape that was a gross incarnation mocking the true Incarnation of Christ and the absolute opposite of the spirit of God. Since Platonic/Christian tradition considered pure matter to be that which is farthest from God and closest to nonbeing, Satan is almost pure matter, barely informed with life, and composed of all the densest weights in the cosmos; his shaggy, bestial body emphasizes that he is the polar opposite of reason, truth, and spirit. He is a worm, a monster (Inf. 34.107–108). The feeble, giant Devil, for which numerous literary precedents existed, perfectly symbolized the inner impotence of this being who on earth can seem so powerful and clever.[30] He is the emperor of his wretched kingdom (Inf. 34.28: "lo 'mperador del doloroso regno"), as God is the emperor who rules forever (Parad. 12.40: "lo 'mperador che sempre regna").

The ugliness of this hulking, pathetic creature who had once been an angel of light is in complete contrast to the beauty of God (Parad. 7.64–66). Through pride he dared defy his maker, and his plunge from heaven transformed all his beauty into ugliness.[31] The doomed Devil is grossest in his hideous, eternal mastication of the three traitors, Judas, Cassius, and Brutus. The blind, futile hatred of this act had been prefigured by the fate of the traitor Ugolino, who, himself betrayed by Ruggiero, is trapped in the ice gnawing in eternal rage on the head of the man who betrayed him (Inf. 33). The *Vision of Tundale* and other literary or artistic sources depicted Satan, Hell, or other demons devouring sinners and (often) excreting them into the fiery pit. Dante avoided the crudities of the tradition and thus better brought out the horror. As Satan chews on his human prey, he weeps, and his

30. Among the precedents: the Titans of Greco-Roman religion; the giant children of the Watcher angels in apocalyptic literature; Vergil's Polyphemus, the cannibal giant from whom Odysseus escaped by clinging onto the woolly bellies of sheep, an image Dante must have had in mind when he wrote of Vergil and Dante clinging to Satan's shaggy sides. Just above the Giudecca, Dante encountered the well of giants, themselves raging, vain, and purposeless. In the twelfth-century *Vision of Tundale*, Tundale saw a huge, black demon, larger than any beast, with a hundred heads and mouths in which he gulped down a thousand sinners at once; he lay bound on a gridiron, thrashing his huge tail, vomiting the sinners up and swallowing them again. Another of Tundale's hideous demons, with great black wings and fiery eyes, sat up to his waist in a frozen lake. On *Tundale* see Chapter 6 above; on the Devil's shape see Chapter 7 above. See also S. Cosmos, "Old English 'Limwaestm' ('Christ and Satan,' 129)," *Notes and Queries*, (1975), 196–198; S. Frascino, "La 'terra' dei giganti ed il Lucifero dantesco," *La cultura*, 12 (1933), 767–783.

31. Inf. 34.28, 35; Parad. 19.46–48. Other references to the Devil: Parad. 9.127–128; Purg. 8.98–99, 32.32; Inf. 6.96, 23.143–144.

tears mingle with their blood and drool down his chin. It is a horrible contrast to Beatrice, who is always smiling for joy (Parad. 18.19; 30.42). Unlike the one tear of repentance that redeemed the sinner Buonconte di Montefeltro (Purg. 5), Satan's tears of frustrated rage serve not to save. Like the gory tears of the cyclops Polyphemus blinded by Odysseus, the bloody weeping of the hideous giant only repels. It repels, and it parodies the blood, water, and tears shed by the heavenly Lord upon his cross.

As Dante descended with Vergil into Giudecca, he distinguished through the murk a huge figure looming before him, shaped like a monstrous windmill or suggesting a distorted outline of the Savior's cross. Lucifer's three faces and three outstretched pairs of wings were like the three points of the cross, the triune Devil an infernal parody of the Holy Trinity. The ironic line "the standard of the hellish king advances" ("vexilla regis prodeunt inferni" [Inf. 34.1]), is a parody of a famous hymn by Fortunatus and also a parody of the cross, for Fortunatus' *vexilla regis*, "royal standard," refers to the cross of Christ.[32] John Freccero linked this parody of the cross with the color of Satan's three faces. Though Dante elsewhere refers to the blackness of the fallen angels (Inf. 21.29; 23.131; 27.113), he gives Satan's three faces three different colors: yellowish white, red, and black. Numerous theories have been coined over the years to explain these colors, but Freccero's is based on careful analysis of the literary background.[33] He begins his explanation with Luke 17.6, in which Christ says that with faith deep enough one could tell a mulberry tree to move and it would move. Saint Ambrose used the mulberry tree as a symbol of the Devil, for just as its fruit begins as white, matures as red, and then turns black, so the Devil begins glorious and white, shines red in his power, and then turns black with sin. But Augustine used the tricolored mulberry as a symbol of the cross, and Ubertino da Casale described the vexilla of Christ as colored in the same way. What Dante did is to draw the cross, the Devil, and the three colors together. Freccero clinches the argument by observing that Dante must have had the actual image of the mulberry in mind, for although the sources used the colors white, red, and black, the mulberry fruit first appears as a waxen, yellowish white, and that is just how Dante describes the color, "tra bianca e gialla" (between white and yellow). Freccero's

32. *Vexilla*, like the Greek *tropaia*, has the root meaning of battle standard(s), but in Christian literature its meaning commonly shifted to connote the cross.

33. J. Freccero, "The Sign of Satan," *Modern Language Notes*, 80 (1965), 11–26. Compare G. Busnelli, *I tre colori di Lucifero Dantesco* (Rome, 1910).

explanation leaves room for further interpretation of the colors. Given sources such as Ambrose and Dante's own ability to pack every detail with meaning, it is plausible that the red face may indicate sin or shame, the black face ignorance or corruption, the whitish face impotence. But what Dante seems to have had chiefly in mind was to extend and deepen the sense of the moral polarization of the cosmos between Christ and Satan.

Another masterwork of medieval literature in which the Devil's influence is felt throughout the moral cosmos is William Langland's *Piers Plowman*. Langland, a clerk in minor orders, had a grasp of nominalist theology, a mystical conception of the world, and a keen, satirical voice. He wrote at least four versions of the poem between 1360 and his death in 1400. The third, the B version is admired for its poetry, the C version for its reflection of the author's more mature thought.[34]

Different in style, conception, and viewpoint as *Piers Plowman* is from the *Divine Comedy*, it is, like the *Comedy*, a work of vision literature, and it has at its heart a similar mystical view of reality. Langland, like Dante, believed that the way to salvation was through love more than intellect, a view that he derived from, and shared with, both nominalists and mystics. *Piers* differs from the *Comedy* in that its mystical view is centered in this world more than in the other. *Piers* presents plowmen, priests, brewers, lawyers, merchants, street cleaners, and friars at their daily labors, as wide a view of society as Dante's but set in the daily life of street and field. Langland was a poor man, and his down-to-earth mysticism was similar in spirit to that of the Brethren of the Common Life and Thomas à Kempis on the Continent. The central character, Piers Plowman, may be understood as Christ, Saint Peter, Everyman, or as the type of the good Christian, the good ruler, or the honest laborer. The vision is that true priests, monks, plowmen, and kings keep their attention upon God at the center of things and so journey in a world of reality and light toward unity with God, while their false counterparts blind themselves with illusion and wander off toward nowhere. We can look at things straightly and clearly and see God through them, or we can muddy them with the dirt of our own desires until no light can shine through. The Devil squats stupidly behind the scenes, pulling our vision awry,

---

34. For editions of and works on *Piers Plowman* see the Essay on the Sources. I am grateful to my graduate student Cassandra Potts, whose seminar work did much to advance this section on *Piers Plowman*.

Demons torment sinners according to their vices: avarice and usury. Fresco by Taddeo di Bartolo (1362–1422) at San Gimigniano, Italy. Courtesy of the Duomo di San Gimigniano.

twisting our view, drawing us down into darkness until we see and understand nothing.

The choice is ours. Influenced by the nominalism and voluntarism common in late fourteenth-century theology, Langland asserted the freedom of the human will. When the Devil attacks the Tree of Charity (C.16), which represents Christ, the just person, or the individual Christian, Piers defends the tree by summoning "Liberum Arbitrium," the personification of free will, which, when it obeys Piers (here Christ or justice), defeats the Devil. When it fails to obey Piers, it has no power against Satan. The will is really free only when it chooses the good; otherwise it sinks in bondage to sin. The analysis resembles that of the anonymous mystical treatise *Theologia germanica* (c. 1350), where the will's natural purpose is seen as serving God, but it can be wrenched by sin from its true course. Langland's emphasis upon human freedom and his concern for this world meant that humanity, rather than angels and demons, has center stage. Yet although the Devil seldom appears in person in the poem, he manifests himself constantly in the affairs of this world, and allegorical personifications such as Wrong, Falsehood, and Deceit are his avatars. Lucifer is ever watchful and active, but his works can take shape only when summoned or welcomed by individual human beings. It is ours to decide whether we prefer the freedom of seeing things as they are or the heavy task of maintaining the illusion that they are as our desires would have them be. We can align ourselves with truth or with idolatry. Idolatry is to choose a limited good in preference to the ultimate good. For Langland, money and profit are the chief idolatry, but any lie, falsehood, or evasion, any preference of fame, fortune, or pleasure over God, even the setting of church or theology over the simple, clean truth, is service to the Dark Lord.[35]

Langland emphasized the Devil's works in the unjust activities of the humans who follow him. Justice is the state of affairs that prevails when the affairs of this world are conducted straightforwardly in accord with God's will and plan. Injustice is the state of affairs that usually prevails and that arises from human perversity and stupidity getting in the way of right order. Langland is contemptuous and furious at injustice; he hates its unshakeable stupidity and treats those

35. B.1.128–129: "Alle þat werchen with wrong wende þei shulle after hir deþday and dwelle with þat sherewe [the Devil]." Compare B.2.102–104; B.7.117–118. See B. Harwood, "Liberum-Arbitrium in the C-Text of *Piers Plowman*," *Philogical Quarterly*, 52 (1973), 680–695.

who perpetrate it harshly. The chief idolatry is the pursuit of gain, whose personification is Lady Meed (B.24 and C.24). Meed can be seen as representing the nascent capitalist economic system, and had Langland thought in such terms he would probably have agreed, but closer to his own world view was the identification of Lady Meed with *cupiditas* or *avaritia*, the ancient cardinal sin of avarice. Langland's belief that avarice is the most deadly of the sins was common in the later Middle Ages, when commercial development enabled a true money economy to develop, making money the measure of all things. Langland's contempt for money appears in his satire of the greedy friars as well as in the passages on Lady Meed, and the venal friars are associated with Antichrist (C.21–22). Like the other six vices, Meed is the daughter of the Devil, or of his avatars Fraud or Deceit.[36]

The marriage of Meed with Fals (Falsehood) is a satire of bureaucracy and law as well as of money. Favel (Deceit) has arranged the marriage, and Fals draws up a legal contract stating that Falsehood, Guile, and Deceit are all pleased at Meed's cupidity and grant her formal license to backbite, boast, bear false witness, despise poverty, and rejoice in avarice, usury, idleness, and all the vices. They give her leave "after her death to dwell day without end in lordship with Lucifer, as this document shows, with all the appurtenances of purgatory and the pain of hell (C.2.106–108)." The charter is given and sealed in the "date of the Devil" instead of in the year of our Lord.[37] Those who choose to follow Meed live false lives and abet injustice, such as the brewer who cries out, "Bah, by Jesus, I won't be ruled, in spite of your jabbering, by the spirit of justice, or by conscience, by Christ, when I can sell dregs and lees and draw either thick ale or thin from the tap as I please. I am the kind of person who doesn't grub after holiness, so hold your tongue, conscience, it isn't doing you any good to talk about the spirit of justice" (C.21.296–402).

The fall of Lucifer is set in the context of the struggle between Wrong and Truth. Though Lucifer is not merely a metaphor, he is chiefly that. It is not so much that Lucifer introduced sin and evil into the world as that his behavior violated eternal principles of truth and justice. God

36. T. P. Dunning, *Piers Plowman*, 2d ed. (Oxford, 1980), pp. 54, 126. Compare C.6.330, where Robbery is "Luciferes aunte." See L. K. Little, "Pride Goes before Avarice," *American Historical Review*, 76 (1971), 16–49.

37. B.2.69–114; C.2.69–115. D. J. Burton, "The Compact with the Devil in the Middle English *Vision of Piers the Plowman* B. II," *California Folklore Quarterly*, 5 (1946), 179–184, misunderstands this as a pact with the Devil; in fact it is a parody of greed and the law.

created ten orders of angels; one of those orders fell. Lucifer, who had been "archangel of hevene, on of goddes knyghtes" (C.1.107), sinned, drawing down the many angels of the tenth order with him. As they fell they took on hideous form, "lepen out in lothly forme" (C.1.109). They fell for nine days, some into the dense air, some to the earth, and some underground, depending upon the gravity of their sin, and Lucifer fell lowest of all. The essence of his sin was that he and those who fell with him "helden nat with treuthe" (C.1.108), the result being that he is bound in hell.[38]

The Devil's great scene in *Piers* is at the harrowing of hell, but Langland uses it quite differently from his contemporaries. The libera-

---

38. C.1.120. See B.1.111–129; C.1.103–128; C.16.210–211. See also A. Kellogg, "Satan, Langland, and the North," *Speculum*, 24 (1949), 413–414; R. Risse, Jr., "The Augustinian Paraphrase of Isaiah 14.13–14 in *Piers Plowman* and the Commentary on the *Fables* of Avianus," *Philological Quarterly*, 45 (1966), 712–717. In C.1.111 and B.1.119 Langland changed Augustine's paraphrase in *Ennaratio in Ps.* 47 from "ponam sedem meam in aquilone" (I shall place my throne in the north) to "ponam *pedem* meam," a shift from "seat" or "throne" to "foot." Kellogg and Risse explain *pedem* as meaning pride and self-love. The fall of the angels to various levels: "Wonder wyse holy wryt telleth how þei fullen, summe in erthe, summe in ayr, summe in heele depe as Lucifer lowest lith of hem all; for pruyde" (C.1.125–128). This notion goes as far back as Origen: see SATAN, pp. 125–126. For the idea that ten orders of angels existed, of which one order fell, see Chapter 6, n. 57, above. Earlier writers agreed that only nine orders proper of angels existed and that those who fell constitute a tenth group, but not a tenth order. Duns states the point in his *Commentary on the Sentences*, 2.9: "Sed cum non sint nisi novem ordines, nec plures fuissent, etiamsi illi qui ceciderunt perstitissent, moventur lectores quomodo Scriptura dicat decimum ordinem compleri ex hominibus" (Since only nine orders existed, and only nine would have existed even if the angels who fell had actually remained loyal, the reader may ask how Scripture can say that the tenth order will be filled up by humans). Duns observes that people have loosely used the term *tenth order* for the fallen angels and for the humans who allegedly replace them. But this is not accurate, he argues: "Ex quo apparent non esse de hominibus formandum decimum ordinem, tanquam novem sint angelorum, et decimus hominum: sed homines pró qualitate meritorum statuendos in ordinibus angelorum. Quod vero legitur decimus ordo complendus de hominibus, ex tali sensu dictum fore accipi potest, quia de hominibus restaurabitur, quod in angelis lapsum est: de quibus tot corruerunt, ut possit fieri decimus ordo" (It is clear that a tenth order was not formed out of humans, as if there were nine ranks of angels and a tenth of humans; rather, humans are brought up into all the ranks of angels according to their merits. When we read that a tenth order was to be filled up with humans, we ought to understand it to mean that what had been lost among the angels was restored among humans and that as many angels fell as *could have* made up a tenth order). The "tenth order" is thus a loose manner of speaking into which Langland fell, perhaps inadvertently. The nine days that the angels fell correspond to the nine spheres of the cosmos and to the nine orders of angels, numerologically three times a triad. The giants of Hesiod's *Theogony* took nine days to fall to earth (*Theog.* 722). See above, Chapter 4, for the north as evil.

tion of the souls in limbo by the Passion of Christ was originally based upon the ransom theory that the Devil held them by right because of original sin. Even before Langland's time, the idea of Jesus as a ransom paid by God to the Devil yielded gradually to the military metaphor of Christ as a knight come to rescue the oppressed. Langland was thus freed to use the harrowing scene without any assumption of ransom theory. For him the drama of the harrowing is subsumed in a statement about the nature of justice. He has prepared for the harrowing in a number of passages that explain that the Devil eagerly watches to snatch up every apple that falls (every soul that dies) from the tree of life. As a result of original sin, he claims power over mankind and carries sinners to hell. He has even obtained power over the patriarchs, holding them prisoner in limbo.[39] Lucifer claims that he holds just title to these souls, but Langland assumes that Lucifer is a liar, and even Satan finds the claim questionable. Since we got these souls by trickery, Satan observes, we may have no real right to them. Satan's doubts presage the debate between Justice and Mercy and that between Christ and Lucifer. Satan, Mercy, and Christ all maintain against Lucifer that the Devil has no rights over humanity. Lucifer claims justice, but the weight of justice is against him.

Immediately before the harrowing, which occurs in passus 18 of the B version and 20 of the C version, the four daughters of God—Truth, Righteousness, Mercy, and Peace—conduct a debate on the nature of justice.[40] Truth and Righteousness defend the notion of strict justice, according to which mankind ought by right to be in Satan's power, for we broke our contract with God of our own free will, and he is in no way obliged to save us. But Peace and Mercy respond with an argument from equity: justice is not always best served by its strict application; though we have doomed ourselves to die, God's mercy will save us. Equity—justice tempered by mercy—is far from being a violation of justice; rather, it is its highest expression. It is the way the real world is constructed. The Old Law, good in itself, was not the truest expression of justice, for it lacked equity and mercy. The New Testament proclaims this perfect reality. The debate among the four

39. C.16.79–85; C.18.111–117. C.18.115: "and made of holy men his hoerd *in limbo inferni.*" Cf. B.10.423–425: Adam, the prophets, and Isaiah held by Satan.

40. The idea of the daughters of God is an old device based on Ps. 84.11. It was frequently used by late medieval poets and dramatists; see for example *The Castle of Perseverence,* below, Chapter 9.

daughters of God prefigures the debate between Christ and the Devil at the gates of hell.[41]

Now it is Holy Saturday, and Christ draws near. From the outset Christ is no lawyer come to pay the Devil his due, but a warrior come to tear down the infernal city: "For Jesus comes yonder like a giant to break and beat down all who stand against him and to have out of hell all that he chooses."[42] Jesus is a knight, a jouster with helmet and mail riding up on his warhorse to challenge the Devil in combat and, having defeated him, to bring the prophets up out of hell. As Jesus the Jouster approaches, the demons hold a frantic colloquy that is an inversion of that of the daughters of God. The number of the demons present varies between the B and C texts. In the B there are two—Lucifer and Satoun (also called Gobelyn), and a third semidemon, the personified Helle.[43] In the C text a number of other demons are added to the council: Mahond, Ragamoffyn, Belial, and Astarot. Langland seems to have cared little which was the chief Devil. Lucifer fills that role most frequently, but it is Satoun who in the C text barks orders to Ragamoffyn, Belial, and Astarot to bar the doors and prepare to repulse the advancing army of Christ (Satoun seems to imagine that Jesus has marshaled a great host, including cavalry, against him). And it is Lucifer, rather than Satan, who has gone up to Eden to tempt Adam and Eve. The division of speeches among the demons is purely a literary device to permit lively debate.

As a great light pierces the darkness of hell, a voice thunders, "Open up the gates!" Satoun, recoiling, mutters to Hell that this is just the kind of light that came to wrest Lazarus away from them; now it is come to save all of humanity. Lucifer is outraged, for he believes that God has promised him rights over the human race and that Christ has come to deprive him of his just due, "for by right and by reason the ranks that are here belong to me body and soul, both the good and the

41. J. A. Alford, "Literature and Law in Medieval England," *Publications of the Modern Language Association*, 92 (1977), 941–951; W. J. Birnes, "Christ as Advocate: The Legal Metaphor of *Piers Plowman*," *Annuale medievale*, 16 (1975), 71–93.

42. C.20.261–263: "For Iesus as a geaunt with a gyn cometh ȝende to breke and to bete adoun all þat ben agayne hym and to haue out of helle alle of hem þat hym liketh."

43. This reading is preferable to one making Gobelyn different from Satoun or one making "þe deuel" yet another demon. In B.18.286ff. a speech is split between Satoun and Gobelyn, and both are equated with "þe deuel and þe fend"; as one being they address Lucifer in B.18.311. The C text implies the same identity. That "þe deuel" is a common noun here is further clear from C.20.340, where "deueles" appears in the plural.

bad." Satan rounds on him: "Yes, well, you got us into this, didn't you? It was your fault that you went up to tempt Adam and Eve in the first place. We would be much better off if you hadn't gone. Now all our prey is lost to us because of your lies."[44] But Lucifer stands up to challenge Christ at the gates. "What lord are you?" he demands, but then the light rushes in and strikes him blind.[45] A debate between Christ and Lucifer ensues, Lucifer arguing that he has the right to humanity for two reasons. First, God gave humanity to him at the time of original sin, and God must not go back on his word. It is a nice irony that the Devil should argue from the justice of the Lord whom he hates and daily betrays, and it is an argument from the strict justice of the Old Law, a law of retaliation untempered by mercy. The second reason is derived from English common law, and Langland wants his audience to note how Lucifer, like unjust landholders on earth, tries to turn the common law to his advantage. According to law, he says, I hold humanity by just custom, for I have had possession of them for 7,000 years. In effect, Lucifer is bringing a suit of novel disseisin against Christ.[46]

Christ rebuts Lucifer's arguments with the argument that he is come to fetch out the souls in fulfillment of justice, not in violation of justice: I ransom my servants through both right and reason.[47] But Langland

---

44. "For bi riht and by resoun þe renkes þat ben here body and soule beth myne, bothe gode and ille" (C.20.300–301). Satan blames Lucifer: C.20.312–321; cf. B.18.311. Lucifer had taken a snake's form in Eden: "not in fourme of a fende bote in fourme of an addre" (C.20.315). Gobelyn/Satoun reports that he had been tempting Jesus in vain for over thirty years and has yet to find out whether he is the Son of God: "and som tyme ich askede where we were god or godes sone? He gaf me short answere" (C.20.330–331). Suspecting the worst, Gobelyn/Satoun tried to stop the crucifixion: "Y wolde haue lenghed [lengthened] his lyf, for y leved [believed], if he deyede, that if his soul hider cam, it sholde shende [ruin] vs all" (C.20.335–336).

45. What lord: C.20.360. Blinding light: C.20.368 ("Lucifer loke ne myhte, so liht hym ablende"); cf. B.5.494: "The liʒt þat lepe out of þee, Lucifer it blente"; B.18.325; C.20.141.

46. "Sethen we haen ben sesed seuene thousand wynter," we have possession by right (C.20.309–311). Satan doubts it: C.20.312–313, and Gobelyn adds that God cannot be cheated or mocked: "And God wol not be gylde . . . ne byiaped. We haen no trewe title to hem, for thy tresoun hit maketh" (C.20.323–324). For the Devil's lawsuits against Christ see Chapter 9 below.

47. C.20.443–444: Christ has at this time come to take from hell only those who believed in him before his coming, but he promises to save all at the Last Judgment. C.20.413–414: "And thenne shal y come as kynge, with croune and with angeles, and haue out of helle alle mennes soules." C.20.395: "thorw riht and throw resoun [I] ransoun here my lege [security, pledge]."

uses the term *ransom* loosely: Christ is not come to pay the Devil, but rather to wrest humanity away from him with a force that springs from justice itself. Christ puts forward three arguments. First, even under the strictness of the Old Law he is justified in taking the souls because of Lucifer's use of trickery in Eden, and "the Old Law teaches that cheaters may be cheated and brought down by their fraud."[48] Second, the New Law provides for equity as well as justice, grace and mercy as well as punishment. Thus mercy wins back what was lost by guile, and fraud is defrauded by grace.[49] Third, Christ observes that as king he has the royal power simply to pardon the damned and release them from hell, but the use of this power is unnecessary because of the effectiveness of the two arguments from justice. The Devil must yield to justice, and Christ binds him in iron bonds (C.2.55–56). In Langland's vision, as in Dante's, God's world is one of simple light and justice; it is blocked and blurred by the sin and folly of humans and angels; but sin eventually perishes and love prevails.

Langland's rejection of ransom theory, his emphasis upon free will, his focus upon love, and his nominalist and mystical assumptions combined to reduce, but not eliminate, the importance of the Devil in his view of the world. It was the impediment to love caused by the sins of the world, especially avarice, that concerned him most. We cannot, Langland says, solve the problem of evil. Following Augustine's admonition, "Do not seek to know more than is appropriate," and the

48. C.20.377–386; C.20.382: "þe olde lawe techeth that gylours be begiled, and yn here gyle falle."

49. C.20.396; C.20.392: "So þat with gyle was gete, thorw grace is now ywonne. . . . and Gyle be bigyled thorw grace at þe laste." Cf. C.20.163–166: "And riht as the gylour thorw gyle begiled man formost, so shal grace, that bigan al, maken a goed ende and begile þe gilour, and þat is a goed sleythe: ars ut artem falleret." The last phrase is derived from Fortunatus' famous hymn "Pange lingua," but Langland shifted the original meaning. Fortunatus was using the ransom theory that God tricked Satan into seizing Christ so that he could deprive him of his booty. In Langland this idea is submerged in the more edifying principle that since Satan's original temptation of Adam and Eve was by fraud, he was never legally entitled to anything at all. God's justice replaces God's trickery. Traces of the old idea remain in "beguiling the guileful," but when Langland says that grace "tricks the trickster," he is using an older vocabulary to cloak a newer viewpoint. That grace and mercy and justice prevail over the Devil is no trickery but a straightforward expression of God's order. But the deluded Devil, who never sees anything straight, thinks of them as trickery. With this viewpoint, Langland can stage the dramatic harrowing of hell without subscribing to the discarded ransom theory that underlay it.

nominalist distrust of intellectual constructions, the poet warns, "Do not wish to know why God permits Satan to cheat his children, but hold to the teachings of the church and ask for God's forgiveness. . . . If you want to know why God allowed the Devil to lead us astray, or if you wish to fathom the purposes of God Almighty, then your eyes ought to be in your arse. Everything happens as God chooses, and thank God it will continue to, worry over it though we may." (B. 10. 120–130).

Geoffrey Chaucer (1344–1400), Langland's almost exact contemporary, was a friend of the nobility and a man of the world. Like Shakespeare later, he was the master of a variety of genres and styles and felt his way into a diversity of characters. Chaucer's underlying theology or philosophy, like Shakespeare's, is difficult to define. That he was a believing Christian is clear from the ending of Sir Thopas' tale, and there is every reason to assume that he believed in the Devil. Yet his emphasis is upon the human, not the cosmic, and his devel, feend, or Sathanas is less often a metaphor of the follies of humanity.[50]

In *The Canterbury Tales* the Devil seldom plays an important role other than as metaphor. "The Monk's Tale" offers a vignette of Lucifer among other great figures who have fallen from high station, such as Adam, Hercules, and Nebuchadnezzar: "O Lucifer, brightest of angels alle, / Now artow Satanas, that maist not twinne [depart] / Out of miserye, in which that thou art falle" (lines 14–16). In "The Friar's Tale" he serves to sharpen the satire of the summoners. A summoner meets the Devil in human shape, and the fiend explains in quite orthodox terms how demons have no fixed shape of their own but can change their shapes, either by creating illusions, or by making temporary bodies out of the elements, or even by animating dead bodies.[51] But they can do these things only with the permission of God. God allows them to tempt only because he turns the temptations to his own purpose of fortifying the just. When a Christian resists a temptation, the result of the Devil's efforts is the opposite of what he intends (lines 169–203). Chaucer might have used the Devil's speech to get inside his character and mock the inverted values of the infernal world, as the

50. The bibliography on Chaucer is enormous. See especially F. N. Robinson, *The Works of Geoffrey Chaucer*, 2d ed. (Oxford, 1957); E. T. Donaldson, *Chaucer's Poetry*, 2d ed. (New York, 1975). On the Devil in Chaucer see J. de Caluwe-Dor, "Le diable dans les Contes de Cantorbéry: Contribution à l'étude sémantique du terme *Devil*," in *Le diable au moyen âge*, pp. 97–116. Caluwe-Dor assembles 106 references to the Devil. R. Kaeuper has a useful article forthcoming in *Studies in the Age of Chaucer*.

51. Lines 161–168, 204–216; see discussion of Dante, above.

dramatist Arnoul Gréban did (Chapter 9 below), but the poet's attention is fixed as usual on human greed and folly. The Devil and the summoner ride off in company for a while with the understanding that each will show the other how he works. They encounter a man cursing his horse and consigning it to the Devil, and the summoner wonders why the Devil does not carry off the animal. The Devil replies that it is clear that the man did not mean what he said. Disgusted with Satan's faintheartedness, the summoner shows him how to work without any such scruple. Going to the house of an old widow of impeccable character, he tries to extort a shilling from her. Angrily she curses him: "The Devil, quod she, so fecche him er he deye," unless he repents. The summoner refuses to repent, "and with that word this foule feend hym hente; body and soule he with the devel wente" (lines 328–340).[52]

The summoner replies in his own tale by satirizing the friars. Satan, he observes in the prologue, keeps 20,000 friars up his arse in hell:

> Right so as bees out swarmen from an hyve,
> out of the Develes ers ther gonne dryve
> twenty thousand freres on a route [in a mob],
> and thurghout helle swarmed al aboute,
> and comen agayn as fast as they may gon,
> and in his ers they crepten everychon. (Prologue 30–35)

But the poet's attention is on the friars, not the demons: the tale is broadly scatological, with more to say about farts than about fiends. The Devil's farts upon the stage, his ingestion and excretion of souls, his tendency to thrust out his backside toward audiences or, in the dark of night, to expose his private parts for the veneration of witches, his emission of sulphurous odors, all combine the disgusting with the comic. The Devil is funny, but he is also repulsive, and he is funny in a way that makes us despise and shun him rather than empathize with him. The scatological has certain apotropaic qualities as well, especially in folklore, where the Devil can be driven off by pungent or evil-smelling herbs such as garlic (which can be chewed or hung round the neck) or asafoetida (known in Germany as *Teufelsdreck*).[53]

52. The Devil wears a green jacket (*courtepy*) in this tale. See Chapter 4 above (see Chapter 4 also for the motif of the fulfilled curse in folklore) and D. W. Robertson, Jr., "Why the Devil Wears Green," *Modern Language Notes*, 69 (1954), 470–472.

53. R. P. Clark, "Squeamishness and Exorcism in Chaucer's *Miller's Tale*," *Thoth* 14 (1973/1974), 37–43; though weighting his case down with leaden Freudianism, Clark makes a valid point in drawing attention to the association of the Devil with the scatological.

In "The Pardoner's Tale" a group of young people in Flanders hold drunken orgies "thurgh which they doon the devel sacrise withinne that develes temple, in cursed wise, by superfluytee abhomnyable" (lines 7–9), but the reference is not to the witches' sabbat but merely to their drunkenness, lechery, and other vices. This was the very eve of the great witch craze, when stories of sabbats were already in circulation, but the poet, if indeed he means to refer to the sabbat at all, does so very much with tongue in cheek.[54]

Of all the tales, that of the Prioress shows the most intense religious feeling, though it is the character of the Prioress, not necessarily Chaucer himself, who is speaking. It is a fiercely anti-Semitic tale, and though the Devil does not appear in person, the audience could have had no doubt that his sinister presence is personified in the Jews. The fate of the pious little lad caught in the street as he sang his antiphon "Alma redemptoris mater"—"the cursed Jew him hente [seized], and heeld hym faste, and kitte his throte, and in a pit hym caste" (lines 82–83)—is the fate of the Christian soul waylaid by the Devil as he passes through the narrow streets of life. The Jew, like the "pagan" Muslim and the heretic "witch," was a servant of the Devil, demonized by his close association with the Dark Lord.[55]

Chaucer shifted the center of moral action away from the cosmic struggle between God and Devil toward the struggle between good and evil in the human soul. At least some of Shakespeare's villains—Iago, Lady Macbeth, Edmund—draw upon a deep well of evil, whose waters seep in from we know not where. The Devil is not named as the source. Yet at the same time that this movement toward humanism was reducing the Devil's stature, the sermons and the theater of the fourteenth, fifteenth, and sixteenth centuries made him more colorful and real to the population at large than he ever had been. The great witch craze, which built upon this wide popular belief, was a phenomenon of the Renaissance, and the witch craze was at its height in England at precisely the time that Shakespeare was at his.

54. On "The Man of Lawes Tale" with its misogynistic association of women with the Devil, see Roddy, "Mythic Sequence." On "The Merchants Tale," where Pluto and Proserpine are figures of the Devil and his wife, see M. A. Dalbey, "The Devil in the Garden," *Neuphilologische Mitteilungen*, 75 (1974), 408–415. Dalbey shows the origin of the identification in the fourteenth-century "Ovide moralisée," which says that "Pluto denote le dyable," and in Petrus Berchorius ("allegorice . . . per Plutonem intelligitur dyabolus"). Pluto's rape of Proserpine symbolizes Lucifer's rape of souls. Compare Dante's use of classical figures, including Pluto, to represent the Devil.

55. See Chapter 5 above.

9 Lucifer on the Stage

Nowhere did the Devil put in a more convincing appearance than in the mystery and miracle plays of the later Middle Ages. These plays were for the most part written by clerics for the purpose of edifying (or terrifying) as well as entertaining. Like sermons and exempla, they were composed by an elite but were designed to appeal to a larger, uneducated audience. The Devil had broad popular appeal at this time owing to the plagues, famines, and wars that ravaged the fourteenth and early fifteenth centuries.

The playwrights' efforts to achieve dramatic unity produced the first coherent chronological accounts of the Devil's activities from his creation to his final ruin. Because this book is a history of the Devil, not of the theater, I do violence to the plays as works of art by fitting scenes from various plays together in the interest of conceptual coherence. Taken thus together, the plays constitute a version of salvation history and the history of opposition to salvation: *Höllegeschichte* as well as *Heilsgeschichte*.

The medieval drama derived primarily from the liturgy and was originally in Latin, but the Latin liturgical plays were soon paralleled and eventually superseded by vernacular plays. Political motivations brought liturgical drama to an abrupt end in the mid-sixteenth century.[1] The medieval plays are traditionally (recent scholarship has reservations) divided into three groups: mystery, miracle, and morality plays. The mystery plays seem to have sprung directly or indirectly from the liturgy. At first, single plays appropriate to certain feast days were staged on the day; later, cycles of plays portraying wide sections of salvation history from the creation of the world to the Last Judgment developed: Passion plays, Easter plays, and Corpus Christi plays. The miracle plays, which began in the twelfth century, were based upon the lives of saints. The morality plays, which flourished in the fifteenth and early sixteenth centuries, drew upon sermons and penitential literature. They described the tension between good and evil in the life of an ordinary human being making free moral choices. Everyman begins his life in innocence; he falls into sin and corruption; with the help of grace he repents and is saved. The Devil is often present onstage in the morality plays and always lurking offstage, for he is the ultimate source of the sin that drags us down and away from God; he may appear in person, or indirectly in the form of the vices or characters associated with the vices.[2]

The history of the world begins with creation.[3] For scholastic theology and philosophy as well as for modern science the world begins in an instant, at the point where time and space begin. After that point the cosmos develops gradually, whether the metaphor is the biblical six days or the eons of evolution. Usually it was supposed that God created the angels first of all beings. Some plays assume the creation of the physical world first, but this notion could not be reconciled with the prevailing theological view that God created humanity (and the physical universe, whose point and purpose is humanity) in order to replace the fallen angels. God made nine orders of angels and created Lucifer the highest angel of the highest order, second in the cosmos only to God himself. God is proud of him: "I have made you closest to me of all the powers; I make you master and mirror of my might; I create you beautiful in bliss, and I name you Lucifer, bearer of light."[4]

1. For bibliography on the Devil and the medieval theater, see the Essay on the Sources.

2. The standard work on the morality plays is R. Potter, *The English Morality Play* (London, 1975).

3. In the medieval view the real history of the world was not the succession of kings or the development of agricultural techniques, but rather the consecutive account of God's saving work in the world and of his creatures' response to it.

4. "Of all þe mightes i haue made moste nexte after me, / I make þe als master and merour of my mighte, / I beelde þe here baynely in blys for to be, / I name þe for Lucifer, als berar of lyghte" (York, "Fall of the Angels," 33–36).

Thus to set Lucifer apart is necessary to a view in which the evil is presumed to be focused in one malevolent personality rather than diffused through many. Many demons may exist, but the unity of the one Devil is necessary.

In medieval literature the Devil is usually called Lucifer or Satan. "Lucifer" was unusual earlier in the Middle Ages because of the tradition applying the name to Christ, the lightbearer, but it became as common as "Satan" in later medieval literature.[5] No significant distinction ever prevailed between Lucifer and Satan, though the two were often distinguished in order to enhance the literary dialogue. Eloy d'Amerval's *Le livre de la diablerie*, for example, is a learned, satirical dialogue between Lucifer and Satan, permitting the author to develop an ironic exposition of a Devil's-eye view of the world, as C. S. Lewis would do centuries later in *The Screwtape Letters*.[6] The name Lucifer was often given to the Devil in both his fallen and unfallen states, but the name Satan was reserved for his condition after the fall.[7] For this reason, Lucifer enjoyed a somewhat higher status, and some writers made him ruler of hell and Satan his lieutenant. In Guillaume de Digulleville's vision, Lucifer remains bound in hell while sending Satan up on the business of trying to get hold of Guillaume's soul; the tension between Lucifer as master and Satan as servant was exploited by Arnoul Gréban for comic purposes.[8]

Although some modern writers have emphasized Satan's subordination to Lucifer, it appears neither in theology nor in most major literature—not in Dante or Langland or consistently in the Corpus Christi plays.[9] The N-Town plays specifically equate the two when Lucifer

5. Rupert of Deutz, "De trinitate et opera eius," CCCM 21, p. 215, gives a *lucus a non lucendo* derivation of the name: "Ille autem cum sit tenebrarum potitor, per contrariam Lucifer appellatus est" (since he is the ruler of shadows, he is contrariwise called "Lightbearer"). See H. Spilling, *Die Visio Tngdali*, 2d ed. (Munich, 1982), pp. 216–225.

6. W. Rice, "Le livre de la diablerie d'Eloy d'Amerval," *Cahiers de l'association internationale des études françaises*, 3/4/5 (1953), 115–126; C. S. Lewis, *The Screwtape Letters* (London, 1942).

7. P. Dustoor, "Legends of Lucifer in Early English and in Milton," *Anglia*, 54 (1930), 211–268.

8. J. Subrenat, "Lucifer et sa mesnie dans le 'Pelerinage de l'ame' de Guillaume de Digulleville," in *Le diable au moyen âge*, pp. 507–525. For Gréban, see G. Paris and G. Raynaud, eds. *Le mystère de la Passion d'Arnoul Gréban* (Paris, 1878).

9. M. Rudwin, *Der Teufel in den deutschen geistlichen Spielen* (Göttingen, 1915), pp. 83–86, and M. Lazar in virtually all of his works, emphasize the distinction. It is found most frequently in the French and German Passion cycles. For the German plays, see R. Froning, ed., *Das Drama des Mittelalters*, 3 vols. (Stuttgart, 1891).

says, "I am your lord Lucifer that came out of hell, the prince of this world and great duke of hell, wherefore I am called Sir Satan."[10] In *La discesa di Gesu*, the ruler of hell is Inferus (hell personified), who sends Satan out on his evil errands. In the *Contrasto del povero e del ricco* Satan (Satanasse) is prince of hell and sends Beelzebub (Balzabouth) up to fetch the rich man's soul. In Huon de Meri's *Le torni* Satan is general of the forces of evil defending the City of Despair against Christ's besieging army.[11] Sometimes, as in *Piers Plowman*, it is Lucifer who goes up onto the surface of the earth to tempt Adam or Christ or do other Devil's business. The writers who subordinated Satan to Lucifer did so without any theological justification and for purely literary purposes. The subordination is occasional, arbitrary, and trivial, having no conceptual significance whatever for the idea of the personification of evil. "Satan," "Lucifer," and occasionally other names such as "Beelzebub," all designate the one ruler of darkness.

In contrast, the distinction between the Devil and minor demons is clear in theology and usually clear in literature. Of the hundreds of names given to demons in medieval literature, only a few were bestowed upon the Devil himself. The seven names given to the demons of the seven vices in the fifteenth-century *Lanterne of Light* are those most commonly associated with the Dark Lord: Lucifer (pride), Beelzebub (envy), Sathanas (wrath), Abadon (sloth), Mammon (avarice), Belphegor (gluttony), and Asmodeus (lechery).[12] Other names given to the Devil were Belial, Behemoth, Berith, Astaroth, Inferus, and Baal.[13] Sometimes a minor demon such as Tutivillus could be-

10. N-Town Passion Play, 1–3: "I am ȝour lord lucifer þat out of helle cam, prince of þis werd and gret duke of helle, wherefore my name is clepyd sere satan." Cf. York, "Harrowing of Hell," 117–119, where Beelzebub places Satan above Lucifer. In this chapter I will cite the Middle English in the text where the meaning is clear but translate it when it is less clear. When the Middle English appears in the text I will modernize it by regularizing the use of *v* and *u* and by using *f* for *ff*, *th* for þ, and *y*, *g*, or *gh* for ȝ.

11. M. W. Bloomfield, *The Seven Deadly Sins* (East Lansing, Mich., 1952), pp. 134–136.

12. Bloomfield, pp. 214–215.

13. For the names "Beelzebub" and "Belial" see DEVIL, p. 228; A. B. Gomme, "The Character of Beelzebub in the Mummers' Play," *Folk-lore*, 40 (1929), 292–293. For "Leviathan," "Asmodeus," and "Behemoth," see DEVIL, pp. 215–216. "Astaroth" derives from Ashtoreth, Ashtoroth, or Astarte, the Near Eastern fertility goddess. "Abadon" or "Abaddon," meaning "destruction" in Hebrew, designated Sheol in Job 26.6 and the Devil in Rev. 9.11. "Mammon" derives from the New Testament use of the term to personify wealth (Mt. 6.24, Lk. 16.11). "Belphegor" is the Greek form of

come a major one, as in the morality play *Mankind*, where he represents all the vices. Tutivillus was usually a parody of the Recording Angel, a minor demon who carried about a sack containing lists of sins or verses skipped by careless monks during the office or omitted by bungling scribes in the scriptorium.[14]

Some names were modifications or translations of the major names, such as Luciper, Lussibiaus, Lightberend. Others, usually applied to minor demons, derived from classical gods or from beings considered evil by the classical authors themselves. Among them were Apollo (reinforced by the Apollyon of Rev. 9:11, actually a version of the Hebrew Abaddon and no relation to the Greek god), Cerberus, Charon, Diana, Jupiter, Neptune, Orcus, Pluto, Proserpine, Tantalus, Venus, and Vulcan. Some, such as Ammon, Moloch, and Berith, derived from Scripture. Some were ironic, such as Tenebrifer (shadowbearer), Cocornifer (hornbearer; the allusion also touches cuckoldry), and Schonspigel (pretty mirror), or Spigelglantz (mirror gleam), these last two a pointed observation on the vanity of women. Other names were more bluntly descriptive or insulting: Robber, Murderer, Ragamuffin, Ribald, Cacodemon (evil demon), Krumnase (crooked nose), Hörnli (horny one), Slange (snakey), Gobli, Barbarin, or Hellhundt. Names of supposedly evil humans were applied to demons: Aggrapart (Herod Agrippa), Annaball (Hannibal), Herodias, Muhammad, Pharos (pharaoh), and Pilate. Some were allegorical: Abisme (hell), Desesperance (despair), Inferus, Aversier (adversary), Maufé (bad faith), Jrtum (error), Nyd (envy), Untrew (false), Fals (Falsehood), or Frauenzorn (woman's wrath). Some came from folklore, especially that of giants. Fergalus derives from the two giants Fergusius and Cornallus, and demon names such as Mauferas and Angingnars resemble the giant names Agolafre, Astrragut, and Ascopard.[15] Other names drew from the little people: Jack, Robin, Oliver, Greedigut, Rumpelstiltskin. Some names were mocking: Pantagruel (the origin of Rabelais' character), Gorgorant, Galast, Malost,

---

the name of a Moabite god, the "lord of Mount Phegor" (Num. 25.3). "Berith" derives from Judges 8.33: "Baalberith." "Moloch" (a god of the Ammonites), "Baal" (Canaanite "lord"), and Zabulon (from *diabolos*) were also used. See W. Arndt, *Die Personennamen der deutschen Schauspiele des Mittelalters* (Breslau, 1904), pp. 27–30.

14. M. Jennings, *Tutivillus* (Chapel Hill, 1977).

15. T. McAlindon, "The Emergence of a Comic Type in Middle-English Narrative: The Devil and Giant as Buffoon," *Anglia*, 81 (1963), 365–371. V. Kolve, *The Play Called Corpus Christi* (Stanford, 1966), has an excellent section on humor on pp. 124–144. See Chapter 4 above for the names of the Devil in folklore.

Libicocco, Cagnazzo, Radamanto, Lisegangl, Puk, Rosenkrancz (but not Guldenstern), Krüttli, Räppli, Ruffo, Lykketape, Funkeldune.[16] Some simply derived from nature: Foudre, Tempeste, Orage, Spavento, Fracasso.

Lucifer is created the wisest and most beautiful of the angels, but when God makes him their "governor," the bright angel's head begins to turn. God's throne is center stage, with the angels grouped around it singing their songs of praise. When God rises and proceeds to exit, Lucifer quickly begins to contemplate the empty throne and to muse upon his own glory:

> Aha, that I ame wounderous brighte. . . .
> All in this throne yf that I were,
> then shoulde I be as wise as hee. [Chester, "Lucifer," 126–130]

Lucifer scorns the angels for dutifully singing the Sanctus and bids them look at him instead and "see the beauty that I bear. To worship whom do you sing this sing, God or me? For I am the worthiest that ever may be."[17] The good angels recoil in horror: "wee will not assente unto your pride" (Chester 134). But Lucifer is undeterred:

> A wurthyer lord forsothe am I
> and worthyer than he evyr wyl I be.
> In evydens that I am more wurthy
> I wyl go syttyn in goddys se [throne]. [N-Town, "Fall of Lucifer," 53–57]

Lighteborne, Lucifer's accomplice, encourages him with gross flattery: "The brightnes of your bodie cleare / is brighter than God a thousandfoulde" (Chester, "Lucifer," 164–165). The good angels make a last effort: stop, they cry, or "Alas, that beautie will you spill" (Chester, "Lucifer," 166). Contemptuous of their caution, Lucifer decides to take the throne.[18] And now he enjoys the fullness of his pride: "All the joy in the world is marked in me, for the beams of my brightness are

16. See R. Griffin, "The Devil and Panurge," *Studi francesi*, 47/48 (1972), 329–336.
17. "And see the beautie that I beare" (Chester, "Fall of Lucifer," 143. "To whos wurchipe synge ʒe þis songe / to wurchip god or reverens me . . . / ffor I am þe wurthyest þat evyr may be" (N-Town, "Creation of Heaven," 40–43).
18. In the Towneley play the whole scene is compressed into one naively elegant stage direction; "hic deus recedit a suo solio et Lucifer sedebit in eodem solio" (here God leaves his throne, and Lucifer shall sit in the same throne).

burning so bright. In glorious glee my glittering gleams; I shall be like him who is highest on high."[19]

This dramatic scene, presenting anthropomorphized angels arguing around God's throne, is in contrast to the theologians' idea of a single moment of cold choice made at the beginning of time by a great cosmic power. The angels of theology are intelligences of great wisdom and power, but the stage angels are limited beings made in man's image: we understand what it is to yield to the absurdity of putting ourselves at the center of the cosmos. The requirements of drama swamped the scholastic refinement that Satan could not have been foolish enough to try to become God's equal but must have worked only to achieve his own beatitude through his own efforts and before God's good time. The grab for power was too dramatic for the dramatist to resist. The drama of the scene also helped underscore an important theological assumption that had been common since the fourth century. If the original sin of humanity is viewed as a terrible calamity and the source of all human evil, then the being precipitating such a horrible event must be wholly evil. To be wholly evil he must have been evil from the very beginning, and thus hatred must have been directed at God from the beginning rather than having been occasioned by the creation of humanity.

The weak-minded angels agree that Lucifer looks splendid in God's chair, and he invites them to worship him: "All angells, torne to me I read (advise), / and to your soveraigne kneele one your knee" (Chester, "Lucifer," 190–191). The good angels refuse, but the weak ones fall at his feet, and Satan, Beelzebub, Astaroth, and the others welcome him as their leader: "Vous serez nostre capitaine" (Gréban, 358). The angels who follow the Devil follow him in pride and folly; after their fall they will become his demons. Lucifer now utters his proudest blasphemy: "Though God come, I will not hense, / but sitt righte here before his face" (Chester, "Lucifer," 212–213). And that seals his doom. God returns in anger and denounces the proud rebel: "Lucifer, because of your great pride I bid you fall from heaven to hell, and with you all who take your part; never more will they dwell in bliss with

19. "All the myrth þat es made is markide in me, / þe bemes of my brighthode ar byrnande so bryghte. . . . / For in a glorius gle my gleteryng it glemes. . . . / I sall be lyke vnto hym þat is hyeste on heghte" (York, "Fall of the Angels," 49–50, 82, 91). Compare the large part played by the fall of Lucifer in the fifteenth-century *Mistere du Vieil Testament*, ed. J. de Rotschild (Paris, 1878).

me."[20] God reproves Lucifer in an echo of the liturgical reproaches on Good Friday:

> Lucifer, who set thee here, when I was goe?
> What have I offended unto thee?
> I made thee my frende; thou arte my foe.
> Why haste thou tresspassed thus to me? [Chester, "Lucifer," 222–225]

Lucifer's abrupt, undignified, and coarse expulsion from heaven accentuates the transformation of the bright angel into an ugly fiend: "Now I make my way to hell to be thrust into endless torment. For fear of fire I crack a fart."[21]

After Lucifer's expulsion, God proceeds to fashion the material universe, while the fallen angels in hell, shocked by their sudden ruin, lament their fate. Lucifer and his comrades are horrified to discover that they have become "feeyndes blacke" (Chester, "Lucifer," 251), and one of them cries out:

> Alas, alas, and wele-wo!
> Lucifer, whi fell thou so?
> We, that were angels so fare,
> and sat so hie aboue the ayere,
> now ar we waxen blak as any coyll [coal],
> and ugly, tatyrd as a foyll [fool]. [Towneley, "Creation," 132–137]

Lucifer himself is miserable, admitting that because of his accursed pride "now I am a devyl full derke that was an aungell bryt" (N-Town, "Fall of Lucifer," 77–78). In some versions the Devil's plaint is a pathetic inversion of the angelic song in Daniel 3:52–92:

> I complain to you, both wind and air, I complain to you, rain, dew and mist, I complain to you, heat, cold and snow, I complain to you, flowers and green meadows. . . . I complain to you, sweet song of birds, I complain to you hills and deep valleys, I complain to you rocks and all stones, I complain also to the

---

20. "Thu Lucyfere ffor þi mekyl pryde / I bydde þe ffale from hefne to helle / and all þo þat holdyn on þi syde / in my blysse nevyr more to dwelle" (N-Town, "Fall of Lucifer," 66–69).

21. "Now to helle þe way I take / In endeles peyn þer to be pyht. / Ffor fere of fyre a fart I crake" (N-Town, "Fall of Lucifer," 79–81).

whole world, which God in his mercy created: on these today I make my cry, that they should in kindness pray for me to the Almighty.[22]

The Devil's view is that God has unjustly hurled him out of heaven, added to his humiliation by creating humanity to take his place in the heavenly ranks, and planned his further defeat by taking on human form. Finally he insulted him by preferring the form of a human to that of an angel, first by creating humanity in his own image, and second by planning his incarnation in human flesh.[23] Satan complains: "Since we were fair and bright, I thought that he would take our form; but I was disappointed; he plans to take human shape, and that makes me envious."[24] How could such a crude creature as man, made of mere clay, have such bliss? (Chester, "Lucifer," 177–178).

As the fallen angels discuss their state in this, the first of many councils or parliaments that they hold in the course of their history of blocking salvation, their thoughts turn to revenge. Their complaint gradually transposes into a plot to destroy the new creation, especially its precious jewels Adam and Eve. Satan says that he will

> shewe mankynde greate envye.
> As soone as ever he [God] can hym make,
> I shall sende hym to destroye,
> one—of myne order shall bee—
> to make mankinde to doe amisse. [Chester, "Lucifer," 255–259]

The parliament decides to send one of their number up to the Garden of Eden to do the job. The original story of Genesis presented the serpent as the tempter in Eden, but the sin of Adam and Eve had from at least the third century onward been regarded as the source of all human evil and the tempter therefore identified with the Devil or at least the Devil's representative. The form the Devil took on his mission to Eden had to be one in which lines could be physically uttered and one that would appear attractive and persuasive to Eve. This meant that the conventional grotesque costumes of the demons were

22. From the Egerer Fronleichnamspiel, translated by R. Woolf, *English Mystery Plays* (Berkeley, 1972), p. 371.

23. "Ha voullu creer homme et fame / doués de si haulz privileges, / qu'ilz seront pour remplir les sieges" (Gréban, 663–665).

24. "And we were faire and bright, / þerfore me thoght þat he / the kynde of vs tane myght, / and þer-at dedeyned me. / The kynde of man he thoght to take, / and thereatt hadde I grete envye" (York, "Fall of Man," 8–13).

inappropriate to the tempter in Eden. The Devil therefore usually
appeared as a serpent with a human head or else in noble form, either
angelic or human. Sometimes the two were combined: he would first
appear in human form to explain his purpose and then reappear as a
snake. If the serpent had lines, he was given a human head, usually
that of a woman. By making the serpent look like Eve, the dramatist
could render the temptation more believable—and make a misogynistic comment on the side.[25]

The closest link between the Devil of art and the Devil of literature
is the stage demon. The elaborate vision literature about hell influenced the representational arts as well as Dante, and some paintings
are virtually illustrations of such visions. Art and theater influenced
one another from at least the end of the twelfth century, when the
vernacular theater began to be popular. The representation of the
Devil on the stage was derived from visual as well as literary impressions, and in turn artists who had seen stage productions modified
their own views.[26] The little, black imp, which could not easily be
represented on the stage, declined in the later Middle Ages. The desire
to impress audiences with grotesque costumes may have encouraged
the development of the grotesque in art, for there were animal costumes with horns, tails, fangs, cloven hooves, and wings; monster
costumes, half-animal and half-human; and costumes with faces on
buttocks, belly, or knees. Masks, clawed gloves, and devices to project
smoke through demon faces were also used.

In most plays Satan is elected to go up to Eden, and he plans his
strategy: "I shall take a virgin's face and the body and feet of a serpent." Gréban's stage direction reads: "Here Satan shall go on all fours
like a serpent and wind himself around the tree."[27]

In a worme liknes wille y wende. [York, "Fall of Man," 23]

25. J. Bonnell, "The Serpent with a Human Head in Art and in Mystery Play,"
American Journal of Archeology, 21 (1917), 255–291. For the treatment of the fall of Adam
and Eve in medieval literature, see J. Evans, *"Paradise Lost" and the Genesis Tradition*
(Oxford, 1968). See Ignatius Diaconus, *Drama de primi parentis lapsu*, MPL 117.1163–
1174.

26. M. Lazar, "Les diables," *Tréteaux*, 1 (1978), 56–69; M. Anderson, *Drama and
Imagery in English Medieval Churches* (Cambridge, 1963), pp. 143–177 and the plates
(e.g., 12B) of the Norwich cathedral bosses.

27. "Je prendrai virginalle face, / les piez et le corps serpentin" (Gréban, 677–678).
The stage direction: "Icy s'en va Sathan a quatre piez comme un serpent entortiller
autour de l'arbre."

A manner of an edder is in this place,
that wynges like a bryde (bird) shee hase,
feete as an edder, a maydens face—
her kynde I will take. [Chester, "Adam," 193–196]

In the *Mystère d' Adam*, the earliest full dramatic representation of the
temptation in Eden, "Diabolus" first appears in a form unspecified by
the stage directions and makes his argument; later he reappears in the
form of a speechless, artificial serpent.[28]

The Diabolus in *Adam* tempts Adam unsuccessfully before trying
Eve. This departure from the Genesis story goes back as far as the Old
English *Genesis B*. The popularity of this scenario, which occurs in
many of the plays, is the result of feudal and sexist assumptions. The
Devil is a great lord, who naturally chooses to address the man and
master first rather than his inferior, the woman. Adam's resistance to
the temptation underlines Eve's own weakness.

The Devil first offers Adam knowledge, then power. He first approaches his intended victim with a mocking challenge: "Que fais,
Adam?" (What are you doing?) (*Adam* 113), to which Adam responds
that he is living happily and getting along very well. Ah, the tempter
replies, but you could be doing much better still, and I can tell you
how. Adam admits that he does not know why God has forbidden the
fruit, and the Devil explains that it is the fruit of wisdom that gives
knowledge of all things. "If you eat it, you will do well;" indeed, you
will become God's equal.[29] The Devil easily transposes to the second
temptation, the temptation to power, telling Adam that if he eats he
will no longer need a lord, for he shall reign in majesty and share God's
own authority.[30] But the twelfth-century Adam well knew the vanity
of trying to be without a feudal lord. Recognizing who the tempter is,
he sends him packing, accusing him of being a faithless traitor—
traitres and *sanz foi* (*Adam* 204)—the worst of feudal crimes. "Get out
of here," he cries. "You are Satan" (*Adam* 196).

---

28. Stage direction: "Tunc serpens artificiose compositus ascendit juxta stipitem
arboris vetit[e]" (then a mechanical serpent comes up next to the trunk of the forbidden
tree).

29. "Ço est le fruit de sapïence de tut saveir donc scïence. Se tu le manjues, bon le
fras" (*Adam*, 157–159); God's equal: *per* (*Adam*, 167).

30. "Que porras estre senz seignor. . . . Tu regneras en majesté. Od Deu poez
partir poësté" (189–194).

Having failed with Adam, Diabolus turns his attention to Eve.[31] Eve recognizes the Devil at once and calls him by name, but she naively fails to grasp that he is evil. Satan offers her a bouquet of temptations: he wants to help her and her husband; God has selfishly denied them the fruit because if they eat it they will become his equal; Adam is too insensitive to understand what is good for them both, and he is certainly not good enough for his beautiful, delicate wife; Adam is stupid and needs his wife's help; since Eve is more capable than her husband she must become his equal; she can satisfy her curiosity by consuming the fruit; she will become queen of the world if only she will taste it; and when all is said and done it has a marvelous taste. Satan explains that God is jealous of his privileges and wishes to keep humanity from sharing them: "He cleverly keeps you from eating the fruit, well I know it, because he doesn't want anyone else to enjoy the great powers that it bestows."[32] Like Adam, Eve remarks that they seem to be perfectly happy as they are, but Satan brushes this aside as unworthy:

> To gretter state ye may be broughte.
> Ay! goddis shalle ye be!
> of ille and gode to haue knawyng,
> for to be als wise as he. [York 61, "Fall of Man," 71–73]

Lucifer invites Eve to precisely the same sin of pride that had brought him down: "Of this Appyl yf ye wyl byte / evyn as God is so shal ye be" (N-Town, "Fall of Man," 182–183). You will have the crown of heaven as the Creator's equal.[33] You will have all knowledge, and on *saver*, "to know," and *savor*, "taste," the author of *Adam* turns a pun. The fruit will give you the power "de tut saver," Satan says, and Eve replies, "Quel savor a?" to which Satan responds, "Celestial!" (*Adam* 251–252).

Satan's flattery of Eve is shameless; he admires her face, her figure, her eyes, her hair; he behaves like a courtly lover insinuating himself

---

31. He goes directly to Eve in most of the plays because he is confident of his success with her, since women are dominated by sensual passion: "wemen they be full licourouse" (Chester, "Adam," 199).

32. "To ete þer-of he you defende, / I knawe it wele, þis was his skylle, / by-cause he wolde non othir kende / thes grete vertues þat longes þer-till" (York, "The Fall of Man," 45–48).

33. "Del ciel averez sempres corone, al creator serrez pareil" (*Adam* 264–265).

between a man and his wife.[34] While Eve is still undecided, the Devil departs, only to return shortly in the shape of an artificial serpent. She goes to the serpent, makes as if to listen to it, and then abruptly bites into the fruit. In the English plays, where the tempter can still speak, the moment of the sin is a little less abrupt: Satan cries out: "Byte on boldly, be nought a-basshed!" (York 80). After eating, Eve experiences a little vision, which, as in the Old English *Genesis B*, the audience is intended to recognize as a delusion of the Devil, and then she returns to Adam, repeating the Devil's own words to her husband: "Byte on boldely, for it es trewe, we shalle be goddis and knawe al thyng" (York 102–103). In most versions Adam yields quickly. The action is best worked out in *Adam*, where Auerbach's analysis of the human motivation is convincing.[35] At the beginning of the play Eve had chattered on like a dependent child, but in the end she took matters into her own hands, biting into the apple herself and then handing it to her husband. In doing so she put him in a terrible position: either he must repudiate his wife (literally the only woman in the world) and allow her to face unknown dangers (or reap unknown delights) alone, or he must follow her lead. Surprised and disoriented, he follows her. This capitulation of husband to wife would have shocked the medieval audience, and the author made sure that they did not miss the point: "You are my equal," Adam tells her ("tu es ma per"). Eve, who had sought to become God's peer, at least became her husband's. Both were shocking ideas: this disruption of proper order was a sign of the disorientation of nature by sin.

God returns angry, reproaching Adam and Eve and cursing Satan roundly: "Thou wyckyd worm full of pryde!" (N-Town, "Fall of Man," 341). The Devil tries to explain himself to God:

> For I am ful of gret envy
> of wreth and wyckyd hate
> that man shulde leve above the sky
> where as sum tyme dwellyd I. [N-Town, "Fall of Man," 319–322]

But such apologies can have no effect, and God sends him packing back to hell. The fiend's response in Gréban's version is to be pleased with himself for having accomplished his mission: "I have played my

---

34. Richard Axton, *European Drama of the Early Middle Ages* (London, 1974), p. 125.
35. E. Auerbach, *Mimesis* (Princeton, 1953), pp. 124–151.

Eve and the serpent. The serpent is the Devil's mouthpiece in the temptation of Adam and Eve. Eve, who fell first and therefore often received more than her share of the blame, is here shown as temptress to Adam as well as tempted herself. She fondles the dragon, or serpent, whose master's will she has freely chosen to do. Statue at Reims Cathedral, thirteenth century. Courtesy of Cathédrale de Reims.

part well and can go home, for no devil will ever do such a good day's work as I have done."[36] But in the English versions his departure from paradise is a gross and humiliating reprise of his initial ejection from heaven: "By God's order I foully fall and creep home to my stinking sty, for both the hall of heaven and the pit of hell must do your [God's] bidding well. A foul fellow, I fall down here quaking, and burst my britches with a fart. My sorrow is coming soon."[37] Gréban allows him his brief triumph, but when he returns to hell to make his report to Lucifer, his reward is, according to the inverted values of hell, further punishment. "Praise me, Lucifer," he exclaims, "for I have just caused the worst disaster that will ever be."[38] Splendid, Lucifer replies, we'll make you a crown. "What shall we make it of, roses?" asks Astaroth. "Why no," Lucifer replies, "of thick irons burning like lightning."[39]

How did the terrifying prince of this world, the mighty enemy of God, become a figure for parody, satire, or even broad humor? A tendency toward the comic Devil began in the theater as early as the twelfth century under the influence of folklore and the folk performances of mimes, jugglers, and maskers.[40] The function of the funny demon was to produce comic relief, which both entertained the audience and relaxed them in order to prepare them for the next tragic action. The comic function was filled by the rustic in ancient drama and by the fool in Renaissance drama. In fact rustics and fools did appear on the medieval stage, along with apes, dwarves, monsters, and giants, who also underwent a transformation from the frightening to the comic.[41] Nevertheless, demons were the most effective comic figures for the paradoxical reason that they provoked the most fear. They were far more immediately terrifying than other comic figures, and

36. "J'ay bien joué mon parsonnage; / je puis bien faire retournee, / car jamès si haulte journee / ne fera deable que j'ay faict" (Gréban 861–864).
37. "At þi byddyng ffowle I falle. / I krepe hom to my stynkyng stalle; / helle pyt and hevyn halle / xul do þi byddyng bone. / I ffalle down here a ffowle freke / ffor þis ffalle I gynne to qweke; / with a ffart by brech I breke. / My sorwe comyth ful sone" (N-Towne, "Fall of Man," 349–356).
38. "J'ai fait le plus cruel besitre qu'oncques fut ne jamès sera" (Gréban, 916–917).
39. Astaroth: "De roses?" Lucifer: "Mes de gros barreaux, ardans comme feu de tonnoirre" (Gréban, 936–937).
40. M. Lazar, "Diables"; T. McAlindon, "Comedy and Terror in Middle English Literature: The Diabolical Game," *Modern Language Review*, 60 (1965), 323–332; McAlindon, "Emergence"; A Wünsche, *Der Sangenkreis vom geprellten Teufel* (Leipzig, 1905).
41. McAlindon, "Emergence," pp. 367–371.

this made their taming and defeat more of an emotional release. The comedy lay in knowing that their vaunting boasts would be foiled.

The defeat of the demons derived from hagiography and homiletic literature. The Devil (or a demon) would afflict the saint with terrible threats and temptations, but the saint would humiliate and sometimes even manhandle him, creating a joyful and comic ending to the tale. The message was that the terrible dark power, no matter how huge it looms, can always be done down by Christ and his saints. The more the audience feared plague, war, and other catastrophes, and the more guilty they felt about their own sins, the more they could enjoy comic relief at the discomfiture of the Devil. The audience was not invited to empathize with the demons and laugh with them, but rather to laugh *at* them and revel in their ruin. Thus the demons were always portrayed with contempt and disgust as vulgar, crude, and mean.[42] Many scenes are broadly funny and meant to appeal to an unsophisticated and uneducated audience, but the jokes were always at the Devil's expense. Real comedy requires the creation of some measure of tension, fear, or apprehension that can be released by the punch line. The persistence of jokes about the Devil at cocktail parties today, where jokes about Minerva or Persephone would fail, indicates that he retains some measure of his formidability.

Several levels of comedy exist in medieval demon plays. The lowest is slapstick, in which the demons run about the stage or out into the audience, screaming, leaping, farting, shouting oaths and insults, making obscene gestures, and executing pratfalls. A distinction was usually made between the great demons—Lucifer and his lieutenants—who could represent the Devil himself, and the minor demons, the *diablots* with their pratfalls, but in some plays, such as Gréban's *Passion*, the broad humor reaches up to the princes of hell and pulls them down, too, in the direction of farce.

The second level of humor was a broad satire reserved for the higher demons. Lucifer blesses his demons by placing his hand on their groins while insulting them in parody of priestly benediction. Hell is the place where all values are inverted: every praise is a curse, every song a cacophony. Sometimes this humor resembles a good-natured religious joke. In the thirteenth-century poem *Saint Pierre et le jongleur* Lucifer sends out his demons onto the earth to fetch souls down to hell, and they return leading prelates, nobles, and merchants. Lucifer

42. S. Kahrl, *Traditions of Medieval English Drama* (London, 1974), pp. 111–112.

is delighted, but one demon returns who has been able to secure only a lone naked jongleur who has lost all his goods gambling. He offers to sing for Lucifer, but the Dark Lord recoils at the suggestion and instead assigns him to stir the cauldrons of hell. One day Lucifer and his colleagues return to the surface of the earth in search of more damned souls, but while they are away Saint Peter descends into hell, plays dice with the jongleur, and wins back a number of the fallen spirits.[43] In such stories, the Devil is already being tamed and trivialized, but satire could be fiercer, particularly when the demons exhibit human vices and sins. The "trial of the human race" (see Chapter 4 above), which featured the Devil as prosecutor, appears in many of the miracle plays, for example the *Miracle de l'enfant donné au dyable* and the *Actes des Apôtres*.

The third level was satire of demonic human behavior. In 1484 Sebastian Brandt published his *Ship of Fools*, which had great influence. Humans are fools sailing on a ship captained by a fool. The fools represent the follies, hence the vices, and hence ultimately the demons. Brandt himself emphasized the foolish more than the demonic, but later writers, especially Lutheran pastors, crewed the ship with demons and tied human behavior closely to the Devil. As the personalities of the demons became more developed and their motivations more psychologically understandable, they became humanized; at the same time exploration of human emotions and motivations led to an internalization of demons in the human mind, and humanity became demonized. The two trends converged, the demons becoming more human and humans more internally evil. This convergence laid the basis for the replacement of the medieval Devil with Shakespeare's human villain, in whom evil is restricted to the individual human personality.[44]

The fourth level of humor was elevated irony. The Devil is truly powerful and threatening, yet God always brings his grandiose plans to nothing. When the Devil is portrayed seriously as God's great adversary, his ruin provokes, not ribald laughter, but a sense of release and joy. Auguste Valensin called this humor mystical hilarity.[45] We

43. D. D. R. Owen, *The Vision of Hell* (Edinburgh, 1970), pp. 206–207.

44. L. Schuldes, *Die Teufelsszenen im deutschen geistlichen Drama des Mittelalters* (Göppingen, 1974), pp. 33. See B. Spivack, *Shakespeare and the Allegory of Evil* (New York, 1958).

45. A. Valensin, "The Devil in the Divine Comedy," in Bruno de Jésus-Marie, ed., *Satan* (New York, 1952), pp. 366–378.

The Devil as an amorphous monster devouring sinners. Fresco by Giusto da Menabuoi (d. 139) in Viboldone parish church. Courtesy of Archivi Alinari.

see the world as it is, and we see that the Devil does not. We fear him because we know that he works horrors in the world through blind and malicious people who also do not see the world as it is. But we also know that his doom is sure, that his muddying of harmony, order, and justice is local and temporary and will pass away into the night without a trace. God is full; the Devil is empty; we can even pity "the poor Devil" as a fool and wish he could be otherwise. But a glance at the darkness does not steal our zest for the light. The cosmic joke is always on the Devil, and that is his choice: he refuses to have it any other way.

The next chapter in the dramatic history of the world was life under the Old Law before the Incarnation. The Devil continues to prompt every vice. The first sin after the expulsion from the Garden is the murder of Abel by Cain, whom Astaroth and Beelzebub urge to commit the crime.[46] Each successful corruption of a human is an occasion for rejoicing. The demons are satisfied with the results of original sin, which entitled them to take all souls to hell, the good as well as the bad, and so the murder of Abel provides them with their first prisoner. This assumption that the Devil has rights over the human race is of course the old ransom theory; long retired by the theologians, it lent itself to dramatic treatment far better than Anselm's satisfaction theory or Abelard's mystical love. The struggle between Christ and Satan for the rights to humanity persisted in literature and popular imagination in spite of the theologians' efforts to replace it. When Cain slays Abel, a jarring dramatic moment occurs: demons come and fetch away, not the murderous Cain, but his innocent brother. Lucifer orders him dragged off to limbo, which he can never leave because the gates of heaven are closed to the entire human race.[47] Or so Lucifer and Beelzebub think. But dramatic tension now begins to build, for the audience knows that they are mistaken and that the Savior will open the gates again, harrow hell, and free the saints from the demons' clutches. Meanwhile Adam and Eve are also taken down to hell when they die, as Satan reports to Lucifer: "They are down there in limbo too."[48] The Devil continues his lordship of the world throughout the entire Old Testament period, sometimes intervening directly, as in the

46. Luzerner Osterspiel; see Rudwin, p. 47.

47. Lucifer: "Elle (the soul) est juste, porte la, porte / lassus au limbe, at la la mectz. / Belzebuth: D'icy ne partirez jamès, / meschant ame, je le suppose: / la porte du ciel vous est close / et a tout le lignage humain" (Gréban, 1224–1229).

48. "Ilz sont la en ce limbe assis" (Gréban, 1708); cf. Gréban 1642–1651, 1698–1717.

temptation of Job, the sins of Sodom and Gomorrah, the sale of Joseph by his brothers, the worship of the golden calf, and Nebuchadnezzar's attack upon the Hebrews.[49]

The demons meet again in solemn conclave at the time of the Annunciation. When they hear of this puzzling event, they come together in the stinking pit of hell to quarrel over its meaning.[50] Gréban uses the occasion to create a comedy of inversion. "God curse you," Lucifer tells Satan, and Astaroth shouts, "Get the devil out of here."[51] Lucifer bewails the effects of the inversion: "My nobility and beauty are become deformity, my song a lament, my laughter desolation, my light a shadow, my glory sorrowful rage, my joy incurable mourning."[52] Satan jeers at Lucifer that whenever he tries to sing or laugh he howls like a famished wolf.[53] Lucifer orders his lieutenants to sing for him, and Astaroth, Satan, Beelzebub, and Berich make up a little choir and sing a ditty about death and damnation. But their singing is so hideous that the Dark Lord cannot bear it: "Hey, you clowns," he calls out, "you are killing me with your noise; by the Devil stop it; you're all off key."[54]

Finally they get down to the business of discussing the Annunciation, and Lucifer asks his associates if they think that anyone really could get the power to wrest the imprisoned souls away from them. Astaroth and Berich assure him that it could never be, as the audience smiles grimly, knowing that the harrowing is in store. Berich insists that the lost souls will never escape, but Satan is not so sure, for he remembers the Old Testament prophecies about the Messiah, and Lucifer muses that Mary's pregnancy may have some bearing on the question. The council sends Satan up to tempt the Virgin, but he tries and fails a hundred thousand times and must report back to Lucifer that she is incorruptible. And, he continues, "it gets worse. This

---

49. Job: Heidelberger Passionspiel; Sodom and Gomorrah: Künzelsauer Fronleichnamspiel; Joseph and his brothers, the golden calf, and Nebuchadnezzar: Luzerner Osterspiel. See Rudwin, pp. 47–48.

50. Hell is "tous puans de feu et de souffre" (Gréban 3707).

51. "Dieu te puist maudire" (Gréban, 3726); "Or va, de par le deable va!" (Gréban, 3758).

52. "Ma noblesse et ma grant beaulté / est tournee en difformité, / mon chant en lamentacion, / mon ris en desolacion, / ma lumiere en tenebre umbrage, / ma gloire en douloureuse rage, / ma joye en incurable dueil" (Gréban, 3729–3735).

53. "Lucifer, roy des ennemis, vous hurlez comme ung lou famis, quand vous voulez chanter ou rire" (Gréban, 3723–3725).

54. "Haro! ribauls, vous m'estonnez, / tant menez cry espouvantable; / cessez, cessez, de par le deable, / vostre chant s'accorde trop mal" (Gréban, 3860–3863).

virgin has had a baby, a fine son, who is going to cause us even more trouble, for rumor now has it that this is the Messiah himself come to redeem all of humanity."[55] Lucifer orders Satan punished for bringing such bad news, and Satan cringes and pleads, "Ha! mercy, maistre!" (Gréban, 7389). Thinking fast, Satan proposes to redeem himself by going back up to tempt King Herod to massacre the children, and Lucifer's mood changes immediately: "What an outstanding idea!"[56] Later, when Herod dies, the demons pull him down to hell; later still, the Devil encourages Herod the Younger to execute John the Baptist and tempts Mary Magdalene to lead a life of prostitution.[57]

The demons are still unsure whether Jesus is a magician, a prophet, the Messiah, or God himself. Though Aquinas and other theologians had referred to Christ's dissimuluation of his true identity at the time of the temptation, the point was made more emphatically in the theater. "Quel deable d'homme est ce Jhesus?" Berich exclaims (Gréban, 10,455). Satan explores the problem: "Listen to a story that is giving me a stomachache. I am very worried about this Christ. I would really like to know who his father is. If he is God's child and born of a virgin, then we have been badly outmaneuvered, and our success will be but short."[58] The demons meet in parliament to discuss the meaning of the Incarnation, which they do with hopeless stupidity and confusion. The prophets have foretold that Christ was coming, they observe, but apparently they do not need to worry, because Mary's son is named Jesus, not Christ.[59] Their confusion mounts: "Once people called him

---

55. "Encor vous diroy je plus fort: / ceste vierge a eu un enffant. . . . / elle a eu ung beau filz, / dont nous serons tous desconffis, / car le bruit vole maintenant / que c'est Christus propre venant / pour tous les humains racheter" (Gréban, 7363–7372).

56. "O quel conseil de noble sorte!" (Gréban, 7446).

57. Deaths of Herod and John: Künzelsauer Fronleichnamspiel; Mary Magdalene: Benediktbeuer Passionspiel, Egerer Fronleichnamspiel, Wiener Passionspiel. See Rudwin, pp. 50–54. In the Wiener Passionspiel, 325–328, two demons approach the Magdalene; one flatters her while the other urges her to dance: "Hoer, Maria, wag ich dir sage: du solt an vroeden nit versage, du solt mit mir tanzen unt hubeschlichen swanzen!" (Listen to me, Mary, you shouldn't renounce pleasure; dance with me and kick up your heels).

58. "Herke now what I sey a tale I xall ȝow telle / þat trobelyth sore my stomak þer of I haue grett dowte. / The dowte þat I haue it is of cryst i-wys. . . . / Ffayn wold I knowe who were ffadyr his. . . . / If þat he be goddys childe / and born of a mayd milde / than be we rygh sore begylde / and short xal ben oure spede" (N-Town, "The Temptation," 3–25). Compare Aquinas, *ST* IIIa.44.1.

59. The stupidity of the demons is clearest in the fourteenth-century poem "The Develis Perlament," or "Parliament of Fiends." The parliament of demons is a useful rhetorical device for getting into the psychology of the demons for moral or satirical purposes. It opens with a blasphemous pun: "Whan Marye was greet with Gabriel"

John the Baptist, but now he has changed, and Jesus is his name. But he who was first called Jesus is now known as Christ. . . , and he calls himself God's son."[60]

Belial and Beelzebub beg Satan/Lucifer to go up and tempt Christ in order to find out who he is. The Devil goes up and tempts the second Adam in much the same way that he tempted the first, but with a quite different outcome. As Nelson pointed out, Christ refused to allow the Devil to learn the truth. Had Lucifer succeeded in tempting Jesus to hurl himself off the pinnacle of the temple, one of two results could have occurred: Jesus would have died, proving that he was not God, or he would have been held up by the angels, proving that he was. By refusing to respond, Christ both showed his contempt for the Devil and kept him in suspense.[61] Satan skulks home to hell:

> What that he is I kan not se
> whethyr god or man what that he be
> I kan not telle in no degre
> for sorwe I lete a crakke. [N-Town, "Temptation," 192–195]

And so he departs, farting miserably. On returning home, he receives an uncomfortable welcome. "Go, Satan," Lucifer rages, "may God curse you! May the Devil carry you off!"[62] Astaroth still blusters that Jesus is nothing but a false prophet, but Lucifer's fear, which commenced at the time of the Annunciation, is slowly growing. The literally monstrous stupidity of the demons as they try to start and

---

(when she was greeted by Gabriel, or when she was impregnated by Gabriel). "The Devil's Parliament" was edited by F. J. Furnivall, *Hymns to the Virgin and Christ* (London, 1868), but a new edition is being prepared by Patricia Silber of the State University of New York at Stony Brook. See her article "'The Develis Perlament:' Poetic Drama and a Dramatic Poem," *Medievalia*, 3 (1977), 215–228, and her unpublished article "Councils and Debates: Two Variations on the Theme of Deceiver Deceived." I am grateful to Professor Silber, who is now working on the topic of the Devil and the law, for sharing unpublished material and comments with me.

60. "Oon men clepid him iohne þe baptist, / but now he haþ turned, ihesus is his name! / þat first hiȝte ihesu, now is clepid crist. . . . / But "goddis sone" he him silf dooþ calle" ("Devil's Parliament," 102–104; 168; see 19–20).

61. A. H. Nelson, "The Temptation of Christ; or the Temptation of Satan," in J. Taylor and A. H. Nelson, eds., *Medieval English Drama* (Chicago, 1972), pp. 218–229; D. L. Wee, "The Temptation of Christ and the Motif of Divine Duplicity in the Corpus Christi Cycle Drama," *Modern Philology*, 72 (1974), 1–16.

62. "Va, Sathan, Dieu te puist maudire. . . . Or, va, que le deable te maine" (Gréban, 10711, 10719).

stop the crucifixion is an essential part of their character: they are simply incapable of grasping things as they are. They unfailingly act against their own interests because they do not understand that what-ever they do, God's will and providence are simply and inevitably done.

When Jesus begins his ministry, the demons cannot keep track of him; he seems to be everywhere at once. Lucifer asks, "Satan, tell me where Jesus is now, and in what place?" "The Devil *I* know," Satan replies, "he is getting worse every day with his teaching and his preaching."[63] The raising of Lazarus and his liberation from hell pro-vide the demons with proof of Christ's unstoppable power. They understand that if Christ can save one soul from hell he can save all. Yet still they continue to hope. Their empire on earth has lasted so long that they cannot really believe that its ruin is at hand.[64]

Increasingly desperate and still unsure as to the nature of their adversary, they plan to kill him. They send Lucifer's daughter Despair up to Judas in order to persuade him to betray his master. When Judas has done the deed, Despair prompts him to suicide, and the demons rejoice at his eternal damnation.[65] Meanwhile Christ is being led be-fore the Sanhedrin and Pilate for judgment, and Satan is delighted with his work. He rushes down to hell to give out the good news: "Harrow, how happy I am!"[66] But Lucifer has second thoughts: if Jesus is really divine, then their plan to kill him will only bring down worse ruin upon their heads. "False Satan," he shouts, "you've ruined everything."[67] Go on up and put a stop to it before it is too late. And so Satan, scorned by his fellows, rushes back up to earth with a last desperate and futile plan to stop the crucifixion. He decides to appear to Pilate's wife Procula in a dream and tell her that a terrible calamity

63. Lucifer: "Sathan, or me dis maintenant ou est ce Jhesus n'en quel place." Satan: "Je ne sçay: le deable le sache! . . . il va tousjours de pis en pis: il presche, il enseigne, il sermonne" (Gréban, 17413–17420).

64. M. C. Pilkinton, "The Raising of Lazarus: A Prefiguring Agent to the Harrow-ing of Hell," *Medium Aevum*, 44 (1975), 51–53; K. Roddy, "Epic Qualities in the Cycle Plays," in N. Denny, ed., *Medieval Drama* (London, 1973), pp. 155–171.

65. "Saultez dehors, Deseperance, ma fille" (Gréban, 21780–21781). See also the Alsfelder Passionspiel, Augsburger Passionspiel, Benediktbeuer Passionspiel, Egerer Fronleichnamspiel, Frankfurter Passionspiel, Luzerner Osterspiel, Sterzinger Os-terspiel; Rudwin, pp. 55–57. For the scriptural bases for blaming the crucifixion on Satan see Jn. 13.2, 13.27.

66. "Haro! comment joyeulx je suis!" (Gréban, 23342).

67. "Faulx Satan, tu as tout gasté!" (Gréban, 23378).

awaits her husband if he should condemn this innocent man. Procula is deeply affected by the dream and rushes to inform her husband.[68] But Caiphas, the high priest, shrugs her off, telling her that Jesus has caused the dream by witchcraft in order to save his skin, and Pilate dismisses doubt on the grounds that he must not falter in his service to Caesar. This episode, which appears in several of the plays, has the dramatic disadvantage of blunting the effect of the harrowing, which is sharpest when the demons do not understand Christ's nature until he is actually battering down their doors.

The demons do not appear at the death of Christ itself, since the comic side of their character was pronounced enough that their presence would have detracted from the dignity of the moment.[69] But they are right there after his death, carrying off the soul of the unrepentant thief. Now Lucifer calls another council in which he orders Satan and a few companions to make their way back up to the cross and seize the soul of Jesus; Satan obeys, but he is met at the foot of the cross by the archangel Gabriel, who drives him off with a sword. The demons retreat back to hell in terror. This is a turning point. Until now, they have taken offensive action against God, but from now on they will be on the defensive only.[70]

For now, driven back into the hold of hell, they must deploy their defense. Yet they are still boasting. Satan exlaims, "If Jesus comes down here and dares say one word, I'll singe his hair off."[71] He still fails to grasp who Jesus is: "I knew his father by sight; he earned his living as a craftsman, so what makes this Jesus so high and mighty? He is nothing but a man really, so, you demons, go get that boaster and bind him in hell torments. We hanged him on the cross, and we'll take care of him now. Go get him and knock that dastard down."[72] But into

68. Pilate's wife is variously named Procula, Pilatissa, Portula, or simply "Uxor Pilaty."

69. T. N. Grove, "Light in Darkness: The Comedy of the York 'Harrowing of Hell' as Seen against the Backdrop of the Chester 'Harrowing of Hell,'" *Neuphilologische Mitteilungen*, 75 (1974), 115–125.

70. Donaueschinger Passionspiel; Alsfelder Passionspiel; Egerer Fronleichnamspiel; Heidelberger Passionspiel; Frankfurter Passionspiel; Rudwin, pp. 59–61.

71. "Se Jhesucrist veut dire mot, je li brulerai le toupot" (Palatinus play, 1383–1384).

72. "Thy fader knew I well by syght, he was a wright, his meett to wyn. . . . Say who made the so mekill of myght?" (Towneley, "The Deliverance of Souls," 245–249). "A man hee ys fullye, in faye . . . therefore this bolster look ye bynde in bale of hell-brethe" (Chester, "Harrowing of Hell," 105–112). "Dynge that dastard doune" (York, "Harrowing of Hell," 180).

the depths of the darkness of hell a great light begins to shine.[73] And the unaccustomed sound of souls rejoicing penetrates the dark council. "What is that noise?" Lucifer demands, and Berich replies, "It is the human race; their salvation is at hand."[74] "I knew it," Lucifer says, "I always knew he would come and steal our inheritance."[75]

And now the decisive moment in the history of salvation is at hand. The soul of Jesus comes to the gates of hell and utters the great words from Psalm 24:7–10: "Attollite portas" (Open up your gates)![76] Now at last the demons know the truth for sure. "Alas, alas, oh no,"cries Belial, "we must bow to your orders; we know now that you are God."[77] Satan or Lucifer makes a desperate effort to argue with Jesus. Wait, Satan cries. Look, I was promised that I could keep the damned souls! All right, Jesus replies, I don't care, go ahead and keep Cain, Judas, and all sinners and unbelievers.[78] Yes, Satan pursues, but if you get to steal my souls, then I get to continue to wander the world and corrupt your servants. But Christ's majesty refuses the bargain: No, fiend, he replies, you shall not, for I shall bind you fast in hell.[79] Jesus summons Michael, who sets Satan in chains, and the Lord leads the happy souls in triumph out of hell: "Then Jesus took Satan, who once was lord and sire, and in thralldom bound him to burn in endless fire."[80] The chronology of the binding of Satan is one of those points on which there was no theological consistency, and here the theological incoherence invades the plays. Satan is bound just after his fall from heaven; or after his temptation of Adam and Eve; or at the Passion or harrowing; or at the Last Judgment. Structurally all these events are

73. Lucifer: "Und ist nie kömen solicher schein in dise gruntlose helle pein" (Pfarrkircher Passionspiel 5.377–378).
74. Gréban, 23,270–23,275. Cf. Alsfelder Passionspiel 5.7078–7080: Lucifer: "Sathanas, was betudet das, singen und frohlich syn alhye in der helle pyn?"
75. "Je l'ay tousjours ymaginé, et ainsi nous en advendra et que ce faulx Cristus vendra despoiller tout nostre heritage" (Gréban, 23302–23305).
76. N-Town stage direction: "The sowle goth to helle gatys and seyth. . . ."
77. "Alas alas out and harrow: onto þi byddynge must we bow þat þou art god now do we know" (N-Town, "Descent into Hell," 1002–1004).
78. York, "Harrowing of Hell," 305–312. Alsfelder Passionspiel 5.7255: "Blibet, ir Verfluchten, in der ewigen Pin!"
79. Middle English Harrowing, 119–122: "ȝef þou reuest me of myne y shal reue þe of þyne; y shal gon from mon to mon and reue þe of mony on."
80. York, "Harrowing of Hell," 335–336; Middle English Gospel of Nicodemus: "þan Ihesu Criste toke Satanas, þat are was lorde and syre, and hym in thraldom bunden has at bryne in endles fire." Erlauer Passionspiel 5.442–443: "Lucifer du solt gepunkden wesen, von disen panden solt du nimmer genesen."

one, and it leads only to confusion to try to straighten them out chronologically. If Satan had been bound at his fall, or at the Passion, how is it that he can still wander the world seeking the ruin and destruction of souls? If Christ stopped him from doing that at the harrowing, how is it that he still is free to tempt us today? But if he is not bound until the Last Judgment, then was the triumph of Christ over death and hell only a limited one? Behind the incoherencies of chronology lies the even deeper theological difficulty: Christ both broke the power of Satan and did not break it, for after the Passion and the harrowing the Devil's power is still strong in the world.

The defeat of Hell at the harrowing was the decisive turning point in the dramatic history of salvation. At the time of the Resurrection the demons are still scurrying about trying to check the course of events, but now that the crisis is passed, they can be only comic or pathetic. When Lucifer reproaches Satan for not following Christ and the patriarchs on their way out of hell to see if he could pick off a few stragglers, Satan finally rounds on his master: You can sit there in hell talking at ease, while I go out and do all your dirty work![81] The Devil's fate has been sealed by the harrowing; now his doom is sure.

And yet he is active in the world until the final day of doom, and these continued activities are attested by miracle plays, poetry, and sermons that describe his attacks on the saints and his perpetual defeat by them. *The Castle of Perseverance*, a fifteenth-century morality play, contains an early scene in which the protagonist, Mankind, confronts the good and evil angels that dwell within him, each trying to pull him toward an opposite goal. The evil angel is aided by the Devil, the World, the Flesh, and the seven cardinal sins, whose personifications are very much like the demons. Belial leads the sins in an assault upon the castle of the soul, where humanity has taken refuge for safety. The stage direction for Belial is colorful: "And he that schal pley Belyal loke that he have gunne-powdyr brennynge in pypys in hys handys and in his erys and in hys ars whanne he goeth to batyl." When Mankind dies, the good and evil angels dispute possession of his soul. In the last scene, the four daughters of God plead before the throne of the Almighty, Justice and Truth demanding the damnation of humanity, Peace and Mercy its salvation. God decides for mercy, and the action is resolved.[82]

81. Gréban, 33,451–33,454.

82. *The Castle of Perseverance*, in M. Eccles, ed., *The Macro Plays: The Castle of Perseverance; Wisdom; Mankind* (London, 1969), pp. 1–111.

Throughout the period between the Resurrection and the Last Judgment, it is the Blessed Virgin who is the most active adversary of the Devil, Christ having withdrawn as it were to his solemn seat above, and Mary having become the compassionate mediator between humanity and Christ the judge. Mary became the leader of the forces of good in the war for the world, so the miracle stories pitted the "top teams" of good and evil against one another, one team captained by Mary, the other by Lucifer.[83] The message was clear: the good team always wins in the end; as Moshé Lazar put it, "The white Queen inevitably checks the black King."[84] We are told that we cannot serve two masters, that we will obtain no lasting profit from following the Devil, that it is never too late to make the decision to turn to the good, and that the Virgin will protect a truly repentant sinner from the punishment due under strict justice.

The final act in the history of salvation is the Last Judgment. It opens with the story of the wise virgins who prepare for the coming of the bridegroom and the foolish virgins who waste their lives and are led off to hell, where Lucifer rejoices at their arrival.[85] The audience knows that this play anticipates the separation of the saved from the sinners at the moment of final doom. Just before the second coming, however, Satan mounts one last desperate attack on the kingdom of God. The demons hold a final parliament and decide that their only hope now is for the Devil to beget a child, the Antichrist, and send him out into the world.[86] When the birth of the Antichrist is reported,

83. K. Roddy, "Mythic Sequence in the Man of Law's Tale," *The Journal of Medieval and Renaissance Studies*, 10 (1980), 1–22, cites the *Speculum humanae salvationis* (p. 18): "Et sicut Christus superavit diabolum per suam passionem, ita etiam superavit eum Maria per maternam compassionem" (just as Christ overcame the Devil with his passion, so Mary overcame him with her compassion). On the tradition of the struggle of the Devil versus Our Lady, see Lazar, "Satan and Notre Dame." The Virgin's defeat of the Devil is the most common theme of Gautier's *Miracles de Notre Dame*; see, e.g., "Dou jovencel que li dyables ravi, mais il ne le pot tenir contre Nostre Dame," vol. 2, pp. 205–223; "De un moigne que Nostre Dame delivra dou Dyable," vol. 2, pp. 114–121; "De celui qui se tua par l'amonestement dou dyable," vol. 2, pp. 237–245.

84. Lazar, "Satan and Notre Dame," p. 6. Cf. Rutebeuf, lines 2471–2473: "Ahi, nostre douce Advocate, tu n'es ne peus estre mate mès tu mates bien le Déables" (Ah, sweet Advocate of ours, you are not checked, nor can ever be, but you check the Devil).

85. Künzelsauer Fronleichnamspiel; see Rudwin, pp. 62–64.

86. K. Aichele, *Das Antichristdrama des Mittelalters, der Reformation und Gegenreformation* (The Hague, 1974); R. K. Emmerson, *Antichrist in the Middle Ages* (Seattle, 1981); L. U. Lucken, *Antichrist and the Prophets of Antichrist in the Chester Cycle* (Washington, D.C., 1940); J. Wright, ed., *The Play of Antichrist* (Toronto, 1967).

the parliament of hell rejoices. The Devil visits the young Antichrist and, in a parody of the temptation of Christ, offers him the kingdoms of this world, a temptation to which the evil lord yields eagerly. Antichrist goes out into the world, working false miracles, deluding the populace, persecuting the saints, encouraging unjust rulers and corrupt bishops, and preparing for the final battle against Christ. His defeat is swift and sure. He cries out in vain:

> Helpe, Sathanas and Lucyfere!
> Belzebubb, bould batchellere!
> Ragnell, Ragnell, thou art my deare!
> Nowe fare I wonder evyll. . . .
> Nowe bodye and soule both in feare
> and all goeth to the devyll. [Chester, "Antichrist," 645–652]

When he dies, two demons appear and carry his body down to hell to remain forever with his father in eternal pain: "With Lucyfere, that lord, longe shall he lenge; / in a seate aye with sorrowe with him shall he sytt" (Chester, "Antichrist," 687–688). The reaction of the demons to the descent of Antichrist, itself a parody of the harrowing, is mixed. They rejoice to see their comrade; they rejoice to see him damned, for he adds to their treasury of souls; yet they know that his ruin makes their own final destruction inevitable. The position of Antichrist in hell is also, like that of his father, ambivalent. He is a damned soul condemned to eternal imprisonment in hell, yet he is also a dark prince, heir apparent to the ruined kingdom.

It is now doomsday, and the demons are still suffering their eternal confusion. They are happy, because now hell will be eternally filled with all the damned sinners. They run here and there with books listing sinners and bags full of documentation. They rejoice over the arrival of each prisoner. It is an exciting moment for them, rather like an inverted Christmas. Hordes of damned sinners file into hell, and the demons delight in their moans.[87] Yet it is now that Satan is bound finally and forever. God says to him: "You, Lucifer, have never been willing to take responsibility for the great sin that you have committed. Instead you have daily persisted in your malevolence, like Pharaoh and Judas, who also did not repent of their sins; because of this, I

87. York, "Last Judgment," 143: The wailing damned go "in helle to dwelle with feendes blake," and the demons rejoice, for "if þe domisman do vs right, full grete partie with vs schall gang" (York, "Last Judgment," 223–224).

curse you."[88] The demons are horrified at the final destruction of their kingdom, which they have feared from the moment of their age-old sin. Lost is their kingdom, lost their power to obstruct the kingdom of God. The cosmos is restored to its perfect harmony, and death, sin, and sorrow are no more. Each member of the audience is left with a double feeling, comparable to the ambivalence of the demons: a joy at the triumph of the light, and a fear that at the Last Judgment he or she will be cast out into the outer darkness with ruined Lucifer. The very last action on the stage of the world is abrupt and final and leaves one introspective: Christ shuts the door of hell, locks it, and takes away the key.

88. M. Lazar, ed., *Le jugement dernier (Lo Jutgamen General)* (Paris, 1971), lines 281–288: "Mas tu, Lucifer, no as vuolgada aver conoisensa / de ton gran pecat que avias comés, / mas a tot jorn perseverat / en ta granda malvestat, / coma ha fach Pharao he Judas / que jamais sertas de lor malecia / no an vuolgut aver conoisensa. / He per so ieu vos doni la maladictio."

10 Nominalists, Mystics, and Witches

The fourteenth and fifteenth centuries were misunderstood until recently. To medievalists and Catholics they seemed to show a steep decline from the glorious twelfth and thirteenth centuries; to Protestants they seemed both an age of corruption and an age when the first stirrings of the glorious Reformation appeared; to the aesthetic they were the Renaissance of arts and letters; to some social historians they seemed an age of decomposition and fear, a dark period when the witch craze began. Elements of truth exist in all these views, but recently a new consensus has been emerging, in which these centuries appear complex and varied, a period in their own right rather than the tail end of the Middle Ages or the preface to the Reformation. To draw a line between the Middle Ages and the Reformation is as arbitrary as any such distinction. The transition was on the whole varied and gradual, and the intellectual and social similarities between the fourteenth and sixteenth centuries are greater than the differences. To end this book about 1500 is artificial, and the best that can be said for it is that it is no more artificial than any periodization.[1]

1. On the period in general see especially G. Leff, *The Dissolution of the Medieval Outlook* (New York, 1976); F. Oakley, *The Western Church in the Later Middle Ages*

None of the main intellectual currents of the period was conducive to diabology. Scholastic realism had already played the Devil down, and now nominalism, mysticism, and humanism were even more inclined to ignore him. Yet at the same time the great witch craze began, a product of inquisitorial theory impressed upon a population prepared by a diabology passed down by saints' lives, homilies, and the mystery and morality plays. The popular theology of the sermon kept belief in the Devil immediate and compelling, and the dominance of the sermon in Protestant thought explains how diabology remained a powerful element in a religion that dismissed so many other earlier traditions. The Council of Trent of the Catholic Reformation deemphasized the Devil, but his power in Protestant thought grew, finally producing, in seventeenth-century England, his finest monument, Milton's *Paradise Lost*.

The most powerful intellectual trend of the fourteenth and fifteenth centuries was nominalism.[2] The roots of nominalism go back to the twelfth-century debates on universals, but its immediate origins lie in the theological tensions of the late thirteenth century, especially the condemnation of "Christian Averroism" by the University of Paris in 1277. From the early fourteenth to the sixteenth century, nominalists such as William of Ockham, Pierre d'Ailly, Jean Gerson, Nicholas of Cusa, and Gabriel Biel vied with realists such as Duns Scotus, John Wyclif, Jan Hus, and Cajetan for control of the schools. Since the term *nominalism* was invented in modern times, some contemporary historians suggest giving it up altogether, but as no other word commands assent, it seems to remain useful in classifying certain tendencies of late medieval thought, so long as one understands that a great variety of "nominalists" existed.

(Ithaca, 1979); H. Oberman, *Forerunners of the Reformation* (New York, 1966); H. Oberman, "Fourteenth-Century Religious Thought," *Speculum*, 53 (1978), 80–93; H. Oberman, "The Shape of Late Medieval Thought," in C. Trinkaus and H. Oberman, eds., *The Pursuit of Holiness in Late Medieval and Renaissance Religion* (Leiden, 1974), pp. 3–25; S. Ozment, *The Age of Reform, 1250–1550* (New Haven, 1980).

2. On nominalism see especially W. Courtenay, "Nominalism and Late Medieval Religion," in Trinkaus and Oberman, pp. 26–59; W. Courtenay, "Nominalism and Late Medieval Thought: A Bibliographical Essay," *Theological Studies*, 33 (1972), 716–734; C. Davis, "Ockham and the Zeitgeist," in Trinkaus and Oberman, pp. 59–65; P. Kristeller, "The Validity of the Term: 'Nominalism,'" in Trinkaus and Oberman, pp. 65–66; F. Oakley, "Pierre d'Ailly and the Absolute Power of God," *Harvard Theological Review*, 56 (1963), 59–73; H. Oberman, "Some Notes on the Theology of Nominalism," *Harvard Theological Review*, 53 (1960), 47–76; S. Ozment, "Mysticism, Nominalism, and Dissent," in Trinkaus and Oberman, pp. 67–92.

The first general tendency of nominalism was to reject the realist belief in universals. William of Ockham (c. 1285–c. 1347), the Oxford Franciscan who was the earliest nominalist leader, held this position strongly.[3] For Ockham and his followers Platonic idealism and realism were false and a source of the unnecessary complications of earlier scholastic theology. Ockham's razor (the simplest explanation consonant with the evidence is usually the best) slashed away the abstract "realities" that earlier theologians had invented. We know that Socrates and Plato are both human, Ockham observed, by direct experience and intuition. We have no need to refer them both to an abstract quality "humanity" in order to know this. People could tell a man from a finback whale before Plato invented realism. We have no evidence that "humanity" exists, only individual humans; no evidence that "finback whaleness" exists, only individual finback whales. Propositional knowledge is thus a creation of human beings rather than a statement about the "real world." Ockham's view influenced Kant, who in turn influenced modern phenomenology. When we say we know abstractions, we in fact know only human conceptions and cannot assume that they correspond with some "absolute reality" beyond. In the fourteenth through sixteenth centuries this doctrine tended to lead in two directions: the first was fideism, reliance upon faith rather than natural reason in understanding religious truth; the second was empiricism, knowledge built upon sensory observation of physical objects.

When applied to God himself the doctrine had several effects. First, whatever we say about God is a human proposition that cannot be assumed to describe the true nature of God. For example, we use the term *being* to categorize things that we experience with our senses, and if we apply the term *being* to God we cannot expect it to mean the same thing. There is no abstract "being" in which all things share; the being of one thing is different from that of another; the being of God is radically different from that of the physical things we observe. Terms are "equivocal": that is, they mean something quite different when applied to God from what they mean when applied to a human or a rock. Ockham believed that we can know God by experience and

3. On Ockham see L. Baudry, *Guillaume d'Ockham: Sa vie, ses oeuvres, ses idées sociales et politiques*, vol. 1, *L'homme et les oeuvres* (Paris, 1949); L. Baudry, *Lexique philosophique de Guillaume d'Ockham* (Paris, 1958); R. Guelluy, *Philosophie et théologie chez Guillaume d'Ockham* (Louvain, 1947); G. Leff, *William of Ockham: The Metamorphosis of Scholastic Discourse* (Manchester, 1975).

intuition, but as soon as we try to construct a natural theology, a rational process, to get at the nature of God we are obliged to use equivocal terms and thus get no nearer to God than human conceptions of him.

For Ockham, no universal exists anywhere. Thomas Aquinas had been willing to admit that universals do not exist in things, but he had affirmed that universals existed prior to things; he thought that an idea of humanity existed in the mind of God as a prototype of individual humans. This Ockham denied. There are no ideas in the mind of God, no prototypes that the Deity had logically to choose among or use as patterns. God is absolutely free, unbound by any necessity internal or external. The nominalists distinguished between God's *potentia absoluta*, his absolute power to do whatever he wishes, and his *potentia ordinata*, the way he has in fact set the cosmos up. God could have made the physical and moral laws of the cosmos quite different. This does not imply that God is whimsical. He has chosen the cosmos he has chosen, and we can learn about it because he created us with senses and intelligence. Every event in the cosmos is immediately contingent upon God: God could make hydrogen and oxygen combine to produce fruitcake if he wished, but in fact he has ordained things so that they ordinarily produce water. God has the power to do many things that he has never done and will never do. His "absolute power" is limited only by the principle of contradiction, but the "ordained power" is simply a description of what is. Evil is evil because God declares it evil, not because God recognized an intrinsic quality of evil that it possessed before he declared it so.

These assumptions led to two quite different traditions about free will and determinism. On the one hand, the absolute freedom and inscrutability of God led some nominalists to emphasize determinism. God may save or damn according to whatever principle he chooses or according to no principle at all. All we can do is throw ourselves upon the inexplicable will of God and hope. For some nominalists, such as Thomas Bradwardine, God selects those whom he wishes to save and gives them a grace that they cannot resist. A human being becomes an instrument of God for whose good or evil God himself must be responsible. The majority of nominalists, however, emphasized God's faithfulness to the "ordained power" and the order that he had created, an order that included free will and a grace that was freely offered but did not compel. Many permutations of these views continued to be debated for centuries. Those taking a generally predestinarian position included Aquinas, Scotus, Bradwardine, Staupitz, Luther, Calvin, and the Jansenists; those taking a largely free-will position included Ockham, Gabriel Biel, Pierre d'Ailly, the Jesuits, and the Arminians. It was against the predominantly free-will Ockhamists that Luther and Calvin reacted to their emphasis upon predestination, though Calvin was also attacking the Neoplatonic-magical emphasis on the capriciousness of fate or fortune as opposed to the benign providence of God.

A moderate position combining elements of both free will and predestination had existed from the time of Augustine. God knows your moral choices in all eternity. Whether this is because God exists outside time, as Augustine thought, Ockham himself refused to say. But he insisted that God at least could be said to know the truth about any disjunctive proposition about the future. Either there will be a war in 2034 or not. God knows whether the proposition "there will be a war in 2034" is true or not, although he does not interfere with human free will in its choice to wage that war or not. God predestines you to salvation if he knows that your life is a good one, but he does not determine your goodness. This idea was expressed as God's predestination "after foreseeing merits." He wills you to be free; he sees (without determining it) that you choose to live right; he predestines you to heaven. Ockham's free-will position was moderate compared with that of Duns Scotus. Duns said that one could earn salvation with one's natural, unaided powers. Ockham argued that you could never earn salvation by any good works. Only God's grace can save, but God may choose to give that grace to those whom he knows are seeking him. The determinists refused the compromise. Bradwardine insisted that God predestines "prior to foreseen merits." God predestines you to good first, and your goodness comes from that predestination; those who do evil do so because right from the outset God does not extend them the grace without which they are incapable of doing good.

The predestinarian position makes God responsible for evil, for he could have given to the Devil the grace that would have prevented his sin, but he chose not to. In spite of Luther's and Calvin's commitment to predestination and their condemnation of Scotist and Ockhamist free will as unbiblical, modern Protestants like modern Catholics tend to be believers in free will. From the time of Augustine preachers have recognized the pastoral difficulty of preaching predestination from the pulpit, for the practical effect can easily be to persuade people that they can do what they like because they are already saved or that they might as well do what they like because they are already damned.

But even Ockham's free-will position was rooted in the assumption of the absolutely unrestrained powers of God. Evil is evil because God ordains it so; God could have made fornication good and friendship evil. God creates the cosmos with evil in it, and nothing external or internal forced him to do so. If God concurs in evil, he must be at least its partial cause, and Ockham thought he might be said to be its total cause. "God concurs, as universal creator and conserver, in any act, even in an act of hatred of God. But he could also cause, as total cause, the same act in which he concurs as partial cause. Thus God can be the total cause of an act of hatred against God.[4] Ockham stopped short of positing evil in God by calling up the nominalist principle that what we call evil may not be evil in God's eyes. Nonetheless, his position could, if he had allowed it, have made God directly responsible for those things that we experience and intuit as evil.

Nicholas of Cusa (1401–1464), a nominalist and mystic whose chief work was *On Informed Ignorance*, came even closer to imputing evil to God.[5] Nicholas' central assumptions were nominalist, though he also drew upon Neoplatonism and Dionysius. Humanity cannot know anything in itself. Absolute truth, whatever that may be, is forever beyond our grasp. Of God we can know only that he is *maximum*, totally exceeding every object of experience and therefore incomprehensible in himself, though we can know something about his manifestations in the cosmos. "All affirmations, therefore, that are made about God in theology are anthropomorphic" (Ig. 1.24). We cannot even say that God is maximum being, for he transcends our conception of being, nor does maximum have to do with mass or force or any observable phenomenon. Since God has no proportional relationship with anything finite, whatever we say about him is merely equivocal, and the only way we can grasp anything about God is to understand

---

4. Ockham, *Commentary on the Sentences*, 2.19; see also 3.12 and 4.9.

5. *On Informed Ignorance* (*De docta ignorantia* [*Ig.*]), was written about 1440. It has been edited by E. Hoffmann and R. Klibansky, *Nicolai de Cusa: De Docta ignorantia* (Leipzig, 1932). On Nicholas see also H. Bett, *Nicholas of Cusa* (London, 1932); M. de Gandillac, *La philosophie de Nicolas de Cusa* (Paris, 1941); E. Meuthen, *Nikolaus von Kues 1401–1464; Skizze einer Biographie* (Munster, 1964); E. Meffert, *Nikolaus von Kues: Sein Lebensgang; Seine Lehre vom Geist* (Stuttgart, 1982). P. M. Watts, *Nicolaus Cusanus: A Fifteenth-Century Vision of Man* (Leiden, 1982).

that we must deny any disjunctive proposition about him. We cannot say that God is the beginning if by that we exclude the end, or that he is great, if by that we exclude the small. We can begin to understand the maximum only by setting apart everything that derives from our observation of created things.

God is absolutely without restriction: there is no quality that his nature excludes or to which it is opposed. His nature includes all qualities. In a statement that daringly denied the assumptions of Aristotelian dialectics, Nicholas insisted that all opposites are united in God. God exists and does not exist; he is being and not being; he is greatest and smallest; he is transcendent and immanent; he is beginning and end; he creates the cosmos from nothing yet extends it from himself; he is unity and diversity; he is simple yet embraces all distinctions. This "coincidence of opposites" or union of contraries is beyond all reason; Nicholas confesses that he cannot understand it, but he is sure that it is the only thing we can say about God with confidence (Ig. 1.24). Reason can lead us only so far as to understand that we cannot define God, for he is his own definition and it is by him that all things are defined. Yet "in a way that we cannot comprehend, absolute truth enlightens the darkness of our ignorance" (Ig. 1.26). For though God cannot be known, he can be directly experienced, directly intuited, and the simple can do this as well as the learned. Since God gives us minds, we try to understand him, but love brings us infinitely closer to God than the most subtle reasoning.

God in himself is the *maximum absolutum*. The cosmos is also maximum, also God, but it is *maximum contractum*, God's extension of himself or, more properly, his *contraction* of himself; it is God's descent, his visible manifestation of himself (Ig. 2.2). We may say that God created everything out of nothing, but we should understand that nothing is really nothing and not a name for something, however shadowy and vague. Nothing is literally no thing, complete absence of anything. The traditional doctrine of creation from nothing was designed to assert that no other principle than God existed from which God created the cosmos. There was nothing, only God, so the cosmos that was created "from nothing" really comes from God. God extends all things from himself and includes all things within himself.[6] But this

---

6. *Ig.* 2.3: "Deus ergo est omnia complicans, in hoc quod omnia in eo; est omnia explicans, in hoc quia ipse in omnibus" (God folds all things into him, in that they are all in him, and draws all out of him, so that he is in everything).

statement is not pantheistic.[7] God is in all things "in such a way that all things are in him," which means that all time and space, all life and all thought are in God. It does not mean, however, that God is limited to the cosmos. The cosmos is God, but God is more than the cosmos. The cosmos is a manifestation of a God who transcends, exceeds, and incorporates it, as a roaring fire includes a tiny spark (Ig. 2.5).

The universe, the maximum contractum, lies within God-in-himself, and it lies there in all eternity. God's being includes creating, which is necessary and proper to him. Inside the cosmos time comes and time passes, but for God all is present at once. What is, is and cannot be conceived to be other. In a sense God may have created the world to increase goodness, but in a deeper sense the cosmos simply follows necessarily from his eternal will. It follows that our whole lives are necessary products of the eternal will. We are born, we live, and we die, but our whole lives are present all at once to God. Thus we are in one sense mortal but in a broader sense eternal (Ig. 2.1–2.2).

What is, is. Since God's providence is unchangeable, everything that happens does so necessarily (Ig. 1.22). Yet God's eternal will also embraces human freedom. God knows in all eternity that I choose good or ill, but his immediate knowledge of everything grasps and provides for that choice. The perfection of the cosmos requires the Incarnation, which links the Creator with his creation; it would be needed, Nicholas implies, whether or not any sin had ever been committed (Ig. 3.3–4).

Nicholas was on the verge of taking the final step and perceiving evil as part of the deity. If God includes light and darkness, greatness and smallness, time and timelessness, and all opposites, then he also can be said to include both good and evil. But Nicholas could not face this logical consequence of his theory. He looked at it, flinched, and turned away, and his treatment of evil is therefore thin and blandly traditional.[8] Evil is the failure to seek the absolute that alone must be sought. On the whole it is a lack of spiritual understanding that proceeds from our limited, animal nature. It is also privation, nonbeing, a necessary consequence of God's limiting or contracting himself in the cosmos. God permits this privation so that his glory can be manifested in his transcendence of it. These ideas are more Neoplatonic than

---

7. In the *Apologia divinae ignorantiae*, ed. R. Klibansky (Leipzig, 1932), Nicholas took great pains to repudiate pantheism.

8. Bett, pp. 150–157.

biblical, and Nicholas' brief treatment of the subject indicates that his heart was not in it. Nicholas' theory provided a great opportunity for understanding evil as part of the coincidence of opposites (C. G. Jung saw this clearly five centuries later), but Nicholas thought it blasphemous or dangerous to make the point.

The idea that Nicholas used to evade the issue of evil was the Neoplatonic doctrine of privation, which most Christian theologians had embraced since the time of Augustine. It is now time to point out the fundamental shortcomings of the doctrine. What, fundamentally, is evil? A nominalist or a modern relativist would respond that it is nothing but an abstraction, a generalization that our minds create in order to categorize certain kinds of things. Yet we seem to recognize the similarity and common basis of these things by intuition. Evil, whether taken as a universal or as the sum total of intuited evil experiences, seems to be built into the cosmos. If, then, the cosmos is a manifestation or expression of God, it follows that evil is built into the manifestation of God. One cannot say anything about God's essence, the absolute God in himself, but one can say things about God as manifested in the cosmos, Nicholas' maximum contractum. At least in this sense evil seems to be in God.

But here the Neoplatonist doctrine of privation enters to argue that evil cannot be in God because evil is really nothing, simply a lack of Godness. This argument is a trap. We need not define God as absolute good and absolute being and equate goodness with being. When we observe the cosmos we intuit the immediate reality of evil just as much as we intuit the immediate reality of good. Suffering *is*, just as joy *is*; pain *is*, just as contentment *is*; ill will *is*, just as goodwill *is*. It may be that God prefers joy and harmony and good will to suffering and ill will; it may be that the former draw things closer to him, and that he has put resistance to evil into his cosmos as well as evil itself. But none of these possibilities means that evils do not exist. Evil may be said to be nonbeing only in the special sense that it may not express the fullness of the divine nature, but if we say this, we must be aware that we are using the term *existence* in a special sense indeed. To say that evil does not exist at all because it does not fully express the divine nature is to muddle two quite different meanings of the word *exist*. And this confusion leads to an evasion of the responsibility of God for evil, a quick way out of the apparently horrifying notion (though not horrifying to the early Hebrews!) that evil does exist in God. The manifestation of God that we call the cosmos is a world in which evil proliferates. We would not call a human ruler who permitted such a state of affairs in his nation good, and we need not hold God to lower standards than a human ruler. In a sense God may indeed be good, the supreme good, passing all our understanding, but his goodness is not univocal with òur idea of goodness. God's goodness transcends our idea of goodness. It follows that his "goodness" may logically include what we call "evil."

Nicholas could have avoided the Neoplatonist pitfall and posited both good and evil in God, simply making it clear that what he meant was that God includes both what *we call good* and what *we call evil*, which allows for God's being wholly good with a goodness that differs from and transcends our own. This clarification would have allowed him to develop the theology of the Devil. The Devil is the name that Christians used to describe the evil power that we experience and intuit in the cosmos. That power must be a part of the maximum contractum, God's manifestation of himself in the cosmos. Our hatred of that evil and our courageous desire to overcome evil are part of the coincidence of opposites in God. This theory would have been consonant with Hebrew and Christian tradition, which always perceived the Devil as the creature and servant of God as well as God's enemy.

Nicholas did not dare go so far. A bit earlier the English reformer John Wyclif had dared to express an analogous view, which was cited as one of the many charges of heresy against him. On several occasions between 1382 and 1418 Wyclif was accused of having argued that "God ought to obey the Devil." This shocking statement was meant to convey the absolute extent to which God is committed to the *potentia ordinata*, the design of the cosmos as it is. Whatever powers, kings, and rulers exist in the cosmos are those that God has placed there, and so they ought to be obeyed. Since God creates a king and places him in power, knowing full well what kind of king he is, then God clearly plans for the king to be what he is and do what he does, and God is committed to the order that he himself ordains. Thus it can be said that God "ought" naturally to "obey" a ruler that he ordains, and this applies by extension to the Devil himself.[9]

Mysticism provided another new point of view. Because the term

9. The condemned article, "Deus debet oboedire diabolo," was the seventh condemned at the council of 1382 and the sixth condemned in 1418. See Denzinger, no. 586; J. Dahmus, *The Prosecution of John Wyclif* (New Haven, 1952), pp. 93–98; R. L. Poole, *Illustrations of the History of Medieval Thought* (London, 1884), p. 301; H. Workman, *John Wyclif*, 2 vols. (Oxford, 1926), vol. 2, pp. 268, 283. Some of Wyclif's followers sought unsuccessfully to explain the proposition as meaning only that God owed the Devil love, as he owes it to every created being.

mysticism was not invented until the eighteenth century, and because it is currently widely abused by its application to the occult, the older Christian term, *the contemplative tradition*, may be better. Yet *mysticism* does refer to phenomena that are also recognizable in religions other than Christianity.[10] Everyone has a sense of radical incompleteness: no matter how hard we try, we can never fully understand the physical universe around us; we can never fully understand other human beings; we can never fully understand ourselves. Yet we sense that life has ultimate meaning and long to transcend these limitations so that we can know the truth.[11]

In the mystical experience a transcendent reality (whether named God or something else) is seen as the reality underlying all other realities, of which the physical universe is only one. Though we humans cannot reach God through the intellect or the senses, we are able to experience him directly through experience and intuition, which indicates that we are in some way similar to God. The nature of each human being is twofold, consisting of an ego and also of a ground of being, which is the similarity to or identity with God, the "spark" in which God's presence is felt. The point of our lives is to open ourselves to that spark and identify ourselves with that ground of being, our true being.[12]

The reason for the similarity of the mystical experience in all religions is that it is direct and intuitive prior to any description or definition of it. As soon as one defines or describes the content of the experience, as being of Jesus, Krishna, or whatever, one subjects it to human conceptualization. The very term *God* carries assumptions. Mystics are keenly aware of the ineffability of God, his absolute and total transcendence of every human concept. Thus Buddhist tradition does not speak of a god, and it is even possible for Christians to be "atheists" in realizing that whatever one sets in place of the absolute, even the traditional Christian concept of God, is idolatry. Mysticism draws one away from egotistical clinging to one's own concepts, even of God. Mysticism replaces the egocentricity of most religion with true theocentrism, in which one loves God for no reason other than

10. For works on mysticism and a list of the Christian mystics, see the Essay on the Sources.

11. The idea of radical incompleteness was coined by the late Professor Philip Wheelwright.

12. Adapted from F. Happold, *Mysticism*, 2d ed. (Harmondsworth, 1970), pp. 20–21.

love itself. One who understands "has *only* God and thinks only God and everything is nothing but God to him. He discloses God in every act, in every place. The whole business of his person adds up to God."[13] The fourteenth-century *Theologia germanica* says, Whoever seeks, loves, and pursues the good for nothing else but the love of the good will find it.[14]

The direct, intuited experience cannot be described without its losing its essence, and the description here can thus only touch upon its components. One component is a sense of the absolute totality of God, who embraces all things in his tremendous energy. God is absolute stillness and rest and at the same time brims and overflows with energy. A second component is a sense of the unity of all things in and with God. Everything that is has its being in God. The cosmos lies wholly in God, who yet surpasses and transcends the cosmos. A third component is a sense of one's own unity with God. The Hindus speak of the identity of the Atman within the soul with the Brahman that embraces the cosmos; Christian mystics speak of union in two ways: divinization (*theosis, vergottung*), in which a human being is transformed by grace and faith into Christ and is united with God's *energeia;* and the return of the individual to God when at the end of time all things return to God. Fourth, the ego is transformed in this process, so that "I live no longer, but Christ lives in me," as Saint Paul put it.

At no time was mysticism more influential than in the fourteenth and fifteenth centuries. There seems not only to have been a rise in the contemplative tradition itself, but also a wider audience and constituency than at any other time. Many Christians who were not themselves contemplatives sought understanding from those who were. Perhaps the insecurity and fears occasioned by famine, plague, and war drew wider numbers to seek a fuller reality. Perhaps the widely perceived corruption of the institutional church led many Christians to seek a purer way. In any event the age produced a number of popular religious movements among unlearned men and women, who found in mysticism an egalitarianism lacking in the institutions of the church. God might seize the soul of a simpleton as well as that of a scholar.[15]

Mysticism was also encouraged by nominalism. It was once thought that mysticism and nominalism were incompatible, because where

13. R. Petry, *Late Medieval Mysticism* (Philadelphia, 1957), p. 200.

14. Paraphrase of B. Hoffman, ed., *The Theologia Germanica of Martin Luther* (New York, 1980), chaps. 44–45.

15. S. Ozment, *Mysticism and Dissent* (New Haven, 1973), pp. 1–9.

Aquinas had thought of contemplation as a means of perceiving transcendental reality, the nominalists denied that we have any way of reaching such a reality. Yet the nominalists did not deny such a reality so much as they denied the ability of human reason to begin to comprehend it. Nominalism and mysticism shared the assumptions that God could be reached through experience, intuition, and love rather than through reason. The nominalist Jean Gerson (1363–1429) recognized the essential compatibility of the two traditions in his treatise *On Speculative Mystical Theology*, written in 1402/1403. Gerson saw the distinctions between mystical and scholastic theology: the scholastics emphasized disciplined reason, God's external effects, and the search for God as truth; the mystics emphasized disciplined love, God's internal effects, and the search for God as love.[16] Considerable differences also existed among the mystics: one tradition, associated with Augustine, Bernard, Bonaventure, and Gerson, spoke of the soul and God embracing; another tradition, derived from Dionysius and identified with Eckhart and the other Rhineland mystics, spoke of a union in which the soul becomes God as a drop of water becomes the sea. The influence of Dionysius the Areopagite grew as his works were translated into Latin and then into the vernacular.[17] But whereas Dionysius had spoken of the yearning and desire of God and the soul for one another in abstract and austere terms, the late medieval mystics spoke of love—love as act of will but also as emotional longing.

The mystics' perception that the cosmos is an aspect of God himself, produced by God in love and drawn back lovingly to God, points the question of evil more poignantly than any other Christian tradition. If everything is in God, and the cosmos is full with overflowing divine love, there seems to be no room at all for evil and the Devil. Then how to cope with the presence of evil in the world? The mystics, like many other theologians, were drawn to embrace the old and untenable argument that evil was privation. For Eckhart only God is absolute being; creatures have being only insofar as they exist in God; otherwise they

16. Jean Gerson, "On Speculative Mystical Theology," in A. Combes, ed., *Ioannis Carlerii de Gerson: De mystica theologia* (Lugano, 1958).

17. Hitherto Dionysius' influence had been only indirect, since his work was not known in the original but only as mediated by Christian thinkers through the centuries. But Thomas Gallus, abbot of Saint Andrew's in Vercelli, translated Dionysius into Latin in the thirteenth century, and vernacular versions followed. The author of *The Cloud of Unknowing* drew upon Gallus in his own translation, *Deonise hid divinite*, ed. P. Hodgson, 2d ed. (Oxford, 1955).

are a "pure nothing." If evil does not have its being in God, it may be
regarded as pure nothingness.[18] But this formulation gets no further
than other privation theories. Elsewhere Eckhart faced the problem
more squarely. We cannot assume that the goodness of God is the
same as our goodness; we have no right to impose human conceptions
and human words upon God. In God is neither goodness, better, nor
best, and a person who calls God good is as wrong as one who would
call the sun black.[19] The existence of what we call evil "is required by
the perfection of the universe, and evil exists in what is good and is
ordered to the good of the universe."[20] Julian of Norwich also saw that
God's goodness transcends our ability to understand good and evil.
"For a man regards some deeds as well done and some as evil, and our
Lord does not regard them so, for everything which exists in nature is
of God's creation, so that everything which is done has the property of
being of God's doing. . . . Our Lord does everything which is good,
and our Lord tolerates what is evil. I do not say that evil is honourable,
but I say that our Lord God's toleration is honourable."[21] Ultimately
God must somehow include what we call evil in himself, but God
himself suffers the same evil that he asks us to suffer. The Incarnation
and Passion of Jesus Christ are signs of God's willingness to partake

18. A pure nothing: *unum purum nihil.* God's absolute being: *esse simpliciter,* as opposed to the contingent being (*esse*) of creatures.

19. Meister Eckhart, Sermon 24, in K. Weiss, ed., *Meister Eckhart: Die deutschen und
lateinischen Werke* (Stuttgart, 1936–), vol. 4 (1964), pp. 211–229.

20. Eckhart, *Commentary on Genesis.* Cited by B. McGinn and E. Colledge, eds.,
Meister Eckhart (New York, 1981), p. 90. McGinn observes that this is consistent with
Aquinas' views in *ST* Ia.22.2, 48.1, 48.3. On Eckhart, see J. Caputo, "Fundamental
Themes in Meister Eckhart's Mysticism," *The Thomist,* 42 (1978), 197–225; E. Col-
ledge, "Meister Eckhart: His Times and His Writings," *The Thomist,* 42 (1978), 240–
258; V. Lossky, *Théologie négative et connaissance de Dieu chez Maître Eckhart,* 2d ed.
(Paris, 1973); B. McGinn, "The God beyond God: Theology and Mysticism in the
Thought of Meister Eckhart," *Journal of Religion,* 61 (1981), 1–19; B. McGinn,
"Eckhart's Condemnation Reconsidered," *The Thomist,* 44 (1980), 390–414; T.
O'Meara, R. Schürmann, J. Campbell, P. Stein, and T. McGonigle, "An Eckhart
Bibliography," *The Thomist,* 42 (1978), 313–336.

21. E. Colledge, ed., *A Book of Showings to the Anchoress Julian of Norwich,* 2 vols.
(Toronto, 1978), the Long Version, chaps. 11 and 35: "For man beholdyth some dedys
wele done and some dedys evylle, and our lorde beholdyth them not so, for as alle that
hath beyng in kynde is of gods makyng, so is alle thyng that is done in properte of gods
doyng. . . . For alle that is good oure lorde doyth, and þat is evyll oure lord sufferyth.
I say not that evylle is wurschypfulle, but I sey the sufferance of oure lorde god is
wurschypfulle." I have used the translation of J. Walsh in *Julian of Norwich* (New York,
1978), pp. 198, 237.

with us in the effects of this evil. Our limited minds cannot grasp the sense of it, but God makes all things right. "See, I am God. See, I am in all things. See, I do all things. See, I never remove my hands from my works, nor ever shall without end. See, I guide all things to the end that I ordain them for, before time began, with the same power and wisdom and love in which I made them; how should anything be amiss?"

God has made the cosmos in such a way that all things are in him and point toward him; yet often things seem to point away. Everything is like a crystal or lens in which God may be seen. Some lenses are clear and sharp and magnify reality; other lenses are less clear; some are so opaque that only the keenest, most enlightened eye can penetrate through them. Such opaque lenses deflect people from God, rather than pointing them toward him. Yet any lens, even a plague or a war, *can* point the way to God if one's sight is very clear. Eyesight in its natural condition is keen and enlightened by God's light, but it can become dim through ignorance and sin, when we are "distracted by cares, clouded by sense images, drawn away by concupiscence."[22] Failure of eyesight is explainable as an effect of sin, but why are some lenses or crystals so opaque? Some crystals sin makes opaque, such as war and quarrels. But some, such as plague, God himself makes opaque. Why should this be? Julian replies, "And to this I had no other answer as a revelation from our Lord except this: What is impossible to you is not impossible to me. I shall preserve my word in everything, and I shall make everything well. . . . And he will make well all which is not well. But what the deed will be and how it will be done," she does not know.[23] The Lord's Prayer says "Liberate us from evil," and we should concentrate on the liberation more than on the evil. The author of *Theologia germanica* issued a blunt warning: "Whoever among men and other beings demands to know the hidden counsel and will of God, desiring to learn why God has done this or that or left this or that undone, that person insists on the same as Adam and the devil. . . . For the urge to know God's plan rarely revolves around

22. McGinn and Colledge, p. 31.
23. Walsh, p. 233; Julian, chap. 32: "And as to thys I had no other answere in shewyng of oure lorde but thys: That þat is vnpossible to the is nott vnpossible to me. I shalle saue my worde in alle thyng, and I shalle make althyng wele. . . . And he shalle make wele all that is nott welle. But what þe dede shal be, and how it shall be done, there is no creature beneth Crist that wot it."

Witches bestow the *osculum infame* on the Devil's posterior while their fellows ride through the air on their way to a "sabbat," or "synagogue." The witches are twelve in number, in parody of the apostles. Illumination from a fifteenth-century French manuscript. Photograph courtesy of the Bibliothèque Nationale, Paris.

anything but . . . sheer pride. . . . A truly humble, illumined person does not demand that God disclose His secrets."[24]

The mystics' fundamental vision was unitive: all things, including sinful creatures, are united with God. The Devil can have no ultimate significance in the cosmos. The Devil, ultimately, is nothing, emptiness. Emptiness has three meanings for the mystics. One meaning is positive: the emptying of the soul from all attachments so that the soul can realize and encounter God; one is ontological: the nonbeing of that which is not God; one is moral: the nonbeing and meaninglessness of that which is directed away from God. For the mystics, the Devil is complete meaninglessness and emptiness. Thus the Devil is like a great vacuum, pulling us away from reality toward unreality. The mystics' desire to avoid defining entities and their hesitation to press for explanations deterred them from dwelling upon the Devil intellectually. Yet in practice they felt his presence more often and more immediately than most.

The contemplatives believed that the Devil bent his evil attention upon them more than upon others because they were seeking union with God more intensely than others, and the soul's union with God is that which Satan envies and loathes most deeply. The mystics felt him to be the source of all that blocked and obstructed contemplation, the process of union. The Devil attempts to interfere with the process of prayer and contemplation. He tells us that we do not have time for it, that it is all an illusion, that it leads nowhere, that it is a waste of time, that we are not worthy of it, that it is better to do good works, that we look foolish to others in doing it. Worse, he twists and perverts contemplation itself, making us proud of our spiritual achievements, causing us to think that we are spiritually superior to others and giving us false sensations of warmth or lightness or inducing visual or auditory hallucinations. When sensations or visions are really from God, the Devil will seize upon them to make us attached to the experiences and thus distract us from our real purpose, which is openness to God. The more we overcome such obstacles, the more the Devil exerts himself to block us from the unitive path. These accounts of the mystics correspond closely to the experiences of anyone pursuing the unitive life in any religious context: the enormous power and thrust of the negative against the process of union is surprising and terrifying.

The Devil's attacks on the contemplatives ranged from spiritual

24. *Theologia Germanica*, chap. 48.

temptation to physical assault. Bonaventure reported that the Devil persecuted Saint Francis with temptations to lust, gluttony, and above all to fear and despair. Teresa of Avila experienced Satan directly, as one spirit touching another, and he appeared to her visibly in hideous forms and frequently beat her. The author of the *Cloud of Unknowing* had terrifying glimpses of the Devil: once he saw him as a hideous figure with huge, yawning nostrils through which one could see the fires of hell. Julian of Norwich, whose visions were concrete and specific, gives a detailed picture of the fiend who tried to choke her to death.[25]

The mystics believed that their intense sensitivity to spiritual experiences might open them to the immediate intuition of powers of evil as well as powers of good. The Devil never ceases tormenting and distracting them. He makes suggestions that at first appear good but then produce only aridity and disgust. He tempts them to pleasure, backbiting, gossip, spite, unforgivingness, envy, despair, depression, self-righteousness, and false humility. Tauler warned, "if you want God to love you, you must renounce all this sort of thing."[26] The Devil sees that Jesus is showing the mystics the light of truth, so he hastens to invent false lights in order to deceive them.[27] Even more dangerous is the false knowledge and spurious warmth that the Devil may infuse into the contemplative, making him think that he is experiencing God, when it is really the Evil One playing upon his soul.[28] The test of

25. Phyllis Hodgson, ed., *The Cloud of Unknowing and the Book of Privy Counseling* (London, 1944), *Cloud*, chap. 55; M. Lépée, "St. Teresa of Jesus and the Devil," in Bruno de Jésus-Marie, ed., *Satan* (New York, 1952), pp. 97–102; E. Cousins, ed., *Bonaventure* (New York, 1978), "Life of Saint Francis," pp. 177–327; Julian, chap. 67: "Me thought the fende sett hym in my throte, puttyng forth a vysage fulle nere my face lyke a yonge man, and it was longe and wonder leen. I saw nevyr none such: the coloure was reed, lyke þe tylle stone whan it is new brent, with blacke spottes there in lyke frakylles, fouler than þe tyle stone. His here was rede as rust, not scoryd afore, with side lockes hangyng on þe thonwonges. He grynnyd vpon me with a shrewde loke, shewde me whyt teth and so mekylle me thought it the more vgly. Body ne handes had he none shaply, but with hys pawes he helde me in the throte, and woulde a stoppyd my breth and kylde me, but he myght not"; cf. chap. 69. See C. S. Nieva, *This Transcending God: The Teaching of the Author of the Cloud of Unknowing* (London, n.d.).

26. Johann Tauler, *Spiritual Conferences*, ed. and trans. E. Colledge and M. Jane (Chicago, 1961), pp. 37–48; *Cloud*, chap. 8.

27. Walter Hilton, *The Scale of Perfection*, 2.26, trans. M. L. Del Mastro (New York, 1979). See J. Milosh, *The Scale of Perfection and the English Mystical Tradition* (Madison, Wis., 1966).

28. Hilton, 1.10; *Cloud*, chap. 48.

whether it is God or the Devil is to see whether the experience makes one excited and confused (a sure sign of evil) or content, quiet, and harmonious (a sign that it is God). For, as Julian observed, "everything which is opposed to love and peace is from the fiend."[29] Most dangerous of all is the Devil's desire to lead us into despair by showing us the sorry state of the world and of our own souls. The Devil tries to make us believe that our sufferings and temptations exist because God has abandoned us, when in fact they lead to fuller understanding of God. If we despair, we perceive love as futile, which is the worst illusion and the worst sin. If we believe the Devil's counsel of despair, we lose confidence in God, and the Devil wins us through our lack of trust in the Lord.[30] Thus contemplatives must be constantly vigilant in rejecting the distractions that the Devil offers us to deter us from the life of prayer and love.

The contemplatives urged those who feel demonic temptations not to try to resist directly, but rather to turn their thoughts away and pray for God's grace, for the Devil has no real power against us.[31] Tauler observed, "for a man to let the Devil get the better of him is just like a well-armed soldier giving in to an insect and letting it sting him to death."[32] Protected by God's grace, we fend off the Devil with faith, humility, obedience, love, and hilarity. Many of the mystics recommended laughter and hilarity as effective defenses against the Evil One, who longs to terrify us into despair. Walter Hilton said, "it gives us the hilarity and joy of one who sees evil overthrown to see the Devil, the chief of all evil, shown as a clumsy scoundrel bound by the power of Jesus, whom he cannot injure. He is overthrown and made powerless. . . . No creature is as powerless as the Devil is, and people are cowardly to dread him so much."[33] And Julian saw "our Lord scorn his malice and despise him as nothing, and (our Lord) wants us to do so. Because of this sight I laughed greatly. . . . I see sport, that the Devil is overcome, and I see scorn, that God scorns him, and he will be scorned, and I see seriousness, that he is overcome by the

29. Walsh, p. 329; Julian, chap. 77: "Alle that is contraryous to loue and to peace, it is of þe feende and of his perty." See also the *Cloud* author's "Discernment of Spirits," in *A Study of Wisdom* (Oxford, 1980), pp. 43–45.
30. Julian, chaps. 33, 76–77; *Cloud*, chaps. 3, 9–11, 23, 44–46, 50–52.
31. Hilton, 1.38; Tauler, pp. 39–47.
32. Tauler, p. 44.
33. Hilton, 2.45.

blessed Passion and death of our Lord Jesus Christ."[34] The ultimate answer to evil is not to cudgel the brain but to live a life of love and laughter.

The Devil was even less central a figure for the humanists. The naturalistic, this-worldly, and classical bent of the humanists predisposed them to ignore the Devil. The revival of Platonism and Neoplatonism provided them with a theoretical basis for doing so. Neoplatonism had from its inception allowed for natural magic. It assumed that hidden, "occult," but natural forces existed in the cosmos that could be manipulated by the wise. Those who understood the occult properties of stones, herbs, and stars could work with these properties to attain a desired end. In the early Middle Ages, when various forms of Platonism were dominant, it was assumed that between divine miracle and demonic delusion a middle ground of natural magic existed that was morally neutral. Such natural magic is really a variant of technology: one man sprinkles powders over his field to increase its fertility, another man sprinkles chemicals. The Aristotelianism dominant in the thirteenth and fourteenth centuries caused a radical shift in these views, for it had no room for such occult forces. Thomas Aquinas and other Christian Aristotelians abolished the middle ground between divine miracle and demonic delusion. All wonders that were not the works of God must be works of the Devil. All magic became the work of Satan. Magicians, whether they were aware of it or not, had made a pact with the Devil.[35] But the new magical world view of the late fifteenth and sixteenth centuries revived a natural view of the occult and offered occult explanations within a highly sophisticated and coherent intellectual system. Many early modern "scientists" such as Ficino and Giordano Bruno (c. 1548–1600) were really magicians in this sense. Alchemy, astrology, herbology, and other such subjects formed part of a powerful and respectable intellectual system that into the seventeenth century offered effective opposition to emerging scientific materialism. Further, the Neoplatonist-occult-magical system

34. Walsh, pp. 201–202; Julian, chap. 13: "Also I saw oure lorde scornyng hys malys and nowghtyng hys vnmight, and he wille that we do so. For this syght, I laght myghtely, and that made them to lagh that were abowte me. . . . I see game, that the feend is ovyrcome, and I se scorne, that god scorneth hym, and he shalle be scornyd, and I se ernest, þat he is overcome by the blessydfulle passion and deth of oure lorde Jhesu Crist."

35. Aquinas, *ST* IIaIIae.96.2. See J. B. Russell, *Witchcraft in the Middle Ages* (Ithaca, 1972), pp. 111–116, 142–144.

Aquelarre (the witches' sabbat), a parody of the fifteenth- and sixteenth-century belief that witches met at night to worship Satan in the form of a goat. Goya (1746–1828), oil on canvas, 1794/1795. Courtesy of the Museo Lazaro Galdiano, Madrid.

emphasized the role of fate or fortune in governing the universe, and thus had little room for the miraculous and providential and less for interventions by the Devil. Humanists such as Pico della Mirandola (1463–1494) and Ficino perceived natural magic as morally good or at least neutral. They even adopted the Neoplatonic position that good demons existed in addition to the evil ones equated with the fallen angels and that these good demons could legitimately be deployed in natural magic.[36] Human nature was seen less as corrupted by original sin than as a balance between good and evil, a balance that allowed a wide scope to free will and that discounted the Augustinian view of human nature in bondage to sin as well as the influence of the Devil. For Desiderius Erasmus (1466–1536) and other humanist leaders of the fifteenth and sixteenth centuries, the demons and the Devil become primarily metaphors for the vices and evil tendencies arising within the human heart. Their existence is not denied, but it is thrust into the background in a system that has no real use for them. Erasmus' practical guide to living a Christian life, the *Enchiridion christianum*, describes the moral conflicts of the individual with rare and almost purely metaphorical use of the idea of the Devil. "Consider as the devil," he says, "anything that deters us from Christ and his teaching."[37] Thomas More (1478–1534) takes the Devil seriously in his *Book of Comfort*, but his discussion of temptation dwells much more upon the natural and worldly sources of sin.[38]

At the end of the fifteenth and beginning of the sixteenth centuries, then, a number of intellectual systems were in competition. Two of them, the Neoplatonic/magical and the nominalist/mystical, tended to downplay the importance of the Devil. Scholastic realism, based upon Augustinianism and Aristotelianism, gave the Devil an important role in the world; this view would soon find strong support both in post-Tridentine Catholicism and in Protestant theology, which drew heavily both upon Augustine and, oddly, upon scholastic demonology. Augustinianism and Aristotelianism continued to dominate the scene,

36. D. Walker, *Spiritual and Demonic Magic: From Ficino to Campanella* (London, 1958); D. Walker, *Unclean Spirits: Possession and Exorcism in France and England in the Late Sixteenth and Early Seventeenth Centuries* (Philadelphia, 1981); F. Yates, *Giordano Bruno and the Hermetic Tradition* (London, 1964).
37. Desiderius Erasmus, *Handbook of the Militant Christian*, trans. J. P. Dolan (Notre Dame, Ind., 1962), 2.4–19, pp. 99–145; quotation from p. 99.
38. Thomas More, *Utopia, and A Dialogue of Comfort* (London, 1951), *Dialogue*, 2.9–17.

and except for a few spiritual leaders such as Pius II (Aeneas Silvius Piccolomini, pope from 1458 to 1464), few of the ecclesiastical elite adopted the newer views. It was upon the assumptions of the Aristotelian scholastics that the structure of witchcraft beliefs was erected at the end of the Middle Ages, a structure that dominated much of European society until the eighteenth century.

Witchcraft has had three quite different meanings. It sometimes refers to simple sorcery, the charms or spells used by simple people in all times and all over the world to accomplish such practical ends as healing a child, assuring the fertility of crops or the abundance of game, or warding off the hostility of an enemy. Recently it has referred to modern neopaganism, a late twentieth-century revival limited to small groups mainly in the Anglo-Saxon countries. The third meaning is the only important one for the history of the Devil: the allegedly Satanic witchcraft of the period of about 1400 to 1700.[39] Whether the accused witches ever believed or practiced the Satanism attributed to them or whether it was wholly projected upon them by their enemies, the conviction that Satanic witchcraft was real pervaded Western society for three centuries and provoked a persecution that killed as many as a hundred thousand victims and brought untold suffering and terror to millions.

By the fifteenth century a stereotype of diabolical witchcraft emerged: On a Thursday or Saturday night, some men, but more women, creep silently from their beds in order to avoid disturbing their spouses. The witches who are near enough to the meeting place or "synagogue" make their way on foot, but those who live inconveniently far away rub their bodies with an ointment that enables them to fly off in the shape of animals, or else astride broomsticks or fences. They join ten or twenty fellow witches at the "synagogue." When a neophyte is to be initiated, the ceremony begins with the new witch's swearing to keep the secrets of the group and promising to kill a child and bring its body to the next meeting. The neophyte renounces the Christian faith and stamps or befouls a crucifix or Eucharistic host. He or she then proceeds to worship the Devil or his representative by kissing his genitals or backside. After the initiation, the assembly proceeds to eat and drink. At table they enact a parody of the Eucharistic feast. The witches bring

---

39. On witchcraft see Russell, *Witchcraft in the Middle Ages;* Russell, *A History of Witchcraft* (London, 1980); C. T. Berkhout and J. B. Russell, *Medieval Heresies: A Bibliography 1960–1979* (Toronto, 1981), items 1809–1868.

children to be sacrificed, or they bring the bodies of the children they have already murdered. The children are offered as a sacrifice to the Devil, and their fat is used to confect the ointment used for flying or for poison. The witches partake of the child's body and blood in a blasphemous version of the Eucharist. After supper, the lights are extinguished, and the witches fall to a sexual orgy, seizing the nearest person, whether male or female and whether mother, father, son, or daughter. Sometimes the witches had intercourse with the Devil himself.[40]

How did such fantastic ideas gain wide credence? The phenomenon of diabolical witchcraft developed over centuries from many sources. Elements of simple sorcery entered into the formation of the concept: Bardonneche, wife of Lorent Moti of Chaumont, called up a demon named Guilleme to help her blunt her husband's sexual appetite; the Devil appeared to her as a pale young man in a long tunic, and on another occasion as a rooster. One Marguerite summoned a demon named Griffart, who helped her take revenge on her enemies; he took the shape of a black rooster or of a ruddy man in a black hood and red tunic. Michel Ruffier summoned "Lucifel" who, in the form of a huge black man, helped him get rich.[41] In the earlier Middle Ages, numerous incantations and spells were used to affect sexual desire, exact revenge, or obtain riches, but they were not assumed to involve demons; rather they were supposed to manipulate hidden natural forces. But later, under the influence of the dominant Aristotelian scholasticism, it was believed that natural magic did not exist and that magic could be effective only through the aid of Lucifer and his minions.

The second ingredient of witchcraft consisted of certain elements incorporated from pagan religion and folklore, for example the blood-sucking female demons who have the double function of seducing sleeping men and of killing infants. Charges of orgy, incest, infanticide, and cannibalism were drawn from ancient descriptions of the Roman Bacchanalia, from the accusations of Antiochus IV Epiphanes against the Jews, from the Roman accusations against the early Christians, and from Christian accusations against the Gnostics and Manichéans.[42]

40. Similar summaries appear in J. B. Russell and M. Wyndham, "Witchcraft and the Demonization of Heresy," *Medievalia*, 2 (1976), 1–22, at pp. 1–2, and in Russell, *A History of Witchcraft*, p. 37.

41. J. Marx, *L'inquisition en Dauphiné* (Paris, 1914), p. 53.

42. See Russell and Wyndham for a history of these charges.

The witch of Berkeley being carried off by the Devil after a lifetime of faithful service as a sorceress. Fifteenth-century German woodcut. Photograph courtesy of the Bibliothèque Nationale, Paris.

The third element was medieval heresy. Heretics, persons who persistently denied accepted Christian doctrine, were deemed to be in Satan's service, and beginning with a trial ordered by King Robert of France at Orleans in 1022, they were subject to accusations of orgy, infanticide, and the other obscene outrages against God. From the 1140s, Cathar dualism, with its insistence upon the enormous power of Satan, sometimes considered to be independent of that of God, increased the widespread terror of his ability to interfere with terrible effectiveness always and everywhere.

Scholastic theology was the fourth and most important element. Witchcraft was less a popular movement than an imposition of ideas by the intellectual elite upon the uneducated. The fundamental theological assumption bolstering the idea of witchcraft was rooted in the New Testament and fathers. Just as the saved constitute the mystical body of Christ, so the Devil's followers constitute the mystical body of Satan. All who oppose Christ's saving mission on earth, whether pagans, sinners, Jews, heretics, or sorcerers, are limbs of Satan. Christians are by duty obliged to reform them if possible and eliminate them if necessary. And such was thought to be Lucifer's powers to protect his followers that fire and sword were often deemed necessary.

The central stone in the edifice of witch beliefs was the idea of pact. The idea went back as far as the story of Theophilus, but it had developed in several critical ways well beyond its state in that early tale.[43] In "Theophilus" the pact was a simple contract between two consenting parties assumed to be almost equal, and the pact was explicit: Theophilus signed a written contract with the Devil. But in the later medieval theory of pact these two elements changed. It was now assumed that the person making the pact did so as a groveling slave, renouncing Christ, trampling the cross, worshiping Satan, and doing him homage on bended knee, offering him the obscene kiss, and even submitting to sexual intercourse with him. Pact was now assumed to exist implicitly where it did not explicitly. Heretics and other evildoers had put themselves under Lucifer's command whether or not they had made a conscious and deliberate submission.

In this way witchcraft was brought under the rubric of heresy. As the inquisitor Bernard Gui observed about 1320, witchcraft implies pact, and pact implies heresy, which lies under the jurisdiction of the inquisition. Pope John XXII (1316–1334), one of the least balanced of

43. See Chapter 4 above.

popes, counted among his other peculiarities an obsessive fear of witchcraft. He ordered a doctor, barber, and cleric at the papal court tried for necromancy, geomancy, and invocation of demons with the purpose of killing the pope and a number of cardinals. The accused were supposed to have made aphrodisiacs, adored the Devil, had sexual intercourse with demons, confected mortal potions, and used wax images of the pope for piercing and melting. John ordered the inquisition to proceed against all sorcerers for adoring demons and making pact with the Devil.

Thus the fifth element, almost as important as theology itself, was the inquisition. Since the inquisition was never an organized bureaucracy directed from Rome or anywhere else, its influence and activities varied widely from time to time and region to region.[44] Yet the inquisitors kept one another informed, and after a while certain common assumptions came to be made about witches, assumptions that were collected into inquisitors' manuals as lists of questions to be put to the accused. Most were leading questions that assumed the answers. Under torture or threat of torture, many of the accused readily confessed to these stock accusations; then, each such confession was used as further evidence for the validity of the assumptions.

The trial of an old man named Pierre Vallin in southern France in 1438 is typical. Seized by the inquisition for witchcraft, he was repeatedly tortured, then removed from the place of torture and interrogated, and then given the choice of confessing or being returned for more torture. Under such pressure, Vallin confessed that he called up Beelzebub daily and offered him tribute. He admitted to having been the Devil's servant for sixty-three years, during which time he had denied God, desecrated the cross, and sacrificed his own baby daughter. He went regularly to the witches' synagogue, where he copulated with Beelzebub and devoured the flesh of children. The inquisition condemned him for heresy, idolatry, apostasy, and the invocation of demons. He was then returned for torture for another week until he named a number of accomplices. Neither Vallin's fate nor those of the other innocent "accomplices" that he was forced to name are known, but it is likely that their property was confiscated before they were burnt at the stake.[45]

Witchcraft was thus for the most part invented by the scholastics

44. R. Kieckhefer, *Repression of Heresy in Medieval Germany* (Philadelphia, 1979).
45. Based on Russell, *A History of Witchcraft*, pp. 78–79.

and the inquisitors, but popular belief in witchcraft was promoted by the sermons and exempla of Caesarius of Heisterbach, Jacques de Vitry, and other popular preachers. The sermon was the chief vehicle for linking elite with popular culture, and when the people heard frequent vivid homilies about the power of the Devil, the approaching end of the world, and the vast hosts of heretics and witches that Lucifer commanded, they were increasingly prepared to believe and to fear. Through sermons the Devil's image was kept fresh and vivid in the popular mind even while it was fading in theology under the influence of nominalism, mysticism, and humanism. Even such a great mystic as Johann Tauler used detailed stories of Satanic activity in his didactic sermons. The diabological emphases of the sermons explain the persistence of scholastic demonology in Protestantism, for the Protestants made the sermon the backbone of their theology.[46]

The witch craze constitutes one of the most important episodes in the history of the Devil. Belief in his immediate and terrible powers was revived throughout society to an extent unsurpassed even at the time of the desert fathers. And it revealed the most terrible danger of belief in the Devil: the willingness to assume that those whom one distrusts or fears are the servants of Satan and fitting targets of hatred and destruction. Though the projection of absolute evil upon one's enemies is not the exclusive property of those who believe in the Devil—atheist commissars practice it with as much zeal as inquisitors—belief in Satan did lend itself handily to the particularly grotesque manifestation of demonization that was witchcraft. The witch craze, at its height in the Renaissance and Reformation periods in both Catholic and Protestant regions and peaking in the period from 1550 to 1650, eventually faded owing to the philosophical ideas of the Enlightenment and the disgust that the patent excesses of the witch hunters had engendered among responsible and reflective people. The discrediting of witchcraft did much to discredit the belief in the Devil upon which it was based. The phenomenon that did the most to advance belief in the Devil for several centuries was largely responsible for its decline from the eighteenth century onward.

46. A. Bernstein, "Theology and Popular Belief: Confession in the Later Thirteenth Century," unpublished paper. Professor Bernstein of the University of Arizona is preparing a major work on later medieval sermons.

11 The Existence of the Devil

Moral relativism is fashionable in many circles today, but more profess to believe it than actually behave as if they did. If good and evil truly do not exist, then one has no grounds on which to complain about anything, nothing real to hope for, and one's own ideas and values are arbitrary and artificial and need be taken seriously by no one. Few really practice such a faith; most understand intuitively that real evil exists, that torture, starvation, and cruelty are unacceptable and cannot be ignored. Evil consists of the nexus of suffering and the conscious intent to cause suffering.

Is the concept of the Devil helpful in understanding evil? The Devil is a Judeo-Christian-Muslim idea, yet it may also have value for others, at least as a metaphor of the irreducible nature of evil and of the evil that transcends individual human responsibility. Evil need not be restricted to human beings; it may exist in other beings, in the cosmos, even in the deity itself. Evil seems to arise from a malevolent force that exploits human faults and translates the unbalanced urges of a Hitler or a Stalin into death and destruction for millions. This transcendent evil may originate outside humanity, in the collective consciousness of humanity, or from some other source within humanity. In any case it manifests itself as a real and purposive force that transcends the borders of consciousness. As Jung once said, you might just as well call this the Devil.

Now the value of the metaphor may have become diluted and hopelessly trivialized in modern perception. But if the figure—Satan, Lucifer, or whatever its name—has been trivialized, the reality for which it stands is more powerful than ever in the world of Auschwitz and Hiroshima. We may need a new metaphor, but the concept behind the metaphor can seem trivial only to those who lack the courage to face the evil that now threatens to consume the earth. If we hope to survive, this evil must be faced without illusion and without empty words. If the Devil has become an empty word, he must be eliminated, but we must not eliminate the concept for which he stands.

Non-Christians may use a variety of terms and metaphors for the principle of evil, but to elect to be a Christian is to elect to use Christian terms. One may modify or enrich them with concepts from other traditions, but one may not discard them. Hence the Devil is significant for Christians (and Muslims) in a way that it is not for those holding other points of view. Recently some Christian theologians have argued that Christianity must be "purified" of belief in the Devil. The difficulty is that any unbiased, educated agnostic observing the phenomenon of Christianity will perceive that belief in the Devil has always been part and parcel of Christianity, firmly rooted in the New Testament, in tradition, and in virtually all Christian thinkers up into very modern times. The opponents of Christian belief in the Devil must persuade the impartial observer that Christianity "really" is not what its history shows it to be. Such an observer will not be impressed with the way some contemporary Christians blandly excise from Scripture and tradition any element they find embarrassing or unpopular. If the historical development of Christianity, based on Scripture and tradition, is abandoned, it is difficult to see how any philosophically meaningful definition of Christianity can be obtained. This does not mean that no innovations may be introduced, but it does mean that they must be in reference to the historical development. The creative thrust is always in the tension between tradition and innovation.

Because the Devil is so firmly fixed in Scripture and tradition the burden of proof lies on those seeking to remove the Devil from Christianity. An extraordinarily powerful and firmly based set of arguments is needed to offset the claims of Scripture and tradition. One must assume that one has access to knowledge derived from a source other than Scripture and tradition, that one knows the "real" Christianity lying behind that which the unbiased observer perceives it always to have been. Where could such knowledge come from? Not from science, which does not address such questions. Not from personal revelation, for such cannot be tested or validated by anyone else. Not from what may be congenial to any given time or place, because times and places shift unceasingly. Of course, if one believes Christianity to be wrong, one must adopt a different position and cease calling oneself a Christian. Christianity—or anything else—must be attacked or defended on the basis of what it is, not on the basis of an arbitrary or unilateral declaration. Nor is the question of the principle of evil an arcane cranny of scholastic theology; rather, it is a central question of both philosophy and theology. Thus it is possible for a Christian to reinterpret, but not to excise, the concept of the Devil.

Why is there a tendency to reject belief in the Devil today? It is undeniably an unpopular idea in contemporary intellectual Western circles, but that these should be assumed to have some peculiar claim to truth is merely chronocentrism, a currently popular variety of ethnocentrism. Belief in the Devil as the personification of the purposive force of evil is ascientific, but it is not unscientific, for science does not and cannot investigate evil. That science has evolved more practical ways of investigating disease than by attributing it to demons is irrelevant, for the belief that demons cause disease is a statement about the physical, not the moral, world. Science does not treat moral questions at all. Another obstacle to belief is semantic. People avoid the expression "I believe in the Devil" because it sounds parallel to "I believe in God." But the two statements are not parallel, because "I believe in God" ordinarily implies both intellectual assent to the existence of God and personal commitment to God, whereas "I believe in the Devil" implies only intellectual assent to the existence of the Devil, not moral commitment.[1]

Another problem lies in determining what definition of the Devil to

1. On a deeper level the "existence" of God is not the same kind of thing as the "existence" of the Devil. The Devil exists (or not) as a table or a human may exist (or not), as a created entity in the cosmos. But God is not like any created entity. In the proposition "God exists" the verb *exists* has a radically different meaning from the verb *exists* when attached to any creature. Latin expresses the distinction where the vernacular fails. One may *credere Deo* and *credere diabolo*, that is, believe in their existence. One may *credere in Deum*, place one's trust in God, but one may not *credere in diabolum*, place one's faith in the Devil.

deal with. There is no "biblical view" as such, since the concept underwent considerable change in the Old Testament and from the Old Testament through apocalyptic literature into the New Testament. The Reformation theologians who claimed to rely only upon Scripture in fact read back into the biblical Devil virtually everything that medieval scholastics and playwrights had elaborated. Nor do the theologians and poets agree among themselves. It is more satisfactory, then, to define the Devil within the boundaries set by the historical development of the concept. The only sure knowledge we have about the Devil is our knowledge of his historical development. Everything else that one may say about the Devil, no matter how learned or sophisticated, is speculation without fundation.

The historical development of the concept yields a fairly coherent view in spite of the many inconsistencies that occur along the way. Some of these inconsistencies appear trivial: Is the Devil the chief of the angels or a lesser angel? Does he have a body of any kind? Was his sin natural or supernatural? Such questions illustrate the impracticality of extending reason to the point of losing touch with experience. Some such inconsistencies can be removed in structural terms. The Devil fell to the air, the earth, or the underworld. Structurally all three views simply illustrate his ruin. Is it Christ or Michael who defeats him? The two are structurally identical, the point being that God arranges his defeat. Is Satan bound after his fall from heaven, or at the Passion of Christ, or at the Last Judgment? The meaning is structurally identical. Some inconsistencies were important but resolved over time, as in the ultimate exclusion of ransom theory.

Yet some important questions have remained unresolved. Is the Devil largely responsible for the original sin of humanity, or is his role unnecessary and tangential? Whether Christ's Incarnation or Passion destroy the Devil's power is a central question only fumblingly resolved by the argument that the Passion finally destroyed his power but that the effects would be incomplete until the Last Judgment. The biggest question is to what extent the evil symbolized by Lucifer is ultimately part of God's plan. These large inconsistencies pose a rational obstacle to belief in the Devil; the impartial observer will also note that the historical Christian idea of God also contains some large inconsistencies. Yet focusing attention on the inconsistencies blurs the picture, because in most essential points the tradition is reasonably consistent and well defined.

The essential part of the concept is that a real force is actively present in the cosmos urging to evil. This evil force has a purposive center that actively hates good, the cosmos, and every individual in the cosmos. It urges us too to hate good, the cosmos, other individuals, and ourselves. It has terrible and immense effects, but it is ultimately futile; every individual can defeat it in himself or herself by drawing upon the loving power of God. For Christians, then, the person of the Devil may be a metaphor, but it is a metaphor for something that is real, that really brings horror to the world every day and threatens to lay the entire earth waste. For this reality some concept, some metaphor is needed, call it what one will. Yet the figure of the Devil has become so trivialized that it may actually stand in the way of understanding evil. What then is to be done?

What is not to be done is the subtraction of the idea of the Devil from Christianity. This would violate Scripture and tradition, and it also violates the principle that rich reservoirs of human thought should never be drained dry. To abandon two thousand years of widely based and widely. shared human experience cannot enrich, but only impoverish. It is sometimes thought that to subtract from the Christian experience is to remove barriers and to be ecumenical; it has the appearance of reaching out and may have some short-term benefits. But in fact it depletes treasuries of experience, makes it difficult to reach people at deep psychological levels, and narrows, rather than widens, wisdom. Oddly, it ends by becoming the opposite of what it intends: a version of the narrowmindedness that has prevented religious traditions from appreciating the richness of other religious traditions. We must not subtract from the human experience in order to find the lowest common denominator, for that is always close to zero; we must reach out and absorb all the richness and texture of the world, following wisdom ever outward as it expands toward reality. The creative encounter between Christianity and Hinduism (for example) is not in subtracting from both until some level of agreement is found but rather in bringing together all the wisdom of both traditions and thus seeing through both toward truth.[2]

The subtraction of the Devil has in fact led some modern theologians to evade or trivialize evil. It is curious that at a time when evil threatens to engulf us totally, when evil has already claimed more victims in this century than in all previous centuries combined, that

2. See, for example, R. Panikkar, *The Unknown Christ of Hinduism,* 2d ed. (Maryknoll, 1981).

one hears less and less on the subject from theology. Any religion that does not come to terms with evil is not worthy of attention. Instead of subtracting the Devil, we need to transcend him. Such action responds to the powerful argument that the metaphor of the Devil is now so weak as to obstruct understanding of what it represents; it retains the strength of Scripture and tradition; and it leads toward a possible resolution of the problem of evil. We transcend the idea of the Devil not by abandoning tradition, but by moving it forward into a larger context and onto a deeper level. The question is what the rich tradition of the Devil can tell us about the cosmos, about God, about reality.

The Devil is a metaphor. Even as such he is not to be dismissed, for we have no access to absolute reality and must always rely upon the metaphors that our minds manufacture from sense observations, reason, and unconscious elements. The idea of the Devil is a metaphor; so is the idea of God, in the sense that anyone's view of God—Christian, Muslim, Hindu, or whatever—is a metaphor for that which passes understanding. Physics too is a metaphor.[3] If we transcend the metaphor of the Devil we may arrive at an understanding that is still a metaphor but a metaphor at a deeper level of understanding.

The most poignant aspect of the problem of evil for Judaism, Christianity, Islam, and all monotheist religions is the reconciliation of God's power and goodness with the existence of evil. Urban and Walton show that this is a philosophically meaningful question.[4] The problem is often expressed in a syllogism:

1. God is omnipotent (all knowing and all powerful); he is capable of creating a cosmos in which evil does not exist.
2. God is all good; God desires a cosmos in which evil does not exist.
3. Therefore evil cannot exist.
4. But we observe that evil does exist.
5. Therefore God does not exist.[5]

Traditional theological responses to this argument have not been sufficient or conclusive.[6]

3. R. S. Jones, *Physics as Metaphor* (Minneapolis, 1982).
4. L. Urban and D. Walter, *The Power of God: Readings on Omnipotence and Evil* (New York, 1978).
5. A sophisticated presentation, modification, and analysis of the problem is D. R. Griffin, *God, Power, and Evil* (Philadelphia, 1976).
6. Urban and Walter, pp. 6–8; DEVIL, pp. 221–228; SATAN, pp. 225–230.

It is impossible to respond adequately to this powerful argument for atheism without qualifying either the omnipotence or the goodness of God, or both. If God is defined in such a way as to be not totally omnipotent or not totally good, the disproof of the existence of God is empty. Such a modification of the definition of God would be no evasion; it would be compatible with the traditional view that any qualities that humans assign to God derive from human understanding and cannot describe God absolutely or fully. The term *omnipotence*, for example, cannot be applied to God meaningfully in an unqualified manner, because it has a number of inherent logical limitations.[7] The concept *goodness* has similar limitations. Human ideas of omnipotence and goodness have only limited, analogical, or metaphorical application to God. This being so, the traditional definition of God can properly be qualified, and the atheist argument fails.[8]

The option of limiting or qualifying God's omnipotence has been developed by modern process theologians, who argue that it is properly limited not only by logic (e.g., God cannot make a square that is a circle) but also by the restrictions inherent in creating an actual cosmos. An actual cosmos is a cosmos in which beings have real self-determination, freedom, or indeterminacy. God could have created no cosmos. God could have created a cosmos in which every event was the effect of his direct will, in which case it would be essentially indistinguishable from God himself. God could have created an actual universe, one essentially different from him in its possession of indeterminacy. The last, process theology argues, is the cosmos that God did in fact create. A cosmos that is truly indeterminate is one that is not perfect and that requires time and divine persuasion to improve. The evolution of the cosmos proceeds away from discord and triviality toward greater and greater harmony and intensity. Meanwhile, the

7. Urban and Walter, pp. 8–13.
8. Suppose God is defined differently from omnipotent and omniscient; suppose he is defined only as the conscious, organizing principle of the cosmos. Is this compatible with the existence of evil? Yes, because the following statements about God are then consistent with the existence of evil: God is evil; God is good but not omnipotent; God is both good and evil; God is neither good nor evil. If it is argued that *no* conscious organizing principle of the cosmos exists, then no values can be absolute, evil cannot be an absolute; and evil cannot be adduced against the existence of God. Thus the argument from evil to atheism fails. Some atheists have insisted that the argument continue to be debated in the old, indefensible, traditional terms; but this is to insist on fighting a straw man and to deny that theists have the right to make the problem of God and evil more intelligible.

freedom and indeterminacy of created beings are truly dangerous and will necessarily cause evil unless and until the perfection of the cosmos is attained.[9]

One way to advance the problem is to reconcile the omnipotence of God with the free will or indeterminacy of creatures. God's omnipotence is compatible with his choosing to limit his power in the area of creaturely free will, permitting the absolutely free choice of evil or good. Moral evil can then be perceived as the absolutely uncaused free choice of creatures to do evil. And God will have created the cosmos in such a way as to embrace that free will and those choices. He will have permitted evil as a necessary concomitant of that freedom, a freedom without which no moral goodness could exist. By this argument, God chooses to limit his own omnipotence to allow the goodness of autonomy to come into play. The argument has two important drawbacks. One is that the *amount* of suffering in the world exceeds that necessary for the exercise of free will. The other is that it says nothing about meningitis and tornadoes, for creaturely free will seems to have little to do with causing natural disease and disaster. God remains responsible for a world in which the amount of suffering greatly exceeds that necessary for the existence of human free will. The dilemma is ameliorated by positing the existence of the Devil, for it is possible that the superabundance of suffering is the result of the free choice of evil by the angel Lucifer, that natural evil is the consequence of his sin. Yet this does not resolve the dilemma, for then God is still responsible for a cosmos in which he permits horrors to exist as the result of a choice on the part of one creature. God might have created the cosmos with a greater restraint upon the action of evil. Process theodicy suggests that the problem can be avoided by extending autonomy to all creatures (not just humans and angels) and by denying or limiting God's knowledge of the future.

Another approach is to accept the totality of God's being, including the existence of the cosmos as an extension or manifestation of God. In this argument the human concept of "goodness" is seen as being of only limited applicability to God. God is all that *is*. There is nothing other than God. It is better not to use the term *existence* to apply to God, since existence is something pertaining to creatures, and the "existence" of God completely surpasses and transcends the meaning of the word. God is simply what is: I AM WHO AM. The mystical

9. The best statement of process theodicy is Griffin's.

doctrine of creation expresses this boldly. Other than God there is nothing: no chaos, no primal matter, no independent power of evil. There is no other principle from which anything can come. "Nothing" is simply not anything, and nothing can come from it. The "nothing" from which the cosmos is made is not anything, and what exists must come, not from nothing, but from God. Everything is made of God's "stuff"; everything is an extension, manifestation, expression of God: everything is theophany.[10] Everything that is, is God's stuff; evil is; therefore evil is part of God's stuff. The suffering of the starving and the tortured is real suffering, and it is part of the cosmos that is made of God's stuff.[11]

How can evil exist in God's stuff? One may see three progressive stages in human understanding of the Devil. Stage one, represented by most monist religions and early Hebrew thought, was characterized by a lack of distinction between good and evil analogous to the early stage of human psychological development when good and evil are not fully differentiated. Stage two, represented by Iranian, Gnostic, and Manichean dualism, postulated that good and evil are totally different, opposed, and unconnected; this stage is analogous to individual development in youth, when things are seen in terms of black and white. The third stage, hinted at by Nicholas of Cusa and expressly stated by C. G. Jung, is the notion of a unity transcending good and evil; this suggests that evil can be overcome not by denying it but by transcending it.[12] If evil exists in God, the desire to struggle against that evil also exists and is manifest in the life and work of many people. This desire, too, God has made; this, too, is part of God. Thus the totality of God includes not only evil but resistance to evil. God creates the cosmos with evil in it, and with the struggle against evil also in it. Deeper than the ambivalence of God is the love of God, which generated the cosmos in love and summons it to return in love.[13]

10. This is neither Neoplatonic emanationism nor pantheism; technically it is panentheism, which has precedents in Dionysius, Eriugena, and other Christian mystics.
11. This is not to deny that the privation argument may be valid in a limited sense, for evil may lack the fullness of God's being. But to use the privation argument to suggest that God is not responsible for the evil in the cosmos is an evasion.
12. See especially E. Neumann, *Depth Psychology and a New Ethic* (New York, 1969).
13. I do not claim to make any statement about the true nature of God in himself, which is always hidden. When I say that evil is in God I do not posit it in his essence; I do not even know what it would mean if one tried to do so. But to use a distinction of Dionysius, evil seems to be in God's *energeia*, his manifestations, which include the cosmos.

The Devil is a metaphor for the evil in the cosmos, an evil that is both in God and opposed by God; he represents the transconscious, transpersonal evil that exceeds the individual human evil will; he is the sign of the radical, unmanageable, yet ultimately transcendable evil in the cosmos. We may now be in need of another name for this force. Let it be so, if one can be found. But let it be one that does not evade, blur, or trivialize suffering.

Essay on the Sources

Dionysius the Areopagite

The most important works of Dionysius the Areopagite are: (1) *Celestial Hierarchy* (περὶ τῆς οὐρανίας ἱεραρχίας, ed. and trans. René Roques, Günter Heil, and Maurice de Gandillac, *Denys l'Aréopagite: La hiérarchie céleste*, SC 58 [1958]); (2) *Ecclesiastical Hierarchy* (περὶ τῆς ἐκκλησιαστικῆς ἱεραρχίας, MPG 3.369–584); (3) *Divine Names* (περὶ θειῶν ὀνομάτων, MPG 3.585–996); (4) *Mystical Theology* (περὶ μυστικῆς θεολογίας, MPG 3.997–1064); (5) Letters (ἐπίστολαι, MPG 3.1065–1131). The works were translated by J. Parker, *The Works of Dionysius the Areopagite*, 2 vols. (Oxford, 1897–1899); C. E. Rolt, trans., *Dionysius the Areopagite: The Divine Names and the Mystical Theology* (London, 1920); T. L. Campbell, *The Ecclesiastical Hierarchy* (Washington, D.C., 1955); R. F. Hathaway, *Hierarchy and the Definition of Order in the "Letters" of Pseudo-Dionysius* (The Hague, 1969); M. Gandillac, *Oeuvres complètes du Pseudo-Denys l'Aréopagite* (Paris, 1943). See W. Völkler, *Kontemplation und Extase bei Pseudo-Dionysius Areopagitica* (Wiesbaden, 1958); R. Roques, *L'univers Dionysien: Structure hiérarchique du monde selon le Pseudo-Denys* (Paris, 1954); J. Vanneste, *Le mystère de Dieu: Essai sur la structure rationelle de la doctrine mystique du Pseudo-Denys l'Aréopagite* (Brussels, 1959), which includes an edition and translation of the *Mystical Theology;* V. Lossky, "La théologie négative dans la doctrine de Denys l'Aréopagite," *Revue des sciences philosophiques et théologiques*, 28 (1939), 204–221; C.-A. Bernard, "Les formes de la théologie chez Denys l'Aréopagite," *Gregorianum*, 59 (1978), 39–69. On the Neoplatonic influence, see S. Gersh, *From Iamblichus to Eriugena* (Leiden, 1978); I. P. Sheldon-Williams, "Henads and Angels: Proclus and the Pseudo-Dionysius," *Studia patristica*, 11 (1972), 65–71.

Maximus Confessor

The most relevant works of Maximus Confessor are the *Questions to Thalassios* (πρὸς Θαλάσσιον, MPG 90.243–786; questions 1–55 in *Quaestiones ad Thalassium*, CCSG 1); the *Disputation with Pyrrhus* (πρὸς Πύρρον, MPG 91.287–354); the *Chapters on Charity* (τὰ κεφαλαία διαφορά, MPG 90:959–1080, and *Centuries sur la charité*, SC 9); A. Ceresa-Gastaldo, "Appunti dalla biografia di S. Massimo il Confessore," *Scuola cattolica*, 84 (1956), 145–151; W. Soppa, *Die diversa capita unter den Schriften des heiligen Maximus Confessor in deutscher Bearbeitung und quellenkritischer Beleuchtung* (Dresden, 1922); L. Thunberg, *Microcosm and Mediator: The Theological Anthropology of Maximus the Confessor* (Lund, 1965); A. Riou, *Le monde et l'église selon Maxime le Confesseur* (Paris, 1973); R. E. Asher, "The Mystical Theology of St. Maximus the Confessor," *American Benedictine Review*, 29 (1978).

John Damascene

The major work of John Damascene is the *Font of Wisdom* (ἡ πηγὴ γνώσεως), divided into three parts: "Dialectics" (τὰ διαλεκτικα, or τὰ κεφάλαια φιλοσοφικά, ed. Bonifatius Kotter, *Die Schriften des Johannes von Damaskos*, 4 vols. [Berlin, 1969–1975], vol. 1 [1969]); *On Heresies*" (περὶ αἱρεσέων, MPG 94:677–780); and *The Precise Exposition of the Orthodox Faith* (ἡ ἔκδοσις (ἔκθεσις) ἀκριβὴς τῆς ὀρθοδόξου πίστεως, ed. Bonifatius Kotter, vol. 2 [1973]); Slavonic version, ed. Linda Sadnik (Wiesbaden, 1967); Latin version, ed. E. M. Buytaert (Leuven, 1955). Another significant work is the *Dialogue against the Manicheans* (ὁ κατὰ Μανιχαίων διάλογος, MPG 94:1505–1584). See also the *Homélies sur la Nativité et la Dormition*, SC 80. Section D25 of *Sacred Parallels* (τὰ ἱερά) is devoted to the Devil; however the work exists only in abridgment, and its authenticity as a writing of the Damascene is now generally doubted. See Hans-Georg Beck, *Kirche und theologische Literatur im byzantinischen Reich* (Munich, 1959), p. 482. On Damascene see J. M. Hoeck, "Stand und

Aufgaben der Damaskenos-Forschung," *Orientalia christiana periodica*, 17 (1951), 5–60.

Michael Psellos

The significant works of Psellos are *On the Work of the Demons* (περὶ ἐνεργείας δαιμόνων, or Τιμόθεος ἢ περὶ δαιμόνων, MPG 122.819–876); the "Life of Saint Auxentius," ed. Perikles-Petros Joannou, *Démonologie populaire, démonologie critique au XIe siècle: La vie inédite de S. Auxence, par M. Psellos* (Wiesbaden, 1971). The treatise *The Opinions of the Greeks on the Demons* (τίνα περὶ δαιμόνων δοξάζουσιν Ἕλληνες, MPG 122:875–882), deals with the pagan Greeks. See also E. Renauld, "Une traduction française du περὶ ἐνεργείας δαιμόνων de Michel Psellos," *Revue des études grecques*, 33 (1920), 56–95; José Grosdidier de Matons, "Psellos et le monde de l'irrationel," *Recherches sur le XIe siècle* (Paris, 1976), pp. 325–349; K. Svoboda, *La démonologie de Michel Psellos* (Brno, 1927); P. Joannou, "Les croyances démonologiques au XIe siècle à Byzance," *Actes du VIe congrès international d'études byzantines*, vol. 1 (Paris, 1950), pp. 245–260 (not seen); C. Zervos, *Un philosophe néoplatonicien du XIe siècle, Michel Psellos* (Paris, 1920; not seen).

Bogomilism

The medieval sources for Bogomilism are the *Sermon against the Heretics* by Cosmas the Priest, written about 972 (see C. Backvis, "Un témoignage bulgare du Xe siècle sur les bogomiles: Le *Slovo* de Cosmas le prêtre," *Annuaire de l'institut de philologie et d'histoire orientales et slaves*, 16 [1961–1962], 75–100); Michael Psellos' *On the Work of the Demons* (see preceding paragraph); the work of Euthymius Zigabenus, a twelfth-century monk who at the command of the emperor Alexius Comnenus defended Orthodoxy in a treatise entitled the *Panoplia dogmatica* (ἡ πανοπλία δογματική, MPG 130). Most of the *Panoply* is a résumé of patristic sources against the ancient heresies, but Title 24 deals with the Paulicians, drawing upon the writings of the ninth-century patriarch Photius, Title 26 deals with the Messalians or Euchites, and Title 27 treats the Bogomils. G. Ficker, *Die Phundagiagiten* (Leipzig, 1910), published two related treatises of Zigabenus against the Bogomils: a letter (pp. 1–86) and a narrative account (pp. 89–125). *The Ascension of Isaiah*, including the ancient, Gnostic *Vision of Isaiah* (ed. R. H. Charles, *The Ascension of Isaiah* [London, 1900]) was widely adopted by the western Cathars. See W. Wakefield and A. Evans, *Heresies of the High Middle Ages* (New York, 1969), pp. 447–458.

Another important work is the *Interrogatio Johannis* or *Secret Supper* (ed. R. Reitzenstein, *Die Vorgeschichte der christlichen Taufe* [Leipzig and Berlin, 1929], pp. 297–311); see Wakefield and Evans, pp. 448–449; 458–465 Secondary works on the Bogomils and dualists include: S. Runciman, *The Medieval Manichee* (Cambridge, 1947), pp. 21–93; M. Lambert, *Medieval Heresy* (London, 1976), pp. 3–23; N. Garsoian, *The Paulician Heresy* (The Hague, 1967); D. Obolensky, *The Bogomils* (Cambridge, 1948); J. V. A. Fine, *The Bosnian Church* (New York, 1975); J. Ivanov, *Livres et légendes bogomiles* (Paris, 1976); H. A. Puech and A. Vaillant, *Le traité contre les Bogomiles de Cosmas le prêtre* (Paris, 1945); M. Wellnhofer, "Die thrakischen Euchiten und ihr Satanskult im Dialoge des Psellos . . . ," *Byzantinische Zeitschrift*, 30 (1929–1930), 477–484; J. Duvernoy, "L'église dite bulgare du catharisme occidental et le problème de l'unité du catharisme," *Byzantinobulgarica*, 6 (1980), 125–148; P. Koledarov, "On the Initial Hearth and Center of the Bogomil Teaching," *Byzantinobulgarica*, 6 (1980), 237–242; B. Primov, "Spread and Influence of Bogomilism in Europe," *Byzantinobulgarica*, 6 (1980), 317–337; D. Gress-Wright, "Bogomilism in Constantinople, *Byzantion*, 47 (1977), 163–185. See also items 213 to 289 in C. T. Berkhout and J. B. Russell, *Medieval Heresies: A Bibliography 1960–1979* (Toronto, 1981); E. Bozóky, ed., *Le livre secret des cathares: Interrogatio Johannis, Apocryphe d'origine Bogomile* (Paris, 1980).

Gregory the Great

On Gregory the Great in general see J. Richards, *Consul of God: The Life and Times of Gregory the Great* (London, 1980); the best intellectual study is C. Dagens' *Saint Grégoire le Grand: Culture et expérience chrétiennes* (Paris, 1977). On the *Moralia in Job* see R. Wasselynck, "Les compilations des 'Moralia in Iob' du VIIe au XIIe siècle," *Recherches de théologie ancienne et médiévale*, 29 (1962), 5–32; Wasselynck, "L'influence de l'exégèse de S. Grégoire le Grand sur les commentaires bibliques médiévaux (VIIe–XIIe siècle)," *Recherches de théologie ancienne et médiévale*, 32 (1965), 157–204; Wasselynck, "Les 'Moralia in Job' dans les ouvrages de morale du haut moyen âge latin," *Recherches de théologie ancienne et médiévale*, 31 (1964), 5–31; Wasselynck, "La présence des *Moralia* de S. Grégoire le Grand dans les ouvrages de morale du XIIe siècle," *Recherches de théologie ancienne et médiévale*, 35 (1968), 197–240, and 36 (1969), 31–45; P. Catry, "Epreuves du juste et mystère de Dieu: Le commentaire littéral du 'livre de Job' par Saint Grégoire le Grand," *Revue des études augustiniennes*, 18 (1972), 124–144; editions of the *Moralia*: R. Gillet and A. de Gaudemaris, eds. and trans., *Grégoire le Grand: Morales sur Job*, books 1–2, 2d ed., SC 32bis; A.

Bocognano, ed., books 11–16, SC 212, SC 221; M. Adriaen, ed., *S. Gregorii Magni Moralia in Iob Libri I–X*, CCCM *143*. The best editions of the *Dialogues* are U. Moricca, ed., *Gregorii Magni Dialogi Libri IV* (Rome, 1924); A. de Vogüé and P. Antin, eds. and trans., *Grégoire le Grand: Dialogues*, 3 vols., SC 251, 260, 265; bk. 2, of the *Dialogues* on Saint Benedict, has been translated frequently, recently by C. Fursdon (Ilkley, 1976). See also P. Boglioni, "Miracle et nature chez Grégoire le Grand," in *Epopées, légendes, et miracles* (Paris, 1974), pp. 11–102; G. Dufner, *Die Dialoge Gregors des Grossen im Wandel der Zeiten und Sprachen* (Padua, 1968); M. Gatch, "The Fourth Dialogue of Gregory the Great," *Studia patristica*, 10 (1970), 77–83.

Isidore

Isidore's *Sententiarum libri tres* date from 612–615 and were edited in MPL 83.537–738. The *Etymologies* was edited by W. Lindsay, *Isidori Hispalensis Episcopi "etymologiarum" sive originum libri XX*, 2 vols. (Oxford, 1911); the *De fide catholica contra Iudaeos* is in MPL 83:449–538. On Isidore see the festschrift for M. Díaz y Díaz entitled *Isidoriana* (León, 1961); H.-J. Diesner, *Isidor von Sevilla und das westgotische Spanien* (Berlin, 1977); Diesner, *Isidor von Sevilla und seine Zeit* (Stuttgart, 1973); J. Fontaine, *Isidore de Séville et la culture classique dans l'Espagne wisigothique*, 2 vols. (Paris, 1959); J. N. Hillgarth, "Review of the Literature (on Isidore) since 1935," in *Isidoriana*, pp. 11–74; F.-J. Lozano Sebastian, *San Isidoro de Sevilla: Teologia del pecado y la conversión* (Burgos, 1976); R. E. McNally, "Isidorians," *Theological Studies*, 20 (1959), 432–442.

Bede and Saint Cuthbert

The only edition of Bede's *Ecclesiastical History* that is fully up to date is B. Colgrave and R. A. B. Mynors, eds. and trans., *Ecclesiastical History of the English People* (Oxford, 1969). On the life of Saint Cuthbert see C. B. Colgrave, ed., *Two Lives of Saint Cuthbert* (Cambridge, 1940); for the *Commentary on Luke* see D. Hurst, ed., *In Lucae evangelium expositio*, CCSL 120.5–425.

Alcuin

Alcuin's *Commentary on Genesis* is found in MPL 100.515–566, *Commentary on Psalms* in MPL 100.569–639, *Commentary on Ecclesiastes* in MPL 100.665–722, *Commentary on John* in MPL 100.733–1008, *Commentary on*

Titus and Philemon in MPL 100.1007–1086, *Commentary on the Song of Songs* in MPL 100.639–664, and Commentary on the Apocalypse in MPL 100.1085–1156. On Alcuin in general see E. S. Duckett, *Alcuin: Friend of Charlemagne* (New York, 1951); A. Kleinklausz, *Alcuin* (Paris, 1948).

Gottschalk

Gottschalk's works and fragments are edited by C. Lambot, *Oeuvres théologiques et grammaticales de Godescalc d'Orbais* (Leuven, 1945). The chief works in the controversy were the *De praedestinatione Dei* of Ratramnus of Corbie (MPL 121.11–80), the *De praedestinatione* of Hincmar (MPL 125.65–474), and the *De divina praedestinatione* of Eriugena, G. Madec, ed., *Iohannis Scotti De divina praedestinatione liber* (CCCM 50). On Gottschalk in general see K. Vielhaber, *Gottschalk der Sachse* (Bonn, 1956).

Eriugena

Eriugena's most important works are *De divisione naturae (Division of Nature)*, or *Periphyseon*, the best (but incomplete) edition of which is I. P. Sheldon-Williams and L. Bieler, eds. and trans., *Johannis Scotti Eriugenae Periphyseon (De Divisone Naturae)*, 3 vols. (Dublin, 1968–1981) (the work has also been translated and summarized by M. Uhlfelder and J. A. Potter, *Periphyseon: On the Division of Nature* [Indianapolis, 1976]); *De divina praedestinatione*, see above; J. Barbet, ed., *Expositiones in ierarchiam caelestem*, CCCM 31; E. Jeauneau, ed. and trans., *Commentaire sur l'évangile de Jean*, SC 180. P. Meyvaert is preparing an edition of Eriugena's translation of Maximus Confessor's *Quaestiones ad Thalassium*. On John's thought see H. Bett, *Johannes Scotus Eriugena* (Cambridge, 1925); M. Cappuyns, *Jean Scot Erigène* (Brussels, 1964); G. Bonafede, *Scoto Eriugena* (Palermo, 1969); M. Dal Pra, *Scoto Eriugena ed il neoplatonismo medievale* (Milan, 1941); G. Madec, "Jean Scot et les pères latins: Hilaire, Ambroise, Jérôme, et Grégoire le Grand," *Revue des études augustiniennes*, 22 (1976), 134–142; J.-E. Manières, "Les articulations majeures du système de Jean Scot Erigène," *Mélanges de science religieuse*, 20 (1964), 20–38; B. McGinn, "The Negative Element in the Anthropology of John the Scot," in *Jean Scot Erigène et l'histoire de la philosophie* (Paris, 1977), pp. 315–325; J. J. O'Meara, "Eriugena's Use of Augustine in His Teaching on the Return of the Soul and the Vision of God," in *Jean Scot Erigène*, pp. 191–200; O'Meara, *Eriugena* (Dublin, 1969); O'Meara, "The Present State of Eriugenian Studies," *Studies in Medieval Culture*, 8–9 (1976), 15–18; O'Meara and L. Bieler, eds., *The Mind of Eriugena* (Dublin, 1973); R. Roques, "Traduction

ou interprétation: Brèves remarques sur Jean Scot traducteur de Denys,"
in O'Meara, *Mind*, pp. 59–77; Roques, "Remarques sur la signification de
Jean Scot Erigène," *Divinitas*, 11 (1967), 245–329; G. Schrimpf, *Das Werk
des Johannes Scottus Eriugena im Rahmen des Wissenschaftsverständnisses seiner
Zeit* (Münster, 1982); I. P. Sheldon-Williams, "A Bibliography of the
Works of Johannes Scottus Eriugena," *Journal of Ecclesiastical History*, 10
(1959), 198–224; Sheldon-Williams, "Eriugena and Cîteaux," *Studia monastica*, 19 (1977), 75–92; Sheldon-Williams, "Eriugena's Greek Sources,"
in O'Meara, *The Mind*, pp. 1–15; J. Trouillard, "Erigène et la théophanie
créatrice," in O'Meara, *The Mind*, pp. 98–113.

Genesis A and Genesis B

Genesis A and *B* form the first part of the famous OE manuscript Oxford
Bodley Junius 11, which also contains the OE *Exodus, Daniel*, and *Christ
and Satan*. The best and most recent edition is A. N. Doane, *Genesis A: A
New Edition* (Madison, Wis., 1978); the standard edition of *A* is G. P.
Krapp, *The Junius Manuscript* (New York, 1931), pp. 3–9, 29–87. Translations are C. W. Kennedy, *The Caedmon Poems* (London, 1916), pp. 7–96
for all of Genesis, and L. Manson, *Genesis A: A Translation from the Old
English* (New York, 1915). *Genesis B* is consistent logically with *Genesis A*
but gives greater color. The latest and best edition is B. J. Timmer, *The
Later Genesis: Edited from Ms. Junius 11*, 2d ed. (Oxford, 1954); the standard
is Krapp, pp. 9–28; the translation is by Kennedy. A new, critical edition
of *Genesis B* by Kathleen E. Dubs is forthcoming. See Kathleen E. Dubs,
"Genesis B: A Study in Grace," *American Benedictine Review*, 33 no. 1
(1982), 47–64. The Junius manuscript itself dates from 1000 to 1025 and is
illustrated by an artist of that period. See M. Dando, "The Moralia in Job
of Gregory the Great as a Source for the Old Saxon Genesis B," *Classica et
medievalia*, 30 (1974), 400–439; J. M. Evans, "*Genesis B* and Its Background," *Review of English Studies*, 14 (1963), 1–16; 113–123; A. Lee, *The
Guest-Hall of Eden* (New Haven, 1972); S. Greenfield, *The Interpretation of
Old English Poems* (London, 1972); Greenfield, *A Critical History of Old
English Literature* (New York, 1965); E. Irving, Jr., "On the Dating of the
Old English Poems *Genesis* and *Exodus*," *Anglia*, 77 (1959), 1–11.

Christ and Satan

Of *Christ and Satan* the best and most recent edition is by R. E. Finnegan, *Christ and Satan: A Critical Edition* (Waterloo, Ont., 1977); the
standard older edition is in Krapp and Dobbie, pp. 135–158. Works of

criticism include Finnegan, "Christ and Satan," *Classica et medievalia*, 30 (1974), 490–551; J. R. Hall, "The Old English Epic of Redemption," *Traditio*, 32 (1976), 185–208; T. D. Hill, "The Fall of Satan in the Old English *Christ and Satan*," *Journal of English and German Philology*, 76 (1977), 315–325; H. T. Keenan, "Christ and Satan," *Studies in Medieval Culture*, 5 (1975), 25–32; G. Mirarchi, "Osservazioni sul poema anglossassone *Cristo e Satana*," *Aion*, 22 (1979), 79–106; C. R. Sleeth, *Studies in "Christ and Satan"* (Toronto, 1981).

Beowulf

The standard edition of *Beowulf* is F. Klaeber, *Beowulf and the Fight at Finnsburg*, 3d ed. (New York, 1950); another standard is E. Dobbie, *Beowulf and Judith* (New York, 1953); an up-to-date edition is C. L. Wrenn, *Beowulf*, revised by W. F. Bolton, 3d ed. (New York, 1973). A good verse translation is by K. Crossley-Holland, *Beowulf* (Cambridge, 1968). The scholarship on *Beowulf* is immense: see Greenfield and Robinson; and D. K. Fry, *Beowulf and the Fight at Finnsburh: A Bibliography* (Charlottesville, Va., 1969). Among useful works are S. C. Bandy, "Cain, Grendel, and the Giants of *Beowulf*," *Papers on Language and Literature*, 9 (1973), 235–249; N. K. Chadwick, "The Monsters in Beowulf," in P. Clemoes, ed., *The Anglo-Saxons* (London, 1959), pp. 171–203; C. Chase, ed., *The Dating of Beowulf* (Toronto, 1981); C. Donahue, *"Beowulf* and Christian Tradition," *Traditio*, 21 (1965), 55–116; M. Goldsmith, *The Mode and Meaning of Beowulf* (London, 1970); J. Hill, "Figures of Evil in Anglo-Saxon Poetry," *Leeds Studies in English*, 8 (1976 for 1975), 5–19; R. E. Kaske, "Beowulf," in R. M. Lumiansky, ed., *Critical Approaches to Six Major English Works: "Beowulf" through "Paradise Lost"* (Philadelphia, 1968), pp. 3–40; Kaske, "Beowulf and the Book of Enoch," *Speculum*, 46 (1971), 421–431; Kaske, "The *Eotenas* in Beowulf," in R. Creed, ed., *Old English Poetry* (Providence, 1967), pp. 285–310; K. S. Kiernan, *Beowulf and the Beowulf Manuscript* (New Brunswick, 1981); L. Malmberg, "Grendel and the Devil," *Neuphilologische Mitteilungen*, 78 (1977), 241–243; R. Mellinkoff, "Cain's Monstrous Progeny in *Beowulf*: Part I, Noachic Tradition," *Anglo-Saxon England*, 8 (1979), 143–162; Mellinkoff, "Cain's Monstrous Progeny in *Beowulf*: Part II, Post-Diluvian Survival," *Anglo-Saxon England*, 9 (1980), 183–197; M. Puhvel, *Beowulf and Celtic Tradition* (Waterloo, Ont., 1979); E. Stanley, "Beowulf," in Stanley, *Continuations and Beginnings* (London, 1966), pp. 104–141; J. R. R. Tolkien, "Beowulf: The Monsters and the Critics," *Proceedings of the British Academy*, 22 (1936), 245–295; S. M. Wiersma, "A Linguistic Analysis of Words Referring to

Monsters in *Beowulf*," (Ph.D. diss., University of Wisconsin, 1961); D. Williams, *Cain and Beowulf* (Toronto, 1982); H. G. Wright, "Good and Evil; Light and Darkness; Joy and Sorrow in Beowulf," *Review of English Studies*, 8 (1957), 1–11.

Aelfric's Homilies

The standard edition of the first series of Aelfric's homilies (HomI) is B. Thorpe, *The Homilies of the Anglo-Saxon Church: The First Part, Containing the Sermones Catholici or Homilies of Aelfric*, vol. 1 (London, 1844). A new edition of HomI is being prepared by P. Clemoes. The second series (HomII) has been edited by M. Godden, *Aelfric's Catholic Homilies: The Second Series*, EETS n.s. 5 (London, 1979). The supplementary collection (HomIII) has been edited by J. Pope, *The Homilies of Aelfric: A Supplementary Collection*, 2 vols. EETS 259–260 (London, 1967–1968). For *The Lives of Saints*, see W. W. Skeat, ed., *Aelfric's Lives of Saints*, 2 vols. EETS 76, 82, 94, 114 (London, 1881–1900, repr. 1966). Note that Skeat's items 23, 23B, 30, and 33 are now known not to be Aelfric's. The *Hexameron* (*Hex*): S. J. Crawford, *Exameron Anglice* (Hamburg, 1921); Crawford, *The Old English Version of the Heptateuch*, EETS 162 (London, 1922). On Aelfric see P. A. M. Clemoes, "Aelfric," in E. G. Stanley, ed., *Continuations and Beginnings* (London, 1966), pp. 176–209; Clemoes, "The Chronology of Aelfric's Works," in Clemoes, *The Anglo-Saxons* (London, 1959), pp. 212–247; M. M. Gatch, *Preaching and Theology in Anglo-Saxon England: Aelfric and Wulfstan* (Toronto, 1977); N. Halvorson, *Doctrinal Terms in Aelfric's Homilies* (Iowa City, 1932); J. Hurt, *Aelfric* (New York, 1972); M. R. Godden, "The Development of Aelfric's Second Series of *Catholic Homilies*," *English Studies*, 54 (1973), 209–216.

Liturgical Works

Among the most important liturgical texts are L. Mohlberg, ed., *Sacramentarium Veronense* (Rome, 1956); L. Mohlberg, ed., *Sacramentarium Gelasianum Sangallense* (Münster, 1918); L. Mohlberg, ed., *Sacramentarium Gelasianum* (Rome, 1960); L. Mohlberg, ed., *Missale Gallicanum vetus* (Rome, 1958); H. Lietzmann, ed., *Das Sacramentarium Gregorianum nach dem Aachener Urexemplar* (Münster, 1921); E. A. Lowe, ed., *The Bobbio Missal: A Gallican Massbook*, 3 vols. (London, 1917–1924); J. M. Neale and G. H. Forbes, *The Ancient Liturgies of the Gallican Church* (London, 1855); M. Ferotin, ed., *Le Liber mozarabicus sacramentorum et les manuscripts mozarabes* (Paris, 1912); H. Wilson, ed., *The Gregorian Sacramentary under*

Charles the Great (London, 1915). On the Devil in the liturgy see A. Angenendt, "Der Taufexorzismus und seine Kritik in der Theologie des 12.
und 13. Jahrhunderts," in A. Zimmermann, ed., *Die Mächte des Guten und
Bösen* (Berlin, 1977), pp. 388–409; E. Bartsch, *Die Sachbeschwörungen der
römischen Liturgie* (Münster, 1967); R. Béraudy, "Scrutinies and Exorcisms," in *Adult Baptism and the Catechumenate*, Series Consilium vol. 22
(New York, 1967), pp. 57–61; D. M. Jones, "Exorcism before the Reformation" (master's thesis, University of Virginia, 1978); H. A. Kelly, *The
Devil, Demonology, and Witchcraft*, 2d ed. (New York, 1974), pp. 39–45; H.
A. Kelly, *The Devil at Baptism: The Demonic Dramaturgy of Christian Initia-
tion* (forthcoming; I am indebted to Professor Kelly for his helpful com-
ments on this topic); F. Dölger, *Der Exorzismus im altchristlichen Taufritual*
(Paderborn, 1909); H. Kirsten, *Die Taufabsage* (Berlin, 1954); K. Thraede,
"Exorzismus," *Reallexikon für Antike und Christentum*, vol. 7, pp. 44–117;
G. Lukken, *Original Sin in the Roman Liturgy* (Leiden, 1973).

Saint Anselm

The best edition of Anselm's works is F. S. Schmitt, ed., *Sancti Anselmi
opera omnia*, 2 vols. (Stuttgart, 1968); this edition was originally issued in
six volumes, indicated in brackets: *De casu diaboli [The Fall of the Devil]*, ed.
Schmitt, vol. 1[1], pp. 231–276, trans. J. Hopkins and H. Richardson in
their *Anselm of Canterbury*, vol. 2 (Toronto, 1976), pp. 127–177, and in
their *Truth, Freedom, and Evil* (New York, 1967), pp. 145–146; *Cur Deus
homo [Why God Became Man]*, ed. Schmitt, vol. 1[2], pp. 37–133, ed. and
trans. R. Roques, *Anselm de Cantorbéry: Pourquoi Dieu s'est fait homme*, SC
91, and trans. Hopkins, *Anselm*, vol. 3, pp. 39–137; *De conceptu virginali et
de originali peccato [The Virgin Conception]*, ed. Schmitt, vol. 1[2], pp. 135–
173, trans. Hopkins and Richardson, *Anselm*, vol. 3, pp. 139–179; *De
concordia praescientiae et praedestinationis et gratiae Dei cum libero arbitrio [The
Congruity of Predestination and Free Will]*, ed. Schmitt, vol. 1[2], pp. 243–
288, trans. Hopkins and Richardson, *Anselm*, vol. 2, pp. 179–223. On
Anselm in general and on evil and the Devil, the most helpful works are J.
P. Burns, "The Concept of Satisfaction in Medieval Redemption Theo-
ry," *Theological Studies*, 36 (1975), 285–304; M. J. Charlesworth, *St. An-
selm's Proslogion . . . with an Introduction and Philosophical Commentary* (Ox-
ford, 1965); D. E. DeClerck, "Questions de sotériologie médiévale,"
Recherches de théologie ancienne et médiévale, 13 (1946), 150–184; G. R. Evans,
Anselm and Talking about God (Oxford, 1978); Evans, "Why the Fall of
Satan?" *Recherches de théologie ancienne et médiévale*, 45 (1978), 130–146; R.
Haubst, "Anselms Satisfaktionslehre einst und heute," *Trierer theologische*

Zeitschrift, 80 (1971), 88–109; J. Hopkins, *A Companion to the Study of Saint Anselm* (Minneapolis, 1972); A. E. McGrath, "Rectitude: The Moral Foundation of Anselm of Canterbury's Soteriology," *Downside Review*, 99 (1981), 204–213; J. Rivière, *Le dogme de la rédemption au début du moyen âge* (Paris, 1934); R. W. Southern, *Saint Anselm and His Biographer* (Cambridge, 1963); R. W. Southern and F. S. Schmitt, *Memorials of St. Anselm* (London, 1969); E.-H. Wéber, "Dynamisme du bien et statut historique du destin créé," in A. Zimmermann, *Die Mächte des Guten und Bösen* (Berlin, 1977), pp. 154–205; S. Vanni Rovighi, "Il problema del male in S. Anselmo," *Analecta Anselmiana*, 5 (1976), 179–188; C. Armstrong, "St. Anselm and His Critics," *Downside Review*, 86 (1968), 354–376; A. Atkins, "Caprice: The Myth of the Fall in Anselm and Dostoevsky," *Journal of Religion*, 47 (1967), 295–312; G. S. Kane, *Anselm's Doctrine of Freedom and the Will* (New York, 1981).

Saint Thomas Aquinas

The complete works of Thomas Aquinas will soon be found in a convenient seven-volume edition, R. Busa, ed., *Sancti Thomae Aquinatis Opera Omnia*, 7 vols. (Stuttgart, 1980–); the edition collects the most reliable texts of the Leonine and other editions (*Editio Leonina*, 51 vols., Rome, 1882–). The computer text of the Busa edition was used to prepare the exhaustive computer index of the complete works, R. Busa, ed., *Index Thomisticus*, 50 vols. (Stuttgart, 1974–1980). Less complete indexes are P. de Bergamo, *In opera Sancti Thomae Aquinatis Index* (Rome, 1960); R. J. Defarrari and M. I. Barry, *A Complete Index of the Summa Theologica of Saint Thomas Aquinas* (Washington, D.C., 1956). The four most relevant works are *Commentarium super libros sententiarum*, in Busa, *Opera omnia*, vol. 1 (1980); *Summa contra gentiles*, in Busa, vol. 2 (forthcoming), in vols. 13–15 of the Leonine edition (1918–1930), and in the translation by Anton Pegis, *Saint Thomas Aquinas on the Truth of the Catholic Faith: Summa contra Gentiles*, 5 vols. (Garden City, 1955–1957); *Summa theologiae*, in Busa, vol. 2 (forthcoming), and *St. Thomas Aquinas, Summa Theologiae*, ed. T. Gilby, 60 vols. (London, 1964–1975); and *De malo*, in Busa, vol. 3 (forthcoming), and in vol. 23 of the Leonine edition (1981). The secondary bibliography on Aquinas particularly useful for studies of the Devil includes J. de Blic, "Peccabilité de l'esprit et surnaturel," *Mélanges de science religieuse*, 3 (1946), 163; C. Boyer, "De l'accord de S. Thomas et de S. Augustin sur la prédestination," in *Tommaso d'Aquino nel suo VII centenario* (Rome, 1975–1978), vol. 1, pp. 217–222; F. Copleston, *Aquinas* (Baltimore, 1955); C. Courtes, "La peccabilité de l'ange chez Saint Thomas," *Revue thomiste*, 53

(1953), 133–163; M. B. Crowe, "On Re-writing the Biography of Aquinas," *Irish Theological Quarterly*, 41 (1974), 255–273; M. DeCourcey, *Theory of Evil in the Metaphysics of Saint Thomas and its Contemporary Significance* (Washington, D.C., 1948); E. Dubruck, "Thomas Aquinas and Medieval Demonology," *Michigan Academician*, 7 (1974), 167–183; P. M. Farrell, "Evil and Omnipotence," *Mind*, 67 (1958), 399–403; A. S. Ferrua, *Sancti Thomae Aquinatis vitae fontes praecipuae* (Alba, 1968); E. Gilson, *Le Thomisme: Introduction à la philosophie de Saint Thomas d'Aquin* (Paris, 1948); E. Harris, *The Problem of Evil* (Milwaukee, 1977); A. Hayen, "Engelfall nach Thomas," *Teoresi*, 9 (Cataria, 1954), 83–176; C. Journet, *The Meaning of Evil* (New York, 1963); R. E. Marieb, "The Impeccability of the Angels Regarding Their Natural End," *The Thomist*, 28 (1964), 409–474; J. Maritain, "Le péché de l'Ange: Essai de ré-interprétation des positions thomistes," *Revue thomiste*, 56 (1956), 197–239; J. Maritain, *St. Thomas and the Problem of Evil* (Milwaukee, 1942); E. J. Montano, *The Sin of the Angels: Some Aspects of the Teaching of St. Thomas* (Washington, D.C., 1955); R. D. Padellaro de Angelis, *Il problema del male nell'alta scolastica* (Rome, 1968); G. Van Riet, "Le problème du mal dans la philosophie de la religion de saint Thomas," *Revue philosophique de Louvain*, 71 (1973), 5–45; J. A. Weisheipl, *Friar Thomas d'Aquino: His Life, Thought, and Work* (New York, 1974); B. Welte, *Über das Böse* (Basel, 1959).

Medieval Literature about the Devil

Medieval literary works dealing substantially with the Devil include *Sir Gawain and the Green Knight:* for the demonic element in this poem see D. J. Randall, "Was the Green Knight a Fiend?" *Studies in Philology*, 57 (1960), 479–491; T. McAlindon, "Comedy and Terror in Middle English Literature," *Modern Language Review*, 60 (1965), 323–332. On "The Develis Perlament" see P. Silber, "'The Develis Perlament:' Poetic Drama and a Dramatic Poem," *Mediaevalia*, 3 (1977), 215–228; P. Silber, "Councils and Debates: Two Variations on the Theme of Deceiver Deceived," unpublished paper. I am grateful to Professor Silber of the State University of New York at Stony Brook for her help in this and other related topics. W. H. Hulme, ed., *The Middle English Harrowing of Hell* (London, 1907), has been treated, with dramatic literature, in Chapter 9. For the thirteenth-century *Story of Genesis and Exodus*, the *Lyff of Adam and Eve*, and the *Cursor Mundi*, see P. E. Dustoor, "Legends of Lucifer in Early English and in Milton," *Anglia*, 54 (1930), 213–268. For *The Lantern of Liȝt*, A Lollard tract of 1409–1410, see M. W. Bloomfield, *The Seven Deadly Sins* (East Lansing, Mich., 1952), pp. 214–215. On French literature and the

Devil in this period see G. Ashby, "Le diable et ses représentations dans quelques chansons de geste," in *Le diable au moyen âge* (Paris, 1979), pp. 9–21; C. Brucker, "Mentions et représentations du diable dans la littérature française épique et romanesque du XIIe et au début du XIIIe siècle," in *Le diable au moyen âge*, pp. 39–69; F. Carmody, "Le diable des bestiaires," *Cahiers de l'association internationale des études françaises*, 3/4/5 (1953), 79–85; R. Ciérvice, "Notas en torno al libro de Miseria de Omne," *Estudios de Duesto*, 22 (1974), 81–96; R. Deschaux, "Le livre de la diablerie d'Eloy d'Amerval," in *Le diable au moyen âge*, pp. 185–193; J. Frappier, "Châtiments infernaux et peur du diable d'après quelques textes français du XIIIe et du XIVe siècle," in Frappier, *Histoire, mythes et symboles* (Geneva, 1976), pp. 129–136; G. Gros, "Le diable et son adversaire dans l'Advocacie nostre dame (poème du XIVe siècle)," in *Le diable au moyen âge*, pp. 237–258; J. Larmat, "Perceval et le chevalier au dragon," in *Le diable au moyen âge*, pp. 295–305; J. Lods, ed., *Le roman de Perceforest* (Geneva, 1951); D. Owen, *The Vision of Hell* (Edinburgh, 1970); W. Rice, "Le livre de la diablerie d'Eloy d'Amerval," *Cahiers de l'association internationale des études françaises*, 3/4/5 (1953), 115–126; M. Ward, ed., *Le liure de la deablerie of Eloy d'Amerval* (Iowa City, 1923); B. Schmolke-Hasselmann, " 'Camuse chose:' Das Hässliche als ästhetisches und menschliches Problem in der altfranzösischen Literatur," in A. Zimmermann, ed., *Die Mächte des Guten und Bösen* (Berlin, 1977), pp. 442–452; J. Subrenat, "Lucifer et sa mesnie dans le 'Pèlerinage de l'âme' de Guillaume de Digulleville," in *Le diable au moyen âge*, pp. 507–525; M. Rossi, "Sur un passage de la 'Chanson d'Esclarmonde,' " in *Le diable au moyen âge*, pp. 461–472; Bloomfield, p. 134. In German literature, too, the Devil usually appears for metaphorical or rhetorical purposes, as in Hartmann von Aue's *Gregorius* and *Der arme Heinrich* and in Wolfram von Eschenbach's *Parzival*. See D. Buschinger, "Le diable dans le *Gregorius* de Hartmann von Aue," in *Le diable au moyen âge*, pp. 71–95. See also H. Backes, "Teufel, Götter, und Heiden im geistlichen Ritterdichtung," in Zimmermann, pp. 417–441; H. Zieren, "Studien zum Teufelsbild in der deutschen Dichtung von 1050–1250" (Ph.D. diss., Universiy of Bonn, 1937); M. Dreyer, *Der Teufel in der deutschen Dichtung des Mittelalters: Von den Anfängen bis in das XIV. Jahrhundert* (Rostock, 1884); H. Stapff, "Der 'Meister Reuaus' und die Teufelsgestalt in der deutschen Dichtung des späten Mittelalters" (Ph.D. diss., University of Munich, 1956). For Konrad of Regensburg's version of the *Song of Roland* see the edition by C. Wesle, *Das Rolandslied des Pfaffen Konrad*, 2d ed. (Tübingen, 1967), and the translation by D. Kartschocke under the same title (Munich, 1970). See P. Geary, "Songs of Roland in Twelfth Century Germany," *Zeitschrift für deutsches Altertum*, 105 (1976), 112–115.

Dante

On Dante and Langland the bibliographies are enormous: I cite only the most recent general works and those most pertinent to the Devil. On Dante generally see W. Anderson, *Dante the Maker* (London, 1980); T. Bergin, *Dante* (New York, 1965); T. Bergin, *Dante's Divine Comedy* (Englewood Cliffs, N.J., 1971); A. Bernardo and A. Pellegrini, *A. Critical Study Guide to Dante's Divine Comedy* (Totowa, N.J., 1968); T. C. Chubb, *Dante and His World* (Boston, 1966); G. Mazzotta, *Dante: Poet of the Desert* (Princeton, 1979); R. Quinones, *Dante Alighieri* (Boston, 1979); J. Oeschger, "Antikes und Mittelalterliches bei Dante," *Zeitschrift für romanische Philologie*, 64 (1944), 1–87; D. Sayers, *Introductory Papers on Dante* (London, 1954); D. Sayers, *Further Papers on Dante* (London, 1957). The best editions of *The Divine Comedy* are the scholarly Princeton Dante, C. Singleton, ed. and trans., *The Divine Comedy*, 6 vols. (Princeton, 1970–1975), with commentary, and the poetic California Dante, A. Mandelbaum, trans., *The Divine Comedy* 3 vols. (Berkeley, 1980–). The best edition of the *Convivio*, written 1304–1308, is by M. Simonelli, *Il Convivio* (Bologna, 1966). On the place of the Devil in Dante see A. Cassell, "The Tomb, the Tower, and the Pit: Dante's Satan," *Italica*, 56 (1979), 331–351; F. Fergusson, *Dante* (New York, 1966); J. Freccero, "Infernal Inversion and Christian Conversion (Inferno XXXIV)," *Italica*, 42 (1965), 35–41; J. Freccero, "The Sign of Satan," *Modern Language Notes*, 80 (1965), 11–26; A. Graf, "Demonologia di Dante," in Graf, *Miti, leggende e superstizioni del medio evo*, 2 vols. (Bologna, 1925), vol. 2, pp. 80–112; A. LoCastro, *Lucifero nella "Commedia" di Dante* (Messina, 1971); B. McGuire, "God, Man, and the Devil in Medieval Theology and Culture," University of Copenhagen, *Institut du moyen âge grec et latin: Cahiers*, 18 (1976), 18–79; R. Palgen, *Dantes Luzifer: Grundzüge einer Entstehungsgeschichte der Komödie Dantes* (Munich, 1969); G. Busnelli, *I tre colori del Lucifero Dantesco* (Rome, 1910); U. Donati, *Lucifero nella Divina Commedia* (Rome, 1958); A. Valensin, "The Devil in the Divine Comedy," in Bruno de Jésus-Marie, ed., *Satan* (New York, 1952), pp. 368–378; K. Verduin, "Dante and the Sin of Satan: Augustinian Patterns in Inferno XXXIV, 22–27," *Italianistica*, 12 (1983).

Langland

Three texts of *Piers Plowman* were first edited by W. W. Skeat, *The Vision of William Concerning Piers the Plowman, in Three Parallel Texts*, 2 vols. (Oxford, 1886), reprinted 1954 with a bibliography by J. A. W. Bennett.

The A text was later reedited by T. A. Knott and D. C. Fowler, *Piers the Plowman: A Critical Edition of the A-Version* (Baltimore, 1952) and by G. Kane, *Piers Plowman: The A Version: Will's Vision of Piers Plowman and Do-Well* (London, 1960). The B version was reedited by G. Kane and E. T. Donaldson, *Piers Plowman: The B Version: Will's Vision of Piers Plowman, Do-Well, Do-Better, and Do-Best* (London, 1975). The C version was reedited by D. Pearsall, *Piers Plowman: An Edition of the C Text* (London, 1978). Translations into modern English include D. and R. Attwater, *William Langland: The Book Concerning Piers the Plowman* (London, 1957), and J. F. Goodridge: *Langland: Piers the Ploughman* (Harmondsworth, 1959). A newly edited text has recently appeared: A. G. Rigg and C. Brewer, eds., *William Langland, Piers Plowman: The Z Version* (Toronto, 1983). Good general works on *Piers* are D. Aers, *Piers Plowman and Christian Allegory* (London, 1975); R. J. Blanch, ed., *Style and Symbolism in Piers Plowman* (Knoxville, 1969); M. W. Bloomfield, *Piers Plowman as a Fourteenth-Century Apocalypse* (New Brunswick, N.J., 1961); M. W. Bloomfield, "Present State of *Piers Plowman* Studies," in Blanch, pp. 3–25; A. Colaianne, *Piers Plowman: An Annotated Bibliography of Editions and Commentary 1550–1977* (New York, 1978); T. P. Dunning, *"Piers Plowman": An Interpretation of the A Text*, 2d ed. by T. Dolan, with preface by J. A. W. Bennett (Oxford, 1980); G. Hort, *Piers Plowman and Contemporary Religious Thought* (London, n.d.); G. Kane: *Piers Plowman: The Evidence for Authorship* (London, 1965); D. Murtagh, *Piers Plowman and the Image of God* (Gainesville, Fla., 1978); D. W. Robertson, Jr., and B. F. Huppé, *Piers Plowman and Scriptural Tradition* (Princeton, 1951); E. Salter and D. Pearsall, *Piers Plowman* (Evanston, Ill., 1967); H. W. Troyer, "Who Is Piers Plowman?" in Blanch, pp. 156–173; E. Vasta, ed., *Interpretations of Piers Plowman* (Notre Dame, Ind., 1968).

Medieval Theater

On the theater in general and the Devil's role on the stage see M. Anderson, *Drama and Imagery in English Medieval Churches* (Cambridge, 1963); T. Andrus, "The Devil on the Medieval Stage in France," (Ph.D. diss., Syracuse University, 1979); K. Ashley, "Divine Power in Chester Cycle and Late Medieval Thought," *Journal of the History of Ideas*, 39 (1978), 387–404; K. Ashley, "The Fleury *Raising of Lazarus* and Twelfth-Century Currents of Thought," *Comparative Drama*, 15 (1981), 139–158; K. Ashley, "The Specter of Bernard's Noonday Demon in Medieval Drama," *The American Benedictine Review*, 30 (1979), 205–221; R. Axton, *European Drama of the Early Middle Ages* (London, 1974); H. Bekker, "The Lucifer Motif in the German Drama of the Sixteenth Century," *Monatshefte für deutsche Sprache und Literatur*, 51 (1959), 237–247; H. Craig, *English Religious Drama of the Middle Ages* (Oxford, 1955); L. Cushman, *The Devil and the Vice in English Literature Before Shakespeare* (London, 1900); E. DuBruck, "The Devil and Hell in Medieval French Drama," *Romania*, 100 (1979), 165–179; G. Frank, *The Medieval French Drama* (Oxford, 1954); E. Haslinghuis, *De Duivel in het Drama der Middeleeuwen* (Leiden, 1912); F. Heinemann, "Die Rolle des Teufels bei den Auferstehungsspielen der luzerner Landschaft," *Innerschweizerisches Jahrbuch für Heimatkunde*, 11/12 (1947/8), 117–136; S. J. Kahrl, *Traditions of Medieval English Drama* (London, 1974); V. Kolve, *The Play Called Corpus Christi* (Stanford, 1966); M. Klostermeyer, "Hölle und Teufel im deutschsprächigen Theater des Mittelalters und der Renaissance'" (Ph.D. diss., University of Vienna, 1966); H.-S. Lampe, *Die Darstellung des Teufels in den geistlichen Spielen Deutschlands* (Munich, 1963); M. Lazar, "Les diables: serviteurs et bouffons (répertoire et jeu chez les comédiens de la troupe infernale)," *Tréteaux*, 1 (1978), 51–69; M. Lazar, "L'enfer et les diables dans le théâtre médiéval italien," *Studi di filologia romanza offerti a Silvio Pellegrini* (Padua, 1971), pp. 233–249; M. Lazar, "Enseignement et spectacle: la 'disputatio' comme scène à faire dans le drame religieux du moyen âge," in A. Sachs, ed., *Studies in the Drama* (Jerusalem, 1967), 126–155; M. Lazar, "The Saint and the Devil: Christological and Diabological Typology in Fifteenth Century Provençal Drama," in N. J. Lacy and J. C. Nash, eds., *Essays in Early French Literature Presented to Barbara M. Craig* (York, S.C., 1982), pp. 81–92; M. Lazar, "Satan and Notre Dame," in N. Lacy, ed., *A Medieval French Miscellany* (Lawrence, Kans., 1972), pp. 1–14; R. Lebègue, "Le diable dans l'ancien théâtre religieux," *Cahiers de l'Association internationale des études françaises*, 3/4/5 (1953), 97–105; A. Nelson, *The Medieval English Stage* (Chicago, 1974); F. Pitangue, "Variations dramatiques du Diable dans le théâtre français du moyen âge," in *Etudes médiévales offertes à M. le Doyen Augustin Fliche de l'Institut* (Montpellier, 1972), pp. 143–160; R. Potter, *The English Morality Play* (London, 1975); R. M. Rastall, *The Chester Mystery Cycle: Essays and Documents* (Chapel Hill, 1983). K. Roddy, "Epic Qualities in the Cycle Plays," in N. Denny, *Medieval Drama* (London, 1973), pp. 155–171; E. Roy, *Le mystère de la Passion en France du XIVe au XVIe siècle* (Dijon, 1903); M. Rudwin, *Der Teufel in den deutschen geistlichen Spielen des Mittelalters und der Reformationszeit* (Göttingen, 1915); L. Schuldes, *Die Teufelsszenen im deutschen geistlichen Drama des Mittelalters* (Göppingen, 1974); S. Sticca, *The Latin Passion Play* (Albany, 1970); D. Stuart, "The Stage Setting of Hell and the Iconography of the Middle Ages," *Romanic Review*, 4 (1913), 330–342; W. Tydeman, *The Theater in the Middle Ages* (Cambridge, 1978); H. Vatter, *The Devil in English Literature*

(Bern, 1978); G. Wickham, *The Medieval Theatre* (New York, 1974); R. Woolf, *The English Mystery Plays* (Berkeley, 1972); K. Young, *The Drama of the Medieval Church* (Oxford, 1933).

Among the most useful plays for the study of the Devil are P. Aebischer, ed., *Le mystère d'Adam* (Geneva, 1963), twelfth century; Rutebeuf's *Miracle de Théophile*, written about 1261, ed. G. Frank, *Le miracle de Théophile*, 2d ed. (Paris, 1969); see M. Lazar, "Theophilus: Servant of Two Masters," *Modern Language Notes*, 87, no. 6 (1972), 31–50; R. Petsch, ed., *"Theophilus:" Mittelniederdeutsches Drama in drei Fassungen herausgegeben* (Heidelberg, 1908); the late thirteenth-century *Passion du Palatinus*, ed. G. Frank, *La Passion du Palatinus* (Paris, 1922); Arnoul Gréban's *Mystère de la Passion*, written about 1450, ed. G. Paris and G. Raynaud, *Le mystère de la Passion d'Arnoul Gréban* (Paris, 1878); see R. Ménage, "La mesnie infernale dans la *Passion* d'Arnoul Gréban," in *Le diable au moyen âge* (Paris, 1979), pp. 331–349; the York Corpus Christi plays, ed. L. Smith, *York Plays* (London, 1885); the N-Town cycle (formerly known as the Ludus Coventriae), ed. K. Block, *Ludus Coventriae* (Oxford, 1922); the Chester cycle, ed. R. Lumiansky and D. Mills, *The Chester Mystery Cycle* (Oxford, 1974); the Wakefield or Towneley plays, ed. G. England and A. Pollard, *The Towneley Plays* (London, 1897); see M. Rose, *The Wakefield Mystery Plays* (New York, 1962); M. Lazar, ed. and trans., *Le jugement dernier (Lo jutgamen general)* (Paris, 1971), fifteenth century; O. Jodogne, ed., *"Le mystère de la Passion" de Jean Michel (Angers, 1486)* (Gembloux, 1959). For other plays, see the list in Haslinghuis, pp. xii–xvi, the excellent bibliography in Lazar, "L'enfer," and the list of the editions of the German plays in Schuldes, pp. 149–151.

The Contemplative Tradition in Christianity

On the Christian contemplative tradition see M. Bowman, *Western Mysticism: A Guide to the Basic Works* (Chicago, 1978); J. Clark, *The Great German Mystics: Eckhart, Tauler, and Suso* (Folcroft, Pa., 1949); H. Egan, "Christian Apophatic and Kataphatic Mysticisms," *Theological Studies*, 39 (1978), 399–426; M. Furse, *Mysticism* (Nashville, 1977); Marion Glasscoe, ed., *The Medieval Mystical Tradition in England* (Exeter, 1980); F. Happold, *Mysticism: A Study and an Anthology*, 2d ed. (Harmondsworth, 1970); P. Hodgson, *The Cloud of Unknowing, and Related Treatises on Contemplative Prayer* (Salzburg, 1982); S. Katz, ed., *Mysticism and Philosophical Analysis* (New York, 1978); S. Katz, ed., *Mysticism and Religious Traditions* (Oxford, 1983); H. A. Kelly, *Love and Marriage in the Age of Chaucer* (Ithaca, 1975); D. Knowles, *The English Mystical Tradition* (New York, 1961); D. Knowles,

The Nature of Mysticism (New York, 1966); V. Lagorio and R. Bradley, *The 14th-Century English Mystics: A Comprehensive Annotated Bibliography* (New York, 1981); J. Leclercq, F. Vandenbroucke, and L. Bouyer, *La spiritualité du moyen âge* (Paris, 1961); B. McGinn, "The God beyond God: Theology and Mysticism in the Thought of Meister Eckhart," *Journal of Religion*, 61 (1981), 1–19; R. Petry, *Late Medieval Mysticism* (Philadelphia, 1957); J. Quint, *Textbuch zur Mystik des deutschen Mittelalters*, 2d ed. (Tübingen, 1957); Wolfgang Riehle, *The Middle English Mystics* (London, 1981); U. Sharma and J. Arndt, *Mysticism: A Select Bibliography* (Waterloo, Ont., 1973); M. Sawyer, *A Bibliographical Index of Five English Mystics* (Pittsburgh, 1978); N. Smart, "Interpretations and Mystical Experience," *Religious Studies*, 1 (1965), 75–97; I. Trethowan, *Mysticism and Theology* (London, 1975); G. W. Tuma, *The Fourteenth Century English Mystics*, 2 vols. (Salzburg, 1977); E. Underhill, *Mysticism* (New York, 1955); E. Underhill, *Essentials of Mysticism and Other Essays* (New York, 1976); E. Underhill, *The Mystics of the Church* (New York, 1964).

The most important mystics in the Christian tradition are Paul (d. c. 65); Augustine (354–430); Bernard of Clairvaux (1090–1153); Richard of Saint Victor (d. 1173); William of Saint Thierry (c. 1085–1148); Hildegarde of Bingen (1098–1179); Hadewijck (thirteenth century); Francis of Assisi (c. 1181–1226); Bonaventure (c. 1217–1274); Mechtild of Magdeburg (c. 1212–1290); Angela of Foligno (1249–1309); Gertrude the Great (1256–1302); Meister Eckhart (1260–1327); Jan van Ruusbroec (1293–1381); Heinrich Suso (c. 1295–1366); Johann Tauler (c. 1300–1361); Richard Rolle (c. 1300–1349); Gerard Groote (1340–1384); the author of *The Cloud of Unknowing* (c. 1350); Catherine of Siena (1347–1380); Florens Radewijns (1350–1400); Thomas à Kempis (1380–1471); Julian of Norwich (c. 1342–1415); the author of the *Theologia Germanica* (c. 1350); Nicholas of Cusa (1401–1464); Catherine of Genoa (1447–1510); John of the Cross (1542–1591); Teresa of Avila (1515–1582); Jakob Boehme (1575–1624). Translations of many of these authors are appearing in the series The Classics of Western Spirituality being produced by the Paulist Press in New York.

Bibliography

This bibliography includes only works dealing entirely or in large part with the Devil and demons. Important works dealing with the subject peripherally or generally are cited in the footnotes or in the Essay on the Sources.

Aichele, Klause. *Das Antichristdrama des Mittelalters der Reformation und Gegenreformation.* The Hague, 1974.
Allard, Guy, ed. *Aspects de la marginalité au moyen âge.* Montreal, 1975.
Andrus, Toni Wulff. "The Devil on the Medieval Stage in France." Ph.D. diss., Syracuse University, 1979.
Angenendt, Arnold. "Der Taufexorzismus und seine Kritik in der Theologie des 12. und 13. Jahrhunderts." In A. Zimmermann, ed., *Die Mächte des Guten und Bösen.* Berlin, 1977. Pp. 388–409.
Ashby, Ginette, "Le diable et ses représentations dans quelques chansons de geste." In *Le diable au moyen âge.* Paris, 1979. Pp. 9–21.
Ashley, Kathleen, M. "The Specter of Bernard's Noonday Demon in Medieval Drama." *American Benedictine Review,* 30 (1979), 205–221.
Atkins, Anselm. "Caprice: The Myth of the Fall in Anselm and Dostoevsky." *Journal of Religion,* 47 (1967), 295–312.
Aubin, Paul. "Intériorité et extériorité dans les Moralia in Job de Saint Grégoire le Grand." *Recherches de science religieuse,* 62 (1974), 117–166.
Awn, Peter J. *Satan's Tragedy and Redemption: Iblīs in Sufī Psychology.* Leiden, 1983.

Backes, Herbert. "Teufel, Götter, und Heiden in geistlicher Ritterdichtung: Corpus Antichristi und Märtyrerliturgie." In A. Zimmermann, ed., *Die Mächte des Guten und Bösen*. Berlin, 1977. Pp. 417–441.

Baird, Joseph L. "The Devil in Green." *Neuphilologische Mitteilungen*, 69 (1968), 575–578.

Baltrušaitis, Jurgen. *Réveils et prodiges: Le gothique fantastique*. Paris, 1960.

Bamberger, Bernard J. *Fallen Angels*. Philadelphia, 1952.

Bandy, Stephen C. "Cain, Grendel, and the Giants of *Beowulf*." *Papers on Language and Literature*, 9 (1973), 235–249.

Bartelink, G. J. M. "Les dénominations du diable chez Grégoire de Tours." *Revue des études latines*, 48 (1970), 411–432.

Bartsch, Elmar. *Die Sachbeschwörungen der römischen Liturgie: Eine liturgiegeschichtliche und liturgietheologische Studie*. Münster, 1967.

Batelli, Guido. "Il 'De pugna daemonum' di S. Romualdo e una scultura simbolica a Valdicastro." *Rivista Camaldolese*, 2 (1927), 298–299.

Bazin, Germain. "The Devil in Art." In Bruno de Jésus-Marie, ed., *Satan*. New York, 1952. Pp. 351–367.

Beck, Edmund. "Iblis und Mensch, Satan und Adam: Der Werdegang einer koranischen Erzählung." *Le muséon*, 89 (1976), 195–244.

Bekker, Hugo. "The Lucifer Motif in the German Drama of the Sixteenth Century." *Monatshefte für deutsche Sprache und Literatur*, 51 (1959), 237–247.

Béraudy, Roger. "Scrutinies and Exorcisms." In *Adult Baptism and the Catechumenate*, Series Consilium vol. 22. New York, 1967. Pp. 57–61.

Berkhout, Carl T., and Jeffrey B. Russell, *Medieval Heresies: A Bibliography, 1960–1979*. Toronto, 1981.

Bernheimer, Richard. *Wild Men in the Middle Ages*. Cambridge Mass., 1952.

Bernstein, Alan E. "Esoteric Theology: William of Auvergne on the Fires of Hell and Purgatory." *Speculum*, 57 (1982), 509–531.

———. "Theology between Heresy and Folklore: William of Auvergne on Punishment after Death." *Studies in Medieval and Renaissance History* (1983), 3–42.

Besserman, Lawrence L. *The Legend of Job in the Middle Ages*. Cambridge, Mass., 1979.

Bieder, Werner. *Die Vorstellung der Höllenfahrt Jesu Christi*. Zurich, 1949.

Birnes, William J. "Christ as Advocate: The Legal Metaphor of *Piers Plowman*." *Annuale medievale*, 16 (1975), 71–93.

Blangez, Gérard. "Le diable dans le *ci-nous-dit:* La théorie des sièges de paradis." In *Le diable au moyen âge* (Paris, 1979), 25–35.

Blic, Jacques de. "Peccabilité de l'esprit et surnaturel." *Mélanges de science religieuse*, 3 (1946), 163.

———. "Saint Thomas et l'intellectualisme moral à propos de la peccabilité de l'ange." *Mélanges de science religieuse*, 1 (1944), 241–280.

Blomme, Robert. *La doctrine du péché dans les écoles théologiques de la première moitié du XIIe siècle*. Louvain, 1958.

Bloomfield, Morton W. *The Seven Deadly Sins: An Introduction to the History of a Religious Concept with Special Reference to Medieval English Literature*. East Lansing, Mich., 1952.

Bober, Phyllis Fray. "Cernunnos: Origin and Transformation of a Celtic Divinity." *American Journal of Archeology*, 55 (1951), 13–51.

Bolte, Johannes. "Der Teufel in der Kirche." *Zeitschrift für vergleichende Literaturgeschichte*, n.s. 11 (1897), 247–266.

Bonnell, John K. "The Serpent with a Human Head in Art and in Mystery Play." *American Journal of Archeology*, 21 (1917), 255–291.

Bouman, C. A. "'Descendit ad inferos': Het thema van de nederdaling ter helle in de liturgie." *Nederlands katholieke Stemmen*, 55 (1959), 44–51.

Bourget, Pierre du. "La couleur noire de la peau du démon dans l'iconographie chrétienne a-t-elle une origine précise?" *Actas del VIII congresso internacional de arqueologia cristiana*. Barcelona, 1972. Pp. 271–272.

Bowker, John. "The Problem of Suffering in the Qur'ān." *Religious Studies*, 4 (1969), 183–202.

———. *Problems of Suffering in Religions of the World*. Cambridge, 1970.

Brenk, Beat. "Teufel." *Lexikon der christlichen Ikonographie*, 4 (1972), cols. 295–300.

Brucker, Charles. "Mentions et représentations du diable dans la littérature française épique et romanesque du XIIe et du début du XIIIe siècle: Quelques jalons pour une étude évolutive." In *Le diable au moyen âge*. Paris, 1979. Pp. 39–69.

Bruno de Jésus-Marie, ed. *Satan*. New York, 1952.

Bucher, Gisela. "Le diable dans les polémiques confessionelles." In *Diables et diableries*. Geneva, 1977. Pp. 39–53.

Burns, J. Patout. "The Concept of Satisfaction in Medieval Redemption Theory." *Theological Studies*, 36 (1975), 285–304.

Burton, Dorothy Jean. "The Compact with the Devil in the Middle-English *Vision of Piers the Plowman*, B. II." *California Folklore Quarterly*, 5 (1946), 179–184.

Buschinger, Danielle. "Le diable dans le *Gregorius* de Hartmann von Aue." In *Le diable au moyen âge*. Paris, 1979. Pp. 73–95.

Busnelli, Giovanni. *I tre colori del Lucifero Dantesco*. Rome, 1910.

Calasso, Giovanna. "Intervento d'Iblīs nella creazione dell'uomo: L'ambivalente figura del 'nemico' nelle tradizioni islamiche." *Rivista degli studi orientali*, 45 (1970), 71–90.

Caluwe-Dor, Juliette de. "Le diable dans les Contes de Cantorbéry: Contribution à l'étude sémantique du terme *Devil*." In *Le diable au moyen âge*. Paris, 1979. Pp. 99–116.

Camerlynck, Eliane. "Féminité et sorcellerie chez les théoriciens de la démonologie à la fin du moyen âge: L'étude du *Malleus Maleficarum*." *Renaissance et Reformation*, n.s. 7 (1983), 13–25.

Campbell, Jackson J. "To Hell and Back: Latin Tradition and Literary Use of the 'Descensus ad inferos' in Old English." *Viator*, 13 (1982), 107–158.

Carmody, Francis. "Le diable des bestiaires." *Cahiers de l'association internationale des études françaises*, 3/4/5 (1953), 79–85.

Cassell. Anthony. "The Tomb, the Tower, and the Pit: Dante's Satan." *Italica*, 56 (1979), 331–351.

Castelli, Enrico. *Il demoniaco nell'arte*. Milan, 1952.

Cawley, F. Stanton. "The Figure of Loki in Germanic Mythology." *Harvard Theological Review*, 32 (1939), 309–326.

Cazenave, Annie. "Bien et mal dans un mythe cathare languedocien." In A. Zimmermann, ed., *Die Mächte des Guten und Bösen*. Berlin, 1977. Pp. 344–387.

Chadwick, Nora K. "The Monsters in Beowulf." In Peter Clemoes, ed., *The Anglo-Saxons*. London, 1959. Pp. 171–203.

Champneys, A. C. "The Character of the Devil in the Middle Ages." *National and English Review*, 11 (1888), 176–191.

Ciérvide, Ricardo. "Notas en torno al libro de Miseria de Omne: Lo demoniaco e infernal en el códice." *Estudios de Duesto*, 22 (1974), 81–96.

Clark, Roy Peter. "Squeamishness and Exorcism in Chaucer's *Miller's Tale*." *Thoth*, 14 (1973–1974), 37–43.

Cohn, Norman. *Europe's Inner Demons*. New York, 1975.

Colliot, Régine. "Rencontres du moine Raoul Glaber avec le diable d'après ses *Histoires*." In *Le diable au moyen âge*. Paris, 1979. Pp. 119–132.

Colombani, Dominique. "La chute et la modification: Le renversement diabolique chez Gautier de Coinci." In *Le diable au moyen âge*. Paris, 1979. Pp. 135–154.

Combarieu, Michelin de. "Le diable dans le *Comment Theophilus vint à pénitence* de Gautier de Coinci et dans le *Miracle Théophile* de Rutebeuf (1)." In *Le diable au moyen âge*. Paris, 1979. Pp. 157–182.

Conner, Patrick W. "The Liturgy and the Old English 'Descent into Hell.'" *Journal of English and Germanic Philology*, 79 (1980), 179–191.

Courtenay, William J. "Necessity and Freedom in Anselm's Conception of God." In Helmut Kohlenberger, ed., *Analecta Anselmiana*. Vol. 4/2. Frankfurt am Main, 1975. pp. 39–64.

Courtès, C. "La peccabilité de l'ange chez saint Thomas." *Revue thomiste*, 53 (1953), 133–163.

Crawford, J. P. W. "The Devil as a Dramatic Figure in the Spanish Religious Drama before Lope da Vega." *Romanic Review*, 1 (1910), 302–312; 374–383.

Crook, Eugene J., and Margaret Jennings. "The Devil and Ranulph Higden." *Manuscripta*, 22 (1978), 131–140.

Culianu, Ioan Petru. "Magia spirituale e magia demonica nel Rinascimento." *Rivista di storia e letteratura religiosa*, 17 (1981), 360–408.

Cushman, L. W. *The Devil and the Vice in English Literature before Shakespeare*. London, 1900.

Dalbey, Marcia A. "The Devil in the Garden: Pluto and Proserpine in Chaucer's 'Merchant's Tale.'" *Neuphilologische Mitteilungen*, 75 (1974), 402–415.

Dando, Marcel. "Les anges neutres." *Cahiers d'études cathares*, 27, no. 69 (1976), 3–28.

——. "Satanaël." *Cahiers d'études cathares*, 30, no. 83 (1979), 3–11; 30, no. 84 (1979), 3–6; 31, no. 85 (1980), 14–32; 31, no. 86 (1980), 3–16.

D'Ardenne, Simone T. R. O. "The Devil's Spout." *Transactions of the Philological Society* (London, 1946), 31–54.

De Clerck, D. E. "Droits du démon et nécessité de la rédemption: Les écoles d'Abélard et de Pierre Lombard." *Recherches de théologie ancienne et médiévale*, 14 (1947), 32–64.

——. "Questions de sotériologie médiévale." *Recherches de théologie ancienne et médiévale*, 13 (1946), 150–184.

DeCourcey, Mary E. *Theory of Evil in the Metaphysics of Saint Thomas and Its Contemporary Significance.* Washington, D.C., 1948.

Dedek, John F. "Intrinsically Evil Acts: An Historical Study of the Mind of St. Thomas." *The Thomist,* 43 (1979), 385–413.

Delatte, A., and Ch. Josserand. "Contribution à l'étude de la démonologie byzantine." *Mélanges J. Bidez.* Vol. 2. Brussels, 1934. Pp. 207–232.

Deschaux, Robert. "Le livre de la diablerie d'Eloy d'Amerval." In *Le diable au moyen âge.* Paris, 1979. Pp. 185–193.

Devine, Philip E. "The Perfect Island, the Devil, and Existent Unicorns." *American Philosophical Quarterly,* 12 (1975), 255–260.

Le diable au moyen âge: Doctrine, problèmes moraux, représentations. Paris, 1979.

Diables et diableries: La représentation du diable dans la gravure des 15e et 16e siècles. Geneva, 1977.

Dölger, Franz-Josef. *Der Exorzismus im altchristlichen Taufritual: Eine religionsgeschichtliche Studie.* Paderborn, 1909.

———. "Teufels Grossmutter.: Magna Mater Deum, Magna Mater Deorum: Die Umwertung der Heidengötter im christlichen Dämonenglauben." *Antike und Christentum,* 3 (1932), 153–176.

Donati, Umberto. *Lucifero nella Divina Commedia.* Rome, 1958.

Dreyer, Max. *Der Teufel in der deutschen Dichtung des Mittelalters: Von den Anfängen bis in das XIV. Jahrhundert.* Rostock, 1884.

DuBruck, Edelgard. "The Devil and Hell in Medieval French Drama: Prolegomena." *Romania,* 100 (1979), 165–179.

———. "Thomas Aquinas and Medieval Demonology." *Michigan Academician,* 7 (1974), 167–183.

Ducellier, Andre. "Le diable à Byzance." In *Le diable au moyen âge.* Paris, 1979. Pp. 197–212.

Düchting, Reinhard. "Titivillus. Dämon der Kopisten und solcher, die sich versprechen: Ein Beitrag zur Geschichte des Lapsus linguae." *Ruperto Carola,* 58/59 (1976/1977), 69–73.

Dumézil, Georges. *Loki.* Darmstadt, 1959.

Dustoor, P. E. "Legends of Lucifer in Early English and in Milton." *Anglia,* 54 (1930), 213–268.

Eickmann, Walther. *Die Angelologie und Dämonologie des Koran im Vergleich der Engel- und Geisterlehre der Heiligen Schrift.* New York and Leipzig, 1908.

Emmerson, Richard Kenneth. *Antichrist in the Middle Ages: A Study of Medieval Apocalypticism, Art, and Literature.* Seattle, 1981.

Erich. Oswald A. *Die Darstellung des Teufels in der christlichen Kunst.* Berlin, 1931.

Evans, Gillian R. *Augustine on Evil.* Cambridge, 1982.

———. "Why the Fall of Satan?" *Recherches de théologie ancienne et médiévale,* 45 (1978), 130–146.

Evans, J. M. *"Paradise Lost" and the Genesis Tradition.* Oxford, 1968.

Faggin, Giuseppe. *Diabolicità del rospo.* Venice, 1973.

Farrell, P. M. "Evil and Omnipotence." *Mind,* 67 (1958), 399–403.

Fehr, Hans von. "Gottesurteil und Folter: Eine Studie zur Dämonologie des Mittelalters und der neueren Zeit." *Festgabe für Rudolf Stammler.* Berlin and Leipzig, 1926. Pp. 231–254.

Feng, Helen C. "Devil's Letters: Their History and Significance in Church and Society, 1110–1500." Ph.D. diss., Northwestern University, 1982.

Finnegan, Robert Emmett. "*Christ and Satan:* Structure and Theme." *Classica et mediaevalia*, 30 (1974), 490–551.

——. "God's *Handmaegen* versus the Devil's *Craeft* in *Genesis B.*" *English Studies in Canada*, 7 (1981), 1–14.

——. "Three Notes on the Junius XI *Christ and Satan:* Lines 78–79; Lines 236–42; Lines 435–38." *Modern Philology*, 72 (1974–1975), 175–181.

Frappier, Jean. "Châtiments infernaux et peur du diable d'après quelques textes français du XIIIe et du XIVe siècle." In Frappier, *Histoire, mythes et symboles*. Geneva, 1976. Pp. 129–136.

Frascino, Salvatore. "La 'terra' dei giganti ed il Lucifero dantesco." *La cultura*, 12 (1933), 767–783.

Freccero, John. "Dante and the Neutral Angels." *The Romanic Review*, 51 (1960), 3–14.

——. "Infernal Inversion and Christian Conversion (Inferno XXXIV)." *Italica*, 42 (1965), 35–41.

——. "Satan's Fall and the *Quaestio de aqua et terra.*" *Italica*, 38 (1961), 99–115.

——. "The Sign of Satan." *Modern Language Notes*, 80 (1965), 11–26.

Freytag, Gustave. "Der deutsche Teufel im sechzehnten Jahrhundert." In Freytag, *Gesammmelte Werke*. Berlin, 1920. Ser. 2, vol. 5. Pp. 346–384.

Frick, Karl. *Das Reich Satans: Luzifer/Satan/Teufel und die Mond- und Liebesgöttinen in ihrer lichten und dunklen Aspekten*. Graz, 1982.

Friedman, John Block. "Eurydice, Heurodis, and the Noon-day Demon." *Speculum*, 41 (1966), 22–29.

——. *The Monstrous Races in Medieval Art and Thought*. Cambridge, Mass., 1981.

Gallardo, Próspero G. "Rutas Compostelanos: El demonio del Languedoc." *Boletín del Seminario de Estudios de Arte e Arqueología*, 20 (1953–1954), 217–219.

Galpern, Joyce Manheimer. "The Shape of Hell in Anglo-Saxon England." Ph.D. diss., University of California, Berkeley, 1977.

Gandillac, Maurice de. "Anges et hommes dans le commentaire de Jean Scot sur la 'Hiérarchie céleste.'" *Jean Scot Erigène*. Paris, 1977. Pp. 393–403.

Garidis, Miltos. "L'évolution de l'iconographie du démon dans la période postbyzantine." *L'information d'histoire de l'art*, 12 (1967), 143–155.

Gaston, L. "Beelzebul." *Theologische Zeitschrift*, 18 (1962), 247–255.

Gatch, Milton McC. "The Harrowing of Hell: A Liberation Motif in Medieval Theology and Devotional Literature." *Union Seminary Quarterly Review*, 36, suppl. (1981), 75–88.

Geister, Otto E. *Die Teufelsszenen in der Passion von Arras und der Vengenace Jhesucrist*. Greifswald, 1914.

Gerest, Régis-Claude. "Le démon en son temps: De la fin du moyen âge au XVIe siècle." *Lumière et vie*, 78 (1966), 16–30. Giacomo, Vittorio di. *Leggende del diavolo*. 2d ed. Bologna, 1962.

Gobinet, D. "Sur les membres inférieures d'un démon." *Revue du moyen âge latin*, 15 (1959), 102–104.

——. "Sur les membres inférieurs d'un démon (note complémentaire)." *Revue du moyen âge latin*, 23 (1967), 131–132.

Goddu, André. "The Failure of Exorcism in the Middle Ages." In A. Zimmermann, ed., *Soziale Ordnungen im Selbstverständnis des Mittelalters*. Berlin, 1980. Pp. 540–557.

Goldziher, I. "Eisen als Schutz gegen Dämonen." *Archiv für Religionswissenschaften*, 10 (1907), 41–46.

Gombocz, Wolfgang L. F. "St. Anselm's Disproof of the Devil's Existence in the *Proslogion:* A Counter Argument against Haight and Richman." *Ratio*, 15 (1973), 334–337.

———. "St. Anselm's Two Devils but One God." *Ratio*, 20 (1978), 142–146.

———. "Zur Zwei-Argument Hypothese bezüglich Anselms Proslogion." *Quarante-septième bulletin de l'Académie St. Anselme*, 75 (1974), 95–98.

Gomme, Alice B. "The Character of Beelzebub in the Mummers' Play." *Folk-lore*, 40 (1929), 292–293.

Goulet, Jean. "Un portrait des sorcières au XVe siècle." In Guy Allard, ed., *Aspects de la marginalité au moyen âge*. Montreal, 1975. Pp. 129–141.

Gouttebroze, Jean-Guy. "Le diable dans le Roman de Rou." In *Le diable au moyen âge*. Paris, 1979. Pp. 215–235.

Graf, Arturo. "La demonologia di Dante." In Graf, *Miti, leggende e superstizioni del medio evo*. Vol. 2. Turin, 1925. Pp. 80–112.

Grant, C. K. "The Ontological Disproof of the Devil." *Analysis*, 17 (1957), 71–72.

Griffin, Robert. "The Devil and Panurge." *Studi francesi*, 47/48 (1972), 329–336.

Grivot, Denis. *Le Diable dans la cathédrale*. Paris, 1960.

Gros, Gérard. "Le diable et son adversaire dans l'Advocacie nostre dame (poème du XIVe siècle)." In *Le diable au moyen âge*. Paris, 1979. Pp. 258–260.

Grosdidier de Matons, José. "Démonologie, magie, divinisation, astrologie à Byzance." *Annuaire de l'Ecole Pratique des Hautes Etudes, IVe section: Sciences historiques et philologiques*, 107 (1974–1975), 485–491.

Grove, Thomas N. "Light in Darkness: The Comedy of the York 'Harrowing of Hell' as Seen against the Backdrop of the Chester 'Harrowing of Hell.'" *Neuphilologische Mitteilungen*, 75 (1974), 115–125.

Grunebaum, Gustav von. "The Concept of Evil in Muslim Theology." *Middle East Studies Association Bulletin*, 2, no. 3 (1968), 1–3.

———. "Observations on the Muslim Concept of Evil." *Studia islamica*, 31 (1970), 117–134.

Haight, David, and Marjorie Haight. "An Ontological Argument for the Devil." *The Monist*, 54 (1970), 218–220.

Hammerstein, Reinhold. *Diabolus in Musica: Studien zur Ikonographie Musik im Mittelalter*. Berne, 1974.

Harris, Errol E. *The Problem of Evil*. Milwaukee, 1977.

Haslinghuis, Edward Johannes. *De Duivel in het Drama der Middeleeuwen*. Leiden, 1912.

Haubst, Rudolf. "Anselms Satifaktionslehre einst und heute." *Trierer theologische Zeitschrift*, 80 (1971), 88–109.

Hayen, André. "Le péché de l'ange selon Saint Thomas d'Aquin: Théologie de l'amour divin et métaphysique de l'acte de l'être." *Teoresi*, 9 (1954), 83–176.

Heinemann, Franz. "Die Rolle des Teufels bei den Auferstehungsspielen der luzerner Landschaft." *Innerschweizerisches Jahrbuch für Heimatkunde*, 11–12 (1947–1948), 117–136.

Helg, Didier. "La fonction du diable dans les textes hagiographiques." In *Diables et diableries*. Geneva, 1977. Pp. 13–17.

Henry, Desmond P. "Saint Anselm and Nothingness." *Philosophical Quarterly*, 15 (1965), 243–246.

Hill, Joyce M. "Figures of Evil in Old English Poetry." *Leeds Studies in English*, 8 (1976), 5–19.

Hill, Thomas D. "The Fall of Angels and Man in the Old English *Genesis B*." In Lewis B. Nicholson and Dolores W. Frese, eds., *Anglo-Saxon Poetry: Essays in Appreciation for John C. McGalliard*. Notre Dame, 1975. Pp. 279–290.

———. "The Fall of Satan in the Old English *Christ and Satan*." *Journal of English and German Philology*, 76 (1977), 315–325.

———. "Satan's Fiery Speech: 'Christ and Satan' 78–79." *Notes and Queries*, 217 (1972), 2–4.

———. "Some Remarks on 'The Site of Lucifer's Throne.'" *Anglia*, 87 (1969), 303–311.

Hourani, George F. "Averroes on Good and Evil." *Studia islamica*, 16 (1962), 13–40.

Hübener, Wolfgang. "'Malum auget decorem in universo': Die kosmologische Integration des Bösen in der Hochscholastik." In A. Zimmermann, ed., *Die Mächte des Guten und Bösen*. Berlin, 1977. Pp. 1–26.

Iancu-Agou, Daniel. "Le diable et le juif: Représentations médiévales iconographiques et écrites." In *Le diable au moyen âge*. Paris, 1979. Pp. 261–276.

Iersel, Bastiaan M. F. van, A. A. Bastiaensen, J. Quinlan, and P. J. Schoonenberg. *Engelen en Duivels*. Hilversum, 1968.

Jadaane, Fehmi. "La place des anges dans la théologie cosmique musulmane." *Studia islamica*, 41 (1975), 23–61.

Jennings, Margaret. *Tutivillus: The Literary Career of the Recording Demon*. Studies in Philology, 74, no. 5. Chapel Hill, 1977.

Jones, David M. "Exorcism before the Reformation: The Problems of Saying One Thing and Meaning Another." Master's thesis, University of Virginia, 1978.

Jordans, Wilhelm. *Der germanische Volksglaube von den Toten und Dämonen im Berg und ihrer Beschwichtigung: Die Spuren in England*. Bonn, 1933.

Jourjon, "Qu'allait-il voir au désert? Simple question posée au moine sur son démon." *Lumière et vie*, 78 (1966), 3–15.

Kably, Mohammed. "Satan dans l'Ithia' d'Al-Ghazalī." *Hespéris Tamuda*, 6 (1965), 5–37.

Kappler, Claude. "Le diable, la sorcière, et l'inquisiteur d'après le 'Malleus Maleficarum.'" In *Le diable au moyen âge*. Paris, 1979. Pp. 279–291.

Kaske, Robert E. "Beowulf and the Book of Enoch." *Speculum*, 46 (1971), 421–431.

———. "The *Eotenas* in Beowulf." In Robert Creed, ed., *Old English Poetry: Fifteen Essays*. Providence, 1967. Pp. 285–310.

Kasper, Walter, and Karl Lehmann. *Teufel—Dämonen—Besessenheit: Zur Wirklichkeit des Bösen*. 2d ed. Mainz, 1978.

Keenan, Hugh T. "Satan Speaks in Sparks: *Christ and Satan* 78–79a, 161–162b, and the 'Life of Saint Anthony.'" *Notes and Queries*, 219 (1974), 283–284.

Kellogg, Alfred L. "Satan, Langland, and the North." *Speculum*, 24 (1949), 413–414.

Kelly, Henry Ansgar. *The Devil, Demonology, and Witchcraft.* 2d ed. New York, 1974.

———. "The Devil in the Desert." *Catholic Biblical Quarterly*, 26 (1964), 190–220.

———. "The Metamorphoses of the Eden Serpent during the Middle Ages and Renaissance." *Viator*, 2 (1971), 301–328.

Kiessling, Nicholas. *The Incubus in English Literature: Provenance and Progeny.* Pullman, Wash., 1977.

Kirschbaum, E. "L'angelo rosso e l'angelo turchino." *Rivista di archeologia cristiana*, 17 (1940), 209–248.

Kirsten, Hans. *Die Taufabsage.* Berlin, 1960.

Köppen, Alfred. *Der Teufel und die Hölle in der darstellenden Kunst von den Anfängen bis zum Zeitalter Dante's und Giotto's.* Berlin, 1895.

Kretzenbacher, Leopold. *Teufelsbünder und Faustgestalten im Abendlande.* Klagenfurt, 1968.

Kroll, Josef. *Gott und Hölle: Der Mythos vom Descensuskampfe.* Leipzig, 1932.

Lafontaine-Dosogne, Jacqueline. "Un thème iconographique peu connu: Marina assommant Belzébuth." *Byzantion*, 32 (1962), 251–259.

Lampe, Hans-Sirks. *Die Darstellung des Teufels in den geistlichen Spielen Deutschlands: Von den Anfängen bis zum Ende des 16. Jahrhunderts.* Munich, 1963.

Langton, Edward. *Satan, a Portrait: A Study of the Character of Satan through All the Ages.* London, 1945.

Larmat, Jean. "Perceval et le chevalier au dragon: La croix et le diable." In *Le diable au moyen âge.* Paris, 1979. Pp. 295–305.

Lazar, Moshé, "Caro, mundus, et demonia dans les premières oeuvres de Bosch." *Studies in Art*, 24 (1972), 106–137.

———. "Les diables: Serviteurs et buffons (répertoire et jeu chez les comédiens de la troupe infernale)." *Tréteaux*, 1 (1978), 51–69.

———. "L'enfer et les diables dans le théâtre médiéval italien." *Studi di filologia romanza offerti a Silvio Pellegrini.* Padua, 1971. Pp. 233–249.

———. "The Saint and the Devil: Christological and Diabological Typology in Fifteenth Century Provençal Drama." In Norris J. Lacey and Jerry C. Nash, eds., *Essays in Early French Literature Presented to Barbara M. Craig.* York, S.C., 1982. Pp. 81–92.

———. "Satan and Notre Dame: Characters in a Popular Scenario." In Norris J. Lacey, ed., *A Medieval French Miscellany.* Lawrence, Kans., 1972. Pp. 1–14.

———. "Theophilus, Servant of Two Masters: The Pre-Faustian Theme of Despair and Revolt." *Modern Language Notes*, 87, no. 6 (1972), 31–50.

Lebègue, Raymond. "Le diable dans l'ancien théâtre religieux." *Cahiers de l'association internationale des études françaises*, 3–5 (1953), 97–105.

Legros, Huguette. "Le diable et l'enfer: Représentation dans la sculpture romane (étude faite à travers quelques exemples significatifs: Conques, Autun, Saint-Benoît-sur-Loire)." In *Le diable au moyen âge.* Paris, 1979. Pp. 309–329.

Lionel, Frédéric. "Le bien et le mal et la foi cathare." *Cahiers d'études cathares*, 25 (1974), 51–57.

Lixfeld, Hannjost. *Gott und Teufel als Weltschöpfer: Eine Untersuchung über die dualistische Tiererschaffung in der europäischen und aussereuropäischen Volksüberlieferung.* Munich, 1971.

Lo Castro, Antonino. *Lucifero nella "Commedia" di Dante.* Messina, 1971.

Lohr, Evelyn. *Patristic Demonology in Old English Literature.* Abridged. New York, 1949.

Loofs, Friedrich. "Christ's Descent into Hell." *Transactions of the Third International Congress for the History of Religions*, 11 (1908), 290–301.

Loos, Milan. "Satan als Erstgeborener Gottes (ein Beitrag zur Analyse des bogomilischen Mythus)." *Byzantinobulgarica*, 3 (1969), 23–35.

Lukken, G. M. *Original Sin in the Roman Liturgy: Research into the Theology of Original Sin in the Roman Sacramentaria and the Early Baptismal Liturgy.* Leiden, 1973.

Maag, Victor. "The Antichrist as a Symbol of Evil." In Curatorium of the C. G. Jung Institute, *Evil.* Evanston, 1967. Pp. 57–82.

MacCulloch, John A. *The Harrowing of Hell: A Comparative Study of an Early Christian Doctrine.* Edinburgh, 1930.

Maeterlinck, Louis. "Le rôle comique du démon dans les mystères flamands." *Mercure de France*, 41 (1940), 385–406.

Malmberg, Lars. "Grendel and the Devil." *Neuphilologische Mitteilungen*, 78 (1977), 241–243.

Malone, Kemp. "Satan's Speech: Genesis 347–440." *Emory University Quarterly*, 19 (1963), 242–246.

Margoliouth, D. S. "The Devil's Delusion by Ibn al-Jauzi." *Islamic Culture*, 9 (1935), 1–21.

———. "The Devil's Delusion: *Talbīs Iblīs* of Abu'l-Faraj ibn al-Jawsī." *Islamic Culture*, 19 (1945), 69–81.

Marieb, Raymond E. "The Impeccability of the Angels Regarding Their Natural End." *The Thomist*, 28 (1964), 409–474.

Maritain, Jacques. *St. Thomas and the Problem of Evil.* Milwaukee, 1942.

McAlindon, T. "Comedy and Terror in Middle English Literature: The Diabolical Game." *Modern Language Review*, 60 (1965), 325–332.

———. "The Emergence of a Comic Type in Middle-English Narrative: The Devil and Giant as Buffoon." *Anglia*, 81 (1963), 365–371.

McGuire, Brian Patrick. "God, Man and the Devil in Medieval Theology and Culture." Université de Copenhague, Institut du moyen âge grec et latin, *Cahiers*, 18 (1976), 18–82.

Mellinkoff, Ruth. "Cain and the Jews." *Journal of Jewish Art*, 6 (1979), 16–38.

———. "Cain's Monstrous Progeny in *Beowulf*: Part I, Noachic Tradition." *Anglo-Saxon England*, 8 (1979), 143–162.

———. "Cain's Monstrous Progeny in *Beowulf*: Part II, Post-Diluvian Survival." *Anglo-Saxon England*, 9 (1980), 183–197.

———. *The Horned Moses in Medieval Art and Thought.* Berkeley, 1970.

———. "Judas's Red Hair and the Jews." *Journal of Jewish Art*, 9 (1983), 31–46.

———. *The Mark of Cain.* Berkeley, 1981.

_____. "Riding Backwards: Theme of Humiliation and Symbol of Evil." *Viator*, 4 (1973), 153–176.

_____. "The Round-Topped Tablets of the Law: Sacred Symbol and Emblem of Evil." *Journal of Jewish Art*, 1 (1974), 28–43.

Menage, René. "La mesnie infernale dans la *Passion* d'Arnoul Greban." In *Le diable au moyen âge*. Paris, 1979. Pp. 333–349.

Menjot, Denis. "Le diable dans la 'Vita Sancti Emiliani' de Braulio de Saragosse (585?–651?)." In *Le diable au moyen âge*. Paris, 1979. Pp. 355–369.

Mirarchi, Giovanni. "Osservazioni sul poema anglossassone *Cristo e Satana*." *Aion: Filologia germanica*, 22 (1979), 79–106.

Montano, Edward J. *The Sin of the Angels: Some Aspects of the Teaching of St. Thomas*. Washington, D.C., 1955.

Montgomery, John Warwick. *Demon Possession: A Medical, Historical, Anthropological, and Theological Symposium*. Minneapolis, 1976.

Müller, Carl Detlef G. "Geister (Dämonen): Volksglaube." *Reallexikon für Antike und Christentum*, 9 (1975), 761–797.

Nardi, Bruno. *La caduta di Lucifero e l'autenticità della "Quaestio de Aqua et terra."* Rome, 1959.

_____. "Gli Angeli che non furon ribelli nè fur fedeli a Dio." In Nardi, *Dal "Convivio" alla "Commedia": Sei saggi danteschi*. Rome, 1960. Pp. 331–350.

Naselli, Carmelina. "Diavoli bianchi e diavoli neri nei leggendari medievali." *Volkstum und Kultur der Romanen*, 15 (1941–1943), 233–254.

Nelli, R. *La nature maligne dans le dualisme cathare du XIIIe siècle, de l'inégalité des deux principes*. Toulouse, Université, Travaux du Laboratoire d'ethnographie et de civilisation occitanes, 1. Carcassonne: Editions de la revue *Folklore*, 1969.

Nelson, Alan H. "The Temptation of Christ: Or the Temptation of Satan." In Jerome Taylor and Alan H. Nelson, eds., *Medieval English Drama*. Chicago, 1972. Pp. 218–229.

Obrist, Barbara. "Les deux visages du diable." In *Diable et diableries*, pp. 19–29.

Oliver, Gabriel. "El diable, el sagristà i la Burguesa: Fragmento de un texto Catalán del siglo XIV." *Miscellanea Barcinonensia*, 36 (1973), 41–62.

Orr, John. "Devil a Bit." *Cahiers de l'association intérnationale des études françaises*, 3/4/5 (1953), 107–113.

Owen, Douglas D. R. *The Vision of Hell: Infernal Journeys in Medieval French Literature*. Edinburgh, 1970.

Ozaeta, J. M. "La doctrina de Innocencio III sobre el demonio." *Ciudad de Dios*, 192 (1979), 319–336.

Padellaro de Angelis, Rosa D. *Il problema del male nell'alta scholastica*. Rome, 1968.

Palgen, Rudolf. *Dantes Luzifer: Grundzüge einer Entstehungsgeschichte der Komödie Dantes*. Munich 1969.

Paschetto, Eugenia. "Il 'De natura daemonum' di Witelo." *Atti dell'Accademia delle Scienze di Torino: Filosofia e storia della filosofia*, 109 (1975), 231–271.

Patch, Howard R. *The Other World: According to Descriptions in Medieval Literature*. Cambridge, Mass., 1950.

Patrides, C. A. "The Salvation of Satan." *Journal of the History of Ideas*, 28 (1967), 467–478.

Paul, Jacques. "Le démoniaque et l'imaginaire dans le 'De vita sua' de Guibert de Nogent." In *Le diable au moyen âge*. Paris, 1979. 373–399.

Payen, Jean-Charles. "Pour en finir avec le diable médiéval, ou pourquoi poètes et théologiens du moyen-âge ont-ils scrupulé à croire au démon?" In *Le diable au moyen âge*. Paris, 1979. Pp. 403–425.

Penco, Gregorio. "Sopravvivenze della demonologia antica nel monachesimo medievale." *Studia monastica*, 13 (1971), 31–36.

Perrot, Jean-Pierre. "Le diable dans les légendiers français du XIIIe siècle." In *Le diable au moyen âge*. Paris, 1979. Pp. 429–442.

Petersdorff, Egon von. *Dämonologie*. 2 vols. Munich, 1956–1957.

Philippe de la Trinité. "Du péché de Satan et de la destinée de l'esprit." In Bruno de Jésus-Marie, ed., *Satan*. Paris, 1948. Pp. 44–97.

———. "Evolution de Saint Thomas sur le péché de l'ange dans l'ordre naturel?" *Ephemerides Carmeliticae*, 9 (1958), 44–85.

———. "La pensée des Carmes de Salamanque et de Jean de Saint-Thomas sur le péché de l'ange." *Ephemerides Carmeliticae*, 8 (1957), 315–375.

———. "Réflexions sur le péché de l'ange." *Ephemerides Carmeliticae*, 8 (1957), 44–92.

Pitangue, François. "Variations dramatiques du diable dans le théâtre fançais du moyen âge." In *Etudes médiévales offertes à M. Le Doyen Augustin Fliche de l'Institut*. Montpellier, 1952. Pp. 143–160.

Poly, Jean-Pierre. "Le diable, Jacques le Coupe, et Jean des Portes, ou les avatars de Santiago." In *Le diable au moyen âge*. Paris, 1979. Pp. 445–460.

Psellos, Michael. *Démonologie populaire, démonologie critique au XIe siècle: La vie inédite de S. Auxence, par M. Psellos*. Edited by Perikles-Petros Joannou. Wiesbaden, 1971.

Quay, Paul M. "Angels and Demons: The Teaching of IV Lateran." *Theological Studies*, 42 (1981), 20–45.

Räisänen, Heikki. *The Idea of Divine Hardening: A Comparative Study of the Notion of Divine Hardening, Leading Astray, and Inciting to Evil in the Bible and the Qu'rān*. Helsinki, 1972.

Raphael, Freddy. "Le juif et le diable dans la civilisation de l'Occident." *Social Compass* 19 (1972–1974), 549–566.

———. "La représentation des juifs dans l'art médiéval en Alsace: La 'truie aux juifs de la Collégiale Saint-Martin de Colmar' et le 'diable aux juifs de l'église paroissiale de Rouffach.'" *Revue des sciences sociales de la France de l'Est*, 1 (1972), 26–42.

Rauh, Horst Dieter. *Das Bild des Antichrist im Mittelalter: von Tychonius zum deutschen Symbolismus*. 2d ed. Münster, 1979.

Raymo, Robert R. "A Middle English Version of the *Epistola Luciferi ad Cleros*." In D. A. Pearsall and R. A. Waldron, eds., *Medieval Literature and Civilization: Studies in Memory of G. N. Garmonsway*. London, 1969. Pp. 233–248.

Rice, Winthrop H. "Le livre de la diablerie d'Eloy d'Amerval." *Cahiers de l'association internationale des études françaises*, 3/4/5 (1953), 115–126.

Richman, Robert J. "The Devil and Dr. Waldman." *Philosophical Studies*, 11 (1960), 78–80.

———. "The Ontological Proof of the Devil." *Philosophical Studies*, 9 (1958), 63–64.

———. "A Serious Look at the Ontological Argument." *Ratio*, 18 (1976), 85–89.

Risse, Robert G., Jr. "The Augustinian Paraphrase of Isaiah 14.13–14 in *Piers Plowman* and the Commentary on the *Fables* of Avianus." *Philological Quarterly*, 45 (1966), 712–717.

Rivière, Jean. *Le dogme de la rédemption au début du moyen âge*. Paris, 1934.

——. "Le dogme de la rédemption au XIIe siècle d'après les dernieres publications." *Revue du moyen âge latin*, 2 (1946), 100–112.

Robertson, D. W., Jr. "Why the Devil Wears Green." *Modern Language Notes*, 69 (1954), 470–472.

Robinson, Fred C. "The Devil's Account of the Next World." *Neuphilologische Mitteilungen*, 73 (1972), 362–371.

Roché, Déodat. "Le rôle des entités sataniques et l'organisation du monde matériel." *Cahiers d'études cathares*, 17 (1966), 39–46.

Rodari, Florian. "Où le diable est légion." *Musées de Genève*, n.s. 18 (Jan. 1977), 22–26.

Roos, Keith L. *The Devil in 16th Century German Literature: The Teufelsbücher*. Frankfurt am Main, 1972.

Roskoff, Gustav. *Geschichte des Teufels*. 2 vols. Leipzig, 1869.

Rousseau, O. "La descente aux enfers dans le cadre des liturgies chrétiennes." *La Maison-Dieu*, 43 (1955), 104–123.

Rudwin, Maximilian. *The Devil in Legend and Literature*. La Salle, Ill., 1931.

——. *Der Teufel in den deutschen geistlichen Spielen des Mittelalters und der Reformationszeit*. Göttingen, 1915.

Rüsch, Ernst Gerhard. "Dämonenaustreibung in der Gallus-Vita und bei Blumhardt dem Älteren." *Theologische Zeitschrift*, 34 (1978), 86–94.

Russell, Jeffrey Burton. *The Devil: Perceptions of Evil from Antiquity to Primitive Christianity*. Ithaca, 1977.

——. *Satan: The Early Christian Tradition*. Ithaca, 1981.

Russell, Jeffrey B., and Mark W. Wyndham. "Witchcraft and the Demonization of Heresy." *Mediaevalia*, 2 (1976), 1–21.

Salmon, P. B. "Jacobus de Theramo and Belial." *London Mediaeval Studies*, 2 (1951), 101–115.

Salmon, Paul. "The Site of Lucifer's Throne." *Anglia*, 81 (1963) 118–123.

Salvat, Michel. "La représentation du diable par un encyclopédiste du XIIIe siècle: Barthélemi l'Anglais (vers 1250)." In *Le diable au moyen âge*. Paris, 1979. Pp. 475–492.

Saly, Antoinette. "'Li Fluns au deable.'" In *Le diable au moyen âge*. Paris, 1979. Pp. 495–506.

Schade, Herbert. *Dämonen und Monstren: Gestaltungen des Bösen in der Kunst des frühen Mittelalters*. Regensburg, 1962.

Schimmel, Annemarie. "Die Gestalt Satans in Muhammad Iqbals Werk." *Kairos*, 5 (1963), 124–137.

Schmidt, Philipp. *Der Teufels- und Daemonenglaube in den Erzählungen des Caesarius von Heisterbach*. Basel, 1926.

Schmitz, Kenneth L. "Shapes of Evil in Medieval Epics: A Philosophical Analysis." In Harold Scholler, ed., *The Epic in Medieval Society: Aesthetic and Moral Values*. Tübingen, 1977. Pp. 37–63.

Schuldes, Luis. *Die Teufelsszenen im deutschen geistlichen Drama des Mittelalters.* Göppingen, 1974.

Schulz, Hans-Joachim. "Die Höllenfahrt als 'Anastasis': Eine Untersuchung über Eigenart und dogmengeschichtliche Voraussetzungen byzantinischer Osterfrömmigkeit." *Zeitschrift für katholische Theologie* 81 (1959), 1–66.

Sedlmayer, Hans. "Art du démoniaque et démonie de l'art." In Enrico Castelli, ed., *Filosofia dell'arte.* Rome, 1953. Pp. 99–114.

Seiferth, Wolfgang S. "The Concept of the Devil and the Myth of the Pact in Literature Prior to Goethe." *Monatshefte,* 44 (1952), 271–289.

Silber, Patricia. "'The Develis Perlament': Poetic Drama and a Dramatic Poem." *Mediaevalia,* 3 (1977), 215–228.

Sleeth, Charles R. *Studies in "Christ and Satan."* Toronto, 1982.

Smith, Constance I. "Descendit ad Inferos—Again." *Journal of the History of Ideas,* 28 (1967), 87–88.

Stapff, Heribert. "Der 'Meister Reuaus' und die Teufelsgestalt in der deutschen Dichtung des späten Mittelalters." Ph.D. diss., University of Munich, 1956.

Stearns, J. Brenton. "Anselm and the Two-Argument Hypothesis." *The Monist,* 54 (1970), 221–233.

Steidle Basilius. "Der 'schwarze kleine Knabe' in der alten Mönchserzählung." *Erbe und Auftrag,* 34 (1958), 329–348.

Subrenat, Jean. "Lucifer et sa mesnie dans le 'Pèlerinage de l'âme' de Guillaume de Digulleville." In *Le diable au moyen âge.* Paris, 1979. Pp. 509–525.

Svoboda, K. *La démonologie de Michel Psellos.* Brno, 1927.

Tervarent, Guy de, and Baudouin de Gaiffier. "Le diable voleur d'enfants: A propos de la naissance des saints Etienne, Laurent, et Barthélemy." *Homenage a Antoni Rubiò I Lluch.* Vol. 2. Barcelona, 1936. Pp. 33–58.

Thouzellier, Christine. "Controverse médiévale en Languedoc relative au sens du mot 'nihil': Sur l'égalité des deux dieux dans le catharisme." *Annales du Midi,* 82 (1970), 321–347.

Thraede, Kurt. "Exorzismus." *Reallexikon für Antike und Christentum.* Vol. 3, cols. 44–117.

Trachtenberg, Joshua. *The Devil and the Jews.* New Haven, 1943.

Trask, Richard M. "The *Descent into Hell* of the Exeter Book." *Neuphilologische Mitteilungen,* 72 (1971), 419–435.

Turmel, Joseph. "L'angélologie depuis le faux Denys l'Aréopagite." *Revue d'histoire et de littérature religieuses,* 4 (1899), 217–238, 289–309.

———. "Histoire de l'angélologie des temps apostoliques à la fin du cinquième siècle." *Revue d'histoire et de littérature religieuses,* 3 (1898), 289–308, 407–434, 533–552.

———. *Histoire du diable.* Paris, 1931.

Turner, Ralph V. "Descendit ad Inferos: Medieval Views on Christ's Descent into Hell and the Salvation of the Ancient Just." *Journal of the History of Ideas,* 27 (1966), 173–194.

Valensin, Auguste, S. J. "The Devil in the Divine Comedy." In Bruno de Jésus-Marie, ed., *Satan.* New York, 1952. Pp. 368–378.

Vandenbroucke, François, S. Lyonnet, J. Daniélou, A. Guillaumont, and C.

Guillaumont. "Démon." In *Dictionnaire de spiritualité ascétique et mystique*. Vol. 3. Pp. 142–238.

Van Gelder, J. G. "Der Teufel stiehlt das Tintenfass." In A. Rosenauer and G. Weber, eds., *Kunsthistorische Forschungen Otto Pächt zu seinem 70. Geburtstag*. Salzburg, 1972. Pp. 173–188.

Vanni Rovighi, Sofia. "Il problema del male in Anselmo d'Aosta." *Analecta anselmiana*, 5 (1976), 179–188.

Van Nuffel, Herman. "Le pacte avec le diable dans la littérature médiévale." *Anciens Pays et Assemblées d'Etats*, 39 (1966), 27–43.

Van Riet, Georges. "Le problème du mal dans la philosophie de la religion de saint Thomas. *Revue philosophique de Louvain*, 71 (1973), 5–45.

Vatter, Hannes. *The Devil in English Literature*. Bern, 1978.

Verduin, Kathleen. "Dante and the Sin of Satan: Augustinian Patterns in Inferno XXXIV, 22–27." *Italianistica*, 12 (1983).

Wagner, Werner-Harald. *Teufel und Gott in der deutschen Volkssage: Ein Beitrag zur Gemeinschaftsreligion*. Greifswald, 1930.

Waldman, Theodore. "A Comment upon the Ontological Proof of the Devil." *Philosophical Studies*, 10 (1959), 49–50.

Walker, Dennis P. *Spiritual and Demonic Magic: From Ficino to Campanella*. London, 1958.

Walzel, Diana Lynn. "Sources of Medieval Demonology." *Rice University Studies*, 60 (1974), 83–99.

Warkentin, A. *Die Gestalt des Teufels in der deutschen Volksage*. Bethel, Kans., 1937.

Watté, Pierre. *Structures philosophiques du péché originel: S. Augustin, S. Thomas, Kant*. Gembloux, 1974.

Wattenbach, Wilhelm. "Uber erfundene Briefe in Handschriften des Mittelalters, besonders Teufelsbriefe." *Sitzungsberichte der königlich-preussischen Akademie der Wissenschaften zu Berlin*, 1, no. 9 (Feb. 11, 1892), 91–123.

Wéber, Edouard-Henri. "Dynamisme du bien et statut historique du destin créé: Du traité sur la chute du diable de S. Anselme aux questions sur le mal de Thomas d'Aquin." In A. Zimmermann, ed., *Die Mächte des Guten und Bösen*. Berlin, 1977. Pp. 154–205.

Wee, David L. "The Temptation of Christ and the Motif of Divine Duplicity in the Corpus Christi Cycle Drama." *Modern Philology*, 72 (1974), 1–16.

Wellnhofer, Matthias. "Die thrakischen Euchiten und ihr Satanskult im Dialoge des Psellos Τιμόθεος ἢ περὶ τῶν δαιμόνων." *Byzantinische Zeitschrift*, 30 (1929–1930), 477–484.

Wensinck, A. J., and L. Gardet. "Iblis." In *The Encyclopedia of Islam*. Vol. 3, pp. 668–669.

Wenzel, Siegfried. "The Three Enemies of Man." *Mediaeval Studies*, 29 (1967), 47–66.

White, Lynn, Jr. "Death and the Devil." In Robert S. Kinsman, ed., *The Darker Vision of the Renaissance*. Berkeley, 1974. Pp. 25–46.

Wieck, Heinrich. "Die Teufel auf der mittelalterlichen Mysterienbühne Frankreichs." Ph.D. diss., University of Marburg, 1887.

Wienand, Adam. "Heils-Symbole und Dämonen-Symbole im Leben der Cistercienser-Mönche." In Ambrosius Schneider, A. Wienand, W. Bickel, and Ernst

Coester, eds., *Die Cistercienser: Geschichte, Geist, Kunst.* Cologne, 1974. Pp. 509–552.

Wirth, Jean. "La démonologie de Bosch." In *Diables et diableries.* Geneva, 1977. Pp. 71–85.

Withington, Robert. "Braggart, Devil, and Vice." *Speculum,* 11 (1936), 124–129.

Woods, Barbara Allen. *The Devil in Dog Form: A Partial Type-index of Devil Legends.* Berkeley, 1959.

Woolf, Rosemary E. "The Devil in Old English Poetry." *Review of English Studies,* n.s. 4 (1953), 1–12.

Wünsche, A. *Der Sangenkreis vom geprellten Teufel.* Leipzig, 1905.

Zieren, Helene. "Studien zum Teufelsbild in der deutschen Dichtung von 1050–1250." Ph.D. diss., University of Bonn, 1937.

Zimmermann, Albert. *Die Mächte des Guten und Bösen: Vorstellungen im XII. und XIII. Jahrhundert über ihr Wirken in der Heilsgeschichte.* Berlin and New York, 1977.

Zippel, Gianni. "La lettera del Diavolo al clero, dal secolo XII alla Riforma." *Bulletino dell'Istituto storico italiano per il medio evo e Archivio Muratoriano,* 70 (1958), 125–179.

Addenda:

Bausani, Alessandro. "La liberazione del male nella mistica islamica." In Panikkar, *Liberaci del male.* Bologna, 1983. Pp. 67–83.

Ferré, André. "Il problema del male e della sofferenza nell'Islam." In Panikkar, *Liberaci del male.* Bologna, 1983. Pp. 53–65.

Panikkar, Raimundo, ed. *Liberaci del male: Male e vie di liberazione nelle religioni.* Bologna, 1983.

Rudwin, Maximilian. "Dante's Devil." *The Open Court,* 35 (1921), 513–523.

Index

A

Abaddon, Abbaton, name of Devil, 66, 249
Abbad ibn-Sulayman, 58
Abelard, 94, 160, 172, 174–175, 178, 180–181, 205, 263
Acts of Pilate, see Gospel of Nicodemus
Adam and Eve:
  in Aelfric, 152
  in Anselm, 164, 167–168
  in art, 130, 211, 258
  in Bogomilism, 46–47
  in Duns, 173
  in early Middle Ages, 104–105
  in Eriugena, 122–123
  in Islam, 55–61
  in Langland, 239–241
  in Old English Genesis, 139–141
  in scholasticism, 176
  in the theater, 248, 253–257, 263, 269
Adam, Mystère d', 255–256, 329
Aelfric, 62, 94, 131, 151–154, 158, 208, 321
Aesir and Vanir, 64–65

Alan of Lille, 172
Al-Ashari, 58
Al-Basri, Hasan, 58
Albertus Magnus, 172–176, 178, 181
Alcuin, 92–93, 99–100, 102, 105, 317–318
Aldhelm, 134
Alexander of Hales, 174, 178
Al-Ghazali, 60–61
Al-Hallaj, 61
Al-Maturidi, 58
Altercatio diaboli contra Christum, 86
Angels:
  bodies of, 41, 172–173
  fallen, replaced in heaven by humans, *see* Humanity
  hierarchy of
    cherubim, 32, 94
    in Dante, 223–224
    in Dionysius, 32, 94
    equality within orders, 173
    in Islam, 55
    numbers of orders, 94, 151, 224, 237, 246
    seraphim, 32, 40, 94
    natural angels, 223–224

Shapeshifting (*cont.*)
  Norse, 65
  in scholasticism, 181, 183
Shaytan, name of Devil, 54
Slavic folklore, 44, 48–49, 62, 78
Sneezing, 72
Snorri Sturluson, 65
Solomon, 86
Sparking, trait of Devil, 144, 153
Statuta ecclesiae antiqua (275), 95
Sufis, 61
Sulpicius Severus, 154
Superstition, defined, 22

T

Tail, 49, 68, 130–132, 211, 215, 229, 231, 254
Tauler, Johann, 291–292, 301, 330
Temptation, function of Devil, 50, 72
  in Anselm, 168
  in Aquinas, 202, 205–206
  in Gregory the Great, 100–101
  in Islam, 57, 60
  in Maximus, 36–37
  in mysticism, 291–292
  in Psellos, 42
  in scholasticism, 178, 180, 189
Temptation of Christ, 33, 145, 153–154, 248, 265–266, 272
Teutonic folklore, 62–69, 78
Theater, 213, 245–273, 327–329
Theologia germanica, 235, 285, 288
Theophilus, 75, 80–84, 299
Thomas à Kempis, 233
Thor, 64, 69
Toledo, Council of (447), 69
Tools of Devil, 131, 212, 227
Tournaments of demons, 73
Towneley (Wakefield) plays, 251, 268, 329
Trent, Council of (1546), 95, 275, 295
Trial of soul, 85–87, 261
Tryphon, 66
Tundale, Vision of, 214–215, 231
Tutivillus, 66, 248–249

V

Van Eyck brothers, 209
Vices:
  in art, 208, 234

daughters of Devil, 77
demons specialize in, 50
Devil attracted by, 72
in English literature, 236, 328
in miracle stories, 156
in theater, 246, 248–249, 261, 270
Violence, defined, 20–21
Violet, *see* Color of Devil, blue
Vision literature, 214–215

W

Waldensians, 184
Walter Map, 181
Watcher angels, 148, 231
Wer-animals, 63, 79
Wheelwright, Philip, 31, 284
Wild hunt, 64, 69–70, 73, 78
Wild men and women, 73, 78, 210
William of Auvergne, 127, 161, 175, 177–178, 180–181
William of Champeaux, 177
William of Ockham, 275–279
Wings, 228, 254
  batlike, 68, 132, 211
  feathered, 130–131, 211
  six wings (Dante), 224, 230–232
  in *Tundale*, 215, 231
Witchcraft, 48, 63, 73, 79–81, 150, 155, 190, 244, 275, 289, 294, 296–301
Witelo (Vitellio), 173
Wolf, 65, 79, 236
Wolfram von Eschenbach, 208, 212, 216, 325
"World, flesh, and Devil," 104, 270
Wulfstan, 154
Wuotan, Woden, 64
Wyclif, John, 275–283

Y

Yezidis, 61
York plays, 247–248, 251, 253, 255–257, 268–269, 272, 329
Yvo of Chartres, 173

Z

Zabulon, 249
Zamakhshari, 59

Library of Congress Cataloging in Publication Data

Russell, Jeffrey Burton.
    Lucifer, the Devil in the Middle Ages.

    Bibliography: p.
    Includes index.
    1. Devil—History of doctrines—Middle Ages,
600-1500. I. Title.
BT981.R86 1984   235'.47   84-45153
ISBN 0-8014-1503-9 (alk. paper)